AMERICA'S REAL WAR

RABBI DANIEL LAPIN

Multnomah®Publishers *Sisters, Oregon*

Susan and I gratefully dedicate this book to the late Rabbi Avraham Chayim Lapin,
may his saintly memory be blessed, who, as my teacher and father,
equipped me to be able to write this book; and my late mother Rebbetzin Maisie Lapin, of
blessed memory, whose legacy of courage made me actually do so.

We also dedicate it to the congregation of Pacific Jewish Center in Los Angeles
which we were privileged to serve for fifteen wonderful years
and where the ideas expressed herein were germinated.

AMERICA'S REAL WAR
published by Multnomah Publishers, Inc.

© 1999 by Rabbi Daniel Lapin

Design by Stephen Gardner
Cover photo of flag by Paul Sanders
Cover photo of arms by Stock Imagery

International Standard Book Number: 1-57673-366-1

Printed in the United States of America

Scripture quotations are from *The New Jerusalem Bible*
© 1985 by Darton, Longman & Todd, Ltd.
and Doubleday & Company, Inc.

For information:
Multnomah Publishers, Inc.
Post Office Box 1720
Sisters, OR 97759

99 00 01 02 03 04 05 06 — 10 9 8 7 6 5 4 3 2 1

CONTENTS

Acknowledgments

How do I best encourage you to read these heartfelt expressions of deep gratitude? Perhaps you will consider this page worth scanning were I to divulge more than merely the names of some of the individuals to whom I feel indebted. Perhaps I should disclose that without the help of these people and many others, I would be far less. You see, expressions of gratitude are really admissions of personal inadequacy and I am grateful and happy to owe so much to so many. Can I tell you just a little more about these individuals who have helped me and why they are listed? Well, here goes then.

By all coexisting on one page of my book together in total harmony, these men and women each help to demonstrate a crucial premise. Commitment to God Almighty appears to better bring together individuals of diverse backgrounds in civility and friendship than secularism can possibly do. The names herein are a microcosm of everything wonderful about America and they enshrine our best hope for a complete moral restoration of the land.

Therefore my first thank-you must be reserved for HaKadosh Baruch Hu, The Holy One Blessed be He, who alone enabled me to bring this book to its conclusion. My prayer is that it should serve as a Kiddush HaShem, a sanctification of His Name and perhaps even introduce to my brethren in the American Jewish community the notion of conducting communal politics with an eye to matters of Kiddush HaShem.

Matt Jacobson embodied just the right balance of bullying and cajoling to obtain my commitment to the book and his brother Don heads Multnomah Publishers. No writer could ever wish to be published by a finer group of people or by a company with more integrity than that created by Don and his team. You have all become dear friends, and I hope we do more projects together in the future. Special mention to Nancy Thompson who simultaneously edited this book and arranged a wedding. May both the book and her marriage bring joy.

The debt that I and my family owe to our friends, colleagues, and neighbors of twenty years, Michael and Diane Medved, is more than can ever be repaid. Whatever modest accomplishments have come my way, including this volume, owe much to their inspiration, encouragement, and support. May God bless them with the happiness they so richly deserve.

Jack Abramoff, along with his wife Pam, is surely one of the wisest and most energetic advisors I am privileged to be counseled by. His guidance and generosity have much to do with the book you hold in your hands.

My brothers Rabbi David Lapin and Rabbi Raphael Lapin, both of California, are vital resources to me. The emotional warmth and intellectual stimulation that they provide, along with their help in reconstructing much of our father's teachings, enormously enhance both my life and my work.

Loyal friendship and sage advice are rare commodities which makes the roles played in my life by Adam Pruzan, David Klinghoffer, Lewis Kaufman, Craig Lewis, and Jeff and Judy Gruen all the more appreciated.

The management and staff of Talk Radio 570, KVI in Seattle have been magnanimous, and I both enjoy and appreciate the exposure I have gained on their airwaves. Elie Pieprz capably heads my Washington D.C. office and his help in this project has been invaluable. Ari Alhadeff in my local office never disdains a challenge, and there are many. By assisting us both at home and the office, Judith Wachs helps blend our complex lives into one integrated whole. Pastor Ken Hutcherson and his family, the Tom Hemphill family and the Jeff Parish family have all done so much for us. We thank you heartily.

This book was incubated by Toward Tradition which we founded in 1991. I deeply appreciate those who did so much to establish this organization which now effectively communicates our message throughout America. Mr. and Mrs. David Holder, Mr. and Mrs. Larry Smith, Mr. and Mrs. Alan Lipman, Mr. and Mrs. David Altschuler, Mr. and Mrs. Judd Magilnick, Mr. and Mrs. Elie Gindi, Mr. and Mrs. John Engelman, Alejandro Chafuen, Asher and Sharon Levine, Bill Hall, Tom Phillips, Shelly Kamins, Brian Siegel, Jim Casparie, and Michael and Mary Mann.

Quietly courageous, gracious, and generous, describe our friend Lenore Broughton. Since becoming part of our life she has imparted so much of herself to our family and particularly to our children. Come back soon to Mercer Island, Lenore. I appreciate the encouragement received from a former Secretary of the Treasury. Thank you William Simon. Thanks also to Steve Ferguson whose faith enabled him to see this book long before pen touched paper and to Tom Fuentes who has made so much happen, and who taught me how a good cigar can help make writing a little easier. Susan also says thanks, Tom.

Sometimes we are lucky enough to know people who beam warmth and closeness into our lives. I could not have written this book without Michael and Judi Lapin as well as Dr. Marty and Tami Rabin. The Rabins and Lapins have not only brought added joy to our lives but they have both helped shape my work with practical and timely advice that has always been correct.

There are also others without whom this book would not exist, but I find myself in a dilemma. They have expressed a preference not to be named here, for reasons that I understand and accept. Nonetheless I am under an obligation from a "Higher Authority" to acknowledge my gratitude. While far from a perfect solution, I can think of no better way out of my dilemma than to identify them by initials and state of residence. This way they will know how profoundly I appreciate their friendship and support while their request for anonymity will be partially honored.

Those of you that do recognize them, should; those that don't, perhaps should not.

Thank you Mr. and Mrs. H. A. of Southern California, Mrs. H. H. of New York, Mr. P. H. of Illinois, Mrs. E. P. of Michigan, Mr. R. L. of Pennsylvania, Mr. and Mrs. G. S. of Utah. You know who you are and how keenly Susan and I reciprocate your affection for us.

A special thank-you to my wonderful in-laws, Jack and Bea Friedberg, who, by allowing me the honor of marrying their daughter, made this book along with absolutely everything else in my life, possible and even perhaps inevitable. I hope their many friends in New York do not consider this book to be poor recompense for their many kindnesses. Perhaps they too should have been identified by initials only.

My executive assistant, Mrs. Rachael Whaley cannot be adequately thanked. Along with her husband Dick, she has become part of our family. Her calm and cheerful competence are intimidating. She somehow manages to weave a perfect and seamless set of results out of the many conflicting demands of my professional and home life. God bless you, Rachael.

A few years ago Mr. Yarden Weidenfeld entered my life and quickly won his way into the Lapin family's heart while establishing himself as Toward Tradition's brilliant national director. His dedication and integrity have made him an admired friend and valued *talmid*—disciple. There is no question in my mind that without him, this book would never have been written. I have come to think of him as almost a son, and Susan and I look forward to dancing with him on the day he marries the fortunate young woman whom God will identify as his *besherte*—his bride.

My children are of course full partners in this project. Not only have they willingly and lovingly yielded much of their parents' time and attention to the book, but by their questions and ideas, they have actually contributed substantially to the work. Rebecca has been an intellectual partner of mine since she was three years old. Her strong character and love of *HaShem*—God—has helped shape our family. Lovely Rena was born with a smile on her lips. Her sweetness brings light and laughter into our home. Rachelle possesses generosity, strength, and independence that her parents appreciate more than she could possibly yet understand. Our only son Aryeh, named after one of my outstanding Torah teachers, is living up to his namesake. We are as proud of the battles he wages with himself as we are of the victories he wins. Feminine and selfless with a flair for seeing the world through the eyes of others, warmhearted Ruth is the sister everyone wishes they had. Miriam intoxicates us all with the love she beams at us. Her beguiling outlook turns everyone into a friend. Little Tamara will always be little Tamara no matter how old she is—a bouncing bundle of effervescence whose absences leave the house too quiet and me incapable of writing. This book is partially to help you understand your parents. It is also a tribute to your contributions to our work. May God always bless you all. Thank you for all you do for Mommy and me.

Which brings me to Susan. This book is as much a product of our collaboration as are our children, for she and I have brought these ideas into being together as surely as our children are also the fruit of our unity. We write together, we home build together, we child raise together, why, we even boat and vote together. Although no word of this volume was sent to the publisher until we both agreed, to the extent you find fault, I can assure you it will be with those passages on which she yielded to me. It would make as little sense for me to thank her for her help in this book as it would make for a left leg to thank a right leg for its help in crossing a street. This is our book.

In humble gratitude to God
Rabbi Daniel Lapin
Mercer Island, Washington
Kislev 5759
December 1998

PART I

REFOCUSING OUR OUTLOOK

CHAPTER ONE

WHY WOULD A RABBI ALLY WITH RELIGIOUS CHRISTIANS?

AMERICA IS INDEED IMPERILED. WE JUST DISAGREE WITH ONE ANOTHER ABOUT WHAT THE SOURCE OF THE DANGER IS.

A captured prisoner of war is required to declare only his name, rank, service number, and date of birth. This is because all the truly profound information about him is already revealed by his uniform. That distinctive garment eloquently proclaims the side for which the warrior is fighting. It equally effectively reveals those values for which the soldier is willing to risk his life.

Although not a prisoner of war, I am among those engaged in a fierce American conflict. It may be the fiercest internal conflict in American history since the Abolitionist movement in the 1800s. It is certainly deeply consequential. And I am in the heart of it. This book is my uniform.

In addition to the information contained in my uniform, the U.S. Military Code of Conduct grants you the right to the equivalent of my name, rank, service number, and date of birth. Here is the vital data: I am an Orthodox rabbi. I am the son of a famous Orthodox rabbi and the brother of two more. My teachers were the great scholars who headed the Gateshead Talmudic Academy in England, some of whom were uncles and cousins. I became a disciple of my great-uncle, the revered Rabbi Eliyahu (Elijah) Lopian (the original family name) during my many years of study at the theological academy (or *yeshiva*) of Kfar Hassidim in Israel. Although I often fall short, I do my best to live my life and raise my children according to the laws of the five books of Moses, our holy Torah, and the customs of Moses and of Israel.

Because it is so unusual these days for a rabbi to say nice things about Christians, I consider it necessary to explain that I am not now, nor have I ever been, a Christian. I profess no special expertise of the books known as the New Testament. Being infatuated with Judaism and the God of Abraham, Isaac and Jacob, I dedicate my study time to expanding my familiarity with Jewish theology. In the midst of a lifelong love affair with the searing truth of the Torah, I reject any notion of theological compatibility between Judaism and Christianity; I do not believe a Jew can also be a Christian without betraying his Judaism. One faith, Judaism, has produced the longest-lasting, continuous culture in the history of the world, while the other, Christianity, has been responsible, among other things, for the founding of America, the greatest civilization the world has ever known, and for making America great. This book will describe how a weakened Christianity in America threatens all Americans, including Jews.

WHY I FIGHT THIS BATTLE

My defense of a religion other than my own has earned me considerable hostility from many Americans. This book will also describe why so many secularized Americans and so many Jews wrongly fear Christianity in America today.

Why have I willingly volunteered to fight this battle? Why have I subjected my wife and children, as well as my friends, to all the disruptions, difficulties—and yes, dangers— of this struggle? I find myself driven to defend American Christian conservatives for three compelling reasons.

The first is because I desperately want my children, and one day (God willing) my grandchildren and their descendants, to have the option of living peacefully and productively in the United States of America. I am certain this depends upon America regaining its Christian-oriented moral compass.

The second reason is that I am appalled by the great injustice being perpetrated by those Jewish organizations that engage in anti-Christian bigotry. Although many of them were founded explicitly to fight bigotry, and for many years did just that, today the shrill rhetoric and hate-filled propaganda found in their direct mail is discriminatory and divisive. The very same Jewish organizations would be the loudest protesters were anything even remotely similar being said by non-Jews about Jews. Justice demands that a member of the group doing the defaming also does the defending. God's blueprint clearly included the emergence of Christianity. After all, Christianity has brought monotheism to more people than any other force during the past two millennia. American Jews in particular, owe a debt of gratitude to Christians for the safe haven America has been since its founding.

Third, I wish to counter the *chilul Hashem,* the desecration of God's name, that is caused when His words are misrepresented. Organizations and individuals, many of whom claim to speak in the name of Judaism, are inflicting enormous harm on America by promoting policies that traditional Judaism finds abhorrent. I want to help both Jewish and non-Jewish Americans differentiate between Jewish positions and positions held by some Jews who are more devoted to secularism than Judaism.

In defending Christianity in America, I am not suggesting that Jews ought to embrace the Christian faith. I believe that all Jews should actively embrace traditional Judaism; I have spent many years of my life helping to bring that about. But I am suggesting, at the very least, that Jews should stop speaking and acting as if Christian America is their enemy. I feel that all Americans who love freedom, whether or not they are religious, should be reassured, not frightened, by the reawakening of earnest Christianity throughout the land. I shall try to establish that Jews as well as other minorities have the most to fear from a *post*-Christian America.

A NATION IN CRISIS

I believe America is in decline—not compared to five or ten years ago, but when compared to the years following World War II up until the early sixties. Most Americans who can remember back thirty-five years or so sense that life has become more squalid, expensive, and dangerous. Some attribute this to inadequate government attention to social problems, while others lay the blame on a more fundamental spiritual malaise. One thing is clear however: fewer and fewer Americans remain unaware of, or indifferent to America's decline. Whether it is in the hollow expressions on the faces of some youngsters, the vulgarity of entertainment, or the many other little signs that all is not well in America, most of us are at least concerned about the future.

There is a tug-of-war going on for the future of our country. Some are enthusiastic pullers for one or the other side. Many other Americans remain uncommitted to the entire agenda of either side but feel the need to make their voices heard one way or the other.

What do the two ends of the rope represent? I believe the basic question is whether America is a secular or a religious nation. The very question sizzles with tension. Almost everybody has an opinion on this one. Furthermore, it is becoming less of an opinion and more of a deeply held fundamental worldview. Whichever view people hold, they do so with utter conviction.

One end of the rope is anchored by those who ask, "How can any intelligent, rational person late in the twentieth century view America as a religious nation?" Some put it this way, "Do you really want to live in a theocracy? Look at Iran." To people on this end of the rope, Judeo-Christian tradition represents primitive tribalism and intolerance, the most damning indictment of our age.

The folks on this end of the rope are joined by many citizens who used to occupy the undecided middle ground. While lacking a doctrinal embrace of secularism, these

Americans have come to feel that religious America poses the real threat to our continuity, so they instinctively migrate to the end of the rope opposite from religious conservatives. Although not committed to every nuance of secularism, they consider it the lesser of two evils and lend their not inconsiderable weight to the left of the rope.

Across the field on the other end, are those Americans who feel increasingly alienated by this "enlightened" perspective which denies the importance of America's history and culture. These religious conservatives are joined by many other Americans who, while admittedly unenthusiastic about religion, are even less enthusiastic about the changes that secular liberalism has brought about in their towns and communities.

In the pages following, I will argue that America is a religious nation and the corresponding interpretation of our history and culture is the correct one. But I shall go much further than that. America is not just religious but is rooted in one particular religious tradition. As an Orthodox rabbi, I will make a compelling case for America as a Christian nation and the need for our nation to be based on Judeo-Christian ethics in order to survive. Despite the fact that Judaism and Christianity have totally differing theologies, there is still one Judeo-Christian ethic. Which is to say that how people order their lives and societies; how they organize their families and behave toward one another turns out to be more similar than different. The origins, legal system, ethos and moral sense of America are entirely Judeo-Christian.

A Jew and a Christian at one end of the rope have more in common with one another in terms of vision for this country than each may have with his coreligionists at the other end. This is because the tug-of-war is not about theological or philosophical differences but about real life disagreements about things like taxes, crime, welfare, and family life. No matter the philosophy of belief that brings us to our view of how things ought to be, we tend to agree with others holding the same view regardless of the belief that brought them to that view.

But this begs another question asked by well-intentioned but worried Americans. Many of those pulling for the secular side of the tug-of-war may concede that there is at least some truth to the Judeo-Christian religious foundation of America. At the same time they argue that nowadays a new secular public policy posture has become necessary because of America's increasing diversity. Otherwise, they argue, America will become intolerant of its minorities who may not share in our founding ethic. The question for those who take this position is not, "Is America a Christian nation?" but "Should America be a Christian nation?" As a non-Christian myself, I still insist the answer must be yes. I shall try to demonstrate that the choice is between a benign Christian culture and a sinister secular one.

I feel that although they may seem unrelated, almost every social pathology and nearly every sign of civic disarray can be traced to one thing: the extirpation of religion from American public life during the past three and a half decades. Very little tells us as much about a culture than how it views the transcendent questions of life. A culture's prospects for success and durability are best revealed by examining what it considers the purpose of life, what is death, how sex should be treated, and similar questions that most of us answer in one of only two ways. Either we consult the traditions of our faith, or, rejecting faith, we seek emotionally satisfying answers. Sometimes we later buttress the answers we have already chosen.

WHAT WILL LIFE BE LIKE FOR OUR CHILDREN?

One of the great gifts of serious religion is the idea of hierarchy. Some things are better than others and some things are more evil than others. It is a greater good to bestow charity on a poor man by offering him a net along with instructions for its use rather than to fling him a fish. Attacking a passerby in order to steal her purse is a greater evil than smoking a cigarette. We must renew our confidence in making moral judgments. We have to be able to identify the direction in which trends are moving. If there is moral movement in each generation, we need to know the direction and the velocity of the movement. This helps us understand what tomorrow might look like, and it helps us decide whether we welcome that particular vision of tomorrow for our children. If our culture is changing rapidly, as I think it may be doing, and if we are changing by becoming coarser and more subject to the tireless ministrations of a government determined to become ever more involved in every corner of citizens' lives, then I experience great concern. It means that we are further under water than we were last generation. And if nothing is going to change that course, what will life be like for our children?

This great American civilization, perhaps the greatest the world has ever known, is not facing imminent extinction. However, life deteriorates significantly long before the very end. And it usually deteriorates fastest for those most dependent on society's civilizing institutions. Those not big and fearsome enough to defend themselves suffer more than others when city streets and parks become menacing. Those not wealthy enough to afford private schools for their children suffer most when public education fails. Those who live from paycheck to paycheck are most vulnerable to creeping and constant tax increases. Those trying to raise children who will honor their parents and their parents' values are most hampered by antifamily legislation and antifamily entertainment. Those trying to build new business enterprises find themselves crippled by confiscatory taxation and crippling regulation.

Are you Jewish, Christian, or neither? Are you indifferent to religion, fervently for, or ardently opposed to faith? It matters little. As long as you devoutly wish for America to remain a beacon of hope and freedom in this troubled world, I appeal to you. Ideas do have consequences and big ideas have big consequences. If there exists an idea bigger than

God, I do not know what it might be. What Americans feel about God probably has greater impact on our national future than what we think about almost anything else. Or to put it another way, what we really think about God deep down within our hearts is likely to influence what we think about almost everything else.

I intend to show you how changing attitudes about God have almost entirely reshaped America during the past three or four decades. Furthermore, I want to show how virtually every one of us has been a participant, sometimes unwittingly, in allowing these changes to take place. Some of us have actively helped to bring these changes about in the belief that we have been improving society. Others have been swept along by the loud enthusiasms of the changers and our passive acceptance of each small step has allowed these big changes to envelop our lives.

I intend this book as a guide to what we have done, to what we have allowed to take place, and to where it all might lead. Those readers who applaud the changes will smile knowingly as I identify the milestones on our road downhill. Those who tremble at what we have come to accept as normal will see my words as a road map for retracing our steps and regaining the right path to continue the great story that is American history.

America is indeed imperiled. We all know that. We just disagree with one another about what the source of the danger is. Some think religious fervor threatens while others feel that secularism is the danger.

CHAPTER TWO

STRIKING THE ICEBERG

LIKE THE OVERCONFIDENT PASSENGERS ON THE "UNSINKABLE" OCEAN LINER, WE REFUSE TO ACKNOWLEDGE THAT OUR PROBLEM COULD LEAD TO TRAGEDY.

The sinking of the *Titanic* makes a perfect metaphor for the unexpected demise of a great and apparently invulnerable enterprise. Could the unprecedented popularity of the movie of the same name be caused by a widespread, subconscious awareness that the movie is a metaphor? Did people flock to theaters across America to see what they felt to be a frightening description of our own period of American history?

Although this seems fanciful, it would not be the first time a movie resonated with the public because of a subtle message from the underlying motif. One thinks of the ship of state sailing serenely through time, when suddenly she strikes an iceberg. Is that what has happened to our land? In the much-seen James Cameron movie, more than half the film elapsed before the *Titanic* reached the iceberg. In Walter Lord's 1955 book, *A Night to Remember,* the majestic liner hit the fatal berg on page three. Walter Lord correctly saw that the real story was to be found in the time between the impact with the iceberg and the sinking of the mighty ship.

THE REAL STORY

What exact moment condemned the *Titanic?* Was it the design of the lifeboat systems? Was it the choice of material used in the hull? Was it actually the moment the great ship struck the iceberg? It is hard to say. It is often difficult to pinpoint a precise moment of doom.

What moment sealed the fate of millions of people by making World War II inevitable? Was it when Hitler invaded the Rhineland on a cold Saturday morning in

March 1936? Was it perhaps in 1919 when a treaty was signed at Versailles prohibiting Germany from entering that thirty-mile-wide stretch of land on both banks of the River Rhine? Or could all the carnage of World War II have had its start with the murder of Austrian Archduke Francis Ferdinand at Sarajevo on June 28, 1914, which many historians feel launched World War I and made almost all else during the next three decades a foregone conclusion? The real story that fascinates twentieth-century historians is not when World War II began. The real story concerns the tension between those who understood the long-term implications of what was happening and those who did not.

I believe the same is true in America today.

Aboard the *Titanic,* many people did not know exactly when the iceberg was struck. Most passengers were oblivious to the collision until they were informed by crew members well after the steel plates of the hull had buckled and ripped. And many of these same passengers scoffed at the notion that any collision could imperil the unsinkable ship.

We, too, consider America to be virtually invulnerable since many of our changes *are* for the better. See how the crime rate has recently gone down in some cities? Even New York City is growing safer and more pleasant. Many feel that the economy is in good shape. We constantly reassure ourselves that America is fine and always will be. Yes, now and then something shocking hits the headlines that shakes us. A young, white high school girl from an upper-middle-class family kills her just-born baby and returns to her prom. Two young schoolboys open fire on their schoolmates, killing five of them along with a teacher. But here is the interesting twist. As such alarming stories continue, we experience less discomfort. After the second and third well-publicized cases of babies found in Dumpsters, we become anesthetized. By the time ten or twelve more schools have been attacked by pimply-faced young gunmen, we are less jolted. We hear vague talk of the need for more sex education and for banning all firearms to avoid such tragedies, but that's about it. Life continues, and very few of us stop to realize that these things simply were not happening fifty years ago.

Even looking back nostalgically to a time not so long ago, when schools were safe and women could walk almost anywhere unafraid, brands one as wanting to turn back the clock. I recognize that while some things back in the 1950s were plain evil, many other things were wonderfully right. We have been conditioned to believe that the injustices that existed in the '50s irreparably tainted everything in our post-World War II generation. Many of us endure sneers for wanting a return to an Ozzie-and-Harriet world. Well, there was much that was right about that world.

WHEN DID WE HIT THE ICEBERG?

While debating the precise moment we hit the iceberg is less important than investigating what we Americans have been saying and doing since, if I had to pick the moment in our history that corresponds to the collision of the *Titanic,* I would select the early 1960s. This is the point when most of us should have realized we had encountered a serious problem. However, like the overconfident passengers on the "unsinkable" ocean liner, we refused to acknowledge that the problem could lead to tragedy.

Each warning sign seemed so minor in itself. For example, when Rudi Gernreich, a Jewish socialist from Vienna, settled in Los Angeles and foisted the topless bathing suit on a shocked America, it seemed titillating and daring. Many will recall the newspaper photographs of grim-faced policemen clutching towels around the shapely torsos of giddy young women while escorting them off public beaches. Many viewed this as harmless liberation and frivolous diversion. Others recognized the opening of a Pandora's box that would never again be shut, a challenge to the basic question of the role of sex in a civil society.

A tug-of-war ensued. A few hailed the flagrantly homosexual Gernreich as the hero of the avant-garde. Hoisting him onto their shoulders, they used him as a banner beneath which to gather the forces that would liberate America from its prudish past. Those at the other end of the rope prophetically condemned the new fashion as a trend that would continue to expose ever more flesh to the public gaze with each passing year. These two sides yelled insults at one another as they heaved and pulled, each side hoping to end the struggle quickly with a triumphant surge that would carry the American public along with their view of what was taking place. But the American public, for the most part, ignored the tug-of-war and calmly continued enjoying their picnic as it was. Our postwar recovery had endowed us with the highest living standard in the world, and we were enjoying it.

Another example of a pivotal development of the '60s, which also failed to startle us out of our complacency, was the birth control pill. I need hardly spend time lauding it as a marvel of modern medical technology; that is unarguable. Even now, however, few have recognized its cultural impact. For the first time in our history, men were told that they were free to view sex as a leisure activity. Even responsibility for any unintended outcomes was transferred to the woman. ("Did you remember to take your pill, honey?") This was clearly an iceberg in the path of American history because it literally changed the nature of vast numbers of American men. It was imperceptible at first, but little by little the changes became apparent. Men began to retain adolescence beyond all previously held records. A generation in which twenty-six-year-old men had fought Hitler and come home to marry and start raising families was replaced by one populated by forty-year-old adolescents. How could this not affect our culture?

Even changes that seemed simply harmless and fun affected the country. One example is the emergence of the fast food industry. A few years earlier Ray Kroc had spotted the MacDonald brothers' hamburger stand in Southern California and seen its possibilities. Up until that time, most American mothers advised their offspring not to nibble food between meals. This was simply part of one's moral and physical education. It was an aspect of learning self-discipline and care for the body. In addition, family meal-times were considered sacred, a key time each evening to connect and spend time with one another. The rapid growth of fast food, however, conditioned us to the notion that anytime and anywhere is suitable for a snack or meal.

Once again, imperceptibly at first, America began to change, and not just in terms of obesity. Far more serious were the spiritual and moral changes. Our national person-ality was shifting. We became more self-indulgent and less disciplined; more attuned to immediate gratification than to what was best for the long-term.

We certainly had hit the iceberg, but only a few knew it and even fewer cared. In the first-class ballroom, the dance continued.

CHAPTER THREE

SUBTLE CHANGES

TECHNOLOGY, AS GREAT AS IT IS, SOMETIMES ONLY CONCEALS HUMAN WEAKNESS.

What does the wise person do after his ship has hit an iceberg? He notices that the water entering the ship has lowered the bow a little. He extrapolates and reasons to himself that if water continues flooding in at the present rate, and unless something is done to repair the damage and stem the flow, he has only limited time before he will be treading water.

Think back only a few years; not long in terms of a nation's history. In 1960, as I noted earlier, the parks of most American towns and cities were safe, even for women, at any hour of the day and night. Americans could send their children to almost any public school in the country confident that their children were not only safe but were also receiving the finest education available in the world. Middle-class families could sustain a lifestyle that was the envy of the world on the earnings of only one worker. Inmates of any penitentiary would have been horrified by the lyrics available to children on any radio today.

Had we awakened one morning to find these changes inflicted overnight by a foreign invader, we would surely have risen in righteous revolution. But that isn't how America changed; it all happened ever so gradually.

THE KETTLE AND THE FROG

The old frog story claims that a frog dropped into a pot of boiling water would leap from the pot with one convulsive spasm of its tormented muscles. However, the same frog deposited gently into a pot of cold water would accustom himself to his new condition even as the pot was placed upon the stove. Gradually adapting to each incremental rise in temperature, the frog would finally be boiled to death without attempting to escape the pot.

A study of the Nazi death camps in *The Survivor* by Terence Des Pres reveals a crucial difference between the people who survived and those who immediately lost their will to live. For those who survived, normality progressed very gradually, over time, toward a barbaric hell. First the well-to-do Jews were forced to accommodate several displaced families in their Warsaw mansions. Then they were moved to a small apartment in the Warsaw ghetto. Later their apartment had to house ever larger numbers of strangers while at the same time food became more scarce. Perhaps a year or more elapsed between the earliest signs of trouble and crowded, unsanitary conditions. During that year their cuisine went from five-course meals served by uniformed waiters in an affluent home to dead horses eagerly consumed in a crowded little ghetto apartment. The passage of time allowed them to adjust gradually to additional horrors. By the time they arrived in the Auschwitz death camp, they were already somewhat inured to the mind-numbing filth and cruel violence that marked everyday life.

By contrast, other Jews were yanked from the luxury of a comfortable life directly onto the cattle cars of death. Within just a few days people had to adjust from bland normality to unthinkable brutality and horror. For most, it was just too much.

We humans can accustom ourselves to almost anything, provided we are given a little time in which to do it. Like the temperature of the water surrounding the frog in the kettle, things that change slowly become accepted as normal. That is why we have come to see as normal those things that so dangerously threaten us. It is not worth making a fuss over another two cents tax on a gallon of gasoline, for example. Few of us stop to total up the cumulative impact.

The past thirty-five years in America have slipped by gradually, allowing us to accustom ourselves to some shocking conditions. Can we extrapolate ahead and predict what might happen if we fail to effect repairs and halt the decline?

More than simply halt the decline, we also need to identify what else has caused the ship's bow to go underwater. In chasing after an unattainable and utopian society, which had more to do with a religious kind of yearning than a political vision, I believe we have abandoned those things that had served us well for nearly two centuries. In trying to eliminate material poverty, we impoverished ourselves spiritually. In embracing untried ideas, we forgot the proven ones that had survived the tests of time. Let's face it: We made a wrong turn three or four decades ago. There really is no alternative but to back up to that intersection and take the better path.

MODERNITY VS. MODERNISM

Am I suggesting we forsake modernity? No, I am advising that we forsake modernism. Modernity implies embracing technological progress and being open to change without necessarily considering all old ideas to be bad. Modernism automatically rejects old ideas. Modernism is the odd notion that mankind should view revolutionary change as inherently good. It is the view that, almost by definition, modifying today's society will produce a better tomorrow. "Never ever stop tinkering," urges the modernist. "Mankind is forever malleable."

On the other hand, modernity and the pursuit of better things is best achieved by anchoring ourselves to the world of old, better, time-proven ideas. Let me emphasize that I am not advocating we model ourselves after the Amish people (despite there being much to admire about them) and reject all modern appliances. Neither am I a closet Luddite. I am captivated by technology. I enjoy using the latest computer developments. I enjoy driving sophisticated cars and photographing my family with the latest cameras. Even when boating, an activity which reeks with tradition, I revel in using my computerized charts and global positioning satellite systems for navigation. I view technological accomplishments as testament to the infinite potential that a benevolent God implanted in His children as a little glimpse into His own infinite ability.

Medical advances, for instance, have certainly made life longer and healthier. Technological advances provide the bulk of the bewildering choice of consumer items for sale in any well-stocked suburban shopping mall. Cars are better than they used to be; air travel is safer, quicker and more affordable; and computers, the like of which did not exist twenty years ago, are within reach of almost anybody who really desires one. Compact discs bring musical performances right into our living rooms, or if we walk around with headphones, right into our ears. They accomplish this with a fidelity to the original sounds that was all but unavailable just ten years ago. The Internet can provide us with more information than we could absorb in a hundred lifetimes. Gourmet frozen food and modern microwave ovens turn anyone into a cordon bleu chef in only minutes.

Nonetheless, let us not make the modernist mistake of assuming that all change is for the better. Amazingly, technological advance can conceal a deterioration in the quality of humans. For instance, prior to the easy availability of mechanized transport, many rural children trudged several miles to school each day regardless of weather. That inevitably produced a toughness and an indomitability in children, not to mention a deeper appreciation for education, that can never be reproduced in children who are whisked to school in air-conditioned comfort. Many older Americans who deserve our gratitude for winning World War II grew up under conditions where personal strength and ability had to provide what technology provided to a later generation.

THE HIGH PRICE OF CHEAPER, FASTER

I recall once visiting a boatyard in the south of England that was still building the prettiest little sailing sloops out of fine English oak—and doing so entirely by hand. I had made a point of visiting this yard during the mid 1960s when fiberglass had just started becoming the material of choice for the leisure boat industry; I had a sense that time was rapidly passing should I want to personally see boats being built, much as they used to be built, by skilled craftsmen.

Now fiberglass is a very technologically-advanced material. It combines two substances—resin and glass strands—in order to produce a new kind of hybrid that possesses the outstanding characteristics of each substance. Its chief advantage is that it can be applied to the inside of a mold by relatively unskilled labor and then popped out as soon as it has hardened and cured. Boat hulls can be turned out rapidly and inexpensively because little skill is required.

By contrast, the craftsmen at the Hilyard boatworks in south England had spent a lifetime building wooden boats by hand. Many of these men were the sons of those who had also spent their lives building exquisite yachts out of ancient oak forests. I recall watching one elderly boatbuilder planking what I remember to be about a thirty-foot boat. He had planked the side all the way down from the sheer, or deck line, and all the way up from the keel until all that remained was space for the last plank to be laid up against the frames. The gap was about thirty feet long from stem to stern. Its width varied between about six or seven inches in the middle to about one or two inches at each end. This was because the cross section of a sailing boat varies from narrow at bow and stern to a wine-glass appearance amidships. Since the same number of planks are used from deck to keel, and since the distance is obviously so much greater at the middle of the vessel than it is at either end, each plank must be far wider toward its middle than at either of its ends. I describe this process in some detail not because I think you will ever need to know, but because I want you to comprehend the enormity of the feat I am about to relate.

While I stood and watched the slightly stooped figure of the older craftsman, he stepped back and, with some obvious satisfaction at being so close to finishing his project, gazed adoringly at the lovely ship. Eyeing the last remaining gap to be planked, he ambled over to the pile of fresh lumber and picked out a long slender plank that must have been about thirty-five feet long and about ten inches wide. After placing it in several vises set into a long workbench, he began planing its edge down to reduce its width. I waited to see him take some measurements off the hull; he never did. Every now and again he would glance over his shoulder and narrow his eyes as he stared at the gap in the planking, as if it offended him personally. It finally dawned on me that he was visually measuring his work against the gap into which it would have to fit perfectly. Not only was there the length and constantly varying width for him to contend with, but there was also a bevel that needed to be set into both the upper and lower edges of the new plank to later accept the caulking.

Swinging backward and forward, he planed away so much that his big old work boots were almost concealed by fresh, fragrant shavings. (I can smell them to this day.) The shavings fell from his hissing plane until he finally released the plank from the vise, lifted it to his shoulders, and carried it over to the boat where he offered it up to the gap. He clamped it into position, stepped back again and strolled the length of the boat without taking his eyes off his new plank. Then he took the plank back to the workbench, where he toiled at it for another thirty or forty minutes before returning it to the boat. It fit perfectly. He glued and screwed it into place, quite oblivious to the fact that he had casually carried off a feat of sheer magic. I was incredibly moved as I realized that the world would soon cease to see anything like this again.

There was very little technology to see that afternoon at the Hilyard boat yard in south England. But no more than about sixty miles away, in a spanking-new factory belonging to Russell Marine, twenty new fiberglass boats had been built in molds in less time than it took the Hilyard works to build just one wooden boat. They were going to be considerably less expensive and much easier to own and maintain.

Which was the superior achievement? Using advanced technology, Russell Marine was churning out large numbers of identical plastic boats that sold for reasonable sums of money and, for the first time ever, brought leisure boating to England's ordinary citizens. Russell Marine was also on its way to becoming a successful company that earned outstanding returns for its shareholders by using every latest advance in manufacturing technology. The Hilyard yard represented a dying industry. Wooden boat building of that kind no longer exists. They were producing works of art for connoisseurs. Their boats were expensive and difficult to maintain, but they were beautiful, hand-crafted creations. Which was superior?

I do not think there is much doubt that in spite of our nostalgia for Hilyard, the shiny new factory was doing the better job. The proof was that they remained in business whereas the Hilyard enterprise finally closed. Yet, in spite of all this, we must constantly remain aware that the plastic factory never did and never will produce outstanding craftsmen. Their technology allows them to succeed in spite of the fact that their best employee has none of the skills, quality, or character strength of Hilyard's youngest apprentice.

Though marvelous, technology has the capacity to conceal a decline in the human qualities of people. One dull child with a twelve-dollar calculator can outshine a brilliant nineteenth-century accountant doing mental arithmetic. The juvenile's accuracy and speed will eclipse that of the man who held the finances of large corporations in his head just one hundred years ago. Let us not fall into the trap of considering the adolescent superior to last generation's accountant. Given the choice we might even have to hire the stripling with the calculator over the skilled number expert of yesterday. But we must remain aware that we will be hiring technical skill without virtue, loyalty, or strength of character, let alone comprehension of what the numbers mean. For those qualities, we might do far better to hire the elderly accountant with the green eyeshade. Technology is very useful indeed, but it doesn't automatically produce greatness in people; sometimes it only conceals weakness. Not only that, but on occasion technological advance provides the illusion that we are moving forward when in reality we are sliding backward.

CHAPTER FOUR

GENERATION BY GENERATION

WHAT MISTAKES ARE WE MAKING RIGHT NOW THAT COULD MAKE THINGS INCREASINGLY INTOLERABLE FOR OUR CHILDREN?

How can technology conceal how little our lives have altered?
Camels and canoes may have given way to Cadillac cars and Concorde supersonic airliners, but people still travel mostly in order to increase their income. Furthermore, travel is still basically uncomfortable. Oh, I do not dispute that a sleeper seat in a transatlantic airliner's first-class section beats a ride through the desert on a camel. But racing to the airport, crossing the ocean, and living out of a suitcase for a week is still less comfortable for most of us than staying home would be. A desert trader of two thousand years ago probably did not have a very comfortable home by modern standards, but whatever it was, it was certainly more comfortable than a camel trip. For him then and for me now, travel is dirty, dangerous, and uncomfortable.

Traveling for business has always been a feature of life, and travel has always been arduous. The desert trader of two thousand years ago spent lonely nights at the oasis campground thinking of his distant wife and children. Occasionally he would fall prey to one of the professional women who plied their trade in the vicinity of the oasis. Today's business traveler returns to his hotel room in some distant city and also misses his wife and children. Sadly, he too may head for the Oasis Lounge off the lobby and feel the allure of one of the professional ladies to be found there. You see, not very much has really changed.

Most people who travel for business spend about the same number of days per year on the road as our great-grandfathers did. The reason for this synchronicity is clear. Most people subconsciously calculate the amount of time they are willing to spend away from family and friends and the amount of discomfort they are willing to endure. They then plug this figure into their economic ambition, massage the resulting equation a little, and emerge with a figure representing roughly how many days each year they are willing to travel for business. All of this is done subconsciously; it even gets updated from time to time. It is no wonder that this number reflecting a basic of human life does not change very much from generation to generation. What does change, of course, is how far we range today on airplane business trips compared to how far our grandparents traveled. But is it worse to drown in an ocean five miles deep than in a swimming pool that is only eight feet deep? Is it significant that I am four thousand miles away from my home on business whereas my grandfather was only six hundred miles? I don't think so.

SOME THINGS HAVE HARDLY CHANGED

Most human beings have discovered that the eight-hour work day is a myth, just as our grandparents also found it necessary to work more than eight-hour days in order to advance their family's living standards. Most of us divide the remainder of the day among sleeping, eating, socializing, engaging in hobbies or other adjuncts to life. It does not really make that much difference whether your work is done walking behind a horse-drawn plow or in front of a computer monitor. The fact remains that I still spend more than a third of my day doing something that may not have been my first choice in how to spend my time, just as my grandfather did. I do it now in exchange for money just as he did back then. He called it work while I massage my ego by calling it a career, but not very much has changed.

Just as my grandpa did a hundred years ago, I find a large part of my meaning in life from spending time with my family. Technology has had little impact on that fundamental of human happiness. If anything, with the advent of mass entertainment through television, family dinner times are more difficult to orchestrate for my family today than they were for my grandpa's family back at the end of the nineteenth century.

I would agree that sleeping on a nice soft innerspring mattress in a suburban condominium beats sleeping on a straw-filled bag in a room over the barn. But are the two experiences different from one another in any fundamental way? I would say not. Tumbling onto one's thermostatically-controlled waterbed after an exhausting day at the stock exchange is not fundamentally different from falling onto one's hay bag after a tough day harvesting corn. This is especially true when one recalls that, to the corn farmer, that dry and warm hay bag was state-of-the-art for its day.

The basics of human life are quite simple. They have to do with a sense of spiritual purpose in life and a warm and loving family. Throw in the esteem of good friends along with enough to eat and drink for oneself and for those one supports. Allow for some extra money in order to acquire a little security and perhaps some prestige. Enjoy sexual fulfillment and a comfortable and pleasing shelter. Technology does not change any of these fundamentals in any significant way. These are the things that have always brought most human beings a sense of happiness and harmony and still do in our present day.

AS STANDARDS DECLINE

With that in mind, we should certainly retain the good changes while alerting ourselves to the frightening ones. Senior citizens cowering in fear behind barred doors is a sight that would have horrified well-intentioned policy makers of an earlier generation. School children being herded through metal detectors on their way to class was inconceivable only a short while ago. Virtually every American of the 1950s would have refused to believe that America's governing machine would ever become incapable of guaranteeing the most basic of all claims citizens legitimately make upon their government: safety from violence. They most certainly would have refused to believe that this lamentable outcome would result from sincere but misguided leadership. But result it did.

The question we are obliged to ask ourselves today is this: What mistakes are we making right now that could make things increasingly intolerable for our children? In the Babylonian Talmud, which is faithfully studied by religious Jews to this day, appears an aphorism. "Who is wise? He who can see what has already been born." The sages did not insist that a wise person see the future, for that takes prophecy, not wisdom. We can all be excused for not seeing the future. But, like Rudyard Kipling's character, Rikki-Tikki-Tavi, the mongoose, we ought to be able to see that tomorrow's fully grown cobras will hatch from those innocuous-looking eggs basking in today's bright sunlight.

What mistakes are we making right now that could make things increasingly intolerable for our children? Some might answer this question by saying that there is nothing to fear, that there are natural cycles in the affairs of men and each generation views its times as periods of unprecedented moral decline. Things rise and fall and then rise again. Our parents were just as shocked by the music we listened to as we are by the music that enthralls our children. Everything is fine, say those who remain unconcerned.

While I agree that each generation is shocked by the customs of the next, this in no way tells us that there is not, in fact, a measurable and objective decline in standards. I am sure that my parents were dismayed by the shift from Bing Crosby to Elvis Presley just as many today are by the journey from the Beatles to the vile words of much of today's rap music. It would be preposterously illogical to conclude that the obscene and degrading lyrics pounded out to the primitive drumbeat of rap are morally equivalent to the innocuous crooning of Crosby. The rise in body temperature of a sick child is more threatening when it goes from 103 degrees to 105, than when it goes from 98.6 to 100.6.

One could wonder whether the line should have been drawn at Elvis Presley or perhaps at the Beatles. Perhaps it needed to be drawn at Crosby. But this is not nearly as urgent a matter as trying to understand where we are likely to find ourselves a few years hence. What is to be said to the optimists who calm us with assurances that things will bounce back? Just wait a few more years, they say. Old music styles will return, the illegitimacy rate will shrink, schools will improve. The problem is that this is not a pattern we have ever seen elsewhere in history. Granted, there are often brief little upward blips, short bursts of good news that must have reassured the inhabitants that the worst was over. But no, they turn out to be little sawteeth on the generally down-sloping graph of civilizations.

THE RISE AND FALL OF CIVILIZATIONS

The sad but inescapable fact is that civilizations invariably rise to prominence and stride confidently onto the stage of world history. After they achieve affluence they begin a long, slow slide into decadence and depravity. Whether we scrutinize the Sumerians and the Phoenicians, the Romans, or even the late, great, British Empire, the story is nearly always the same: civilizations that seemed impregnable fade away.

Does all this have anything to do with us? It most assuredly does. America is changing generation by generation. The changes are, for the most part, part of a slow, tragic decline of a once-great nation. Life in America is becoming, for most people, indescribably more stressful, costly and risky. However, we are still a great nation. We still enjoy almost a monopoly of world power and a higher standard of living than most other nations. Our borders are still an irresistible goal for millions of would-be immigrants. So, how bad can things really be? The answer is that things are not unendurable by a long shot. But that is partly because of incremental deterioration. Things have slid downhill so slowly that we have all had ample time to regard the new reality as normal.

There is only one way to gain a more accurate assessment of where we stand. We need to remind ourselves of how things used to be. We need to compare then and now; we need to imagine how America would look to John F. Kennedy today, let alone to Franklin Roosevelt or George Washington. Only by comparing today to yesterday, can we even begin to understand what tomorrow might look like.

CHAPTER FIVE

A STRANGE DOUBLE STANDARD

WHY IS ONLY *CHRISTIAN* PARTICIPATION IN THE DEMOCRATIC PROCESS PERCEIVED AS A THREAT TO CONSTITUTIONAL SAFETY?

C alling for a return to the enduring values that nurtured our nation through both its greatest and darkest days is not radical. Suggesting that we need to allow traditional Judeo-Christian values to inform our public policies is not an act of revolution. If anything, it is an act of return.

Not that long ago, when Americans said something was right or wrong, they meant right or wrong in the eyes of God as revealed in the Bible. In advocating a return to those days, I am not suggesting anything new; I am recommending something old and proven. I am not suggesting further exploration and experimentation down a dark and unknown alley; I am suggesting we turn around and retrace our steps until we once again find ourselves in familiar and safe territory.

During the last few years, one group has begun to respond to the fact that America is on a dangerous, downward slope. Regarded by some with admiration and by others with vilification, the so-called Christian Right has not caused a rift through this land— they simply have recognized and called attention to the fact that one exists. In the time-honored American tradition they have mobilized the political process in an attempt to return America to a safer course. Welcome to democracy.

WHY THE DOUBLE STANDARD?

If one examines several recent events through the eyes of religious Americans, it is hard to see the changes America has undergone as anything other than a deliberate attempt to alter our nation's foundations in a way that denies and denigrates religious faith. I believe it is important that we recognize the recent surge in political activism among Americans of faith to be what it truly is. It is their response to a perceived threat to their interests, a threat to the very foundations of religious faith and liberty on which America was founded.

Let's face it: Participating in the democratic process through this kind of political activism earns admiration when practiced by Jesse Jackson on behalf of African-American causes. It is greeted enthusiastically when practiced by Jewish groups. It is warmly welcomed when practiced by homosexual activists. But when Christian groups organize to protect their interests, they are demonized.

Not only is this intellectually dishonest, it is also inconsistent with the American way. Jews may be encouraged to vote out of office those representatives perceived to be inadequately supportive of Israel. Blacks may be encouraged to vote out of office those representatives who are thought to harbor illicit feelings. Same with pro-gay and lesbian interest groups. Why, then, the double standard? Why is it unacceptable for Christians to encourage one another to vote out of office those politicians who oppose their family-friendly agendas? Why is only *Christian* participation in the democratic process perceived as "intolerance" and a threat to constitutional safety?

Little by little, year after year, those united behind a secular agenda have succeeded in imposing countless changes on Americans. Had the trend sometimes favored tradition and family and sometimes gone the other way, I doubt that a movement of Christian conservatives would be necessary today. But the trend has been overwhelmingly directed to only one end: It has inexorably shifted American society away from policies friendly to Judeo-Christian tradition. No sooner has one unfriendly change been successfully implemented than the next hostile policy initiative has been launched.

A POLICY BORN OF HATRED

Madalyn Murray O'Hair's victory marked one of these major changes. Today, the removal of prayer from the public schools is generally regarded as an enlightened move that spoke against bigotry and with compassion to all Americans, whatever their faith or lack thereof. Most Jews and other religious minorities welcomed this Supreme Court ruling as an improvement that would make them feel more included in American society. Christians saw it entirely differently.

Few Americans are aware that O'Hair actually harbored a maniacal hatred for this country and had tried desperately to emigrate from here to the Soviet Union. In fact, her son Bill Murray's autobiography reveals that instead of being a loving mother concerned for her son's rights or feelings, she was a violent and cruel woman who merely used her son to advance her goals. Bill Murray's book presents a very different picture from that shown in the famous photographs of an all-American boy and his loving mother on the steps of the Supreme Court in 1962. After all, most Americans do not, while denying they are Communists, attempt to emigrate to the Soviet Union.

After doing just that and being refused entrance by Russia, O'Hair returned home and began her crusade. As her son recalls, she was incensed upon hearing that he participated in school prayers:

> "You stupid fool," she said, slapping me hard across the face. "Don't you understand what is going on yet?" Her face was flushed again. "Listen, kid, the United States of America is nothing more than a fascist slave labor camp run by a handful of Jew bankers in New York City. They trick you into believing you're free with those phony rigged elections. Just because we can run around the street free doesn't mean we are really free.
>
> "The only way true freedom can be achieved is through the new socialist man—an entire race that lives for the state. Only when all men know the truth of their animal sameness will we have true freedom. Russia is close but not close enough, or they would have let us in. The CIA probably passed bad information on us.
>
> ..."Well, if they'll keep us from going to Russia where there is some freedom, we'll just have to change America. I'll make sure you never say another prayer in the school!"[1]

On June 17, 1963, in an act of judicial fiat that went against the will of the majority of Americans, the Supreme Court, with only Justice Potter Stewart dissenting, awarded victory to O'Hair and defeat to millions of religious Americans.

Perhaps it does not legally make a difference that O'Hair desired the destruction of this country and was a despicable individual. Or that the "hero" of another landmark decision of those years, Larry Flynt, was by his own admission a "scumbag." Or that Norma McCorvey, the true identity of Jane Roe in *Roe v. Wade,* now admits she was manipulated by others and profoundly regrets her part in the Court's landmark ruling on abortion.

What *should* make a difference is the fact that these issues have not died down. If, almost forty years after a ruling, the issue still causes major conflict between large segments of our society, perhaps the Court was the wrong place for the issue to be decided. The Supreme Court has on occasion reversed itself. The Court is composed of nine human beings who occasionally do need to make a correction when hindsight shows that they allowed misplaced logic to rule. A classic example is the *Plessy v. Ferguson* decision of the 1890s, which allowed legal racial segregation until the Court overruled itself in the legendary *Brown v. Board of Education.* Our Supreme Court, for all its greatness, is not above human error. The Judiciary certainly possesses the incredible power to impose a certain moral view on America. The fact that America has not accepted every view that our courts have attempted to impose does suggest that there is a tug-of-war going on.

My father, a renowned rabbi, repeatedly told me that there is an imaginary fifth section to the four-volume text, the *Shulchan Aruch,* that codifies Jewish law. He used to call it the Volume of Common Sense. Looking back at the judicial rulings of the 1960s, that virtue of common sense seems to have disappeared. Our sense of decency and our belief in the Constitution were used as tools against us. We were manipulated by those who, by their own admission, hated both America and God.

For those of us who believe that restoring prayer to the public schools is an essential element in defeating drug use and promiscuity, it is not uncommon to be dismissed as simplistic. How foolish we must be to blame society's ills on the absence of a three-minute activity at the beginning of each school day! But let us imagine that the ruling never took place. At the time, eleven states already prohibited Bible reading in school. After the decision, the *New York Times* reported that 41 percent of school districts would need to change their practices. If the Judiciary had not been an activist one and had left the decisions in the hands of local school boards and individual states, we would have been able to better judge the impact of removing prayers from schools by comparing school districts. An activist Court took away the option of letting communities determine for themselves what works and what does not and of allowing society to evaluate its own choices.

Liberal doctrine will argue that it is wrong and simplistic to blame the removal of prayer from schools for the astounding increase in violence, pregnancies and drug use over the last few decades. And I agree. Yet it is very plausible to contend that the removal of prayer was a cataclysmic change, an iceberg in our path, which helped lead to all these negatives.

THE NEUTRALITY MYTH

The fallacy at the root of the removal of prayer from schools is the belief that the opposite of religion is neutrality. What is clear to me is that by removing religious references from the classroom, an anti-Judeo-Christian religion has taken its place. Instead of achieving neutrality, we have achieved unfair and intellectually dishonest bias. Nowhere is this more clear than in the creation-evolution debate.

Let us try to understand the unspoken but unmistakable message our children are receiving. Few have been as succinct and honest about the moral message contained in evolutionist dogma as Harvard professor and leading evolutionist, Stephen Jay Gould. In his closing comments for a Canadian Broadcasting Corporation documentary for David Suzuki, called *The Nature of Things* he said, "Now that we know we were not made in anybody's image, we are free to do whatever we wish." I personally suspect that this view has less to do with his paleontological training and more to do with his secular Jewish background and the flag of the USSR that used to decorate his office wall.

Unlike religious Catholics and Jews, religious Protestants tended to rely on the nation's public schools for their children's education: reading, writing, arithmetic, history, science, and so on. But then aggressive secularism was forced onto the nation's schools during the '60s, '70s, and '80s, and it increased in intensity with each passing year. It has reached unprecedented heights of extremism during the '90s. Not only have Christian parents found that academic standards have declined, but when they send their six-year-olds off to first grade, anticipating excited accounts of traditional learning and activities, they discover that they have been naïve—and deceived. For example, in the early 1990s, New York children came home from school speaking of an explicit lesbian advocacy text read in class: *Heather Has Two Mommies*. Christian parents' religious beliefs instruct that the best home situation for a child is a loving mother and father, and that lesbianism (something they never would discuss with a six-year-old) is a sin. Yet their children's teacher taught that their way of thinking showed a lack of compassion, or at best an anti-quated belief.

After justified outrage, the New York school board underwent major changes. But similar examples exist in many other school districts throughout this country, and most instances have not received the national press or the positive result that this one did.

The very moment any parent might suggest that some books are not suitable for elementary school children due to sexual explicitness, the entire academic establishment explodes in indignation at the whisper of censorship. In contrast, whenever a school library discovers some long-forgotten volume which political correctness now decrees might offend one group or another, that book is instantly yanked. When the school inflicts books on youngsters which deliberately undermine the moral and religious convictions of parents, it is termed "education." Should parents complain, they are portrayed as narrow-minded or "intolerant."

Is it any wonder that so many Americans feel an entire new set of values has been shoved down their throats? Is it not clear that a moral tug-of-war is being waged in America's public schools?

Sex education classes routinely promote as normative those ideas that are abhorrent to religious adherents of many faiths, including, once again, the Christian community. There is substantial proof that these classes lead to increased and earlier sexual activity among our youth. When Christian conservatives speak of starting the school day with prayer and allow that a child's parents may ask to have him or her excused from that activity, liberals shout that that would make the child stand out from the crowd and cause his self-esteem to suffer. Why, then, when Christian conservatives complain of children being forced to take sex education courses that conflict with their religious values, liberals are unabashed in answering that the children's parents can always ask to have them excused?

OFFEND NO GROUP, EXCEPT ONE

It seems to me that we have reached a point where it is demanded that the concerns and sensitivities of every group in America must be taken into account—with the sole exception of the concerns of America's Christians. Given that their concerns so often spring directly from the pages of the Bible, it is disturbing to me that Jews so seldom support them on these matters. What is worse is that much too often, those school board members pushing an anti-religious agenda on the schools are themselves Jewish. Recently, in both Texas and Illinois, Christian parents organized to democratically vote out of office school board members who were fighting ferociously to introduce condom programs to small and largely conservative school districts. In both cases, the offending board members were secular Jews. In both cases, the local Jewish communities created a national uproar by alleging anti-Semitism. What are Christian parents to do?

As a citizenry we have allowed our tax dollars to be used to promote the arts. Unfortunately, much of what passes for taxpayer-supported "art" is nothing short of obscene defamation. Can anyone imagine the federal government funding an "artistic" rendering of Martin Luther King dunked in urine, or a map of the state of Israel smeared with excrement? Of course not. If such an abuse of tax dollars had slipped through, the outrage would have filled editorial pages and front pages of newspapers for days. Those responsible would have been rightfully fired. But when tax dollars funded a so-called work of art that depicted a crucifix dipped in urine, we heard only high-minded drivel from the secular Left and the cultural elite about the necessary price of free expression. Once again, Christians were subjected to society's strange double standard and placed in a position where they were forced to fund insults to their faith.

"DON'T FORCE YOUR VALUES DOWN OUR THROATS"

Often, as I speak on these issues across the country, someone in the audience hurls this tired old corker: "The religious Right is trying to force its values down our throats." I have a standard response which I enjoy offering. I inform my listeners that the secular Left has introduced sexual indoctrination and condom distribution to eleven-year-old public school students. It has made the enjoyment of tobacco the moral equivalent of child molestation. It has dramatically increased illegitimacy in America. It has created an entertainment ethos that brings smut and vulgarity into our living rooms. Take an honest look at the values that the secular Left has already succeeded in forcing down the throats of religious Americans. How can anyone honestly confront the changes that have been inflicted by the secular Left and worry about the changes that the religious Right might force down our throats?

I contend that the values concerned Christians desire for America are not really changes, but simply the return to an earlier and legitimate status. If you fling an invader out of your land, back over the border he illegally crossed in the first place, you are not guilty of aggression. It is called self-defense. You are worried that the religious Right might succeed in forcing their values onto us? I am worried they might fail, for they are our values too. Or at least they ought to be.

CHAPTER SIX

THE CURIOUS RISE
OF ANTI-CHRISTIANISM

IF THE TERM "ANTI-SEMITISM" IS TO RETAIN
ANY INTELLECTUAL AND MORAL INTEGRITY,
WE MUST ALSO TODAY ADMIT TO THE TERM
"ANTI-CHRISTIANISM."

A s societal values eroded over the past four decades, not only were the valid concerns of Christians ignored but their growing political involvement was viciously attacked. It was as if only *other* groups, such as Jews, union members or racial minorities were allowed to organize themselves to further their own group interests by democratic process.

For example, whenever Jews organized to advance something they perceived to be in their best interest nobody was allowed to criticize. And why should they? Under our rules of democracy, the Jews were exercising a legitimate right. However, Christians doing the same thing have been immediately reviled and portrayed in sinister terms. The American Jewish Committee was kosher while the Christian Coalition was dangerous and evil. How are Christians supposed to feel?

ATTACKING FREEDOM OF BELIEF

Prominent in the assault against traditional Judeo-Christian values, I am sorry to say, were a number of Jewish organizations. In fact, it was the ferocity and unfairness of the attacks that brought me, and many others, into the fray. One famous battle in this cultural tug-of-war came in 1994 with the publication of two volumes that I consider biased and bigoted. *The Political Activity of the Religious Right in the 1990s: A Critical Analysis,* published by the American Jewish Committee (AJC), harshly criticized religious Christians because they, among other things, "adamantly oppose social acceptance of homosexuality as an alternative lifestyle." Whether one thinks homosexuality is right or wrong, the AJC was attacking the right of Christians to freedom of belief.

Since those beliefs are based on the Bible in which I too believe, I felt I could not remain silent while the AJC suggested that Judaism somehow supported the acceptance of homosexuality. For over three thousand years Jewish tradition and Jewish law have been unambiguous about homosexuality: it is a sin. Now an organization with the word "Jewish" in its title was vilifying Christians for taking the authentic Jewish position on homosexuality. I felt as if I had emigrated to Alice's Wonderland, where logic and ratio-nality were completely turned around. I did everything in my power to remind Americans that Judaism was actually the source for opposing homosexuality as an acceptable lifestyle. I reminded Americans that although many Jews (whose real faith is secular humanism) support the homosexual agenda, this tells us as much about Judaism as the entertainer Madonna tells us about the Roman Catholic faith.

The Anti-Defamation League (ADL) similarly published a book filled with unfair and untrue defamation of religious conservatives. It contained such unrestrained invec-tive as, "The religious Right brings to the debate over moral and social issues a rhetoric of fear, suspicion and even hatred." As a rabbi and as a Jew, I was embarrassed at the tone of both these books. Had any Christian association published anything comparable about the Jewish community, cries of anti-Semitism would have rung out far and wide— and been justified.

I found myself unable to ignore the above diatribes, so the organization I head, Toward Tradition, published a repudiation of the sentiments in a large paid advertise-ment in the *New York Times* that was signed by fifty prominent Jewish conservatives and called for Jewish conservatives to band together. The response was overwhelming. Letters poured in from Conservative and Reform Jews all over the country who, because of their traditional values, had been made to feel unwelcome in their synagogues and local Jewish establishments. Many Orthodox Jews contacted us with gratitude for telling America that the American Jewish Committee and Anti-Defamation League did not represent them. Several Reform rabbis wrote to pledge support while asking to remain anonymous for fear of being fired were their conservative political leanings to become known.

THE DISHONESTY OF ANTI-CHRISTIANISM

Just as there are many seniors who join the American Association of Retired Persons for the benefits (and who would be shocked to discover that they are funding a radical lib-eral agenda), I have found that many well-meaning Jews support groups purporting to fight anti-Semitism and promote fellowship, when in fact these groups use much of their time and money to support aggressively secular and Left-leaning causes. These groups also regularly commit what I call "anti-Christianism." They have declared war against the recent rise of religious conservatism in American politics. Even a quick glance at publications and direct-mail appeals from the Anti-Defamation League, American Jewish Committee, American Jewish Congress and others, reveals a level of rhetoric that far exceeds the bounds of civilized political discourse. Their words demonstrate that many Jewish organizations do not merely consider devout, politically active Christians to be misguided—they consider them evil. I believe that if the term anti-Semitism is to retain any intellectual and moral integrity, we must also today admit to the term anti-Christianism. If one is to be fought, then surely both should be.

For too long, any questioning of the policies and priorities of the American Jewish community has been foreclosed by the fear that potential critics would be stigmatized as anti-Semites. If you condemn Hollywood for its focus on sex and violence, you must be an anti-Semite since so many Hollywood policy makers are Jewish. Do you oppose liberal dogma? Once again you risk being called an anti-Semite. The reflexive impulse to denounce as a bigot anyone who dares question any aspect of liberal life, including Jewish organizational support for it, actually fosters and promotes the hostility toward Jews that these organizations were founded to forestall.

I am aware that there are true anti-Semites in this country. I naturally had to consider the possibility that writing this book would run the risk of supplying them with fuel. However, after looking through some of their literature I rejected that idea, for anti-Semites do not need fuel. They will use whatever is available and twist it or conjure it up themselves. Fortunately they are few in number and small in influence. I do not wish to see their small number or limited influence change, but I see little risk of that, unless, because of the behavior of a small, but very vocal, number of Jews and misguided American Jewish "leadership," decent, ordinary Americans are forced to begin to question whether Jews are bad for this country. I realize how inflammatory this statement is and will expand on it in detail later on. I do know that I am not alone in that concern. A letter to the editor in the October 1998 issue of *Moment* magazine (which bills itself as the "Jewish magazine for the '90s) states: "The Jews in America have often been a great blessing to this country, from the large number of Nobel Prize winners to many thousands of Jewish physicians, judges, teachers, and builders of business enterprises." That said, I must add a fact that is embarrassing me more and more as an American Jew. The scandals in this administration have brought to public attention an entirely different group of Jews, from Monica Lewinsky, whose sexual proclivities have made me burn with shame, to all the spinning defense lawyers on national TV night after night, from Bernard Schwartz of Loral, who apparently sold missile technology to China, to Larry Lawrence, who falsified his war record to be buried in Arlington National Cemetery. This is a new group of Jewish faces, a whole different generation from that of Einstein, and Cardozo, Salk and Buber. Frankly, they strike me as arrogant, shameless, and very foolish. They have all the answers, or so they think, but the people who see them on TV night after night know better.

There was a time when the Jewish community worried about being tarred by the actions of some irresponsible individuals. Apparently this is no longer true. But if anybody thinks there are no potential anti-Semites noticing the number of Jews involved in national scandals, they are only fooling themselves. It is high time for Jews who care about our public image to dissociate themselves from these characters.

I can only add that not only is Jewish leadership silent in not denouncing Jews who behave reprehensibly, they too often are, as I mentioned above and will enumerate further, in the forefront of hateful and reprehensible behavior themselves.

TIME FOR SELF-APPRAISAL

My firm conviction is that we must engage in an honest exploration of the problems and shortcomings of the Jewish community and Jewish communal leadership. Instead of focusing on imagined enemies, we should ask whether dogmatic commitment to a secular-liberal vision is encouraging dislike for the Jewish community. Without such honest self-appraisal, Jews will become more and more disliked—not by crazed individuals but by decent Americans distressed over their rapidly deteriorating culture and the role of Jews in that agenda. It cannot escape the notice of ordinary Americans coping with the challenges of raising responsible children in a hostile world that many Jewish names and groups lead the fight for policies these Americans see as causing the country's decline.

When the moral basis of a nation disintegrates, my people are often the first to suffer. I am convinced that if America abandons her Judeo-Christian heritage, there will be no place here for Jews. This would be particularly true were the role played by secularized Jews in America's slide to socialism to increase. We might well see a replay of what took place in Russia, where secularized and anti-religious Jews, against the advice of many leading Orthodox rabbis, disproportionately supported the Communist revolution. Before long they became persecuted by that same revolution and were clamoring to leave the country. It would be ironic indeed if the country that did the most to rescue Russian Jews from the socialist nightmare that was partly of their own creation, were to be assisted down the road to socialism by her own Jewish community.

In the final analysis, who other than a Jew filled with genuine love for Judaism and his fellow Jews, what we call *Ahavat Yisrael,* can legitimately criticize other Jews who, perhaps unintentionally, are joining in the destruction of this society? Who better than a son of Abraham to come to the defense of God's vision as outlined in the Bible, even if those who most fiercely oppose that vision include those of Jewish ancestry? In defending that biblical vision, I do not seek a radical new religious agenda foisted upon an unwilling country. I seek to encourage those Americans similarly inclined to help return America to its founding moral imperative. This is neither a cry for religious revolution nor a crusade; it is something else entirely. It is a reminder that we have lost our way. It is a suggestion that we return home again.

Why do we now see, as we approach the millennium, America's religious conservatives pushing efforts to pass a school prayer amendment, a defense of marriage act, and other laws codifying moral issues? Until a few decades ago, such acts were not needed. They were part and parcel of what everyone understood to be obviously necessary to American life. The Christians who are leading the above legislative measures are not being proactive—they are being reactive. They are reacting to changes in this country that have not been neutral toward religion, but hostile to it. All of a sudden, Christians in this country have found themselves under selective assault. God has, almost overnight, been removed from the educational, legal, and political institutions of the country.

Newton's third law of motion states that for every action there is an equal and opposite reaction. As a deeply religious and committed Christian, Sir Isaac would, I hope, approve of this application of his great observation: As God was forcibly removed from America's public square and as Christian beliefs were jeered at and reviled in the country's universities and media, a counter-movement arose, whose purpose was to restore God back to His rightful place. During the past thirty-five years we have undergone a terrifyingly effective action; we are now witnessing the reaction. How can anyone blame Christians for protecting biblical belief and defending their values? How can Jews possibly support the preposterous premise that devout religious observance is a national menace?

CHAPTER SEVEN

CULTURE WAR

WE ARE NO LONGER ONE NATION UNDER GOD.
WE ARE TWO SEPARATE NATIONS WITH
TWO DISTINCT AND INCOMPATIBLE MORAL VISIONS.

Most Americans, oblivious to the approaching crisis, regarded the conservative Christian movement as something that suddenly exploded onto the national stage. Not surprisingly, an uproar erupted when the words "culture war" were spoken at the 1992 Republican convention. After all, American citizens profess many different faiths, come from diverse backgrounds, and have two major opposing political parties, but surely we respect each other. Why use fighting words? Why suggest that a war exists between groups of citizens in our country?

I believe that understanding this phrase, "culture war," is imperative for the restoration of our society.

When the Civil War was fought, the individuals participating were not enemies. Often they were neighbors and cousins; in more than one instance they were brothers. On both sides fought upright, valiant soldiers. However, they had reached a point where their conflicting beliefs could no longer coexist in one country. A terrible war ensued, but at the end of the fighting, one idea again prevailed. Once again, we were one country.

This time the culture war, thankfully, is not a bloody one. That makes it no less a war that will, in the end, yield a victor and a loser. The two ideas struggling for supremacy in society today cannot coexist. One needs to dominate. What are these two ideas?

Reduced to their simplest elements, one idea claims that public adherence to biblical values and acceptance of traditional godly direction are essential for the continued existence of this country. The opposing view is that such religion, while perhaps laudable for individuals, is an impediment to progress in the public arena.

What do I believe is meant by the phrase "culture war"? Author Russell Kirk was once asked the source of humankind's many cultures. His reply was that they originally came from cults. While the word "cult" has now taken on a negative connotation, it originally meant a joining together for worship—that is, the attempt of people to commune with a transcendent power. Therefore, when we say that people are unified by a common culture, what we really mean is that they share the same general view of God and His expectations. Conversely, when we speak of a culture war, we are referring to a great rift over the issue of God. What does this have to do with most Americans? The role of God in society is somehow similar to that of sewers, telephone lines and gas pipes. We don't see them running invisibly beneath our streets. We seldom even think about them. However, their sudden removal would dramatically and horribly impact our lives. Likewise, we never used to think about the invisible structure of morality and logic that lay reassuringly beneath our culture. Now, however, it is being ripped up.

TWO NATIONS INSTEAD OF ONE

One of the most profound truths about America as we approach the end of the twentieth century is that we are no longer one nation under God. We are really two separate nations with two distinct and incompatible moral visions. We are two nations occupying the same piece of real estate and engaged in a giant cultural tug-of-war for that real estate. In the last few elections, some politicians attempted to use this concept of two Americas to divide us into warring groups. Blacks were pitted against whites, rich against poor, Democrats against Republicans, Christians against Jews, consumers against capitalists, men against women. The truth is that different people do have different ideas of how America should look. But it is a lot simpler than a complicated smorgasbord of competing interests.

I believe there are just two basic, competing visions for America which encompass all the various special interest groups. The two views can best be characterized as either support for or opposition to Judeo-Christian morality playing a role in American public life. The crucial point I want to make here is that *both* sides attract blacks and whites, rich and poor, Democrats and Republicans, Christians and Jews, and men and women. It is important to note that members of religious, ethnic, and gender groups unite with those of varying religious, ethnic, and gender groups despite media attempts to insist otherwise. California's Proposition 209 banning affirmative action was passed not because whites on one side outnumbered blacks on the other. Blacks and whites lined up on both sides of the issue. *Heather Has Two Mommies,* the aforementioned book that attempted to inculcate first grade students in New York City with the idea that lesbianism was acceptable, was taken out of the schools by a coalition of Protestants, Catholics, and Jews.

California's Proposition 227 English for the Children, was driven by the passion of Jewish conservative Ron Unz and passed overwhelmingly by Californians of every race, color, religion, and socio-economic background. Bill Clinton was not, despite headlines to the contrary, elected because women lined up staunchly for him. Truth be told, married and unmarried women differed in their voting patterns even more than males and females did in theirs.

TWO FUNDAMENTAL QUESTIONS

I would like to make what seems on the surface to be an outrageous suggestion, but one I hope to buttress throughout this book. More often, people are now lining up with each other according to how they answer two essential questions:

1. Do you yearn for an America in which God is allowed and honored outside of our churches and synagogues, or do you want an America in which lip service is paid to Him so long as He is kept out of the real world?

2. Do you accept a view of God that would be compatible with one that your religion held 223 years ago at the founding of this country, or have you reinvented God to fit in with your present-day views?

Dividing Americans along those two fault lines begins to make sense of otherwise confusing data.

Many women are eschewing radical feminism for a reemphasis on being wives and mothers. They are black and white, Jewish and Christian, rich and poor, Democrat and Republican. What unites them is a belief that raising a family is a noble and worthwhile use of their time and talents. Radical feminists, on the other hand, vehemently reject a traditional model for family life. If you doubt this, do what few have bothered to do: find and read the platform of the last United Nations Conference on Women.

Statistics often deceive rather than enlighten. When the McCaughey septuplets were born, columnists delighted in mentioning that they would need close to 30,000 diapers in the next few years. Since my wife and I have seven children, all past the toilet-training stage, I began jokingly telling people that between us, Susan and I had changed that many diapers. That was technically true but utterly deceptive. The diaper changing duties were in no way divided evenly between us. It is also correct, but utterly misleading, to state that a graduating student from Stanford University has a 50 percent chance of giving birth to a baby. Yes, I know that almost 100 percent of the female graduates will one day give birth. Yes, I know that zero percent of the male graduates will ever give birth. But averaging those results confuses rather than enlightens.

There are large families in America today, as there were one hundred years ago. I have been told of studies that inform prospective pediatricians that large families are prone to certain problems. Poor nutrition, sexual abuse, and low IQs are some of the dangers touted. In the large families I know, and I know many, malnutrition is hardly a danger. The only possible candidates for "abuse" are the parents who have chosen to be deprived of leisure, time alone, and many material luxuries. And no one has told the children of these families, who often excel in their studies, that their intelligence is endangered by the presence of their many siblings. How do we reconcile the grim statistics collected about large families with the large and happy families we know and love?

This is not a difficult problem as long as you remember that we are not one, but two nations. Mixing entirely different statistics from the two separate nations, and presenting the averaged results to a trusting populace, confuses the issue rather than shedding light on it.

The two nations of America are not distinguished by their incomes as much as by their religious outlook. In one of these nations, a family with many children means a husband and wife devoting their lives to one another and to their children. It may mean a widow and a widower combining their families; or two divorced people, who recognize their divorce as a major tragedy, combining theirs; or a combination of the above. What these families share is a commitment to the concept that one man married to one woman and raising children is a noble enterprise.

In the other America we find that a large family might well be a never-married woman with many children, none of whom will ever know his father. Or perhaps, there is a succession of fathers, each present for a short time. Or perhaps as marriages and divorces occur, many groups of step-siblings weave in and out of each other's lives. Families in this other America are not distinguished by race, religion or income. They are distinguished by the sad fact that they have abandoned God's plan for human happiness.

This other America is made up of those for whom marriage is either an unnecessary and unsacred concept or perhaps even a recreational activity, to be ignored or to be entered into and exited with a casualness that makes divorce a Hallmark card opportunity. This America includes those who encourage others to think that a family is whatever you want it to be. They like to mix the statistics of the two Americas and pronounce the doom facing large families. It is true that in this America there is a likelihood of the children being hurt by one of the procession of men passing through the mother's life. Psychiatric problems abound as do learning difficulties. But the determinant is not the large number of children. It is the absence of the sacred, holy dimension provided by the biblical model.

There is an important similarity between these two Americas: Both are products of a belief and of a moral vision. Some of the people in each America have thoughtfully and carefully decided where they belong; others are either the fortunate recipients of a tradition or the victims of those who have persuaded them that one vision is correct.

There is only one core difference between these two Americas: the difference in moral vision that each chooses. This is the tug-of-war taking place in our land. It includes the cultural disagreement between women who feel that fulfillment can best be found outside the home rather than within it. Some women, like my wife and six daughters, believe that motherhood, family building, community support, and all-around nurturing are worthy and noble activities. Other women heap scorn on these traditional views, dismissing them in contemptuous terms. The tug-of-war is not between black and white or between rich and poor. The main separation between the majority of traditionally minded women, whether or not they work outside the home, and hard-line feminine careerists is how each views God's guidance.

As the bow of our ship of state sinks deeper into the dark ocean, I believe each American must carefully think about which vision for our nation will lead to success, both for individuals and for the country as a whole. The lines are blurred today. There are indeed upright, staunch citizens in both the Democratic and Republican parties. There are honest politicians and decent leaders who consider themselves liberals, and honest politicians and decent leaders who call themselves conservatives. Likewise, both liberals and conservatives have within their ranks people with whom they should be ashamed to be associated. Nonetheless, we need to understand the two basic pulls tugging at both us and our political representatives.

WHICH GOD SHALL WE SERVE?

Only when we realize that there are two diametrically opposing nations struggling to gain ascendancy in America will we be able to have an open and honest examination of where each will lead. One acknowledges the Judeo-Christian tradition as necessary for America to survive, while the other defiantly insists that religion should stay in the churches and out of the public square. Note that we are not discussing whether Americans should attend worship services or belong to a religious organization. We are speaking instead of ideas that permeate and shape every decision of our lives. We are contemplating whether we should place God and biblical morality in a neat little box labeled "religion" or, as our founding fathers did, regard God and biblical morality as the core value for all of life. It is imperative to know whether our god is the God of all time or a god created in modern man's image, a god to be used merely as a photo op or to justify our "enlightened" positions.

I remember enjoying a fascinating debate on my radio show with Peter J. Gomes, Plummer Professor of Christian Morals at Harvard University. Since I had never met him nor yet read any of his writing, I assumed that his outlook would be similar to that of most of my African-American friends who are Christians. Which is to say that I anticipated a cheery chat with someone with whom I expected to agree on most important issues. Well, Professor Gomes is an extremely likable and engaging fellow, but we agreed on very little. This may well have resulted in a more entertaining radio show than had we agreed, but I was still shocked to find myself so at odds with someone who taught Christian morals at one of the country's great universities.

Attempting to nail things down a bit, I asked him if we could at least agree that the act of homosexuality is a sin. To my astonishment, he burst into good-natured laughter and assured me that under no circumstances was he prepared to consider homosexuality a sin. This served as quite an education for me. Here was one of our society's premier intellects claiming that the Bible is not the defining authority on what constitutes a sin. At that point it became clear to me that whether Peter Gomes was black or white, homosexually-inclined or not, rich or poor, professor or construction worker, Democrat or Republican, mattered not at all in clarifying our relationship. What mattered most was whether we viewed traditional Judeo-Christian principles as relevant to the American experience. He did not and I did. That was all there was to it.

Dr. Gomes was good fun and I remain indebted to him for so honestly identifying for me what the schism is all about. We could be friends but we cannot both be right. Either he is right or I am. If he is teaching morality at Harvard, that esteemed college cannot serve the needs of my children. We disagree on only one issue, but it is a big one: whether God created us in His image and supplied us, for our own good, with His commandments.

People often think that life would be better if we knew for certain whether God created us; if we knew for certain whether death ends it all or is only a beginning; if we knew which lifestyle truly provides lasting fulfillment. These are the identical questions asked by a child reaching the threshold of cognizance. Every young mind disconcerts his parents by persistently questioning his origins and senses the awkwardness caused by his curiosity about death. In contrast to the view held by many child psychiatrists, a child yearns to be told what he is supposed to be doing between birth and death. A country needs to agree on the answers to these questions no less than individuals do.

CHAPTER EIGHT

ORIGINS AND DESTINY

WE SHOULD NOT BE SURPRISED THAT THE SECULAR LEFT TELLS US WE ARE HOPELESSLY DOOMED.

Where do we come from, and what end is in store for us? Judaism's Ethics of the Fathers advises us to mull over this question.

As to where we came from, there are really only two possibilities. Let's characterize them this way: We descended either from apes or from angels. That is it. In other words, was there a godly dimension to man's creation or not? The starkness of this question is what has propelled evolution into being a major focus of science in most schools.

In fact, while it may sound illogical at first, that question actually has nothing to do with whether we believe in evolution. God may have used some form of "evolution" as His method of creation. It also has nothing to do with believing in a literal interpretation of the Bible or in six twenty-four-hour days of creation. What we must do is choose between what I call the godly choice and the anti-godly choice rather than getting caught up in theological details. Details are important, of course, but only within each of our faiths and theologies. For purposes of trying to clarify the cultural tug-of-war, we need only ask the question: Did we get here by a process of unaided materialistic evolution or did God arrange it? Do we come from a Creator or from apes?

To clarify the practical implications of this dilemma, let me tell you what happened to one of my teachers, a great rabbi. On a trip to Israel, he found himself seated next to one of the heads of the Israeli socialist labor movement. Soon after the plane took off, one of my teacher's students, seated several rows behind, came forward and said, "Rabbi, let me take your shoes; I have your slippers here. You know how your feet swell on the airplane." A few minutes later, the student returned and said, "Here are the sandwiches your wife sent. I know you do not like the airline food."

This went on in similar fashion for some time, and finally the head of Israel's socialist labor movement turned to my teacher and said, "I don't get this. I am so impressed with your son. I have four sons. They're grown now. But in all my life I don't recall them ever offering to do anything at all for me. Why is your son doing all of this?" And the rabbi said, "He isn't my son, he's my student. Had my son been here you would really have seen service. But you must not blame yourself. Your sons are faithful to your teachings, and my sons are faithful to my teachings. It is simple, you see. You made the decision to teach your sons that you are descended from apes. That means that you are one generation closer to the ape than they. And that means that it is only proper and appropriate that you acknowledge their status and that you serve them. But, you see, I chose to teach my sons that we came from God Himself. And that puts me one generation closer to the Ultimate Truth, which means it is only appropriate that they treat me accordingly."

Does society as a whole need to answer this question? Well, until we answer that question, how can we decide whether school children ought to start their days with prayer? Until we answer that question, how can we punish criminals? If we got here by a process of unaided materialistic evolution, then we are not significantly different from animals, and everyone knows that animals do not have moral choice. We do not punish a cougar for snatching a rancher's sheep for dinner. That is what cougars do. We may find a way of protecting the farmer's assets but we do not consider the cougar wicked. If we are qualitatively animals, then mugging little old ladies is just what some people do. Labeling their actions as wicked makes no sense, and you cannot punish humans who have done nothing wicked any more than you can punish cougars.

REPLACING ONE RELIGION WITH ANOTHER

The problem is that some people have successfully imposed a false idea upon the rest of us. They have persuaded us that religion is at one end of the spectrum while a bland kind of neutrality is at the other. They assured us that they were not opposed to religion, they just wanted to protect those who professed different religions. They comforted us by telling us that they just wanted to remove the practice of any specific religion from public life. This is a bit like saying that one is not against food, one simply objects to imposing any specific diet upon the hungry. Therefore no food should be provided to people for fear of appearing to endorse any specific diet.

It is a fallacy that removing religion from the growing-up experience of our next generation is a neutral action. It is far from neutral; it is a powerful statement that has been noted by an entire generation. What has become clear is that by removing religious references from the classroom, an anti-Judeo-Christian religion has taken its place.

Nowhere is this more clear than in the creation-evolution debate. Does how we decide the answer really make a difference in our practical lives outside of synagogue and church? It most certainly does.

I hear you saying, "But evolution has been proven. We can't ignore science." The presumptuous teaching of materialistic evolution is one of the greatest proofs that there is indeed a war going on in America today. Newspapers, TV, and school textbooks teach the theory of evolution as a scientific fact. Meanwhile, six-inch, titanium steel nails are being driven into the coffin of Darwinian evolution by many brilliant men and women such as my children's favorite professor, University of California at Berkeley law professor Phillip Johnson. This genial force is changing the face of American academia with his books and lectures. Fortunately for us, courageous men such as Phillip Johnson, author of *Darwin on Trial,* and Michael Behe, in his surprise bestseller *Darwin's Black Box,* have bucked the establishment and produced works that show how evolution is not a fact, but a theory. They expose serious scientific problems with the theory of evolution. They do not claim a more provable thesis; they simply state that "we don't know" is intellectually preferable to insisting that evolution is fact even if it means ignoring the evidence.

I would seriously challenge all educators, but particularly the heads of religious schools and colleges who have not yet exposed their students to Dr. Johnson and his arguments, to do so very soon.

College students have told me that if they question evolutionary doctrine in a class, they are told that no dissent is allowed. What better proof that this is dogma, not science? The elementary or high school science teacher is passing on to the next generation what he has been told. He is often personally religious but separates his beliefs from what he has been taught are irrefutable facts. In contrast, the high priests of the evolution movement comprehend very well what the battle really is. To them evolution *must* be correct because there *must* be the probability of a world without God.

FACT VS. BELIEF

Surely I exaggerate, you may think. But I do not. Professor William Provine of Cornell University is an internationally recognized scientist and proponent of evolution. In a famous videotaped debate against Professor Phil Johnson, author of *Darwin on Trial,* he claimed that there are three indispensable components to accepting Darwinian evolution. These include accepting *as a fact* that there is no life of any sort after death. Now I choose to live my life according to the belief that there is life after death, but I know this to be a belief, not a provable fact. When Professor Provine insists that the scientist must accept the doctrine of no life after death as proven, he is blurring the distinction between facts and beliefs. I can think of no scientific experiment that has conclusively shown that there either is or is not life after death. Professor Provine is, of course, as entitled to his beliefs as I am to mine. The difference is that I do not try to impose my beliefs upon all American students by mislabeling them as scientific fact.

The debate is not between religion and science. The scientists who are now on the cutting edge of human knowledge sound quite different from the popular media scientists. Unlike the book *Shadows of Forgotten Ancestors: A Search for Who We Are* by media star Carl Sagan, a secular Jew, the writings of neurophysiologist John Eccles or cosmologist Stephen Hawking and many others resound with the language of worship. Their use of the word "God" is adoring and unselfconscious. Contrary to popular belief, even Charles Darwin could not conceive of a discussion on the origins of life without invoking God's name. In an earlier time, Sir Isaac Newton wrote more about God than he did about mathematics. He almost certainly felt the fame he earned for his *Principia Mathematica* rightly belonged to the Almighty whom he praised. Gerald Schroeder, Lee Spetner, and other Orthodox Jewish physicists are among the many scientists who likewise see no contradiction between Scripture and science. In his recent book, *The Science of God,* Schroeder quotes Harvard professor emeritus of zoology, Ernst Mayr, who has been a noted authority and advocate of Darwinian evolution. After many years of study Mayr had the intellectual honesty to admit that we may never solve the puzzle of the origin of the species.

No, the debate is not between religion and science but between two competing and incompatible belief systems, one religious and Judeo-Christian, the other secular and materialistic. Either of these two faith-driven systems, if adopted by large numbers of Americans, would produce completely different societies. We saw an example of this above with the story of my rabbi friend on the airplane. Let us examine this issue further.

HOMO SAPIENS REDEFINED

Most people are unaware that the Peabody Museum at Yale University recently reclassified *Homo sapiens* (men and women) so that certain species of chimpanzees are included in the same genus. For the first time in the glorious history of Western civilization, the special uniqueness of the human being is being denied. We are no longer painters of the Sistine Chapel, builders of temples, and composers of music to the greater glory of God; we are simply smarter chimps. Nothing more and nothing less. Already museum exhibits, including those at the Smithsonian Institute, have been changed to fit Yale's new world view.

Since humans seem to possess the one inescapable distinction of speech, it became necessary to try to prove that animals also speak. Thus, during the 1970s, chimpanzees like Washoe and Nim Chimpsky (named in honor of secular linguist Noam Chomsky) along with gorilla Koko, were all being subjected to ill-fated experiments designed to teach them to speak. Their obstinate failure to catch on in no way diminished enthusiasm for the basic postulate that people are just another species of animal.

What has changed in America in the last thirty-five years is that we have replaced an essentially religious foundation with a secular substitute. We have declared that God may have much to do with specific religious rituals, but must be forcibly excluded from anything to do with public policy. We have gone from looking at humans as God's special creation to seeing humans as nothing more than sophisticated animals, slower than many animals and more intelligent than others, but far from unique.

And we must not think of these happenings as arcane matters of the scientific establishment. They are major attacks on man and God that affect all of society. Consider: Will this new view of humanity as just another animal be more or less likely to encourage a teenage boy to restrain his natural animal urge to impregnate as many females as possible? I know the average teenager has not heard of the Peabody Museum and may not understand the implications of efforts to teach chimps to speak. But what he is exposed to through the media and his science textbook do reflect the change in our culture's message, and these changes will impact him powerfully.

How Origin Affects Destiny

Having glanced into the question of where we came from, the question of where we are going also brings significant implications to society. We should not be surprised that the secular Left tells us we are hopelessly doomed, due to whatever seems to be the catastrophe of the moment. Some years it is nuclear war; other times overpopulation or global warming. Whatever the crisis may be, the Left does not accept the premise that man's God-given ingenuity can create solutions. Nor does it look forward to a messianic age. In their view, we are in imminent peril of destruction. And so we must eliminate aerosols, ban freon, and discourage people from having children. Schoolchildren must be taught that it is up to them to save the rain forests and oceans or else the planet is doomed. The sacred sacrament of secularism becomes that of recycling, and children are taught to observe its almost religious rituals.

Not surprisingly, children's psyches are affected by constantly being told that all is eventually for naught. Crisis beckons at every corner. Children as young as four or five are made anxious and worried rather than being made to feel secure and safe. Parents, who should be seen by children of that age as powerful and protective, are obviously impotent to save the planet. Children are taught to look to the government for solutions because only legislation can force people to keep the air clean and the ozone layer intact.

The questions of origins and destiny preoccupy much of humanity's quest for meaning. Almost all men and women have wondered how the human race appeared on Planet Earth and if there is life after death. What is more, most people sense that the answers to these questions are considerably more important than those to questions like "What is the name of the largest island in the southern hemisphere?" Questions of origins and destiny are also harder to resolve definitively than questions about geography, medicine, and nuclear physics.

All people acknowledge that both animals and human beings have physical limitations. When the eminent scientist, Dr. Lewis Thomas, informs us that a frog can see only a moving object, we accept that statement. We comprehend that basic physics, the facts of human metabolism, and the force of gravity will forever prevent a normal human being from jumping unaided over a skyscraper.

We are less willing to accept our intellectual limitations. It is disconcerting to human beings that we cannot scientifically measure whether there is a soul, whether there is life after death, where human beings came from, and if there is a God. What we have refused to acknowledge in America today is the concept that we cannot prove either side of the debate for all to agree.

Yet, in spite of being more difficult, some would say impossible, to answer, these questions frequently vex us because making important life decisions would be far easier if we knew the answers. We would agonize less over dilemmas of whether to marry, whom to marry, whether to raise children and how many, how to balance career and family demands and how to respond to various crises. Questions about the natural sciences are more easily answered but have far less impact on serious life decisions.

Nonetheless, life decisions must be made despite the fact that relevant questions are unanswered. Often, the decision to await all relevant data is itself a decision to not act at all. Upon becoming engaged, nobody knows for sure that the intended is the best possible choice for a spouse. Paradoxically, waiting for that data to become certain is the surest way to never marry. There is no way to determine whether the child being carried in the womb will later bring its mother pleasure or pain. Anyone requiring that certainty must assuredly remain childless. The same is true when starting a business or embarking on a career. We invest our money without knowing every possible fact about the fiscal outcome of our decision. We plan for a career with no assurance that we will not find that it is really an unsuitable one for us.

Similarly, the decision regarding our ultimate origin and destiny must be made before we know for sure, which will not happen until we die. That we must choose before all relevant data is in does not negate the importance of the choice. Whether we choose to accept or reject the God-centered approach defines the cosmic tug-of-war. Whichever side wins, it will have profound consequences for our society. Human nature seeks a unifying principle, something that explains and makes sense of life and its mysteries, and this unifying principle could well be one's view of God. People are unified, often without realizing it, into either one of the two available camps because there are really only two approaches from which to choose. Either we are here because God willed it or we are here by accident, the result of a cosmic roulette ball. Similarly, either death ends it all or it does not. These are questions we all have, and the answer determines our lives. One is the pro-God view; the other is what I call the "anti-God view."

In using the term "anti-God view" rather than a less provocative one like "non-religious view," I am trying to clarify the point that to position one's self on the anti-God team, one need not be militantly or even consciously anti-God. In fact, one may very well be a church or synagogue member with a profession of deep faith. However, by not understanding the connection between one's faith and public policies, the same person who does believe in God can be undermining that very faith by supporting policies that are actually anti-God. One need only subscribe to a seductive canon of superficially appealing ideas.

THE CHOICE

I am suggesting that just as there are only two answers to the questions of where we came from and where we shall end up, there may only be the same two ways to settle the question of what we should be doing during our life: namely, either following the pro-God worldview or the anti-God worldview. The alternative, indifference to God, is unworthy of men or women and is therefore practiced chiefly by non-human life forms such as cows and carrots. In reality there are very few agnostics.

I suspect that most of our cultural institutions are now firmly in the hands of those who reject the Almighty. Those who run our entertainment and news media are consistently shown by polls to attend worship services far less, and to be less likely to have a religious affiliation, than the nation's population as a whole. Those who run our schools, universities, and courts are constantly implementing anti-God doctrines no matter how often they might invoke His name. I am not even too certain of many of our churches and synagogues. It is time for the rest of us to recognize that there is a war being waged and to fight back.

There is a broad, loosely linked coalition of Americans who see it as axiomatic that liberty and religion go hand in hand. Many polls suggest that it is a majority of Americans, but there are of course those who believe just the opposite. They believe religion must be routed out in order for liberty to flourish. If we are to become one nation again, Americans must eventually choose one of these conflicting views. As with the issue of slavery in the nineteenth century, it is too basic a question for one nation to disagree upon.

In this great revolution over whether our culture is, at heart, derived from and linked to religious principles, the final decision will not be dictated by moral compromise. Instead, it will be made on the basis of moral conviction and that gleaming flash of resolve which can capture the minds of men, and which springs from the spiritual foundations of life itself.

CHAPTER NINE

THE REJECTION OF GOD

THE ULTIMATE PRINCIPLE BEING REJECTED BY THE LEFT IS NONE OTHER THAN GOD HIMSELF.

I need to explain the political thrust of the extreme animal rights and evolution movements because they so clearly reveal the hidden and sometimes subconscious agenda of the Left. Most of us do not consider ourselves squarely on one or another side of the conservative-liberal or traditionalist-modernist issue. We correctly do not label ourselves as extreme leftists or radical rightists. We are not fanatics, tending to be either black or white in our thinking. As individuals, we may be for abortion and against capital punishment. We may be against both gun control and school choice.

It is helpful, however, to look at the standard "liberal" (modernist) and "conservative" (traditional) positions to understand what is tugging at each side of the cultural debate. While as individuals increasingly fewer of us unthinkingly vote a party platform, politicians in particular usually do not succeed by standing alone. They need to ally themselves with a party and with specific groups. For the most part, the Republican and Democratic Parties have lined up as traditional versus modernist. Reading the party platforms, something that unfortunately few voters do, makes this clear. As voters, we are wearing blinders if we do not recognize that alliances affect those for whom we are voting. We must prove for the unifying principle of the banner beneath which our representatives choose to stand.

In order to do that, rather than talking about one person's stance, let us examine liberalism as a policy for a moment. We need to determine whether, despite its claims to be motivated by science and reason, liberalism is motivated by its own "religious" convictions.

Could it be chiefly driven by its own search for unity? I continue with my hypothesis that the ultimate principle being rejected by the Left is none other than God Himself.

AN UNLIKELY CONGRUENCE

Of course, the scientific standard for the acceptance of any hypothesis is how well it explains the observed data. I believe my hypothesis stands up very well. The congruence of opinion on the Left is absolutely remarkable. Consider: Why on earth should those organizations that support radical environmentalism, in all its bizarre manifestations, be supported by exactly the same people who endorse the agenda of homosexuality? But they are. Why should the same group of people who enthusiastically advocate wide-spread abortion also, by and large, embrace gun control? But they do. And so on, down the line of liberal causes. The exception proves the rule: It makes the newspapers when a group of Democratic self-proclaimed feminist women oppose partial birth abortion or when a Democratic legislator supports school vouchers.

This is too remarkable to be mere coincidence. We must strip away the black magic and find the cause and effect. My hypothesis does just that. Restated simply, there are many, many ways to worship God but only one way to reject Him. Thus, many different views can share one basic urge: the rejection of God. This, I think, best accounts for both the divided nature of the conservative movement and the congruence of the far Left. It helps explain the unlikely uniformity of the anti-God alliance. Why do gun-control advocates make common cause with militant abortion advocates? What interests do either of these groups share with the homosexual lobby? Why can these groups nearly always be found standing shoulder to shoulder with the multiculturalism militia and the condom counselors? Clearly, they must all share a great unifying principle, which, whether intended or not, is anti-Godism.

I am not saying that anyone who votes for a left-leaning candidate or anyone who likes to think of himself as a liberal hates God. I am trying to show that the foundations of liberalism lie in the bedrock of secularism and rejection of God. We may have very good reasons to support a local liberal candidate. A person may have very good reasons for taking certain positions on specific issues. However, the overarching philosophy that fuels the Leftist agenda is a ferocious determination to extirpate all religious influence in American public life.

THE LEFT AND THE SCRIPTURES

Some might hesitate over my assertion that it is God the Left opposes. Then allow me to further test my hypothesis in a more specific way. I will ask how the basic doctrines of the Left compare with their scriptural counterparts. Scientifically, one must agree that if this were a random matter, if there were no anti-God, anti-Christian theme to liberalism, then we ought to find that liberals sometimes agree and sometimes disagree with biblical social policy. Perhaps we might expect to find a fifty-fifty distribution. Let us examine a few liberal policies with this purpose in mind.

The Bible has some interesting prohibitions. I, along with many of us, possess no tattooing at all on my body. This is in spite of the artistic themes that, from time to time, have occurred to me to place across my chest. All right then, this happens to be one of the biblical injunctions that I find easier to obey than others—right up there with not sleeping with one's grandmother. Nonetheless, the objection to tattooing is very significant. It ties in to a prohibition in the Bible against any self-mutilation of the body.

What drives this prohibition? The fundamental idea here is stewardship and tenancy. God has provided us with a body to occupy during our stay on earth. The Bible tells me that my body does not belong to me. I have the use of it, and I must look after it. The tenant has much less freedom to paint the walls or change the plumbing than the landlord. Biblical law, therefore, severely restricts not just tattooing but also such practices as abortion and euthanasia. The message is consistent: Control over the body, including life and death, must be left with God. Man should not interfere.

Of course, the position of the Left on these issues helps confirm our hypothesis. Liberalism rejects the notion that God gives life and resents the notion that God controls death. So liberals would seize that power and make matters of both life and death into questions of human choice. We now understand why abortion and euthanasia have to be such major themes on the Left's political landscape, in spite of the fact that polls repeatedly show that America is far from sanguine over the expanded practice of abortion. In other words, the Left does not endorse abortion to win elections; it endorses abortion because that is its very purpose. It is part of its religious principle, if you like.

We can also find the exception that proves the rule. The Bible does give society one measure of control over life: It authorizes capital punishment for certain crimes. If human control over life and death, generically understood, were the underlying principle in the Left's position on abortion and euthanasia, then wouldn't liberalism fight for capital punishment as a logical extension of their principle? Either society should have control over life and death or it should not. But instead the liberal position opposes the death penalty at every turn, *even, if the criminal himself desires to be executed.* This moral repugnance for imposing capital punishment is best explained by our hypothesis. The biblical model says that we should welcome new life and revere elderly life, but the lives of murderers should be taken. Liberalism turns this policy on its head: New life and elderly life, if unwanted, inconvenient, or medically challenged, should be taken while murderers should be spared.

What about the peculiar ferocity that devotees of the Left reserve for the cigarette smoker—in the face of its placid acceptance of the AIDS carrier? The Left forges a national movement to prohibit smoking in any public building but urges that the individual with AIDS be left alone. In some states, a person with a sexually communicable disease is legally obliged to tell his or her partner about it. There is only one exception. A person who is HIV-positive does not have to disclose that fact. In other words, you must tell someone they run the risk of pain, sterility, or open sores if they have sex with you, but not that they risk death. It should also be noted that the Left's special compassion showered upon AIDS victims is not duplicated with lung-cancer patients. Why the discrepancy in the treatment of a disease resulting primarily from homosexual behavior and a disease resulting from smoking? The only possible explanation I can find is that cigarette smoking is not singled out as biblically proscribed. Since homosexuality is directly biblically forbidden, any sanctions applied in that direction might look suspiciously like an endorsement of God so must be scrupulously avoided.

THE WAR ON HIERARCHY

As we observed earlier, the beginning of all beginnings, the opening chapters of Genesis, shows us a hierarchical universe. God puts mineral at the bottom of the pyramid, and proceeds, day by day, to add level upon level. Once vegetation is created, we move one level up, to animal. And when animal is created, we go one level above that, to man. After that, the pinnacle of creation is achieved once woman arrives.

Well, naturally, if God approves of hierarchy, then modern liberalism must reject it. And one of the very first victims of the war against hierarchy is education. What education used to mean was that someone who knew more than I, would tell me what he knew. He would teach me how to relate to the world, and he would initiate me into my culture, into my people, into civilization. He could do this only because he occupied a niche above mine. Otherwise, what reason would there have been for me to listen to him rather than him listen to me? I will only learn from my teacher if I am first persuaded that he is superior to me in some way. If we are equals in every way, we should take turns instructing. One day he can talk and I shall listen, and on the next day he will attend my lecture.

What has the war on hierarchy accomplished? For the first time in the American experience, students grade teachers. What is more, students, by sanctioned evaluations or by unsanctioned classroom or building takeovers, tell teachers what to teach. What on earth can account for this? It makes sense only in one context: the overthrowing of hierarchy.

The same people who proudly converted the world's finest education system into a degenerate joke also mock the traditional family. This fits my hypothesis rather well since hierarchy is also one of the organizing principles of the family. If you reject God, you must reject the principle of hierarchy, which means you must reject classical family life.

How backward, sexist and repugnant for the husband to act as spiritual leader of the home! And how old-fashioned for parents to discipline their children, whose aberrant behavior may have been considered wrong in the 1950s but today is regarded simply as a healthy expression of selfhood.

All these things follow logically once a population forgets that greatness can be found in subservience. Understandably, men say "No woman is going to tell me what to do." Children of parents whose vehicles sport bumper stickers that read *Question Authority* will grow up doing just that. They will also become rather hard to live with.

Furthermore, when people forget that one can only acquire true authority by being able to accept it, the economy declines. The most important lesson of one's first job can be learning how to subdue the childish instinct to tell the boss to go jump in the lake. An ability to accept orders will do far more to give young people a chance in the work-force than will increases in the minimum wage. We do not need government to teach entry-level job skills. There are only three of them, they are quite simple, and they are best learned in a religiously founded family, not during midnight basketball games. They are: showing up on time for work, following orders, and acting respectfully to one's boss and coworkers.

Businesses now must teach the basic literacy and computation skills that all high school and even elementary graduates used to have. They have adjusted to the poor aca-demic achievements of today's school-leavers. At the same time, however, businesses are stymied by the lack of a conscientious work ethic in these people. Entry-level workers will not progress past that starting point unless they understand that they must train their characters as much, and perhaps even more, than they train their technical skills. This is the avenue for rising above the minimum wage, not some liberal government edict.

Humans are by nature reluctant to submit themselves to a higher authority. Each one of us finds liberalism, the ultimate liberation from external authority, to be seductive. This is why one of the most conspicuous characteristics of our culture is the hatred of hierarchy. Yet, one of the most telling differences between a nation comfortable in its Judeo-Christian heritage and one engaged in a struggle to reject it is how its people accept authority. Do they manufacture bumper stickers that proclaim *Question Authority,* or do they train children to obey parents, students to venerate teachers, husbands and wives to revere each other, and soldiers to follow their commanders? Children are more likely to obey parents' rules and later, society's too, if they grow up watching adults accept God's rules, even when those rules may seem inconvenient.

Granted, there are abuses of hierarchy just as any other good thing can be abused when taken to the extreme. Nazi Germany was certainly an example of the dangers of total, blind obedience to orders. But we may have gone too far in the other direction. With no ability at all to recognize any authority over us, we lose functionality in almost every area that a healthy civilization needs. Let's not confuse voluntary acceptance of authority, with being forced to conform. In the atheistic USSR, authorities were feared, not respected. When the citizens obeyed laws, it was in response to the whip over their heads. The ability to recognize and be comfortable with valid authority is most reliably nurtured within a religious environment. This is because subservience to God teaches us the inherent value of service. We Jews look at our Egyptian slavery experience as part of God's preparations for our destiny. In order to ultimately become servants of the Almighty, we first had to learn what the alternative felt like: being slaves to humans.

When a society abolishes its religious underpinnings, one of the first casualties is the ability of its people to willingly accept authority. Are we surprised that the younger generation has a growing contempt for the military? Since all military systems depend on lines of authority, this is a natural consequence of people's increasing inability to respect leaders and take orders. In addition, the book of Exodus explicitly calls God a Man of War. War is admissible, the Bible tells us, because there are certain important principles which can only be upheld or resolved by war. To the Left, the military is the enemy.

Another of the Left's fondest conceits is that world peace is attainable. Those of us who view the Bible as a blueprint know that world peace will be one of the fringe benefits of Messianic times. Our current condition, in which some type of war is always going on somewhere, is unpleasant but inevitable. It is arrogant at best to suppose that our government is up to the job of imposing world peace. There is little history of success in this area to serve as evidence that any government is up to this task. Our job is to move toward a moral restoration which, in due course, will result in world peace. Peace is indeed attainable, but not by dispatching members of the United States military on improbable "peacekeeping" misadventures. Peace is attainable, but the Left rejects the only avenue that will ultimately work.

"MY MOTHER MADE ME DO IT"

There is still more evidence for our hypothesis. Whether one considers the Bible light bedtime reading or the Word of God, nobody, but nobody, can miss this fundamental rule found in virtually every page of the Good Book: Every single biblical character is granted the power of moral choice. Every single person is given the ability to make his own decisions, but he is also made to endure whatever consequences arise. Abel's murderer, Cain, is not gently excused on account of traumatic potty training. The population of Sodom is not the victim of its environment. Everyone is accountable for his actions. Humans can't punish each other for their thoughts and motivations, since only God can know these, but punishment certainly can be meted out for behavior.

What is the position of the Left? Absolutely predictable. Evil is found in this world, but never because any people elected to commit evil. Evil is always the result of outside forces making people do things. Would you accept this from your children? Would you excuse little Tommy when he kicks his sister in the stomach and tells us that a bad dream made him do it? I don't think so, because it hands him carte blanche to do so again and again. Yet secular liberalism offers us an unbelievable proliferation of mental and social disorders to explain how factors other than free moral choice make people act the way they do. There is even a frantic attempt to find a genetic component for infidelity. All right, even if men are genetically programmed to be unfaithful, we still have the choice to follow that instinct or to refrain. Instincts are determining factors in animals, not in people. If God said, "Personal accountability," the Left has to say, "No personal accountability." Enormous social dislocation inevitably results from such a seemingly small decision.

The concept of anti-Godism also explains the unrelenting search for life in outer space. In spite of the fact that no conclusive proof has yet been found for the existence of any planet outside of our solar system, large sums of tax money are spent scanning the heavens for some whisper from an alien civilization. After nearly fifty futile years pursuing this endeavor, why not put the radio telescopes in moth balls until some evidence surfaces that there is a planet or two upon which life could endure? There almost appears to be an air of desperation to the search.

And indeed there is. One need only recall the ridiculous media extravaganza that greeted the much-ballyhooed Mars rock. This small rock, supposed to have bounced into our atmosphere from the planet Mars, was said to contain little voids that resembled the shape that certain life forms would leave, had any existed. Yes, the voids were the wrong size by several orders of magnitude, but still, said the experts, it was the shape that counted.

On my radio show at the time, I denounced the Mars rock as a ploy by NASA to increase its funding which coincidentally was up for renewal just then. I was deluged by angry callers who appeared to be clinging desperately to the hope of life in outer space promised by the unremarkable piece of debris. They were not being any more scientific about this matter than I would be about the promise of Divine Redemption. Why should they; it offended their philosophical belief. Following their approach we should spend a fortune seeking hieroglyphics in a Hershey Kiss because it is shaped roughly like a pyramid.

The reason for this determination to see life in outer space where no evidence yet exists is simple to see. It is a rule of mathematics and statistics that no random event happens only once. For instance, if you saw a roulette wheel that turned up the number seven only once during a week of gambling, you would be sure you were watching a rigged wheel. No random or chance event happens only once. I am sure you can see where this leads. If indeed life on earth were a random event; if just by chance bacteria became Bach, then it absolutely and positively must have happened somewhere else in the universe too. Unless, of course, *God* made it happen here, which is an unthinkable proposition because if God did make us, then He also gave us instructions on how to live. This would spell doom to secular liberalism.

To Americans of faith, whether God did or did not create little green men with waving antennae is largely irrelevant. To the secularist, since God did not create us in the first place, the same random forces that put us here must have also put our first cousins somewhere else. If we acknowledge that humans are unique and that we have no reason to suspect life exists elsewhere, then anti-Godists face a crisis of faith.

WATCHING OUR LANGUAGE

Likewise, the origin of language makes almost as fascinating a story as the origin of humanity because of the hurricane of controversy that surrounds the story. Why should an area of scientific analysis be controversial? Why should studying the origin of human speech stir more emotion than studying the origin of, shall we say, whooping cough?

Emotion is exactly what is at work rather than dispassionate scholarship when the subject of language is discussed because, like so much else, it too is impossible to discuss without also discussing God. After all, either the faculty of human speech is God-given and distinguishes us from animals, or it can be explained entirely materialistically—that we humans are nothing more than $6.97 worth of common chemicals and somewhere along the way we picked up speech. Jewish tradition takes the former view, explaining that when God breathed the breath of life into Adam's nostrils as recounted early in Genesis, what was really happening was that God was bestowing upon Adam the gift of speech.

But secularists take a purely materialistic point of view on language, as illustrated by arch-materialist John Maddox in the 1998 yearbook of *The Economist*. Maddox ponders the question, "Why does man speak?"

> So what are the genetic differences between the species [apes and humans]? At least in part, in the arrangement of the genes.... But that cannot be the whole story. People have the faculty of language, which must require that there should be extra genes to regulate the development of the human brain before and after birth. No doubt the reality will turn out to be more complicated than this simple tale. Human language must be far more complex than can be accounted for by a single gene. There must be connections with the sound with which animals other than people communicate, while the innate sense of syntax that Noam Chomsky has predicated must have its genetic representation in the rapidly growing list of developmental genes.[1]

After the completion of the human genome project, some explanation will be needed to account for the fact that there are inadequate resources within the genome itself to assemble all the separate components of the language system. Perhaps then the evidence for man's linguistic uniqueness will trump secularism's commitment to its ideology, but somehow I doubt it. I wouldn't renounce Torah Judaism regardless of the evidence, and it would be foolish of me to suppose that the faith of secularism evokes any lesser commitment in the hearts of its devotees.

If, as secularists believe, various tribes of baboons evolved into early tribes of primitive humans at different times and in different places around the world, we would expect to see many separate and distinct languages. We might find groupings of languages, but we certainly would not expect to find all languages related to one another and to one original mother of all language. If in fact all languages are descended from one original language, it makes it just a little more difficult to accept a purely materialistic account of mankind's origins. Yet that is precisely the direction in which current research is leading and which secularists find so disturbing.

What I am saying is that we must not get bogged down by looking at individual pieces of legislation or the voting record of our congressperson. First we have to see the overall picture. As it is, many decent, caring, God-fearing people look only at the surface of each issue, be it welfare, education, or specific taxes, and do not see the underlying connection between them all. Here is a way to see the unifying framework.

Let us use an earthquake as an analogy. In one part of the city an earthquake might cause a fire. In another it could collapse buildings and in a third area it could cause flooding. A citizen who slept through the actual movement of the earth would awaken to what he perceived as a strange coincidence. To him the city seemed to have coincidentally suffered a fire, collapsed structures and flooding all on the same morning. All of a sudden, an aftershock suggests to him the possibility that an earthquake might have occurred. His ability to deal with the crises will be enormously enhanced once he realizes that a single phenomenon caused all three disasters.

IS IT A CONSPIRACY?

Likewise, our society is encountering an over-arching phenomenon that is destroying key areas of our culture. The phenomena? Liberalism's unrelenting opposition to God. The key areas? Our nation's cultural, economic, and moral vitality. Is it a conspiracy? Not if by conspiracy you mean people meeting in dark rooms to work out a secret agenda to take over America. But imagine racing down the highway on your way to a dentist appointment for which you are already late. All of a sudden the traffic backs up and you are brought to a halt. Little by little you are able to creep forward as you crane your neck trying to gauge the seriousness of the holdup. Soon you see that there has been an accident in the oncoming lanes and everyone ahead of you is slowing down to observe the mayhem on the other side of the road. Strangely enough, although there was no obstacle blocking lanes in your direction, you arrive at the dentist too late for your appointment. You were delayed by nothing but people's morbid curiosity. Did all those drivers ahead of you conspire to delay you? No, there was no conspiracy, only morbid curiosity.

However, someone unaware of the nearby accident and ignorant of human nature could have reasonably concluded that every motorist ahead of you had agreed on a conspiracy to make you late. He would have jumped to the conclusion that all those drivers had met in a darkened cellar just before dawn. At their secret meeting every one of them solemnly pledged that later that morning they would all slow their vehicles to a crawl. In this way they would jam up the highway and thwart your intention to visit your dentist.

Even with no conspiratorial plans, people who don't even know one another will sometimes act in concert and bring about consequences that hardly differ from what a real conspiracy could accomplish. It happens innocently but the consequences can be deadly.

CHAPTER TEN

ONLY ONE WAY WORKS

HUMILITY DOES NOT REQUIRE US TO DENOUNCE AMERICA. ON THIS POINT WE HAVE CERTAINLY MOVED OFF TRACK.

As a child I was encouraged to seek the moral message in almost everything. Being fond of dismantling old clocks and trying to repair them, I became the neighborhood repository for any old piece of junk that had ever ticked. Anyone with an old clock, kitchen timer, broken watch or any non-functioning time keeping device would drop by our home to present me with another treasure for my growing collection of such things. My father encouraged my attempts to resuscitate the deceased timepieces. But I can still recall my mother's slightly forced smile each time some well-meaning neighbor contributed what Mother considered to be yet another act of sabotage in her ongoing fight for a neat and tidy home.

For my part, I happily dismantled the clocks and attempted to get them going again. Almost always, the process of reassembling was stymied by the five or six little cog wheels for which I could find no home. Occasionally I ran out of little wheels, so I would cannibalize one non-working clock in the hope of saving another. My efforts were not blessed with much success; I finally lost interest, as most of us do with projects that yield none of the encouragement that comes from a sense of achievement.

Later, I wanted my father to explain why he had encouraged me to play with the clocks. His response was that he was waiting for me to discover the moral message of mechanical clocks. Moral message? I was only about ten years old; surely this was a bit too early to be burdened with moral messages. But Father believed, and I have since learned, that for religious people there is a moral message in almost everything and the challenge to find it can't start too early.

To this day I recall how my father applied that message: *Although there are countless ways to reassemble clocks, only one way works. There are also countless ways of structuring families and societies. Only one way works.*

BUT ISN'T THAT A BIT ARROGANT OF US?

You might be thinking that this is not altogether true. After all, we seem to be on the threshold of regarding as a family two men living together with adopted children. And look at how many different ways there are of structuring societies. There are eastern countries, there are African cultures, there are South and Central American societies, and many more. Isn't it a bit arrogant to regard western civilization in general, and American civilization in particular, to be the only one that really works?

Fortunately, a humble spirit does not require us to deny the truth. For instance, Judaism does not allow me to express humility by proclaiming myself to be nothing. An old joke goes like this: Overcome by the emotions of the Day of Atonement, the rabbi stepped out into the congregation, fell to his knees and proclaimed in a trembling voice, "Lord, I am nothing." The president of the synagogue, not to be outdone joined the rabbi, fell to his knees and also proclaimed himself to be nothing. Whereupon one of the less important synagogue members, overwhelmed by the mood, ascended the platform, dropped to his knees and informed God that he too was nothing. At this point the president nudged the rabbi and said, "Now look who thinks he's nothing!"

That is the danger with taking things to implausible extremes. Humans are not nothing. We are the result of God's creation; what is more, we are the apex of that creation. Trying to persuade ourselves that we are nothing carries two terrible risks. One is that we laugh at the absurdity of thinking such fine creatures as ourselves to be nothing and we abandon the attempt to find humility. The second risk is even worse: We may actually come to believe that we really are nothing. And if we are really nothing, then none of our actions could possibly mean anything either, could they? So why worry about what we do? If humans are nothing, then nothing matters.

Humility is attainable but not through considering ourselves to be utterly worthless. Anyone who lives responsibly, and invests his time in durable values rather than in the frivolous pursuit of fun, has achieved something. Such a person is not nothing. The key to humility is not to denigrate what you have become, but rather tó renounce any credit for it. You are a real somebody. To begin with, you are utterly unique. You have thoughts that nobody else has ever had. You have dedicated yourself to more than your own gratification. You have supported your spouse. You have labored faithfully at a job. You are raising good children. You have added to your store of knowledge about the world. No, you are nowhere near being nothing. You are somebody!

But who gets the credit for you being you? Taking the credit yourself makes you arrogant. First of all, God created you as a unique, fearfully-and-wonderfully-made individual. Then there are your parents; after all, they endowed you with a pretty useful set of genes. They also imparted crucial knowledge and habits as they raised you. You probably picked up a thing or two as your formal education progressed, so there are teachers to thank. How about that long-forgotten associate who gave you your first leg up in business? You may not be nothing, but you probably had a lot of help in becoming a somebody. For that we must thank others, most notably God Almighty, and avoid the folly of arrogance.

This is why it is not arrogant at all to consider American civilization superior to most others. I believe America is the greatest country of our time. Apparently, so do many others who brave frightful danger to immigrate here. I don't believe I have heard of many other countries in the world with illegal immigration problems. Humility does not require us to denounce America. On this point we have certainly moved off track.

LET'S BE HONEST...

It has become chic to glamorize and adulate most other cultures while denigrating our own. Example after example found in suggested new educational standards reveal the anti-American bias and its warped view of history. What pride in country could a youngster have from new history guidelines that accord Senator Joseph McCarthy, McCarthyism, and the Ku Klux Klan a total of thirty-six mentions while totally ignoring American heroes such as Paul Revere and Thomas Edison? Was the Seneca Falls Declaration of Sentiments so pivotal to the feminist movement (and more important to America than the first gathering of Congress) that it deserves eight mentions to Congress's zero? Do we have no pride in American history? If a nation preserves its national identity by recalling its origins, then it follows that a nation should recall and honor its founding fathers. Three times a day Jews say a prayer that commences with the words, "God of our fathers, God of Abraham, God of Isaac and God of Jacob." For American schoolchildren of all faiths, it used to be a regular part of education to regularly recount stories of our founding fathers. I believe the cost of no longer doing so will be paid for many years to come.

It would be hard to find a more important characteristic of durable nations than an ever-present awareness of fathers. Smart wives and mothers know this. Wise citizens know this. Both ancient Israel and modern America had fathers. To their descendants, they still live.

A number of years ago, one of our summer sailing trips took my family to British Columbia at the time of Expo 86. We docked our boat in Vancouver's False Creek and eagerly disembarked to enjoy the many exhibits from foreign countries. One of the most striking exhibits was Russia's, where we marveled at the gall of portraying Russia's advanced technology without a mention of the recent Chernobyl nuclear plant disaster.

We eagerly anticipated America's pavilion and looked forward to instilling our children with pride in their homeland. To our dismay, this was not to be. Instead of an exhibit that celebrated America's greatness, the entire display was a maudlin, self-flagellating memorial to an American disaster, the Challenger explosion.

One left the pavilion feeling that America was a failure, embarrassed to belong to such a bumbling country. I am not suggesting that, like Russia, we totally ignore our problems and failings. But surely there is a middle course, where we can be honest about both our problems and our triumphs, rather than focus only on the latter in a misguided attempt at revisionistic humility.

My wife was once asked to review the reading list for a third grade class in a private school. She disapproved of many of the books. Let me give you one example why. There wasn't an inherent problem with the choice of an excellent book, Roll of Thunder, Hear My Cry, by Mildred Taylor. The book is a well-written depiction of the injustices suffered by Southern blacks. My wife's concern was that this book was going to be read by students who had not yet learned of the Civil War, had never heard of the greatness of people like Harriet Beecher Stowe, and knew nothing of those who had made incredible sacrifices for racial equality. These students did not yet even know the phrase, "All men are created equal." There was nothing to place the book, with its valid criticisms of societal injustice, in context. Surely, children should be exposed to pride and patriotism in their country first, for only after that base has been established are they able to put in perspective any wrongs the country has committed.

Honoring our country and its history is a traditional Judeo-Christian principle; many schools today teach the opposite. There is a similar pattern among adults as Americans at the Left end of the tug-of-war rope revel in an orgy of disparagement. Jefferson owned slaves! they cry exultantly. He actually was a racist! Washington had an affair! (This is claimed even though there is no supporting proof.) Each tries to better the other by divulging ever more shameful, "newly discovered" information about our founding fathers. Isn't it horrible to listen to someone denigrate his dead parents? He is turning himself into an orphan before your very eyes.

One of the functions religion has for a society is the teaching of repentance. Perfection is not a human trait, but a godly one, and as America has expelled God from its schools the students have the load of the sins of all the centuries laid on their backs. Instead of being able to acknowledge the failures of our forefathers, while still recognizing their greatness, the absence of repentance allows only the first half of the equation to be taught. My guess is that most high school students would be stymied by the question of why we have an illegal immigration problem while Iran and Cuba have people clamoring to get out. Having been taught chiefly the ills of America, how could they understand how truly great this country is? In these and many other ways, parents who do not actively review the messages their children are getting may find that their children are being indoctrinated contrary to their own beliefs.

What should we tell our children? We should say that America is the greatest country on earth, but it is not because Americans are brighter, more competent, stronger, or luckier than other people. No, the credit must go elsewhere. America is what she is because her founders chose to follow the Word of God. America is as successful as she is because of the Christian system of values our founders implanted in this land.

REMEMBER THE MORAL MESSAGE

The moral message my father wanted me to learn from my attempts to fix all those broken clocks is that only one way works. America's founders understood this message as well. They acknowledged that although there may be many different ways to structure human society, only one way works.

But, some may counter, don't we see many societies structured entirely differently that seem to work? The answer is that for brief snatches of time, almost anything can work. Even adultery seems to work during the short moments of stolen bliss. Running your car without regularly changing the oil might seem to be a new and more economic breakthrough in car ownership, but only for a while. Eventually the mistake becomes painfully evident. As mature citizens we have to learn to hear the sinister footsteps of approaching consequences to the well-intentioned policy decisions of today.

We tossed out the moral message of the clocks only a few decades ago. Until the early 1960s most Americans accepted, often without even thinking about it, the basic ethos of Judeo-Christian thought. Until the early '60s few among our populace doubted that the best citizens are produced in a family in which both a man and a woman raise the children. Until the early '60s nearly everyone believed that it was important for all to work for a living and that living on the dole was sad and even a little shameful. Until the early '60s we even understood that shame was a legitimate component in shaping our society. "What will the neighbors say?" was a noble expression of concern for community standards. Today it would be more likely mocked by children raised in the spirit of permissiveness and contempt for any kind of authority.

For less than fifty years we have been living with the result of saying that all ways of organizing families and societies are equally valid. It is still too early to see impending doom. Remember, though, that communism (a disastrous rejection of a biblical blueprint if ever there was one) survived just seventy years. And for those peering ahead into America's future, the signs are becoming dismayingly clearer.

CHAPTER ELEVEN

THE ISOLATION ERROR

WE MUST START LOOKING AT AMERICA AS ONE
INCREDIBLY COMPLEX ORGANISM RATHER THAN AS
MILLIONS OF DISCONNECTED INDIVIDUALS.

Hold on a minute! When we step into the polling booth on election day, most of us do not begin to think in such fundamental terms as pro-God or anti-God. While we certainly do occasionally confront major issues of philosophical faith, most of us do not consult those larger spiritual signposts before we enter the polling booth. From time to time there is a new candidate to support or oppose, or perhaps a new school bond issue to decide. On a national level there are questions of where the candidates stand on a variety of issues. Our concern may be with how our armed services should be used or how far environmental regulation should go. Most of us examine these questions, if at all, in a localized sort of way. Either we ask ourselves how the candidate or the issue might impact our lives or we quickly judge the larger, national question in terms of what "feels right." Some candidates even confess to being swayed chiefly by emotion. We should all feel emotions, but to act upon them can be perilous. Very few of us are likely to analyze the decision we must make in terms of whether the candidate or issue is in accordance with Judeo-Christian principles or is a result of a secular mindset. How in the world would we know that, anyway?

Were we to try to do just that, it would become a formidable challenge. After all, if the candidate is photographed leaving church with a large Bible clutched under his arm, should we support him? Does that superficial piece of public relations really prove anything? Of course it doesn't. Tax increases? New school bond issues? Well, doesn't God want the poor cared for? Doesn't God want children to become educated? Just how can we quickly and easily evaluate whether the proposed legislation or the hopeful candidate will play the appropriate role in God's plan for American civilization?

APPRAISING PROPOSED POLICIES

The only way to appraise a proposed policy in terms of God's biblical blueprint for America is to avoid specialization. It is hard to ask ourselves the complex set of questions that would reveal the broader and long-term impact of a proposed policy, but it is the only way. We have been conditioned to examine candidates and policies in isolation. We ask ourselves, "Is *this* decision a good idea?" Instead, we have to learn to ask ourselves new questions such as "What negative impact might this policy cause in spite of it being very well intentioned?" In other words, we need to start looking at America as one gigantic and complex organism instead of as a million constituent parts, each functioning in relative isolation.

Imagine a person seeking medical advice. One specialist might diagnose high blood pressure and prescribe a suitable medicine while, two days later, a kidney specialist conducts his examination and prescribes an appropriate drug. At that point the patient needs a generalist, as it were. Someone must be able to look at the entire individual. Perhaps the pharmacist says, "Hold on, you can't take both of these medicines simultaneously— the combination will kill you." Each specialist may have been correct in isolation, for neither was aware of what was taking place outside his specialty.

I recognize the need for specialists. Today the complexity of society and the vast knowledge available makes it all but impossible for any one person to know everything about everything. Hence, specialization came into being. But let's remain alert to the flaws of specialization. We should also recognize that it is far easier to be a specialist than to be a generalist. To probe deeply into a subject without ever having to understand how it interacts with all else under the sun, is essentially an indulgence. It is always easy to say, "Sorry, that's not my department."

The old-style family doctor has all but vanished, but he was as close as one could get to the ideal of a generalist. He was aware of my childhood allergy and years later made a connection between that and an eyesight problem. Yes, I then consulted an ophthalmologist but was able to put him on the track that had been intuitively identified by the family generalist. Perhaps we have wrongly come to venerate the specialist. Being a competent specialist takes technical greatness. Being a competent generalist takes enormous human greatness. It is the difference between knowledge and wisdom. Perhaps we have also wrongly venerated specialist-type judgments instead of generalist-type judgments in decisions that responsible citizens are called upon to make.

There is little doubt that it suits the purposes of bureaucrats and career politicians to have us make simple, emotional decisions that view an issue in isolation. It would be difficult to persuade the populace that certain new taxes are required "for the children" if everyone stopped to ask what possible unintended consequences might result from a well-intentioned but flawed tax proposal. Is more funding for college education worthwhile? Easier access to student loans? Obviously. Look how many people's lives have been improved by an education. On the surface, a noble cause. But when we look below the surface we find that our increased tax dollars may be funding frivolous, useless, and sometimes anti-American or ferociously secular college courses. These can't be dismissed as exceptions. They have actually become the norm on many campuses. Don't we need to look at what is actually going on in colleges today before deciding that they deserve more of our money?

If we are told that sending our armed forces to Bosnia or Somalia will "bring peace and stop the killing," only callused citizens would question the policy. However, if we train ourselves to always examine the impact across space and through time, it might well turn out that the best course of action is not what looks or sounds best in a thirty-second sound bite.

Yes, we all want clean air to breathe and crystal-clear water to drink. That is a given. However, when we approve sweeping Environmental Protection Agency legislation that imposes not hundreds, but thousands of new regulations on American businesses, do we fully understand the implications across America for families dependent on small businesses? Do we fully understand the future impact on the American economy? Do we know that sometimes attempting to diminish a problem has sometimes ended up increasing it? Knowing all these things, we may still decide to impose the laws, but we will have decided from the vantage point of knowledge rather than from behind the blindfold of emotions. Americans on the whole are intelligent and want to do what is right. However, it is becoming harder and harder to see behind all the political smoke screens.

SPACE AND TIME: KEYS TO TRUTH

Space and time are the keys. In 1908, the Russian-born, German mathematician Hermann Minkowski addressed the Assembly of German Natural Scientists and Physicians with words that laid the foundation for relativity theory and heralded in the age of twentieth-century quantum physics: "Henceforth space by itself, and time by itself, are doomed to fade away into mere shadows, and only a kind of union of the two will preserve an independent reality."

Without knowing it, Minkowski was echoing the words of rabbis and scholars from hundreds of years earlier. They explained that in the holy tongue of Hebrew, only one word, *olam,* was used for both the concept of infinite time and the concept of infinite space. Reality is indeed a kind of space/time continuum. We find physical principles such as the law of gravity, the law of friction, or the laws of static electricity to be elegant precisely because they are true and apply anywhere in the universe. They are true everywhere in space and time. Jews are instructed to obey most commandments in the Torah regardless of where on earth or in space they live and regardless of when in human history they live. Thus, too, a suitable test of reality is how something impacts us throughout both time and space.

In other words, each and every policy ought to be examined in terms of both space and time. We must know how it will impact space, which is to say the rest of America and not just the narrow area of concern it purports to address. We must also know how it will impact time, which is to say the future of America, not just today and tomorrow but also next year and perhaps even next generation. Yes, clearly, if we wish to analyze trends and policies in American life, we should not behave like specialists. We should certainly consult specialists, but it is up to us to absorb and integrate the data they provide into the bigger picture. In that way there is at least a chance of finding out whether a specific proposal corresponds to the reliable blueprint we have been given.

It is not at all an easy matter. Somehow one has to be able to mentally wrap up 250 million of our fellow inhabitants into one entity. Then we must find it in ourselves to try to evaluate the impact of a new idea on that entire gigantic entity. Then we have to evaluate the impact of our proposed new idea both in terms of our past and in terms of what it might do to our future. It is not easy, but even trying without total success is far, far superior to simply asking, "How does this legislation affect *me today?*" Even just an attempt to escape the blindness imposed by viewing things in isolation is worthwhile.

OF ANTS AND MARTIANS

There are a number of great mysteries that are best resolved by eliminating the isolation error. Think of insects such as ants. They create what appear to be complex societies made up of countless individual insects divided into several categories according to task. There are workers, there are soldiers, there are nest builders, and then, of course, there is a queen ant. Try driving a garden implement into the next ant hill or colony you encounter. One type of ant rushes out to attack your shovel and repel the invasion. Other types of ants immediately start repairing the physical damage you inflicted upon their home. As you watch, you will become amazed to see that they are reproducing the architecture you demolished. Apparently each one of these tiny creatures, with inadequate neurological equipment to store up the ant equivalent of blueprints, somehow knows where to carry the next grain of sand and exactly where to place it. Meanwhile, soldier ants are still busy driving away the invading shovel and other ants are secreting construction glue from one of their glands. Who is orchestrating all the frenzied activity as the ants rebuild their damaged home? Is it perhaps the queen ant? But even she does not possess a large enough brain to handle the entire enterprise. In any event, even were you to lock her into a lead container in the hope of preventing her from communicating her directives to the other ants, it would have no effect. Work would continue and the ant hill would be rebuilt.

The answer, provided by the great African naturalist Eugene Marais, is that we make a mistake when we think of the ant hill as the home of hundreds of thousands of ants. This would be identical to the mistake a Martian could be forgiven for making. He might encounter his first human and, after slashing him with a knife, sit back to watch how this strange thing called a human deals with its damaged condition. First a group of soldiers come racing out of the wound; their task is to fight off the invader. Actually they are the cells whose function is to ward off infection, but the Martian might well view them as thousands of tiny individuals that reside in this strange structure called a human body.

Soon another group of individuals emerge to start the repair process. Not only do they start replacing the muscle and skin that was torn in the attack, but they make it look almost identical to its original appearance. Our Martian is stunned because after examining each individual cell, he can tell that none contains enough neurological matter to store the necessary information on how the rebuilding ought to proceed. Should the original attack have damaged a fingerprint, amazingly enough, the repair job will reproduce the original and unique fingerprint pattern.

Finally our Martian realizes his mistake. He considered the human body he encountered to be no more than a home for many different but isolated little organisms. He saw a heart, lungs, kidneys, millions of blood cells and many more occupants, all living peacefully and somewhat cooperatively within the same structure. In reality, he now sees that this is all one large and incredibly complex organism with thousands—if not millions—of constituent parts, all of which interact with one another all the time.

The lesson of the ants and the Martian? We must start looking at America as one incredibly complex organism rather than as just a home to millions of disconnected individuals. This way we can come to see how similar it is to our own bodies. Never can you do something to one organ without also impacting many, if not all, other organs.

While not providing a scientifically rigorous explanation, this approach can at least provide some satisfying insight into strange phenomena. For instance, it is well known that after enduring a war, a country's sex ratio gets mysteriously altered. In both England after the First World War and in Israel after several of the wars that plagued the embryonic nation, the sex ratio became modified. Normally, roughly the same number of baby boys as baby girls are born. In both England and Israel, as well as other nations that suffered the loss of many men during a war, the sex ratio altered dramatically after the wars, with many more baby boys being born than baby girls. This has always baffled us because we see no way the appropriate sperm can be informed that it is to move to the front of the line. However, viewing a nation as an organism rather than as a collection of disconnected individuals brings us a little closer, I think, to understanding this phenomenon.

At any rate, it should certainly encourage us to think about the nationwide impact of new rules, regulations, laws and policies. Viewing things from this perspective makes it a lot easier to measure what we are doing in terms of God's plan for the extended order of human cooperation that we call civilization or society.

Thinking of what is happening to all of America, not just now but also tomorrow and next year, is important for another reason too. It helps us see that there really are two utterly incompatible visions competing with one another for the soul of the land. One view embraces God's role and welcomes His guidance on how to run our lives both private and public. It insists that, as our founding fathers believed, a secular government and constitution can work only as long as the population conducts itself along religiously informed lines. The second view vigorously rejects any notion of a godly authority external to our own wishes and inclinations. It maintains that the secularism of government must be injected into every corner of American life, displacing the native piety that used to be such a conspicuous element in our national character.

As an Orthodox Jew I must acknowledge that a society can only be successful if it adheres to God's basic plan. By recognizing that a battle is raging and that, right now, Christian conservatives are leading the side I believe is morally, historically, and intellectually correct, I find myself linking arms with those so many of my coreligionists vilify.

CHAPTER TWELVE

LOOKING THE WRONG WAY

ASSAULTS ON RELIGIOUS FREEDOMS OF JEWS AND OTHER MINORITIES WILL COME FROM THE SECULAR LEFT, NOT FROM THE RELIGIOUS RIGHT.

I n allying myself with the Christian Right on so many issues, I am often assaulted with two questions. Aren't I afraid that America will turn into a Christian theocracy? If the Christian Right gets more political power, won't it be harder to live as a Jew in this country?

The notion that the religious liberties of America's Jews are threatened by the rise of the "religious Right" makes little sense. To observant Jews, religious liberty is not an empty slogan. It means some rather specific things. For instance, it means having the freedom to slaughter animals for meat in accordance with the biblical rules for *Kashruth*—the Jewish dietary laws. It means being free to circumcise our baby boys eight days after their birth, just as God commanded Abraham. It means the ability to observe our Sabbath rather than being forced to work or go to school on Saturday, as was the case in the atheistic Soviet Union.

I don't see an immediate threat to any of these laws. But I can see how they could be imperiled over the next few decades, a threat which emanates from contemporary liberalism rather than from Christian conservatism. Something that has occurred in other countries, such as Switzerland and the socialist paradise of Sweden, has been an assault on our practice of ritual slaughtering, by means of which religious Jews can eat meat. The process is conducted by a ritual slaughterer called a *shochet,* who uses an extremely sharp and specialized knife. The purpose in using this kind of knife is that a very sharp knife can cut without the nerves registering pain for the first few seconds. As a rabbi, I have from time to time been called upon to check the *shochet's* knife for smoothness and sharpness. More than once I have inadvertently cut my finger rather badly, and in each case I was oblivious to the gash until I became aware of blood all over the place. The idea is for the animal to lose consciousness before it can become aware of pain.

Anyone who has worked in or inspected a slaughterhouse knows that it is not pleasant. Not surprisingly, the bloody environment seems to have a desensitizing effect on people who work there. This makes one's first encounter with a *shochet* even more shocking. Instead of a toughened exterior immunized to the pain, one sees a man who might slaughter dozens of animals a day, yet whose soul weeps for each and every animal he dispatches to the butcher store. The Psalms and prayers he recites during his work address the difference between humans and animals, his ultimate purpose of providing food for humans, and the moral legitimacy of eating meat.

How It Could Happen

Nonetheless, there have been several attempts to persuade legislators to ban this form of religiously based slaughter. Here is how it has happened during the recent past in Europe—and how it could, and perhaps will, happen here in America. The broad coalition of animal rights enthusiasts and their fellow travelers have unified through the cement of secularism. They derive some legitimacy from the claim that all religions proscribe cruelty to animals. Every trend that becomes dangerous, no matter how far-fetched, can only do so if it contains enough truth to provide it with the launch pad of legitimacy. In the case of animal rights, some legitimacy was provided by the fact that, indeed, all decent people abhor acts of cruelty to animals. From there to trying to eliminate the use of animal furs in clothing and fashion is a gigantic leap. From there to banning the use of animals in pharmaceutical and drug testing is an even greater leap. From there to suggesting that eating meat is somehow morally reprehensible, and certainly that killing an animal without stunning it (rendering it unkosher), is only one more leap.

These great leaps are made with the fervor of genuine faith. I have spent half a lifetime trying to demonstrate that it is possible for people to dedicate themselves to a hatred of God and the extirpation of His influence in society with a fervor and devotion equal to that of any religious person. Nothing arouses passions and conviction like the Almighty does. In their furious determination to refute the first few chapters of Genesis, extreme secularists are driven to insist that animals and people are identical in essential nature; different only superficially. In reality, the entire point of those early chapters is that God is building up to the pinnacle and ultimate purpose of Creation. First come inanimate objects followed by vegetation and animals. Only then do we see man being formed and, as I remind my six daughters, thereafter we reach the pinnacle when God creates woman.

Secularism crouching beneath the banner of the animal rights movement is determined to eliminate any moral endorsement of the differences between man and animal. Using animals in any way at all is distasteful. No, it is evil. After all, would you test a potentially dangerous drug on your cousin before using it yourself? Would you wear the skin of your sister? Would you become a cannibal? The answers to all these questions then become moral justification for eliminating their practice.

Eating meat is bad enough, but eating meat as a form of sacramental experience is too much for these radical extremists. It is intolerable to them that animals should be killed religiously as a daily reaffirmation that God permitted the eating of animal meat. To me, the highest purpose of animals is to assist in furthering the spiritual development of humans. In exactly the same way, the highest purpose of minerals is to allow vegetation to grow and the highest purpose of grass is to enable the higher life-form of animals to thrive. Thus there is a violent collision of philosophies between secularism, as seen through the lens of extreme animal rights advocates, and religion. At its crux is the question of whether any external brake on my desires and appetites exists. I believe that God began His relationship with humanity by telling us which trees we may eat of and which are prohibited to us. The appealing thing about being an animal is that nothing is prohibited. I am devoted to reaffirming the difference between humans and animals, which I do by eating meat every Sabbath. Animal rights secularists rightly recognize the danger that I represent to their worldview and eventually target ritual slaughter as practiced by religious Jews.

They sound very reasonable at first. They raise concerns about animal cruelty, suggesting that kosher slaughter is less humane than other methods. Little by little they work on public opinion, which is gradually swayed. They discuss how all Americans subsidize kosher meat because FDA inspectors need to be trained to deal with this alternate form of slaughter. While their ultimate goal is to eliminate the entire meat industry, attacking kosher meat is a vital interim step. It is important for Jews to realize that whenever this happens in modern, secularized societies it is always instigated by the Left. In Sweden, for example, it was not the traditional Lutheran clergy that supported the ban on Jewish ritual slaughter; it was the Left-wing animal rights enthusiasts.

ANOTHER SCENARIO

Many Jews reading this warning will reassure themselves that since they are not observant of the Torah and its dietary laws, known as the kosher laws, this matter is of little concern. Some may even feel that eliminating kosher meat will help remove some of the guilt they still experience when consuming non-kosher meat. But the same process and social mechanism works toward the elimination of yet another religious practice which most Jews, whether or not they are religiously observant, still practice.

Circumcision is also under attack. In this case the camouflage is provided by the so-called children's rights movement. Public relations campaigns target the pediatric medical community which, not surprisingly, wavers. Initially the protestations specify that they are not referring to circumcision for religious reasons. You will read ominous warnings by one pediatrician or another (usually a secularized Jew himself, because no gentile would have the *chutzpah* to speak like this) about the long-term dangers to the psyche of a child who was circumcised. Sometimes they speak of the trauma suffered by the mother of the infant, but more often of the pain and suffering inflicted upon the infant. They also remind us of how little evidence there is of long-term medical benefits to the procedure. To which I respond that it doesn't matter. Jews don't circumcise our boys because we think it will be healthy for them and their wives, although it wouldn't surprise us to learn that a benevolent God arranged things in this way. The reason we circumcise is only because, in the book of Genesis, God instructs us to do so.

Again it is worth noting that the attacks on circumcision always originate with the thinly veiled forces of secularism that make up the Left-wing political alliances of America. In recent years the practice of female genital mutilation by some primitive cultures has been referred to as "female circumcision." Again, such an association is seldom an innocent mistake. More often it is intended to cast suspicions of primitive cruelty on a holy and exalted practice by which devoted Jews have demonstrated their fidelity to their Creator for thousands of years.

The secular Left will not openly oppose circumcision. They will merely argue that it should be a decision every adult should make for himself rather than allowing adults to inflict the procedure on children.

With the Left's love of centralized government control, there is a simple and insidious way that they will interfere with the religious liberty of Jews to circumcise their sons. They will raise their hands in mock horror at discovering that circumcision is a surgical procedure that can be performed by one citizen upon another with no medical license. They will ignore the fact that Jewish circumcisers (the practitioner is called a *mohel*) perform thousands of flawless circumcisions each year. They will ignore the fact that Queen Elizabeth the Second of Great Britain had each of her sons circumcised by a Jewish *mohel* rather than by a doctor. In fact, one of my father's Bible students, Dr. Morris Sifman, who is now the chief medical officer of the Initiation Society, the Chief Rabbi of England's organization for supervision of *mohelim*, ritual circumcisers, tells us that Prince Charles was indeed circumcised by the late Dr. Snowman, a Jewish *mohel*. It is an old royal family tradition dating back to at least Queen Victoria who was under the impression that the royal family of Britain was somehow descended from ancient Israel, and possibly from the house of King David. Thus King Edward the Eighth, who had abdicated, possessed the name David among his other first names and titles, and in the intimate circle of the family was actually called David. As secularism has spread throughout the west, detractors of circumcision convinced Charles and the late Diana that circumcising their sons would be tantamount to child abuse. This is why the new generation of British royalty is not circumcised. Circumcision was outlawed in the recent Soviet Union, and as far back as the Roman Empire. Why not in America? I suggest that if circumcision survives in America as a legal process it will only be because of a respect for Judaism, not only by Jews, but by their friends in the Christian community.

FAR-FETCHED? NOT REALLY

I know that outlawing kosher meat or circumcision seems far-fetched, but so did many of the crazy excesses that have now become part of the fabric of "political correctness" that binds and restricts the lives of Americans today. Had someone told you that you would be forbidden to mention that an apartment for rent was on an upper floor, or that it had a view, would you have believed it? Yet, major newspapers refuse to run such advertising for fear of a lawsuit by the federal government claiming discrimination against the handicapped or blind.

Consider how all air travel passengers are inconvenienced by the moronic questions asked at check-in and which serve absolutely no safety purpose. How do you suppose notorious international terrorist Abdul Rachman would respond when asked, "Did you pack your bags yourself and have they been in your possession all the time?" Is Abdul really likely to say, "Rats. You nailed me. What can I say? In that bag is a bomb given to me by the mad genius of Baghdad. You Americans are just too smart for us terrorists."

Hardly; this procedure accomplishes only two things, neither having to do with traveler safety. First, it increases airline profits by preventing your cousin Fred from using that ticket you once purchased for yourself and never used. Nowadays the identity of the traveler must match the name on the ticket, so Fred can just go and buy his own ticket while your unused ticket slowly expires. Second, it gives the false impression that the government is actually doing something about airline terrorism, while in reality all that has happened is that government has found yet another way to involve itself in another area of transport.

Imagine being told ten years ago that the day would come when you would be regularly and inconveniently interrogated before boarding a plane in a way that serves absolutely no safety purpose, by a skycap with very little training in criminology or terrorism. Surely you would have been incredulous that anyone could be stupid enough to impose a meaningless and time-consuming formality on American travelers who are already a somewhat frazzled crowd. Even if anyone would be both stupid and reckless enough to try such a dumb bureaucratic grab, the American people would stand up for their rights. Well, it has happened, and we all compliantly and silently put up with it.

Stupid and sometimes even dangerous things do come to pass in a society. Each one, on its own, usually constitutes only a small incremental assault on freedom and common sense. Thus, each little advance against the freedoms and independence of law-abiding citizens takes place with little protest because it just isn't worthwhile to disrupt life for what most of us consider such a small matter. And in this fashion little things gradually begin to add up to big things; before you know it, the quality of life has deteriorated a little further.

Is life in America still much better than anywhere else? Without question it is. However, we must be aware that many of the policy makers and idea generators in government seek their inspiration not from our own glorious past but from other countries' less-glorious present.

LOOK LEFT, NOT RIGHT

Whether you believe, as I do, that outlawing kosher meat or circumcision could easily happen here, and gradually lead to the erosion of other religious freedoms as well, one thing is clear: Assaults on religious freedoms of Jews and other minorities will come from the secular Left, not from the religious Right. The notion that Pat Robertson and Jesse Helms secretly yearn to outlaw Jewish circumcision is ludicrous. In fact, it is not uncommon for traditional Jews to receive greater respect from religious Christians than from secular Jews. In June 1997 I was one of the guest speakers at a Catholic home-schooling convention in Washington State. In the literature mailed out to participants, an interesting note followed the paragraph detailing my topic. It requested the female audience to refrain from extending a handshake to me, as religious Jews reserve physical contact between the sexes, even of the most innocuous type, for close relations such as spouses or siblings. Orthodox Jewish speakers throughout the country have mentioned to me, and I have myself experienced, the great efforts expended by Christian groups in order to acquire kosher food for their Jewish guests. The same speaker at a Jewish Federation event, at least until very recently, was often left with nothing to eat as the "establishment" Jews downed their non-kosher dinners.

The things that threaten most ordinary American Jews are the same as those confronting most ordinary Americans. We are all bothered by how much more stressful and perilous life in America has become. Many of the institutions on which Jews depend even more than most for the preservation of safety and tranquillity are failing due to the failed ideology of the liberal Left. Academic institutions and the media fail to censure the perpetrators of violence and destruction, preferring instead to find excuses. If they ever do attach blame, it is not to the vicious predators that prowl our streets but to inanimate objects or social policies. Police, in some cases unable and in others unwilling to take the necessary steps to restore civility, are failing at their task. The criminal justice system prefers not to impose the penalties that would truly deter crime.

All these trends seriously threaten the life, liberty and happiness of the average American Jew as they do that of the average law-abiding American citizen. And most of us know that Jews do not get raped, robbed, murdered or mugged by Christians on their way home from church on Sunday morning. On the contrary, we are allies. Christian conservatives possess the political muscle to help restore many of the traditional qualities of public life upon which Jewish religious liberty depends.

In America today I have access to everything I require in order to observe my religion fully. Not only can I follow all the tenets of my faith, but I can even wear my *kippah* (religious head covering) when addressing Congress because of a deep respect for religious practice in this country. Most Americans, upon hearing about a religious conflict, go out of their way to accommodate religious needs. On the other hand there are people who, for varied reasons, find things such as ritual slaughter or circumcision highly offensive. Throughout Jewish history, though never in America, each of these religious practices has been outlawed at one or more times. As a Jew I am extremely grateful to be living in a country that, though founded without one Jewish signature on its Declaration of Independence, has legally granted me full religious expression. I am worried that my grandchildren may not have the same freedoms, not because of Christians, but because of a removal of Christian values from this country.

Can I promise that no demagogue will rise in the Christian community or that there will never be church-sponsored hatred of Jews in America? No, I cannot. I can only look at what is, and attempt to see what may hatch from eggs that have already been laid. At the moment, followers of the Christian Right are among the most philo-Semitic citizens of this country. Their sensitivity to Judaism is increasing, not diminishing, each year. I know that few Jews realize this. Those of us who have spent the time getting to know the leaders and platforms of Christians do. What is absolutely irrefutable is that founding a theocracy would entail abrogating the First Amendment to the Constitution as well as pulling together a coalition of groups that have serious theological differences with one another. In other words, the chances are infinitesimal. In my eyes, this is much less likely to occur than prohibitions against Jewish religious practices in the name of children's or animal rights.

To understand more completely why America cannot be easily turned into a Christian theocracy, let's examine another key question: Who is being more faithful to the original vision of the founding fathers of this country—the Christian Right or the liberal Left?

PART II

REAFFIRMING
OUR ROOTS

CHAPTER THIRTEEN

SPIRITUAL GRAVITY

SECULAR LIBERAL GROUPS ARE ATTEMPTING
TO REWRITE AMERICAN HISTORY,
AND IN MANY CASES THEY HAVE ALREADY
BEGUN TO SUCCEED.

After a catastrophic air disaster, countless investigators gather to find out why the airplane fell out of the sky. Without attempting to be flippant or simplistic, I can provide the only accurate answer in one word: gravity. The real question is, Why did the plane ever remain airborne? What an amazing sight! Two hundred humans hermetically sealed in a tube made of one hundred tons of aluminum hurtling through the atmosphere at just below the speed of sound. How does that happen? What kept the airplane up there? It remained airborne because it had engines that could convert the chemical energy stored in fuel into thrust. It had wings that could convert thrust into lift. Remove any of these elements and the natural effect of gravity will take its course. I do not even have to believe in gravity for these events to unfold.

The story of America during the past thirty-five years is likewise a story of an airplane running out of fuel. What will transpire when it does is entirely natural and predictable. The good news is that, for those who wish it, the fuel tanks can be replenished. But what is the fuel? What has kept America airborne for so long? I believe it is loyalty to the basic principles that God laid down in His Bible for the safe and durable operation of the machine we call human society.

REMEMBERING WHO WE ARE

Many years ago I embarked on a motorcycle trip through parts of the African continent that were far off the beaten track. While the decision to undertake this adventure may have been caused by the testosterone poisoning found so often in young males, I certainly learned many lessons that summer that have remained with me.

One highlight of that fascinating excursion was camping one night in an isolated part of the Great Rift Valley, not far from Lake Victoria. I was enjoying the warm evening while lubricating my motorcycle in front of my little tent. The sky was full of stars and I felt a sense of wonder at where I found myself. I had just told myself that there probably were no other humans within fifty miles when I saw what appeared to be a lantern among the trees a few hundred yards away.

Creeping closer, I determined to identify those sharing my corner of the African veldt before I disclosed my presence. You can imagine my astonishment upon finding a clearing in which a small table had been exquisitely laid, complete with fine English china and sparkling crystal. The vision was so incongruous that I assumed I was delirious from dehydration.

My concern was soon alleviated as a dapper old man in full dinner dress descended from a camper vehicle I had not noticed until then. Extending his hand, he assisted a beautifully dressed lady to the table. I could no longer restrain my curiosity. Upon spotting me, they invited me to join them. I soon discovered that they were well-known entomologists on one of their regular scientific expeditions. When I expressed my bewilderment at their mode of dress and dining, they kindly explained. Soon after they were married many years earlier, they agreed that although their work would have them spending up to half a year at a time in the bush, they would cling to their civilization in order to always be able to feel at home back in London's fashionable West End. They decided to accomplish this by disciplining themselves to always dress for dinner and make dinner a formal occasion no matter where they found themselves.

I am ashamed to admit that, at the time, I found the couple's insistence on proper behavior more amusing than admirable. Over the years I have grown more respectful of their ability to know exactly who they were and to retain their essence no matter what the circumstances. I have even come to feel retrospective embarrassment at how inadequately dressed I was when they so graciously invited me to join them. By pretending not to notice my tired Levi's, rough shirt, and heavy boots, they demonstrated that their attempt to maintain the delicate structure of human civilization, even in the furthest corners of the world, had worked perfectly. They knew just who they were—and they have inspired me to do the same since then.

It seems to me that America has lost precisely that certainty over the last few decades. Who are we? What is the "American culture"? What behaviors and beliefs distinguish an American from members of other nationalities? What essential principles can America not abandon and still be America? In other words, what fuel has kept America airborne for two centuries?

To answer these questions we must turn to America's origins.

DECLARATION OF INDEPENDENCE: POLITICALLY INCORRECT?

Studying the United States Constitution gives us a subtle reminder of what the fuel was: "If any bill shall not be returned by the President within ten days (Sundays excepted) after it shall have been presented to him...." Why "Sundays excepted"? For exactly the same reason that, to this day, mail is not delivered in America on Sundays. America was founded as a Christian nation and, as such, Sunday is special. It is the Lord's day. Similarly, Israel was founded as a Jewish nation; mail is not delivered in Israel on Saturday because Saturday is *Shabbat,* the Jewish Sabbath.

It strikes me as unlikely that the Declaration of Independence could ever be adopted today because too many Americans would protest the use of the word "Creator." It probably would be bemoaned by liberals as the endorsement of religion by government, a suggestion that humans did not evolve in an unaided, materialistic manner from primeval sludge to Bach or Beethoven. On July 4, 1776, however, there was no debate over the phrase "endowed by their Creator" (with an upper-case C). That America was founded as a Christian nation is beyond debate. We were a Christian nation with a constitutional government rather than a theocracy, but a Christian nation nonetheless. What is more, we were founded as a Christian nation that took Judeo-Christian principles so much for granted that the founding fathers saw little reason to state the obvious.

What America has become today, we cannot agree upon. And as we debate and protest and argue about what type of fuel has, and should, propel our airliner, we are slowly losing altitude and running out of fuel.

NO THREAT

From the very beginning of our country it was perfectly evident to all, including early Jewish Americans who saw no threat in our nation's Christian orientation, that Christmas was to be a national holiday. Nobody argued that the post office or other government offices should be open on Christmas for fear of inconveniencing or offending non-Christians. In exactly the same way, post offices and much more are closed in Israel on *Yom Kippur,* the Jewish Day of Atonement.

As I speak to Jewish audiences they are often astounded to hear what a high proportion of Americans say a prayer of thanks before eating a meal. Likewise, they are quite unaware of how many Americans attend church at least once a week. Unfortunately the figures for saying grace before meals and for weekly worship attendance are much lower in the Jewish community. As usual, statistics lie—chiefly because we have become accustomed to speaking of the Jewish community as if there is only one. In fact there are at least two Jewish communities. One is fairly small but fervently religious. Members of this Jewish community pray in synagogue more frequently than once a week and say grace both before and after each meal. The other, considerably larger, Jewish community prays seldom (if ever) and doesn't consider grace an indispensable element of a meal.

What is more interesting is how little the second Jewish community knows about the first. As a matter of fact, the second Jewish community is somewhat indifferent, even embarrassed, about the first. There is a small and shrinking group who are non-practicing Jews but who feel a warm nostalgia for the religious ritual of their faith. For the most part, feeling the polarization pressures, their children are either becoming fervently Jewish and religious or abandoning faith altogether.

As a rabbi observing both Jewish and American culture, I believe these two separate Jewish communities are an accurate reflection of how separate the two larger American communities have become. Just as most secularized Jews do not socialize with religious friends or relatives, so most secularized Americans spend little time with people who take their faith seriously. I suspect that by now, far more people socialize across the color barrier. Far more whites have African-American friends, and vice versa, than the secular Americans have religious friends.

This is hardly surprising. Color should indeed be a largely irrelevant factor in human interaction. In economic transactions, everyone's money is green; in neighborhood socialization, values are what counts. If my neighbor and I each respect our fences and look out for one another, our respective colors are irrelevant. Most of us are most comfortable among like-minded people. Some contend we are most comfortable among people who look like we do. If that were true, I'd only want to socialize with bald people. Good-looking women would never be seen with plainer-looking friends. No, it has nothing to do with appearance and everything to do with values. I'd be the first to admit that I am uncomfortable among people who do not share my values. I would go to great trouble, and indeed have done so, to live among people who do share my values.

Let's be honest: Most of us would rather have a next-door neighbor whose practical, day-to-day values correspond to our own—even if his theology and faith were different—than a neighbor who attended our synagogue or church but whose values and conduct were abominable. It is upon this simple premise that America is based. Worship as you will, as long as your behavior and values reflect the basic ethic of the Judeo-Christian tradition.

Thus we are fortunate enough to live in a society whose government is not committed to any particular theology, but which is committed to a broad Judeo-Christian understanding of good and evil in human behavior. Interestingly, much of European history, including many cultures who once were strong but now are weak or non-existent, was built on the reverse: a theologically committed government but a people bereft of any deeply rooted sense of right and wrong.

To this day, more homes per capita in America possess a Bible than in any other country in the world. More Americans attend regular worship services than in any other industrialized nation. More Americans say a prayer before meals than in any other western country. I delight in long drives through the American countryside with my children. One of my chief pleasures is tallying the towns we drive through with biblical names. We recently found a new one as we drove along the banks of the mighty Columbia River in our home state of Washington: Piel. Do enough Jewish hearts swell in pride to know that early settlers of the Northwest felt such a kinship to the God of Abraham, Isaac and Jacob that they named their new home "Piel," Hebrew for "Mouth of God"? What does it mean that this land of ours has so many places with biblical names? America has more Hebrons, Bethels, Canaans, Salems, Pisgahs, Jerichos and Zions than anywhere else in the world. What does it mean that so many early Americans had biblical names? Every third or fourth person was a Jeremiah, Obadiah, Abigail, Abraham, or Sarah. The Bible served as a source for place names, a source for people names and a source for an entire vision of America's future. What does all this mean for us? It helps demonstrate that we Jews have thrived in America, not in spite of America's Christian fervor but because of it.

FREEDOM FROM RELIGION OR RELIGIOUS FREEDOM?

Reading material from only the last few decades, one might emerge with the view that America has always seen itself primarily as a nation of immigrants, a quilt of all different faiths and customs. Today's reader, media watcher, and certainly the student at university, could easily be led to believe that our founding fathers were concerned with freedom *from* religion rather than with religious freedom. I have had a graduate student tell me that the phrase from the First Amendment, *"no law respecting an establishment of religion,"* meant that no religious establishment should be respected! How ignorant can you be and still get a degree in higher education? My extensive readings have left me without a doubt that this nation was founded by Christians and was meant to be based on broad Christian principles. Religion was the bedrock upon which the nation stood, and without it these amazing men and women saw no future for the country they had established.

There was also an unprecedented respect for and tolerance of Judaism. Historical records clearly show that there were Jews, some of them prominent, in the American colonies. They participated in the Revolutionary War and were certainly known to the founding fathers. Could the fact that the Declaration of Independence refers to the Creator, rather than to Jesus, be an acknowledgment that not all Americans of the day believed in the latter? More likely there was a desire not to define America as a Christian nation because doing so would raise the question, "Whose variety of Christianity?" Many of the colonists had fled Christian countries where their specific denomination had been persecuted. The individual colonies which then became states each had their own religious slants. Maryland, for example, had been founded specifically as a Catholic colony; Quakers, expelled from some colonies, eventually found a home in Pennsylvania. Not all groups accepted all others as in fact Christian. While some of the fathers, such as Thomas Jefferson, were Deists, the overwhelming majority, according to the late historian Russell Kirk, were staunch members of more standard churches. Declaring in the Constitution that *"Congress shall make no law respecting an establishment of religion, or prohibiting the free exercise thereof,"* was a necessity for the various *Christian* denominations to be able to live together.

The emphasis, furthermore, was only on the federal level. Several colonies (and later states) did have religious requirements for holding public office and even established churches, with the blessing of those who wrote the Constitution. Most Americans would be surprised to learn that some of these requirements remained in force even into the 1800s. It is not hard to believe that a passing thought was given to the Jewish community. However, history shows that Jews were primarily the beneficiaries of a Christian community's attempts to deal with its own variety of beliefs and practices under the broad Christian umbrella. What is historically insupportable is the idea that God, the Creator, was meant to be excluded and forbidden from the running of this country.

LIBERAL REVISIONISM VS. HISTORICAL FACT

For almost two hundred years, America functioned, grew, and prospered under this tacit agreement. America was a religious country without demanding allegiance to a specific church. Congress opened with a prayer (and still does), and the Ten Commandments were posted on courtroom and schoolroom walls. God was frequently invoked in presidential speeches and community events; the assumption was that Americans were "one nation under God." Not only did religion in general have a respected place in our nation's affairs, but Christianity in particular was a positive undercurrent.

But today one hears over and over that religion, especially Christianity, must be kept out of public policy, and that this was the intent of our ancestors. Supporting this revisionist position is a report of the American Jewish Committee dated September 9, 1996:

> We must continue to emphasize pluralism as a basic value of America to which the AJC is dedicated, and to remind Americans of their history on these issues. *The religious right may be convincing people that this country was founded on religious principles, and that the founders intended to create a Christian nation, since the religious rightists keep saying that.* We must continue to publicize *our* view of American history and make it relevant to people today. (emphasis added)[1]

The majority of liberal policy groups, politicians, and pundits in this country would probably agree with that statement. Others, myself included, would say exactly the opposite. Allow me to counter the above with what I believe to be a more historically correct statement:

We must continue to emphasize religion as a basic value of America to which we are dedicated, and to remind Americans of their history on these issues. *The secularist may be convincing people that this country was founded on pluralistic principles, and that the founders intended to create a secular nation, since the liberals keep saying that.* We must continue to publicize our view of American history and make it relevant to people today.

Questions of pure opinion or belief, because they are not measurable, rarely lead to resolution. We might not be able to find a resolution. If two neighbors quarrel as to whether Mount Rainier or Mount Fuji is higher, they can consult an atlas to ascertain which is correct. However, if one American feels that Van Gogh is a superior painter to Rembrandt, while another is convinced that the opposite is true, there may never be agreement. In fact, there is no correct answer to such a debate. As Americans, we can never resolve whether Christianity, Judaism or any other religion is the true expression of God's will. But religion is an area where we must each respect the other's right to *believe* differently than ourselves.

But when we are debating whether this country was *founded* on religious principles and whether any *convincing to the contrary* is being attempted, there is a plethora of material from which to draw. Secular liberal groups are attempting to rewrite American history, and in many cases they have already begun to succeed. A clever strategy it is, too. To a greater extent than we know, our sense of self is authenticated by a link to our fathers. If you could persuade me that my father never was a wonderful rabbi but was in fact a notorious vagrant, you will have effectively changed my life. At a time in our history when studies often inform us that many high school seniors cannot recognize the Bill of Rights, identify America's southern neighbor, or name our first president, our children are vulnerable to whatever history, factual or otherwise, they are being taught. Thus it is doubly important that America's adults deal in facts rather than in revisionism.

CHAPTER FOURTEEN

ANOTHER LOOK
AT OUR ROOTS

IF IT IS WRONG TO DENY THE HOLOCAUST, SURELY IT IS ALSO WRONG TO DENY CHRISTIANITY'S ROLE IN THE FOUNDING OF AMERICA.

A visitor to these shores comparing two history textbooks, one from the 1940s and one from the 1990s, concerning the Pilgrims and Thanksgiving, would probably have difficulty realizing that the same people and observance were being discussed. Fortunately as we near the year 2000, there is no need to guess what was in the mind of the Pilgrims as they landed in the New World. They bequeathed us a written document, the Mayflower Compact, signed just prior to disembarking their ships on November 11, 1620. The compact reads, in part:

> In the Name of God, Amen, We, whose names are underwritten, the Loyal Subjects of our dread Sovereign Lord King James, by the Grace of God, of Great Britain, France, and Ireland, King, Defender of the Faith, etc. *Having undertaken for the Glory of God, and Advancement of the Christian Faith,* and the Honour of our King and Country, a Voyage to plant the first Colony.... (emphasis added)

It is difficult to interpret that document as anything other than a Christian statement of purpose. Surely, one would think that this document would form an integral part of school textbooks dealing with this period. In many instances, it sadly does not.

There are other undisputed historical facts of the time, such as that Squanto, the Indian who guided the Pilgrims through their first winter, was not simply a good pagan who happened to help, but was himself a believing Christian. There is no doubt, due to primary source material, that the first Thanksgiving was a day of gratitude to the Almighty—not, as is often taught today, gratitude to the Indians. Yet in the recommended Washington State teacher's guide for teaching about Thanksgiving, the historical facts are set aside in favor of secular revisionism.

This problem is not unique to any one state. In 1995 the National Education Association passed a resolution celebrating diversity in Thanksgiving. There is a school district that teaches children an Indian chant for Thanksgiving, not minding that the Indians who used this chant lived nowhere near the east coast in the 1600s. It is one thing for a Disney movie to leave out the fact that Pocahontas converted to Christianity. It is another thing for our schools to neglect that part of her life. It seems that we would rather teach lies to our children than acknowledge the deeply Christian roots of the settlement of the country. Because we Jews loudly loathe attempts to revise Jewish history, we ought also to be among those denouncing attempts at rewriting American history. If it is wrong to deny the Holocaust, surely it is also wrong to deny Christianity's role in the founding of America.

A case might be made that the observance of Thanksgiving denies the native Indians their heritage, and that more citizens today are descended from later immigrants than from those on the Mayflower. Perhaps Thanksgiving should be replaced with a new holiday that would celebrate the diversity of this country. In rebuttal, I would argue the importance of not cutting ourselves off from our roots, that canceling Thanksgiving would be a denial of a key event in our history. We could have an honest debate.

POLITICALLY CORRECT VS. HISTORICALLY CORRECT

But what has happened is insupportable. Those who have been given the job of educating our youth have, on their own, decided that it is imperative to teach an historical event inaccurately. Just as in the old Soviet Union, where all inventions were credited to the Soviets no matter where they actually originated, a higher cause than truth is now the force behind our history textbooks. I agree with the liberal claim that a lot of indoctrination is going on. I just disagree as to who is doing it.

Granted, when the Constitution was signed more than a hundred years after the Pilgrims landed, federal documents did not have the same level of focus on Christianity as in the early 1600s. (There was not the same focus on being loyal subjects of the king, either.) Yet, again, we have no shortage of papers letting us know what the leaders of the American Revolution were thinking. It is hard to find pluralism in the words of John Jay, first Chief Justice of the Supreme Court: "Providence has given to our people the choice of their rulers, and it is the duty of our Christian nation to select and prefer Christians for their rulers."

The much-vaunted pluralism seems to also be lacking when Patrick Henry, writing in the Virginia Bill of Rights, dated June 12, 1776, declared: "All men are equally entitled to the free exercise of religion, according to the dictates of conscience; and that it is the mutual duty of all to practice Christian forbearance, love and charity towards each other."

The fact that statements of founding fathers such as John Adams, George Washington or Patrick Henry have been expunged from our most commonly used history textbooks does not mean they were not said or that they do not reflect what was truly in the minds of these men as they agreed upon the Constitution.

In 1787, the year the Constitution was officially approved by Congress, the Northwest Ordinance was approved by the same body. Article 3 of that ordinance states: "Religion, morality, and knowledge, being necessary to good government and the happiness of mankind, schools and the means of education shall forever be encouraged." It is not an unreasonable leap to propose that a solid case for religious instruction in school is present in that document.

Likewise, George Washington's Farewell Address of 1796 deals with the issue of religion: "Let us with caution indulge the supposition that morality can be maintained without religion. Reason and experience both forbid us to expect that national morality can prevail to the exclusion of religious principle."

From these samplings it is clear that our founders did not afford atheism a respected role in America. Equally clear is that religion was at the very foundation of this country's policies. Even Benjamin Franklin, not regarded as one of the more religious founding fathers, gives us a clear glimpse of what he believed to be described by the word "religion." In a letter to the president of Yale University, Ezra Stiles, he wrote:

> Here is my creed. I believe in one God, the Creator of the universe. That he governs it by his Providence. That he ought to be worshipped. That the most acceptable service we render to him is in doing good to his other children. That the soul of man is immortal, and will be treated with justice in another life respecting its conduct in this. *These I take to be the fundamental points in all sound religion.* (emphasis added)[1]

"SEPARATION OF CHURCH AND STATE"

Perhaps you think that while it is fair to quote from official documents like the Virginia Bill of Rights, I should not build my argument from a personal letter of Benjamin Franklin. Yet the much-touted phrase, "a wall of separation between church and state" comes, not from the Constitution but from a letter written by Thomas Jefferson to Nehemiah Dodge, Ephraim Robbins and Stephen Nelson of the Danbury Baptist

Association. Volumes have been written, and myriad documentaries made, about Thomas Jefferson. I am not going to attempt to analyze his views on religion and government. The fact that he approved the government's role in the "propagation of the Gospel among the heathen," and that he wrote that students at the University of Virginia, which he founded, should be "expected to attend religious worship at the establishment of their respective sects," suggests that whether or not he personally believed in Christianity and/or God, he publicly supported both.

The American Jewish Committee, in the document mentioned previously, brings as proof for its position the Congressional approval in 1796 of a treaty with Tripoli that included the words, "as the government of the United States of America is not in any sense founded on the Christian religion... [it has] no character of enmity against the laws, religion or tranquillity of Muslims." I see no conflict between the assertion that our *government* is not officially Christian and my assertion that Christian thought and traditional Judeo-Christian ethics were meant always to be intertwined with American policy. As the federal government has expanded its reach, and as public government schools have become the norm, government has taken on an entirely different meaning than it had in the late 1700s, when its role was very limited. Government now is in the position of removing religion from the American nation.

As history textbooks used in public and private schools encourage the view that America was meant to be neutral on the subject of religion, it is worthwhile to review George Washington's closing official words to the nation in his famous Farewell Address. Referring to the very issue of removing religion from an exalted position, as was happening in revolutionary France, he warned: "Of all the dispositions and habits which lead to political prosperity, religion and morality are indispensable supports.... Who that is a sincere friend to it can look with indifference upon attempts to shake the foundation of the fabric?"

CHAPTER FIFTEEN

WHY OUR PLEDGE OF ALLEGIANCE WAS CHANGED

EITHER AMERICA HAS NO RELIGIOUS ROOTS AND NO SPECIAL SPIRITUAL DESTINY, OR IT HAS BOTH.

Only recently has part of America challenged the long-held assumption that America is a Christian nation.

Most citizens do not recognize just how quickly we have moved in an anti-Christian direction. Even fewer devote even a few minutes' contemplation to how this extirpation of religion might impact them if it totally succeeds.

Imagine the present-day reaction if a respected judge were to make the following speech: "What then is the spirit of liberty? ...the spirit of liberty remembers that not even a sparrow falls to earth unheeded; the spirit of liberty is the spirit of Him who, near two thousand years ago, taught mankind that lesson it has never learned...."

Yet, in 1944 Justice Learned Hand, named by Jewish Supreme Court Justice, Benjamin Cardozo, as the greatest living American jurist of his time, gave that speech to over one million people in New York City. It was received with great acclaim and gained greater renown as it disseminated over the next few weeks. The speech was delivered to newly naturalized Americans (about 150,000 of those gathered), and yet there was no hesitation in referring both to the New Testament and Jesus, and stating that spirit to be American. In 1954, Chief Justice Earl Warren said, "I like to believe we are living today in the spirit of the Christian religion. I like also to believe that as long as we do so, no great harm can come to our country."

Both of these men are heroes of the modern secular liberal. That they could speak in a manner that today would create an uproar, accentuates the idea that what was routinely accepted in our culture has been, over a very short period of history, overturned.

In the 1950s there was already a perception that this country was moving away from its origins and needed to ask exactly what differentiated us from a country like Russia. In his brilliant address which led to the phrase "one nation under God" being added to the Pledge of Allegiance, the Reverend George M. Docherty answered that question. I can just hear someone saying, "Aha! See, Lapin admits that this whole business of 'under God' is recent. This proves that before the 1950s, God was not part of public American discourse." Just the opposite. Let me explain.

WHY ADD "UNDER GOD"?

When I was still a pulpit rabbi in West Los Angeles, a member of my synagogue came to me in a very disturbed state. A young social worker, she had been unnerved by a meeting with one of her teenage clients. The young girl had told her that a friend of hers had murdered someone in her presence the previous evening, and she didn't know if her obligation was to stay quiet and protect her friend or to tell the police. The young girl was troubled by the moral dilemma in which she found herself and could not discern the right thing to do. Similarly, my friend Dennis Prager, the erudite writer and speaker on moral issues, often tells of a quiz he gives teenagers around the country. He presents them with a hypothetical situation that has the family dog and a stranger drowning at the same time, and it is in their capability to rescue one but not both. He has ceased to be astounded when a large percentage of teenagers opt for the dog over the human being and argue their choice as the truly moral one.

Perhaps we should now post signs in all social workers' offices telling clients that if they know of a murder they must tell the police. Perhaps we should also require public service announcements on TV urging parents to sit down with their teenagers to discuss the difference between animals and humans. It is not too far a leap to see the need for such laws.

Imagine one of our great-grandchildren looking back at the year in which these rules are enacted. "Wow!" they will exclaim. "How backward people were before these rules. It wasn't until 1999 that they became really moral. Until then they really didn't know that murderers should be turned in or that human life takes precedence over dogs." Looking at their history books, they would conclude that until 1999, young women who witnessed murders committed by their friends never reported the crime. How wrong they would be. The fact that these things need to be legislated shows not progress, but how low we have fallen.

In a similar vein, an eleventh-century rabbinic leader in Main Germany, Rabbeinu Gershom, enacted a law that prohibited Jews from opening and reading someone else's mail. Rabbeinu Gershom was not acting in a radical, progressive way. Far from demonstrating moral progress, his ruling sadly acknowledged the depths to which some members of his community had fallen. Until that time it had been ethically unthinkable to invade anyone else's privacy in communication. Now, degeneration of moral values in his community made the ruling necessary.

THE SPEECH THAT CHANGED OUR PLEDGE

So on Flag Day of 1954, when President Eisenhower heard Reverend Docherty's sermon and signed the order adding "under God" to the Pledge of Allegiance, he comprehended the need for *previously understood* words to be *clearly stated*. "Under God" had always been considered a given in America until Docherty, Eisenhower, and others recognized deterioration in the mandate. I cannot improve on Reverend Docherty's magnificent oratory:

> Freedom is a subject everyone seems to be talking about without seemingly stopping to ask the rather basic question, "What do we mean by freedom?" In this matter, apparently, we all are experts.
>
> ...Lincoln in his day, saw this country as a nation that "was conceived in liberty and dedicated to the proposition that all men are created equal." And the question he asks is the timeless, and timely, one—"whether that Nation, or any nation so conceived and so dedicated, can long endure."
>
> I recall once discussing the "American way of life" with a newspaper editor. He had been using the phrase rather freely. When asked to define the phrase "the American way of life," he became very wordy and verbose. "It is live and let live; it is freedom to act," and other such platitudes.
>
> Let me tell what "the American way of life" is. It is going to the ball game and eating popcorn, and drinking Coca Cola, and rooting for the Senators. It is shopping in Sears, Roebuck. It is losing heart and hat on a roller coaster. It is driving on the right side of the road and putting up at motels on a long journey. It is being bored with television commercials. It is setting off firecrackers with your children on the Fourth of July. It is sitting for seven hours to see the pageantry of the Presidential Inauguration.
>
> But, it is deeper than that.
>
> ...And where did all this come from?
>
> It has been with us so long, we have to recall it was brought here by people who laid stress on fundamentals....
>
> These fundamental concepts of life had been given to the world from Sinai, where the moral law was graven upon tables of stone, symbolizing the universal application to all men; and they came from the New Testament, where they heard in the words of Jesus of Nazareth the living Word of God for the world.

...Now, all this may seem obvious until one sits down and takes these implications of freedom really seriously. For me, it came in a flash one day some time ago when our children came home from school. Almost casually, I asked what happened at school when they arrived there in the morning. They described to me, in great detail and with strange solemnity, the ritual of the salute to the flag. The children turn to the flag, and with their hand across their heart, they repeat the words: "I pledge allegiance to the flag of the United States of America and to the Republic for which it stands; one nation, indivisible, with liberty and justice for all."

They were very proud of the pledge; and rightly so.

...I don't suppose you fathers would have paid much attention to that as I did.... But I could sit down and brood upon it, going over each word slowly in my mind. And I came to a strange conclusion. There was something missing in this pledge, and that which was missing was the characteristic and definitive factor in the American way of life. In fact, I could hear little Muscovites repeat a similar pledge to their hammer-and-sickle flag in Moscow with equal solemnity, for Russia is also a republic that claims to have overthrown the tyranny of kingship.

...What, therefore, is missing in the Pledge of Allegiance that Americans have been saying off and on since 1892, and officially since 1942? The one fundamental concept that completely and ultimately separates Communist Russia from the democratic institutions of this country.

...We face, today, a theological war.... It is a fight for freedom of the human personality. It is not simply man's inhumanity to man. It is Armageddon, a battle of the gods. It is the view of man as it comes down to us from Judeo-Christian civilization in mortal combat against modern, secularized, godless humanity.

The Pledge of Allegiance seems to me to omit this theological implication that is fundamental to the American way of life. It should be "one nation, indivisible, under God." Once "under God," then we can define what we mean by "liberty and justice for all." To omit the words "under God" in the Pledge of Allegiance is to omit the definitive character of the American way of life.

Some might assert this to be a violation of the First Amendment to the Constitution. It is quite the opposite. The First Amendment states concerning the question of religion: "Congress shall make no law respecting the establishment of religion."

Now, "establishment of religion" is a technical term. It means Congress will permit no state church in this land such as exists in England. In England the bishops are appointed by Her Majesty. The church, by law, is supported to teinds or rent. The church, therefore, can call upon the support of the law of the land to carry out its own ecclesiastical laws. What the declaration says, in effect, is that no state church shall exist in this land. This is separation of church and state; it is not, and never was meant to be, a separation of religion and life. Such objection is a confusion of the First Amendment with the First Commandment.

If we were to add the phrase "under the church," that would be different. In fact, it would be dangerous. The question arises, which church? Now, I can give good Methodists an excellent dissertation upon the virtues of the Presbyterian Church, and show how much superior John Knox was to John Wesley. But the whole sad story of church history shows how, of all tyrants, often the church could be the worst for the best of reasons. The Jewish Church persecuted unto death the Christian Church in the first decade of Christianity; and for 1,200 years the Christian Church persecuted the Jewish Church. The Roman Church persecuted the Protestants; and the Protestants, in turn, persecuted the Roman Church; the Presbyterians and the Episcopalians brought low the very name of Christian charity, both in Scotland and America. It is not for nothing that Thomas Jefferson, on his tombstone at Monticello, claimed that one of the three achievements of his life was his fight for religious freedom in Virginia—that even above the exalted office of President of the United States. No church is infallible; and no churchman is infallible.

Of course, as Christians, we might include the words "under Jesus Christ" or "under the King of Kings." But one of the glories of this land is that it had opened its gates to all men of every religious faith.

...There is no religious examination of entering the United States of America—no persecution because a man's faith differs even from the Christian religion. So, it must be "under God," to include the great Jewish community, and the people of Moslem faith, and the myriad of *denominations* of Christians in the land.

What then of the honest atheist?

Philosophically speaking, an atheistic American is a contradiction in terms. Now don't misunderstand me. This age has thrown up a new type of man—we call him secular; he does not believe in God; not because he is a wicked man, but because he is dialectically honest, and would rather walk with the unbelievers than sit hypocritically with people of the faith. These men, and many have I known, are fine in character; and in the obligations as citizens and good neighbors, quite excellent.

But they really are spiritual parasites. And I mean no term of abuse in this. I'm simply classifying them. A parasite is an organism that lives upon the life force of another organism without contributing to the life of the other. These excellent ethical seculars are living upon the accumulated spiritual capital of Judeo-Christian civilization, and at the same time, deny the God who revealed the divine principles upon which the ethics of this country grow. The dilemma of the secular is quite simple.

He cannot deny the Christian revelation and logically live the Christian ethic.

And if he denies the Christian ethic, he falls short of the American ideal of life.

In Jefferson's phrase, if we deny the existence of the God who gave us life, how can we live by the liberty He gave us at the same time? This is a God-fearing nation. On our coins, bearing the imprint of Lincoln and Jefferson, are the words "In God We Trust." Congress is opened with prayer. It is upon the Holy Bible the President takes his oath of office. Naturalized citizens, when they take their oath of allegiance, conclude, solemnly, with the words "so help me God."

This is the issue we face today: A freedom that respects the rights of the minorities, but is defined by a fundamental belief in God. A way of life that sees man, not as the ultimate outcome of a mysterious concatenation of evolutionary process, but a sentient being created by God and seeking to know Him well, and "Whose soul is restless till he rest in God."

In this land, there is neither Jew nor Greek, neither bond nor free; neither male nor female, for we are one nation indivisible under God, and humbly as God has given us the light we seek liberty and justice for all. This quest is not only within these United States, but to the four corners of the globe, wherever man will lift up his head toward the vision of his true and divine manhood.[1]

In terming secular Americans spiritual parasites, living off the life force of others, Reverend Docherty foresaw today's tug-of-war. Some are outraged by what they see as his undeserved slur, while others applaud his courage and forthrightness. The issue does need to be settled. Either America has no religious roots and no special spiritual destiny, or it has both. The past is a matter of fact; the future is our choice. But it is a choice that will have to be made. I pray we choose wisely.

THE PREVAILING ETHIC

DO WE REALLY AGREE THAT ANYTHING ANYONE DEFINES AS "HIS RELIGION" MUST BE ACCORDED EQUAL STATUS IN AMERICA?

We Americans like to think of ourselves as having a sense of fair play. Unlike other countries we have no tradition of privilege. We have never believed in only eldest sons inheriting the estate. No segment of the population is granted hereditary titles, and America boasts of being the "land of opportunity" rather than of inheritance. The original colonies were populated by people from different denominations of Christianity and different social classes. Not surprisingly, we are truly disturbed by the idea that we might be elitist, or less than welcoming to all groups.

Yet we now face a crisis. Rather than integrate the differing cultures in our midst into American culture, we attempt to say that there is no inherent American culture and we should not judge anyone's ideas. Ludicrous results follow.

In San Jose, California, a statue is erected in a city park with taxpayer money that celebrates an Aztec god to whom child sacrifices were made. While in San Diego, California, a court rules that a cross that has stood in a park for many years must now be removed. An Aztec god, yes; a symbol of Christianity, no. In parks, schools, and public institutions across the country, this kind of double standard has become more and more common.

Do we really agree that anything anyone defines as "his religion" must be accorded equal status in America? We do need to decide this question. Most Americans feel something has gone amiss when they hear of these occurrences, but are nervous about stating unequivocally that the Judeo-Christian heritage with which this country was founded is superior to any other. There is a difference between the United States attacking say, Pakistan to extend the light of Christendom, and unapologetically condemning child sacrifice as evil. We have no interest as a nation in doing the former, we have no hope as a nation if we cannot do the latter.

THE PROBLEM WITH PLURALISM

Why not simply be pro-religion, without emphasizing the Christian roots of America? First, it would not be historically accurate. The founding fathers were not an amalgam of Shintoists, Jews, Muslims, Christians, and pagans. As we have already seen, our founders were Christians just as no one disputes that the founders of Saudi Arabia were Muslims.

Second, it is important to understand that different religions are incompatible. When the British ruled in India, they had to choose between imposing their beliefs (also derived from Judeo-Christian values) and allowing widows to be burned on their husband's pyres in the name of the religious ritual of *suttee*. There was no middle ground possible. Had the famous Darwinian scientist William Provine, who has publicly proclaimed that science shows there is no life after death, talked with Mother Teresa for hours they would not have reached an agreement on the origins of life. As a scientist I object to his passing his beliefs off as factual. What experiments has he conducted that have proven his thesis? Where are the subjects whom he has resurrected after dying who have come back and reported to him? But even if he would admit that these are beliefs, not facts, we cannot establish the norms for our society on both his views and those of Mother Teresa. Any restaurant can choose whether to serve spaghetti or ravioli just as it can choose whether to serve steak or ribs. However, the same restaurant may well have to choose whether it is an Italian-style pasta restaurant or a steak house. Confusing the two could create confused customers, a marketing disaster and the collapse of the enterprise.

Sometimes in life we just have to choose who we really are. This is as true for groups as it is for individuals. Nobody would contend that a tennis club should also provide equal facilities for mud wrestlers. Its members may dispute whether to play tennis on indoor or outdoor courts, but debating the fundamentals of the club and the purpose of its establishment would assuredly spell doom. Similarly, any society wishing to endure needs to know its basic purpose.

WHEN RELIGIOUS PRACTICES CONFLICT

We have had court cases in which a parent's belief that illness must be treated with prayer alone conflicted with the American belief that an ill child is entitled to a doctor's intervention. If all religions are equally valid, then none are. There is no way to reconcile our civilized desire to help that child with the parents' religious convictions. We need to recover our willingness to clearly state exactly what we do believe in. This will ultimately benefit all Americans, including religious minorities, by conferring durability on our society.

As the debate about doctor-assisted suicide intensifies, a letter to the editor in a local Seattle paper makes the point. Writing as a Buddhist, the letter writer wants to know: Why the big fuss about abortion and euthanasia? After all, we are all reincarnated over and over again in many lives, so why the big deal about ending one? If we are to say that America has no intrinsic religious tradition, and that all faiths are equal in our eyes, we cannot challenge that letter or many like it. But I think most of us when we, for example, board an airplane want to know that the pilot greatly values human life. These values do derive from religious outlook; they are also values that do impact others. A pilot who is entirely fatalistic about life and death would be wrong in supposing that his religious beliefs are exclusively his own business. I have no desire to censor or regulate his beliefs, but I would greatly appreciate knowing that his actions as a pilot will be in accord with the traditional Judeo-Christian understanding of the sanctity of life before fastening my seat belt and returning my tray table to the fully upright and locked position.

There are people in the world whose religious belief persuades them, beyond all shadow of a doubt, that dying in the process of dispatching non-believers is a certain avenue to paradise. Are we unwilling to notify him that his religious beliefs are incompatible with American principles? How about telling him that his beliefs are incompatible with Christian principles and that those Christian principles are the governing principles of American society? It makes you a bit squeamish? I think we are going to have to get over it. How might you feel sending your children to school on a bus driven by someone who, in an emergency, might not do everything possible to save the children's lives because he believes that death actually speeds them along into a better life? Does this mean we have to refuse to grant pilot licenses to Buddhists or prohibit all Muslims from driving school buses? No, not at all. However, it does mean we must be comfortable letting everyone know that the public religious ethic that prevails in this country is a Judeo-Christian one and demanding a public adherence to that standard in terms of behavior rather than belief.

Here is how we might formulate it: *We may all believe as we wish; however, translating our beliefs into the actions sometimes demanded by those beliefs may conflict with Judeo-Christian belief. When they do, it is the actions informed by Christian belief that will prevail.* Read that again. Aloud. There, that wasn't too hard, was it? If we are uncomfortable making that statement, then there can be no glue that binds us together as Americans.

A CASE IN POINT

Earlier in our history, this country faced the issue of whether all religious practices must be accepted. While Montana, with 132,000 residents, and Wyoming, with 61,000, became states in 1889 and 1890 respectively, Utah with 208,000 residents was continually refused statehood. While it is simplistic and inaccurate to say that polygamy was the sole issue, it became the lightning rod. Protestant churches of the time viewed Mormonism as pagan and heretical and fought against statehood that would have made Mormons the dominant voting block of the new state. When the Mormons protested the Poland Act of 1874 that moved jurisdiction in criminal cases (like polygamy) away from local probate courts and into federal courts, their protest was based on interference with their First Amendment rights. In 1879 the case went before the Supreme Court, which ruled that Congress could not regulate religious *belief,* but could regulate religious *practice.*

Only when Mormon church president Wilford Woodruff issued a proclamation that no plural marriages were contracted in the past year and advised Mormons to "refrain from contracting any marriage forbidden by the laws of the land," did the fracas begin to calm. On January 4, 1896, Grover Cleveland issued the proclamation admitting Utah as the 45th state. The new state's constitution outlawed polygamy.

In the years since, members of the Church of Latter-Day Saints have become some of the most outstanding citizens of this country. Utah is one of the safest, most successful, family-friendly and healthy states in the country. While the Mormons can actually lay claim to being a group, perhaps the only group, really to face religious persecution in America, the insistence on accepting what was the Judeo-Christian norm allowed them to become part of the fabric of American life.

What we once felt comfortable demanding from Mormons, we once again need to feel comfortable demanding from everyone else too. Our country's leaders in the 1800s understood that one religious ethic has to prevail and that saying all religions are equal in terms of public policy is the same as rejecting religion outright.

CHAPTER SEVENTEEN

AMERICA: A UNIQUE HAVEN FOR JEWS

AS A JEW I TREMBLE AT WHAT POST-CHRISTIAN AMERICA MIGHT MEAN FOR MY PEOPLE.

A s a Jew I am filled with profound gratitude to America. For more than 2,000 years Jews have immigrated to and settled in whichever countries were then occupying center stage of world history. When Babylon dominated the known world, Jews lived there. Later, as the biblical book of Esther describes, Jews lived under the ruling Persian Empire. From the heyday of the Roman Empire, great Jewish communities arose and survived everything the centuries flung at them, up until the time of Hitler.

Until Spain unceremoniously ejected them in 1492, Jews enjoyed their Golden Age while Spain enjoyed hers (although it should be noted that Jews were seriously persecuted during their sojourn in Spain). While the sun shone upon the British Empire, the chief rabbi of Great Britain traveled the pink parts of the world map and was treated like a dignitary. In each case, for a short slice of history, the wandering Jew found a resting place for his weary feet. Some of these resting places were more hospitable than others; many were downright painful, but they were the temporary abode that God had arranged for His people.

UNPARALLELED HOSPITALITY

When two world wars finally left America as the mightiest economic and military power in the world, the American Jewish community achieved maturity and emerged as the healthiest and wealthiest of all Jewish communities. Nowhere else in the world, and at no other time in Jewish history, have Jews lived in such comfort and safety for such an extended period of time. The hospitality that Jews have enjoyed in America is unparalleled—in recent times and perhaps in all time.

Since I came to this country as an adult and chose to become an American citizen, perhaps I appreciate what this country means to a Jew more than those who have been born here. Before arriving in America I traveled extensively, living in South Africa, England and Israel, and passing through many European countries. My original intention was simply to visit America, thinking that a rabbi needed to see the home of the largest Jewish population in the world. On the first day of my visit, I realized that America was unmatched by any other place. Leaving aside Israel, which would take a book of its own to discuss, there is nowhere else in the world that a Jew can find so little conflict between his religion and his country.

Is there a unique relationship between America and the Jewish people, one that did not exist between Jews and any other country where they resided? I would like to share a story of the great twentieth-century Jewish leader, Rabbi Abramsky. When Rabbi Abramsky was condemned by the Russian communists to a life sentence in the Soviet Gulag, the British government, on behalf of Anglo-Jewry, secured his release. This took place in 1933, after which the Russians expelled him to London where he became *dayan* (judge) of the London *Beth Di* (Jewish law court). Much later, in a public discussion on the Holocaust, the rabbi refuted the notion that anti-Semitism was endemic to the Germans. A member of the audience agreed, suggesting that the Holocaust could have happened anywhere. Then, remembering Rabbi Abramsky's debt of gratitude to the British government, he sensitively added, "Excepting England, of course." Rabbi Abramsky looked sadly at the speaker and replied, "Even in England." Before the stunned London audience could recover, Rabbi Abramsky continued, "But probably not in America."

Years later as a *yeshiva* student, I occasionally visited with Rabbi Abramsky at his Jerusalem home. More than once I referred back to the London lecture and asked him: Why not in America? He would only smile and repeat "No, not in America." I cannot say why Rabbi Abramsky felt so sure that America was intrinsically different from other countries, but I know that I share his conviction. America has been much more than just one more country in the long list of places where the Jewish people have wandered.

No country has been a more stalwart friend of Israel than America; no other society has ever been more hospitable to its Jewish population. It is hard to think of another nation in which a Jewish community has enjoyed a longer period of tranquillity and affluence. The bond that has always existed between America and her Jews is so conspicuous that it has even attracted foreign attention. Books have been published in Europe, Asia and many Islamic countries chronicling the extraordinary prominence Jews enjoy in America.

There have, of course, been instances of anti-Semitic discrimination in America, and we do occasionally encounter the bigoted, hateful extremist in the form of an ill-educated Ku Klux Klan member or a "skinhead." But these tiny, radical factions do not represent America. Neither, despite their ill-educated references to God, Jesus, and Christianity, do they represent God, Jesus, or Christianity. And there is little comparison between anything Jews have experienced in the United States with the terror of the frequent Saturday night pogroms in Eastern Europe, or what it must have been like to be a German Jew from 1930 to 1945. Compared to the heart-stopping uncertainty of daily life that most European Jews experienced over the past few hundred years, being denied admission by a medical school's quota for Jews or not being allowed to buy a home in some choice neighborhood hardly ranks as a serious problem. Life in America has been good for American Jews. It would be churlish to deny it.

WHY THE UNIQUE BOND?

One explanation often advanced to account for the hospitality enjoyed by America's Jews has been the size of the American Jewish community and its economic and political influence. In other words, the argument goes, America has been good to her Jews because their power has allowed her little alternative. In addition to demonstrating astonishing ingratitude, this argument is as wrong-headed as the argument that turning on street lights causes the sun to set. A moment's reflection reveals that American Jews have achieved affluence and political prominence precisely because of the security and tranquillity they have enjoyed here for so many years.

The question remains as to why America has treated its Jews so differently from almost everyone else. I believe there are unique bonds binding America and Jews. One clue to these bonds is that the most visible enthusiasm for Israel today often comes from precisely those politicians who can hardly be said to preside over major centers of Jewish culture. For example, it is hard to make the case that Senator Jesse Helms supports Israel in order to placate the large number of Jewish voters in North Carolina. If America's support for Israel were based entirely on political expediency, that support would originate from the State Department, not our elected representatives. Instead, support of Israel springs from the heartland of America. Clearly something more profound than our numbers or political expediency lies behind the historical and present-day affinity between America and Judaism. The question is, what?

I believe the answer lies in the deep commitment, held by so many mainstream, heartland Americans, to Judeo-Christian morals. The graciousness extended by most religious Christians toward their Jewish friends is not the result of having been intimidated by those friends into a mood of sullen acceptance. Rather, it is a wholehearted embrace based on belief in God's words to Abraham: "I will bless those who bless you, and whoever curses you I will curse" (Genesis 12:3). Many Americans revere those words because they revere God Almighty who spoke them. American Jews have always been the beneficiaries of that reverence. I wholeheartedly believe that the joyous serenity of living as an American Jew is safe *not* because of governmental secularism but only for as long as most Americans continue to subscribe to that biblical belief. It is *only* due to this belief on the part of so many Americans that I could easily imagine any anti-Semitic governmental decree being widely flouted by a majority of Americans.

WHEN CULTURES CLASH: THREE CHOICES

Note that I am not trying to show that Jews live comfortably in a Christian America. I believe Jews live comfortably in America *only* due to that Christian heritage. Indeed, as an Orthodox Jew, there are ways I don't easily fit into the culture. When my children want to take the SATs they need an alternate date, as they cannot write on Saturday, our Sabbath, when the test is routinely given. The school year begins in September, a month replete with Jewish holidays, which makes going to school impossible many days of the month. On the island where I live, community celebrations often take place on Friday night or Saturday, making my family's participation impossible. Becoming President of the United States is not an option for my children as Jewish religious observances negate being able to devote oneself fully to running the country.

I see myself faced with three choices. One is to abandon major tenets of my faith and blend in to the culture, a choice many Jews have certainly made. A second choice is to emigrate to Israel where there might possibly be fewer clashes between my religious and civic life. But I have opted for choice number three. It is to follow my religion faithfully, even if it causes me occasional discomfort in the American culture, while being grateful for the freedom America does grant me. This includes the freedom to exercise the option of sending my children to a Jewish school, where classes do not take place on Jewish holidays, even if it means a tremendous financial sacrifice. It includes the freedom to have meat slaughtered in a kosher manner, even if it necessitates greater expense and trouble to locate it. It includes the freedom to circumcise my son when he became eight days old. Many times in the past, and even in other countries today, those freedoms were not available to Jews. In general, I understand that I live not under a Christian government but in a Christian nation, albeit one where I can follow my faith as long as it doesn't conflict with that nation's principles. The same option is open to all Americans, and will be available only as long as this nation's Christian roots are acknowledged and honored. We cannot survive as a country that doesn't deliver mail on Friday because there are Muslim citizens, on Saturday out of respect for Judaism, and on Sundays to honor Christianity. Neither can we survive, as indeed the USSR did not, if we choose to remove respect for religion altogether and pronounce ourselves an atheistic nation. A point often ignored by those who urge the removal of religion from public life is that hordes never did attempt to emigrate to the atheistic Soviet Union.

This country has held a unique position in the world as a place where all could worship freely, while becoming complete Americans. Ironically, that is only because America had a strong sense of who she was. Immigrants learned the language and the culture, and in doing so integrated themselves into American society. When we dictate that American society must fit itself into each citizen's culture and religion so as to offend no one, we have signed the death certificate for this country.

If all Christians were outstanding citizens and all others were murderers and crooks, it would be simple to see what we should teach our children. As it is, we can point to examples of decent, honorable atheists and cheating reprehensible clergymen. We need to look beyond individuals when we run a society.

Shortly after moving to America, I settled in the San Francisco Bay area. In addition to enabling me to sail frequently, I discovered another great advantage there when I came across a facility that replicated all the complexity of the tidal flows in the San Francisco Bay and delta. If there was a request to build a new marina, rather than speculating how such construction would affect the entire bay, the Army Corps of Engineers would run a simulation on their splendid model and see it. By actually building the marina in this model, you could watch exactly how the larger area would be affected.

Imagine if we could have a miniature model of the United States of America. One that would not only cover geographical information but one that could demonstrate sociological conditions and transcend time. Simply by looking at the model we could see the consequences of a legislative or judicial act. Make abortion legal? Ban school prayer? Remove Christian symbols? We would be able to look into the model and see what effects those steps would have in the near and far away future. Alas, no such model exists. We mere mortals have to live with the unintended ramifications of our actions. The best we can do is look to the Bible, as the leaders at our founding did, and continue on a path that has had amazing success for over two hundred years. As an American, I am grateful for the religious outlook that guided the founders of this country; as a Jew I tremble at the thought of what a post-Christian America might mean for my people.

CHAPTER EIGHTEEN

SPIRITUAL LINKS BETWEEN JUDAISM AND AMERICA

AMAZINGLY ENOUGH, MANY AMERICANS OF THE 1600S AND 1700S WERE APPRECIATIVE OF THE SPECIAL INSIGHTS INTO THE BIBLE AND GOD THAT THE JEWS POSSESSED.

The affection that the founders of America had for the Hebrew language and ancient Israel is startling.

Sir William Bradford, second Governor of the Plymouth colony, explained in the introduction to his *History of the Plymouth Plantation* that Hebrew is the language in which "God, and angels, spoke to the holy patriarchs of old time." He then proceeded to write page after page of Hebrew at the beginning of his book. It would be very difficult for an American child to understand Governor Bradford's English. The "s" looks like an "f," and the spelling is different from our modern version. For example, *"owne"* instead of "own," and *"stoppe"* for "stop." But show any Jewish youngster who has learned to read Hebrew, the words at the beginning of this book, and they will roll off his tongue, with fluency and full comprehension.

CULTURAL CONTINUITY

This observation helps us understand why the early American founders realized the wisdom to be obtained from the Bible and the Hebrew language. Judaism is the hands-down winner in the world's longevity sweepstakes. We Jews even confounded historian Arnold Toynbee's theory of how nations appear on the stage of world history, thrive, fade, and depart. We have survived for so long as a continuous unbroken cultural chain that he felt he had no choice but to label us as "the fossils of history." Some fossils.

The key is the unbroken cultural chain. China has been around for at least as long as the Jews. Greece has been around for quite a long time. However, neither Greece nor

China enjoy an unbroken cultural chain. I recall how, when as a young lad I first traveled to Greece with my father, he signed his name on the official entry permit at Athens Airport. The official became irate. It turned out that my dad was so excited to finally put to some practical use the schoolboy Greek he had studied decades earlier that he had signed his name and completed the questionnaire in the language of Homer in *The Iliad* and *The Odyssey*. This meant absolutely nothing to the mid-twentieth-century Athenian we encountered at the airport. He may well have been a biological descendant of Homer, but he certainly was no cultural descendant.

In the same way, inhabitants of China are certainly descended from early Chinese dynasties. However, in many cases, successive dynasties were not cultural continuations of their dynastic forbears. On the contrary, they frequently recreated the culture each time. This is one reason for the plethora of subcultures in China and the vast number of characters in all their alphabets.

In Judaism, by contrast, even a young child in a *yeshiva* (a Jewish religious school) in say, Dallas, can fluently read and understand the writing of Jeremiah who lived two and a half thousand years ago in Israel. That is what I mean by an unbroken cultural chain. Perhaps not all Jews, but certainly millions of us, still eat only the food that Moses decreed when he descended from Mount Sinai more than thirty-three hundred years ago. That too is part of an unbroken chain. Knowing that each year my family and I celebrate Passover in exactly the same way Moses Maimonides described his own celebration of Passover more than eight hundred years ago is another example of unbroken cultural continuity.

Amazingly enough, many Americans of the 1600s and 1700s were aware, and appreciative of, the special insights into the Bible and God that the Jews possessed. Does this imply that early Americans ate only kosher food that conformed to the Torah or the Old Testament's dietary rules? No, of course not. But they did try to conform to the ethical rather than the ritual features of God's covenant with the Jews.

THE LANGUAGE OF GOD

The love affair with the Hebrew language was not limited to the Pilgrims. After the Declaration of Independence there was a serious suggestion to make Hebrew the new country's language. Any number of the early patriots, such as James Madison, studied the ancient language. Well into the twentieth century, Harvard University always included in its Commencement Day celebration at least one speech in Hebrew. While he was president of Yale University, Ezra Stiles used to visit regularly with a rabbi who was a great friend of his.

Samuel Johnson, the first president of King's College, now known as Columbia University, declared in 1759 that "Hebrew was a gentleman's accomplishment...as soon as a lad has learned to speak and to read English well, it is much the best to begin a learned education with Hebrew, the mother of all languages," In the writings of Cotton Mather (1663–1728) we find interspersed a number of Hebrew words and expressions such as *im yertzeh Hashem*—if God pleases, *baalei nefesh*—men of refinement, *chassidim rishonim*—the first righteous ones. His Father, Increase Mather (1639–1723), delivered discourses in Hebrew and his writings contain quotations from the Talmud, Midrashim, Kabbalah, Saadia Gaon, Rashi, Maimonides, and many other classical Jewish sources. It is not commonly known that Increase Mather's rather unusual first name was itself proof of his family's devotion to Hebrew and the Bible. *Increase* is a very good translation of the Hebrew name Yoseif, or Joseph, at whose birth his mother Rachel declared, "God will increase [Yoseif] me another son" (Genesis 30).

Knowing Hebrew is different from knowing any other language. Much of the reality of the world is revealed through that ancient tongue. Since the founders did not learn Hebrew through a Berlitz course but knew that this was God's special language, we can speculate that they understood some of the truths hidden in it. Let me give you a clue to some of the mysteries of the language which contains compelling clues to the nature of reality.

In Hebrew, each letter is linked to a number reflecting its place in the alphabet. This would be like making A=1, B=2, and so on. Wouldn't it be interesting if the English word YEAR added up to 365, the number of days in a year? Unfortunately it does not. Y=25, E=5, A=1, and R=18, for a total of 49—not even close.

In Hebrew, however, the word for year is *shana,* which adds up to 355. Combine that with the fact that the Jewish calendar operates on a lunar year rather than on a solar year, and the language reflects reality. A lunar year is twelve times the mean period of a lunar month. Since the mean period of a lunar month is 29 days, 12 hours, 44 minutes and 3.3 seconds, twelve of those fixes the Jewish year at—yes, you guessed it—355 days.

There are countless examples of numeric links between Hebrew words and the real-world meaning of those words. Here is one more: What differentiates a human hand from the claw of an animal? It is the ability to bend the fingers. If you count the number of joints that give you that power, you will find two joints on the thumb, and three on each of the other four fingers, for a total of fourteen. Not surprisingly, the Hebrew word for hand is *yad*—with a numerical value of fourteen.

Did some primitive desert band of Bedouins sit around making up this language we call Hebrew? Did they carefully contrive to create words with intrinsic numeric meaning? I don't think so. After all, only one language is known to have been created by committee and, to say the least, it hasn't become a runaway success. Early in the twentieth century some enterprising committee created the language of Esperanto. Although its advocates claim to have several thousand Esperanto language books in print, it simply has not caught on. People speak natural languages, not created ones. Yet Hebrew behaves more like a carefully constructed language than a casually evolved one. For Sir William Bradford and James Madison, and for today's religious Jews and Christians, the reason is obvious. Hebrew was constructed by God.

It is no accident that the Hebrew language has no word for coincidence. Even when things seem to happen randomly, that is only from our human perspective, not from God's omniscient view. I personally find it intriguing that the original colonies numbered thirteen. Thirteen disparate colonies become one, forming the United (united, of course means one) States. It turns out that the Hebrew word for one, *echad,* is made up of three Hebrew letters possessing the numeric values of 1, 8, and 4 for a total of 13. This is one of the reasons a Jewish boy becomes at *one* with the people at the age of thirteen.

Examining a one-dollar bill reveals an abundance of thirteens. There are thirteen letters in both the phrase *ANNUIT COEPTIS,* printed above the pyramid, and in the phrase *E PLURIBUS UNUM,* printed above the eagle. (The latter phrase, of course, means "From many, *one.*") There are thirteen layers of stone in the pyramid, thirteen stars arranged above the eagle's head, and thirteen stripes on the eagle's breast. There are thirteen arrows grasped in its left talon; among the olive twigs in its right talon are thirteen olives, although you will need a magnifying glass to see them. You will find no such symbolic occurrence of the number thirteen on the five-dollar bill, nor on the ten or twenty. Thirteen is not linked to five, ten, or twenty. In Hebrew, thirteen actually means one.

Thus we see deep psychic and spiritual links between the traditions, values, and origins of Judaism and those of America. Paradoxically, some Jewish organizations and their leaders are doing their utmost to shatter these links. Perhaps they would rather see strife between Christian and Jew than admit that the kinship felt for one another by most ordinary and decent Americans of both faiths is religiously based.

CHAPTER NINETEEN

THE NATURAL AFFINITY OF AMERICA'S CHRISTIANS AND JEWS

WE BECAME UNITED IN AMERICA ONLY BECAUSE WE USED TO PASSIONATELY BELIEVE THAT HUMANS ARE SPIRITUAL BEINGS ENDOWED BY THEIR CREATOR.

The similarities between the people of ancient Israel and modern America are endless. For both, an idea preceded having a land. The Jews were welded together in the crucible of Egypt and received their constitution, the Torah, forty years before stepping foot in the land of Israel. The Declaration of Independence was a document of ideas that welded disparate people into a nation long before they had secured their territory. In other words, both Israel and America are nations founded on an idea rather than on real estate. This is why Judaism survived for two thousand years without a land. An idea is a flame kept alive in the hearts of men wherever they may be. As long as Americans share a godly idea rather than simply coexisting on a plot of earth, they will likewise be indestructible.

This is not only the key to our remarkable founding and our two-hundred-year success story, it is also the key to solving some of the problems of today. For instance, it is no coincidence that the scourge of racial separatism finds its highest expression on America's university campuses. The very institutions that breed liberal secularism have, without realizing it, also established new doctrines of race that would warm the hearts of the old rulers of South Africa. How is this so? Simply this: The liberal elite deny that men and women are spiritual beings. If we are not unified by those feelings of divine aspiration that surge spontaneously from the human heart, then we must look to our externals. And if we look to externals, what could possibly be more conspicuous than the color of a man's skin?

BELIEF IN THE SPIRITUAL BEING

Either we are spiritual beings occasionally engaged in material pursuits like plowing fields and building factories, or we are material beings occasionally engaged in spiritual pursuits like prayer. Being one nation absolutely requires that we hold only one view of ourselves. If we are material beings, skin color matters. Do we not often determine the cars we drive and the clothes we wear on the basis of color? Why should we not choose our friends, or for that matter our elected representatives, on the same basis? But if, on the other hand, we are spiritual beings, then our relationships with other spiritual beings transcend such superficialities. The encounter is not a materialistic interaction; it is an interaction between two souls, each of whom was touched by the finger of God.

If I am wrong, then give me only friends who look just like me. If what I say is true, my sons and daughters may marry mates of any appearance, just so long as the souls are congruent.

We became united in America, and we absorbed immigrants from so many backgrounds and cultures, only because we used to passionately believe that humans are primarily spiritual beings endowed by their Creator.

FURTHER SIMILARITIES

Any foreigner could have become a member of ancient Israel, and British soldiers could and did defect to join the colonists. Anyone could, and indeed still can, become a Jew. In the same way, anyone can become an American. If one becomes either an American or a convert to Judaism, one becomes a full American or a full Jew with all rights, save one. As a convert to Judaism, one cannot become king, and as a naturalized American, one cannot attain the presidency. The founding fathers incorporated this principle from the Torah right into our American Constitution.

Contrast this with England, France, Switzerland or Japan. I lived in England for more than five years, but I was always a foreigner. If I was still living there, I'd still be a foreigner. Others have lived in London for a lifetime, but to their English neighbors they will always be foreigners. In the same way you have to have been born in France, Switzerland or Japan to be a Frenchman, a Swiss or a Japanese. The Swiss or the Japanese, for instance, take pride in how little immigration has taken place to their shores. The reason is that these are all nations whose identity springs exclusively from their land. When they speak of national homogeneity, they make us uncomfortable because they are referring to physical appearance. That sort of talk suggests that we are herds of animals who are supposed to all resemble one another. In America, our national homogeneity springs from us agreeing on certain fundamental spiritual principles while celebrating the diversity we enjoy in the more superficial things. In the history of the world, only two nations have been founded on an idea rather than on a land: ancient Israel and modern America.

There is a touching scene in the wonderful film *The Great Escape* in which the American prisoners in a German prisoner of war camp are determined to celebrate the Fourth of July. For weeks leading up to the event, led by the character played by the late Steve McQueen, the American POWs distilled a primitive potato liquor. Finally Independence Day dawned and the proud Americans marched in an Independence Day parade around the camp. Only an American could understand what was happening, and the film depicts well how puzzled the English prisoners were about all that was transpiring. This parallels the heartbreaking stories of how doomed Jews in Nazi concentration camps celebrated joyful holidays like *Chanukah*. Only Jews understood the significance of these grand acts of commemoration and defiance; to the Nazis, they were mystifying.

The predecessors of America, the Pilgrims, were called "separatists" in England; the early Jews, Abraham and his family, were called *Ivrim* (Hebrews) which translates as "separatist." Upon arriving in their respective promised lands, both the children of Israel and the early American settlers found native peoples who knew nothing of the God of the Bible.

So aware were our founding fathers that they were following in the spiritual footsteps of ancient Israel that Benjamin Franklin suggested an unusual motif for the Great Seal of the United States. He wanted the seal to depict the Israelites crossing the Red Sea on their way to the Promised Land.

Both countries found themselves fighting bloody civil wars early in their respective histories. Oddly enough, both the war between the North and the South and the war between Judah and Israel were over moral issues.

Ancient Israel built its capital city, Jerusalem, in such a way that it would belong to no single tribe and would be accessible to all. Modern America adopted the idea from ancient Israel and in so doing, departed dramatically from the European model. Only ancient Jerusalem and Washington, D.C. exist as separate entities from their respective countries. In neither case could any one tribe or state claim control over the capital city and deny admittance to others. The entire principle of federalism conceived by the American founders was not original; it was based on the curious mixture of tribes that made up ancient Israel. The motto was unity through diversity, and it worked brilliantly for both societies. No other nation enjoyed this distinctive form of social organization. But the unity depended then, as it does now, upon the primacy of religious idealism.

We also find more than mere coincidence in the thirteen original colonies. Studying the history of the time shows that opportunities presented themselves to form that great union with fewer than thirteen colonies. Yet, in the final analysis, thirteen prevailed. The number thirteen resonated with our founders for two reasons. As we said earlier, *one* has a numeric equivalent of thirteen in Hebrew. But there is more. Jacob, or Israel as he was sometimes known, launched the nation of Israel by replacing his son Joseph with Joseph's two sons Ephraim and Menashe. He indicated that his two grandsons would be as sons to him when he said, "Ephraim and Menashe will be to me like Reuben and Simon," thus giving him thirteen sons instead of his original twelve. That moment was when the family of Jacob became the children of Israel. Somehow, it was necessary for a great nation to be founded on thirteen elements rather than upon twelve. Once again, America's founding fathers, subconsciously or not, imitated the founding of ancient Israel when they waited for Rhode Island to join in before launching their great enterprise. The number of elements required for the founding of a holy nation had to be increased from twelve to thirteen.

AN AFFINITY WORTH KEEPING

As we have seen, there is a natural affinity between Jewish and Christian Americans. It is evident in neighborhoods around this great land. It is evident from countless stories this writer has been told. These stories tell of long-ago and never-forgotten kindnesses and favors done for one another by Jewish and Christian families. This affinity is evident from the Jewish and Christian names, side by side above the stores that still adorn the main streets of small towns across America. It is an affinity that springs from the very origins of America and which reflects the origins of Judaism.

It is tragic that certain leaders of the American Jewish community, who themselves long ago abandoned their own religious traditions, are determined to shatter this natural affinity. They do so in the name of aggressively imposing an almost unnatural secularism upon America. This not only threatens that affinity and those friendships, it also threatens America herself.

We must be equally determined that they do not win. Our side of the tug-of-war must prevail—or the unique and wonderful fabric that makes America great will slowly but surely unravel.

CHAPTER TWENTY

AMERICA AND THE JEWISH VISION

TO BOTH ISRAEL'S AND AMERICA'S FOUNDERS,
THE BIBLE WAS AS VITAL FOR THE
SAFE OPERATION OF HUMAN SOCIETY AS ANY
MANUFACTURER'S INSTRUCTION MANUAL.

The similarities between America and ancient Israel go even deeper. I have come to believe that there is almost a Jewish vision ingrained in the American soul.

As I said in 1996 when I addressed the Republican National Convention in San Diego, California, both America's Pilgrims and the ancient Israelites under Joshua entered their promised lands bearing nothing but one fundamental conviction. Three millennia ago, those Jews crossed the Jordan carrying only one article of inestimable value.

America's Pilgrims crossed the Atlantic and arrived in America, also bearing no material riches. But they did bring with them that same great spiritual treasure the ancient Israelites had carried with them on their journey to their promised land. For both people, the powerful principle they carried in their hearts was worth more than all the gold imaginable. What is more, they knew that following their Great Truth would eventually bring them gold and make them rich and powerful.

This is surely one of the great secrets behind the almost legendary economic prowess of Jews as well as the unprecedented economic might of the United States. The secret is that wealth never brings values in its wake; however, the right values always breed wealth in those who cling to them. These values first created the nation of Israel, then America. Later these values made those nations great and granted them endurance.

Both ancient Israel and modern America came into being because their founders believed—no, they *knew,* beyond a shadow of a doubt—this misleadingly simple fact:

Whatever we think about God is not nearly as important to know as what God thinks of us. Or to put it slightly more usefully, thinking about what we expect from God is not nearly as valuable as knowing what God expects of us.

GOD'S INSTRUCTION MANUAL

To both Israel's and America's founders, the Bible was as vital for the safe operation of human society as any manufacturer's instruction manual would be for the safe operation of a complex piece of machinery. The only difference was that to those devout and pious Christians, the Bible was the Word of God. To the Jews, the Torah, or Five Books of Moses, was only part of the package. To Jews, the Torah constitutes the written word of God, but there is much more. The oral transmission, captured mystically and sometimes in maddeningly difficult style in the Talmud, completes the picture. Moses was on Sinai for forty days and forty nights. This was far longer than necessary for merely transcribing about six thousand verses. These verses refer to a specific year of human history in a marvelous and mysterious fabric of revelation, according to ancient teaching. It is the Talmud itself which explains that Moses spent the days taking divine dictation. Jewish tradition tells us that during the dark hours of the night, Moses listened while God explained the hidden meanings of the verses he had written that day.

JEWISH ORAL TRANSMISSION

This helps to understand how there comes to be almost universal agreement among Jews for the interpretation of apparently obscure biblical references. For instance, the book of Deuteronomy describes something called *totafot,* often translated as frontlets, to be worn by male Jews as signs "upon your arms and between your eyes" when at prayer. The Torah provides no details at all about the appearance or construction of these frontlets. What on earth are frontlets anyway? Interestingly enough, every set of frontlets, or *tefillin* as we now call them, looks the same. Upon the occasion of their *bar mitzvahs,* millions of Jewish men start wearing these leather boxes during weekday morning prayers. Just recently another link in the chain of Jewish transmission was forged when I purchased a set of tefillin for my son Aryeh, who was turning thirteen.

Just think about it. When did you ever hear of two Jews agreeing about anything? You may recall the old joke about two Jews finally rescued many years after a shipwreck had marooned them on a remote desert island. Surprised to see three elaborately constructed edifices, the Coast Guard officer politely inquired about the buildings. "That one is his synagogue," explained one of the scruffy survivors. "The second building over there is the synagogue I attend," he continued. "And the third one?" asked the puzzled officer. "Oh, that one? Well, neither of us would be seen dead in that one."

Yet, amazingly enough, every tefillin set in the world is constructed in exactly the same way. Many Jews no longer consider the obligation to don tefillin to be binding, but all Jews agree on how these leather boxes are to be made. Not only that, but embedded in each box are several scrolls of parchment upon which are handwritten paragraphs from the Torah. There is no disagreement among Jews as to how tefillin should be made or what Scriptures should be written. Given that the Torah in Deuteronomy gives no details at all, isn't it rather incredible that such agreement exists? To make the case even more compelling, during excavations of Israel's mountaintop fortress of Massada after the 1967 Six Day War, ancient tefillin sets dating back some two thousand years were found. Yes, you guessed right: They too match in perfect detail the set of tefillin just recently constructed for my son. All of this consistency with nary a word of description in the written Torah but with vast back-up data in the so-called oral transmission.

In the same way we find that all religious Jews agree upon the meaning of the puzzling passage, "You shall not cook a goat in its mother's milk." After all, who would even have thought of doing such a thing? The Talmud records that God explained to Moses, who subsequently passed it on to Joshua, that this was His way of prohibiting the simultaneous consumption of meat and dairy dishes by his people. To this day this practice is part of Jewish dietary laws known as *kosher*. There are some Jews who do not observe these laws or who claim they are no longer relevant. There are none who disagree on what the laws are or who claim they do not exist. The eternal magic of the Talmud, the oral transmission, converts the esoteric goat in its mother's milk into the common but prohibited cheeseburger.

One more example is the prohibition, "Do not place a stumbling block before the blind." This is not a warning against deriving childlike merriment from tripping up little old men with dark glasses and white canes. God assumes that anyone already mature enough to study the Bible is beyond such hooliganism. This law simply prohibits us from deriving economic benefit from information that we have deliberately withheld from another. In other words, do not "trip" up someone economically after you have made him "blind." This universally accepted meaning for the original verse is the legal basis for many chapters of civil and mercantile law in the Talmud; is also played a role in the early emergence of the Jew as significant in the development of world trade and banking. After all, no business will result between two people who feel no trust for one another. Feeling assured that your colleague is not concealing material information from you certainly makes it more likely that you would trade with him.

Thus we see that part of the Jewish contribution to the world has always included "filling in the blanks." For instance, with regard to America's founding, one of the thorns in the side of the early colonists that contributed to the War of Independence was the British habit of inflicting floggings on lawbreakers. One record has the colonists indignant over the fact that the British frequently imposed more than the biblically mandated maximum of thirty-nine lashes. The interesting fact is that the Bible allows a maximum of forty lashes. Clearly the colonists had access to Jewish data from the oral transmission. Perhaps parts of the New Testament served as the conduit through which some of this oral transmission was conveyed. At any rate, the oral transmission reduces the practical limit to thirty-nine from the Bible's theoretical maximum of forty. The British violated a biblical principle and infuriated the fervent colonists. Obviously the early Americans regarded that Jewish source limiting flogging to thirty-nine as authoritative. Thus some unknown British soldier may well have significantly contributed to his country's loss of the American colonies by inadvertently whipping an American just one lash too many. Thirty-nine lashes would have been seen as painful but just; forty violated God's will.

SHARED GRATITUDE

Thanksgiving itself is an amazingly Jewish type of celebration. The crops had been reasonably successful and the settlers' survival was assured. They didn't engage in an orgy of self-congratulation or allow the moment to fade away. They gathered together in order to thank God. What a sublime stone with which to lay the foundation for a nation! Despite several school districts around the country trying to indoctrinate youngsters into believing that the first Thanksgiving was an expression of gratitude on the part of the Pilgrims toward the Indians, most Americans still recognize the truth. The first settlers were profoundly religious and, in a gesture that perfectly matches the Jewish principle of expressing gratitude to God, they established a day of Thanksgiving. This is no different from the prayer said by Jews immediately upon awaking each morning which thanks the Almighty for restoring our soul to us. Religious people always seek opportunity to express gratitude, first because it is the correct and moral thing to do. Second, we do so because gratitude is a wonderful gateway to optimism and hope. In a way not found among other nations, Americans are comfortable and not self-conscious about thanking God for our many blessings. This is one of the most obvious examples of the family resemblance between modern America and ancient Israel.

FROM BIBLICAL PRECEDENT TO U.S. LAW

At almost every step, America was led by men who "acted Jewish." John Winthrop, the founding governor of the Massachusetts Bay colony, repeatedly referred to the Puritans as the New Testament Hebrews. Neither George Washington nor Saul wanted to be king, and both men stood far taller than their fellows.

In making just weights and measures a matter of federal law, Article 1, Section 8 of the United States Constitution echoes the words of the third book of the Bible, Leviticus. Indeed, the very idea of a Constitution itself is an endorsement of ancient Israel, the first nation in history to function at the dictate of a Constitution, the Torah. Every aspect of civil and criminal law, as well as all details of ordering society, are to be found there. The king of Israel himself was to be bound by the laws of the Torah. In order to drive home that humbling point to the king and also to reassure every citizen that the king is also subject to the rules of the "Constitution," every Jewish king, including the great King David, had to personally hand-write a complete and letter-perfect Torah scroll which he subsequently was to carry with him wherever he went. Indeed, some of the intense animosity towards President Clinton that is felt by so many Americans, stems from his acting as if he is not bound by law. Modeling themselves once again upon God's ancient people, the founding fathers wrote what they considered to be a modern-day interpretation of the basic biblical principles of government. In designing the three legs of government, they drew inspiration from Isaiah 33:22, "The Lord is our Judge, our lawgiver, and our King." In other words, God is the ultimate government and He considers Himself to be Judge, Lawgiver, and King. Therefore America would need a judiciary, legislative, and executive branch. It was really so simple for people who recognized the Bible as God's blueprint for America.

Finally, let us look at property ownership, an incredible breakthrough for humans. Just think of it. No animals seem to regard themselves as owning property. Oh yes, I know that many animals seem motivated by a territorial imperative and will drive away those they perceive as invaders, but that is different from owning land. That is more like the law of the jungle; the defender retains title only for as long as he is younger and stronger than the invader. Likewise, the invading animal doesn't claim to have right on his side, he merely is counting on survival of the fittest. Humans, on the other hand, enjoy the unique gift of ownership.

I can just imagine how bemused the Hittites and the Jebusites were, not to mention the Canaanites and the Girgashites, to encounter this new group of arrivals, the Israelites, who actually spoke of purchasing the land. It must have been as bizarre as someone planning on buying the sun or the moon. They referred to an ancestor of theirs, Abraham by name, who, years earlier, had purchased a field containing a cave to use as a cemetery.

The peoples who did not know the God of the Bible did not know of the enormous good that could come from having all property owned by people. Let me clarify that this does not mean all property was to be owned by the people at large, but by individual people. This was one of the great gifts God imparted to the Jews and which was later adopted by America. As the Creator, God knew that the creature He had created and called Man would best care for things he owned. Thus, early in the book of Genesis, we find the principles of land ownership laid down as Abraham purchased the field from Efron.

In Europe, countries did all they could to keep all men tenants of the ruler. Until only a few years ago, it was close to impossible to purchase freehold property in London. One could at best purchase a leasehold, usually from the royal family or some aristocratic family that had been granted large holdings years earlier. But America followed the Jewish vision, not England's. The foundations of American affluence were laid when we sought to make as many men as possible masters of their own small holdings. Settlers had only to travel to certain uninhabited parts of the growing country to acquire their own farms.

By following patterns laid down in the Bible, America established itself as a country that recognized the Bible to be a comprehensive blueprint of reality. But what exactly does that mean?

PART III

REBUILDING
OUR FOUNDATION

CHAPTER TWENTY-ONE

THE UNIFYING PRINCIPLE

THE ETERNAL CHALLENGE TO THE PERSON OF FAITH IS TO ACQUIRE SO CLEAR AN UNDERSTANDING OF HOW THE WORLD WORKS, THAT GOD'S ROLE BECOMES OBVIOUS.

A great deal of science has focused on the search for a unified system by which to explain the workings of the world.

Astronomer Johannes Kepler (1571–1630) discovered secrets of the planet's orbits by looking for, in his own words, a harmony of the worlds. As a religious Christian, he was certain that God had built order into the world.

In our century, Albert Einstein devoted the latter part of his life to searching for a unified field theory. He sought one equation or formula that would explain many natural forces such as gravitational, magnetic and nuclear. He was unsuccessful, but why did he search in the first place? We already possess adequate, separate explanations for each force. However, Einstein was convinced that there existed one simple reason that would explain everything; finding it would give his life meaning. His suspicion was right. Although he died without telling us whether he found it, some of his later references suggest that his search led him to realize that God was a necessary component.

Edward Fredkin was a professor of computer science at Massachusetts Institute of Technology where he studied a class of computer programs known as cellular automata. He hoped his research would provide him with a clue to "The prime mover of everything, the single principle that governs the universe." He too was moved by the same yearning for unity.

The search for one—not two or three, but only one—unifying force is no more than a search for God. God in His Oneness is the source of the concept of unity and of our yearning for some framework in which everything else makes sense. Our founding fathers thought they knew what it was and they proceeded to build a nation using it as a blueprint. Today, national restoration pleads for us to recover that conviction.

We all seek to make sense of the world. It would be intolerable to be married to someone, for example, whose moods varied greatly from day to day. This is precisely one of the reasons an alcoholic's or drug addict's family suffers so. A good temper one day may be replaced with violent behavior the next. Were the alphabet to change on a weekly basis, reading would be impossible. While occasional excitement adds spice to our life, we all like relying on thousands of predictable phenomena, from the fact that day turns into night on a regular basis to knowing that friends' personalities are not going to change radically from hour to hour.

THE GIFT OF PREDICTABILITY

Predictability, the benefit of God's patterns in time and space, (which I see as His unity) is one of the great gifts bestowed on us by a benevolent God. Even something that we all take for granted, like being able to hop into a car and drive across town, is a consequence of predictability. In America we can transport ourselves and our goods in a reasonably timely manner, partially because we are blessed with considerable predictability. One of the reasons one can maintain a reasonable speed along America's surface roads is that we count upon nobody unexpectedly entering our path from a hidden side street. We also count on an intersection being clear and safe provided we enter it only after being given the green light. Unlike many other cities around the globe, American people, by and large, obey the authority of traffic regulations.

Even something seemingly as prosaic as the tax code is subject to the deterioration I describe. It is devastating for families and harmful to the country to have no tax predictability. If last year's carefully constructed investment plan is rendered obsolete by this year's new tax regulation, we all suffer. It breeds a feeling of insecurity and encourages us to start thinking short-term in our financial planning, exactly the opposite of what works to maximum advantage. Since unity, predictability, and authority all go hand-in-hand, it is not surprising that constant tampering with the tax code also diminishes compliance on the part of a long-suffering populace. After all, once you strip away the ultimate source of predictability, you have also stripped away the justification for authority. We not only yearn for unity, the stability of our society demands it. Thus a society that abandons God is a society that will eventually be cursed with random chaos, divisiveness and civil anarchy. We struck that iceberg about thirty-five years ago and we are now enduring the conditions that inevitably result.

OUR SEARCH FOR A FOURTH DIMENSION

Taking this concept further, we all seek to bathe the darker corners of our lives in a brilliant light—a laser-like beam that would illuminate both path and obstacles. We want a kind of spiritual road map that would enable us to stop making the mistakes that irritate and distress us as we make our way through life. We need to be able to access that fourth dimension, the spiritual one that tells how the world works.

The Victorian era theologian and mathematician, Edwin Abbott, wrote a book called *Flatland*. In it, he described a land that exists in only two dimensions and how the inhabitants function in what is obviously an inadequate state of awareness. Since Flatlanders know no other reality, they are oblivious to the shortcomings in their world view. They concoct elaborate and incorrect explanations to account for phenomena that are perfectly comprehensible to three-dimension-equipped observers such as ourselves. The inescapable implication for us is that there may exist some *fourth* dimension—without which our own attempts to understand our world are equally absurd. And of course, that is quite true. It is all too easy to miss the point that as humans, our object is to escape our temporal limitations—not adapt to them. Whether we are primitive or modern, we all have our blind spots that obscure the truth for us.

Jamie Uys' charming film *The Gods Must Be Crazy* traces the turmoil brought into the lives of a primitive Bushman tribe by a bottle that was carelessly dropped by the pilot of a private aircraft. The picture is hilarious, but only because the hero has never before seen a bottle or an aircraft. The audience knows that the intense confusion felt by the Bushman hero of the film would vanish were he to become aware of the fourth dimension, or unifying principle. In his case, it would be knowledge of the existence of Western modernity. Were Jamie Uys to produce a sequel about his Bushman hero coming to Manhattan, it might not be as funny as the first film. It could be very thrilling, however, to watch the hero's eyes open as everything he now sees, serves to explain away the mysteries and confusion of his earlier life.

Finding the unifying principle that can explain away confusion brings great satisfaction to the human spirit. On an IQ test, spotting the unifying pattern enables one to predict the next logical term in a series or the diagram that logically should follow the pattern established by the first three. Spotting the pattern just feels good, and that goes for whether it is a pattern in the spiritual world or the physical.

At just about the same time that Abbott wrote *Flatland* in England, Russian scientist Mendeleev discovered chemistry's Periodic Table of the Elements. It turned out to be the single most important unifying principle in chemistry until the nuclear epoch. It made a comprehensible and elegant pattern of predictability out of what had hitherto been an unruly mass of seemingly unrelated observations. Later, when Einstein developed his special theory of relativity into the far more comprehensive General Theory, he too provided a unifying principle that paved the way for twentieth-century physics.

Wouldn't it be comforting if we could find a similar unifying principle to explain all the nuances in the extended order of human cooperation sometimes known as politics?

The Judeo-Christian tradition argues that such a unifying principle does exist. It is God, and it is precisely His quality of "oneness" that unifies and defines monotheism. A religious sensibility, or a capacity to know and feel close to God, satisfies precisely because it projects a comprehensive, consistent guide.

A Beverly Hills tycoon I once knew was dismayed by his son's decision to engage in religious studies instead of joining the family business. The young man had studied the Bible with me in my Venice congregation for a year or two and wished to master more of Judaism's eternal wisdom. I encouraged him to spend some time in a *yeshiva*, a religious academy in Israel. After several years the son returned home to his father's sardonic question, "So what have you got to show for your years of study?" "I know there is a God," replied the young man. Angrily, his father leapt to his feet and pointed out the window at the elderly gardener patiently mowing the vast lawns. "He also knows there is a God!" shouted the older man. "No, father," the boy quietly responded. "He *believes* there is a God. I *know*."

WHEN GOD'S ROLE BECOMES OBVIOUS

The opening sentence of Maimonides' monumental work *Mishne Torah* reads: "The foundation of the entire structure and the pillar of all wisdom is to know that there is a Fundamental Cause (God)." The important word is not "believe" but "know." The eternal challenge to the person of faith is to acquire so clear an understanding of how the world works, that God's role becomes obvious. In the Jewish view, it has nothing to do with fervent proclamations of faith or serendipitous moments of epiphany. It has everything to do with years of disciplined intellectual dedication. It may not be easy, but neither is body building. In both cases, devotees consider the effort worthwhile; what is more, both provide highs along the way. For this reason perhaps, the Hebrew term for God-fearing is similar to the phrase "seeing God."

At quite a young age, my number-three daughter was once candid enough to tell me that she did not believe in an afterlife because she knew of no proof for its existence. She explained that she felt immeasurably saddened at the thought that when she died, there was to be nothing else. I pointed out to her that she accepted many things for which she had no independent proof, in fields such as science, medicine, and economics, simply because experts whom she trusted told her so.

We all accept that neurosurgery, ballet, and plumbing are examples of fields in which he who has studied extensively possesses an advantage. Somehow the error has crept in which allows us to suppose that the deepest mysteries of God are accessible to the ignorant. We are all certainly entitled to a profound and loving relationship with God; we are not all vouchsafed His secrets equally. Those secrets are available to all but remain the reward of individual effort. The knowledge and data is certainly accessible to each of us just as anyone who really desires to master neurosurgery, ballet or plumbing can also do so. But whoever does invest the time and effort will know and understand more than those who do not. I explained to my daughter that she needed to locate an expert in religion whom she trusted and modestly submitted my candidacy for consideration. Over time this helped to reduce her anxiety.

I often think that the depression which has become endemic in our teenage population is another consequence of the secular world view with which we have indoctrinated our young people. We teach the textbooks of science, medicine, and plumbing; it is baffling to me that we would decline to teach the textbook of God.

CHAPTER TWENTY-TWO

JUDEO-CHRISTIAN TRADITION

HUMAN BEINGS ARE ALWAYS SLIGHTLY UNEASY ABOUT PURSUITS THAT HAVE NO SPIRITUAL OVERTONES AT ALL.

When I refer to the Judeo-Christian tradition on my radio show, it invariably sparks controversy. I receive frantic calls from both Jewish and Christian listeners denouncing the term. "There is no such thing," they tell me.

Now I would be the first to agree that there is no such thing as a Judeo-Christian theology. The two theologies are quite separate, distinct, and in many ways incompatible. However, it is hard to deny that there is a common ethic and a common tradition.

Both American Christians and American Jews who are serious about their faith believe that the family is the fundamental building block of society. Remember that not everyone in today's America would go along with that assertion. It is part of the Judeo-Christian tradition. Similarly, both religious Jews and religious Christians would believe that marriage is a religious covenant and that people ought to marry within their faith. Both would agree that fear of the Lord is the foundation of all wisdom and both would agree that parents know better than children and should be respected by their children. What is more, both would agree that these ideas regarding the organization of human society are the direction of God rather than the rational conclusions of clever humans.

What are some other core theoretical principles of Judeo-Christendom? Both Jews and Christians accept the account of Adam and Eve in the Garden of Eden. Jewish tradition teaches that the serpent was the embodiment of the animal world attempting to persuade humanity that its destiny lay not with God but with the animals. The serpent's message was essentially this: If it tastes good, eat it. The Judeo-Christian tradition constantly reemphasizes that we are closer to angels than to apes, that humans and animals are radically different. So much depends on who wins that tug-of-war. So much changes if we view ourselves as animals (very smart animals, to be sure, but animals nonetheless).

Human beings are always slightly uneasy about pursuits that have no spiritual overtones at all. When necessary, we superimpose spirituality precisely to avoid being exclusively physical and thus uncomfortably animal-like. We apply ceremony and ritual to our actions that are also animalistic. Only people read a book or listen to music; hence these activities require no associated ritual. On the other hand, all living creatures eat, defecate, engage in sexual activity, give birth, and die. If we do not confer a uniquely human ritual upon these functions, we reduce the distinction between ourselves and the animal kingdom. Therefore, we celebrate the birth of a child, often by a naming ceremony; no animal does that. Even if our hands are quite clean, we wash them before eating rather than after, like a cat. We prefer to serve food in dishes on a tablecloth rather than straight out of the can, although doing so does not enhance the physical, nutritional qualities one bit. We even say a grace or a benediction before eating, and according to Jewish law, after. After encountering an attractive potential mate, people used not to proceed directly to physical intimacy. An engagement announcement followed by a marriage ceremony served to accentuate to the couple and to all society that all-important distinction; no animal announces its intention to mate and then defers gratification for three months while it prepares its wedding and future home. Likewise, burials traditionally are full of ritual, including annual visits to the cemetery.

The more physical the activity, the more awkwardness and subconscious embarrassment surround it. Nudism is practiced with a certain bravado in order to conceal the underlying tension. Similarly, we express a normal and healthy reticence about bathroom activities. In fact, it is the bathroom that is often the most adorned and decorated room in the house. At the moment I look more like an animal than any other, it is a deep comfort to reflect upon the little soaps cast in the shape of seashells and upon the monogrammed hand towels. They remind me that although I am doing in private what most animals do in public, it would be a mistake to think of myself as an animal. No animal decorates the room in which he relieves himself. I am a human being and I exult in my specialness. On the other hand, as purely spiritual occupations, reading and art evoke no discomfort, and thus demand no ritual.

Our entire approach to manners is based on this aspect of the Judeo-Christian tradition. Anyone born in the English-speaking world before 1980 probably had a mother or grandmother who asked, "What are you doing? What is the matter with you—were you raised on a farm?" following some egregious breach of manners. This wasn't a slur on farmers; in fact my mother was a farmer's daughter. It was a suggestion that your behavior was reminiscent of the barnyard and therefore unacceptable among humans. When your mother told you, just as mine told me, not to comb your hair in public, she was in essence reminding you that we are not animals. Baboons groom themselves in public; humans do not. How many times did your father object to you making animal noises at the dinner table? Mine did so frequently, always explaining that people must not let their bodies sound like animals. We are even embarrassed when our bodies emit involuntary animal sounds, as well we ought to be. Emphasis on manners is the way civilized members of a Judeo-Christian society remind one another that our entire culture is founded on the conviction that we are not merely animals but that we are so much more. We are unique creatures touched by the finger of God. Forgetting this dooms our society to descend into an abyss of animalism and ultimately barbarism.

In direct opposition to the Judeo-Christian tradition stands the "animal rights" movement. It must be clear that no matter how well-motivated many animal rights activists may be, there is an underlying philosophy at work. In the same way that so many American journalists during the 1950s were duped into becoming apologists for Stalin, well-intentioned backpackers, hikers, suburban matrons, college students and many others have been brought aboard the cause of secularism via their concern for animals. They are unwittingly promoting a moral message with frightening implications, namely that humans are qualitatively just animals. We may be smarter than many, although some even contest that too, but animals are what we are.

Activists flinging red paint on women wearing fur coats or breaking the windows of a restaurant that sells meat are acting quite consistently with their own secular vision. Since they view people as just another species of animal, it truly is distasteful to them to wear the skin of one's departed cousin. They would demonstrate a little more bravery by flinging the red paint onto the leather jackets of Hell's Angels motorcyclists, jackets made from the same dead animals.

However, even if not brave, the radical animal rights activists are quite consistent. This is a tug-of-war that has played out in every human epoch. The final days of the British Empire also had their animal rights activists. Some of them called themselves the Anti-Vivisection League; there were many other similar groups.

Certainly every civilized society must prohibit cruelty to animals. The prohibition stems from a biblical law to not cause pain to animals. However, that is very different from saying that animals have rights.

In a religious worldview, either Jewish or Christian, there are very few rights for humans, let alone for animals. God's system is one of obligation and responsibilities rather than rights. I am sure that like my wife and I, you too have discovered that raising your family in a culture of many rights and few obligations elicits a whiny kind of selfishness from your children. On the other hand, teaching all members of a family of their respective obligations means that everyone both gives and receives in an atmosphere more conducive to nobility and joy. The same is true for society. Not surprisingly, secularism promotes a culture of many rights and few obligations, extending the notion even to animals. By arguing that ultimately we must resist any use of animals whatsoever, secularism approaches its philosophical goal of animal-human equivalence. Obviously the deeper purpose for this equivalence is not to grant animals the self-discipline of humans but to seize for humans the freedoms of animals.

Now there is a seductiveness to regarding ourselves as animals. It allows us the indulgence of never evaluating our behavior. After all, animals do not agonize over life. They eat what they feel like eating. They mate when they feel like mating. Being a human means constantly analyzing whether every proposed action is something we really ought to do. If I could be persuaded that I am merely an animal, my life would change dramatically. There are many things I have never done that I would instantly start doing. There are other things I regularly do which I would cease. Oh, yes, becoming an animal has its appeals. It means the abandonment of all notions of conventional morality.

Our concern for emphasizing the distinction between humans and animals in turn depends on the religious belief that the unseen, or spiritual, world is more important than the visible, or material, world. The Talmud addresses both of these principles by laying down the rule that we must feed our hungry animals before we feed ourselves. This rule directs our attention to the fact that animals necessarily suffer from their relative inability to control their appetites and to anticipate the future. We humans, in contrast, can master the rumblings of our bodies (also called, revealingly, "animal instincts") because we are spiritual creatures. I am focusing on the animal rights movement because it illustrates so well the two options between which our society must choose.

Almost all Americans cringed at a statement by an animal rights activist a few years ago after a California girl was mauled by a mountain lion who had come down from the hills. Referring to the plan to find and kill the lion, she said that priorities were wrong because there are many young girls and a diminishing number of mountain lions. People were horrified, yet when a campaign was mounted years ago to discourage wearing furs, many husbands were persuaded to start feeling uncomfortable about their ambition to present their lovely wives with a mink coat. You see, we all recoil from the extreme manifestation of secularism. The trick is for us all to see the iceberg in good time. My most deeply felt prayer for these words is that they serve as an alarm to link ideas that are now viewed as harmless to their very menacing consequences.

"But it takes a long time to go from harmless idiosyncrasy to real threat," you might cry. I agree. But one does lead to the other, perhaps not in five years, maybe not even in twenty. But there is a wisdom in being able to see down the road. The initial campaign against wearing fur centered first on the mistreatment of the animals. It focused on the inhumane conditions in which the animals were raised. Valid point. Judaism teaches, as do other religions, of an obligation not to cause pain to any sentient creature. As such, many decent people did feel uncomfortable with the idea of wearing their minks.

As with almost all secular propaganda, there was truth in the starting point. Having made an inroad, the focus now changed. It did not matter how conditions might change in the breeding of the minks; the real issue was wearing animal skins. After all, they are living creatures like us. Notice too, the class war element in this crusade. Tattooed Harley Davidson bikers did not have their leather jackets pelted, and no fuss was made of leather belts or shoes. But fur, a symbol of wealth, was the enemy.

Having been successful in closing down fur salons in major department stores and devastating the industry, the attack was ready to move on. Cosmetics were being cruelly tested on mice and rabbits. Once again, by dealing with a real abuse, most citizens' sympathies can be had. After all, if you can test a new product with or without animals, why cause needless suffering? But that was only a battle, not the war. The war continued with the cry that, after all, what makes us think that we are more important than animals? Why should animals be used in medical research? Why should we feel a child's life is more important than a monkey's?

We have now reached the crux of the issue. If human beings are no more than sophisticated animals, the activists are right. Some animals are faster than others, some swim better, some have better sight, and humans have their own peculiarities. Who said one was better than the other? Only God. A society that believes in God can be concerned with humane treatment of animals. But they cannot be confused as to whether humans and animals are equal because they know that God made man, and only man, in His own image.

Remove the stipulation that God created the world, and you may argue that man is stronger by virtue of his mind, but that means that we are only bullies in eating and using animals for any purpose whatsoever. Animal rights as they exist today are not a moral urging to show mastery over animals in a compassionate way. Instead the movement attempts to defy God's biblical blueprint and the unique place it gives humans in the universe.

CHAPTER TWENTY-THREE

THE MANUFACTURER'S INSTRUCTION MANUAL

BIBLICAL LAWS ARE BINDING, WHETHER WE ACCEPT THEM AS THE RULES OF THE GAME OR ATTEMPT TO DISMISS THEM WITH A DEFIANT SHAKE OF THE FIST.

By calling the Bible a blueprint of all reality, I do not mean the book of stories that to many secularized people is nothing but accumulated mythology for children or for adults with childlike minds. No, I mean the majestic and mysterious data stream of three hundred thousand letters and the ancient oral wisdom that accompanies them, which I earlier described. My understanding is, of course, totally influenced by Jewish beliefs. Yet I think everyone will find it useful.

Think of the million or so lines of software code that make up a computer operating system such as Windows 98. These lines of code are written using the conventional alpha-numeric characters found on any typewriter keyboard. The lines contain many easily recognizable words like "and," "go to," and "stop." It is not hard to imagine that with a little ingenuity and effort the characters, words and numbers that make up the computer's instructions could be cunningly arranged to read as a piece of prose. Thus one might encounter what appears to be a lengthy, if poorly written, epic poem while remaining oblivious to its higher software purpose. We would endlessly debate the veracity of the saga and the identity of the author without ever realizing the inestimable value the document offers as an operating system rather than as an improbable narrative.

PLANET EARTH'S OPERATING SYSTEM

Likewise, the Bible is Planet Earth's operating system thinly disguised as a piece of literature. Buckminster Fuller, the inventor of the geodesic dome, claimed that the problem with what he called "Spaceship Earth" was that it did not come with an instruction manual. Religious tradition argues that it did.

My friend and well-known economist P. J. Hill of Wheaton College writes of his belief "that the God of the universe has spoken to humankind, and that a large part of that communication has been to a particular group of people, the Jews."[1]

This communication is in the form of the written Bible; religious Jews believe it is also in the form of our oral law, the Talmud, which is meticulously rooted in the Scriptures.

The faithfulness to original formulations throughout the three thousand years of transmission since Sinai shows how fervent is the belief in divine origin and how real the Jewish conviction that "the God of the universe has spoken to humankind." The Creator presented a seamless web of wisdom at Sinai, combining religious, historic, cultural, legal and ethical data into a comprehensive political system that enables human communities to function reliably and durably. Essentially it is a comprehensive and general theory of the totality of all existence.

The traditionally religious perspective of Scripture explains away seeming anomalies. For instance, secular scholars of the Bible (surely as big an oxymoron as vegetarian scholars of beef cuisine) often ask why the Apocrypha's book of Maccabees, a historically verified account of a war, was not included in the biblical canon while a non-verified tale of a voyage and a huge fish recounted in the book of Jonah was included. The traditional and religious answer is that Scripture was not intended by its Author to provide simple history. Unaided, men would prove quite capable of assembling their oral tradition into the needed history books. In Scripture, each story, every law, and all the poems and proverbs have only one purpose: To provide mankind with a deeper understanding of the unifying principles that enable him to live his life, both personal and communal, in the best possible way.

In the Jewish religious view, the biblical chapters describing Noah and the flood are there to inform us of the nature of the contract between humans and animals, a topic particularly useful as America gropes toward an understanding of so called "animal rights." Animal rights is not a new idea; Jeremy Bentham, the father of Utilitarian Ethics whose skeleton appropriately enough can still be seen on grotesque display at University College in London, argued in favor of such rights in 1789. Some agree and others do not, but only religion can escalate kindness to animals from a political squabble to a moral debate.

The tie between the Exodus from Egypt and what is shown to be its sequel, the revelation at Sinai seven weeks later, is told only in order to reveal the truth that contemporary history confirms: Rejecting slavery is an option, but only if an embrace of God accompanies that rejection. The real choice is between slavery to humans or subservience to God.

Although biblical times must have witnessed countless incidents of powerful men desiring unavailable women, the only story of its kind recorded in Scripture is that concerning David and Bathsheba. This is because it is not merely a historic narrative. It also contains technical data on how the appetites for power and sex are blended in human nature. It sheds light on the instinct for evil possessed by even one as great as King David himself. We are able to derive practical information on the subject which, if widely known and practiced in our time, could surely have prevented the disruption in several promising political careers of late.

The Bible's role as "manufacturer's instruction manual" can be seen in how even natural events such as earthquakes and eclipses are interpreted to serve as spiritual lessons. This bears no resemblance whatsoever to primitive people's irrational fear of these natural phenomena. We should not say that God sends earthquakes, for instance, to punish us for evil behavior, although that can hardly be ruled out. What we do say is that there is a moral message in natural phenomena. They are a valid educational device, offered by an ever-concerned God, to drive home to us certain theoretical concepts in a practical and palpable way. They reveal how very jarring are disruptions to man's preference for predictability.

They also highlight the genius of the founder of the Holiday Inn Corporation as well as other successful business franchises. This company was among the first to realize that travelers will pay a little more for familiarity, which is just another word for predictability. As we noted earlier, people do have an innate need that is catered to by the light switch being in the same place in every hotel room. People feel comfortable knowing just what the bathroom in their hotel room will look like. We all like knowing just what a hamburger and fries will taste like and how much it will cost. The identical spiritual forces are at work when a society that constantly meddles with its income tax code experiences economic decline. The effect may be small, but constant and unexpected changes do make people uncomfortable, and uncomfortable people are often less productive.

In criminal and civil law the same principle applies. When yesterday's permitted acts become tomorrow's felonies, people feel themselves to be in the grip of unpredictable forces. One way the old Soviet Union kept their people in subjugation was through legal confusion. One day you could do something with impunity, the next day you found yourself enroute to Siberia for the same activity. The Torah suggests to us that applying the Creator's timeless rules to ourselves saves us from the social evil of legislators who feel that they are wasting their time unless they are continuously promulgating new decrees. The Niagra-like cascade of new regulations that incessantly pour forth from every level of government is seen by many as solving problems and bringing us closer to some ultimate ideal of societal perfection. To others among us, they diminish freedom, constrain creativity and imperil society. Both views may contain valid elements but they are incompatible. As a society, we will have to decide which view will prevail in America.

PHYSIOLOGICAL COMPATIBILITY

Not only does the blueprint embedded in the Law and the Prophets show man's predilection for predictability and unity (in other words, his subconscious urge to know God), but it also reveals his physical compatibility with those ideals. For instance, physiological particulars are not seen as evolutionary coincidences. Instead, the Talmud considers the location of the balance mechanism in the ear as one way that God indicates to us the relative reliability of information acquired aurally. We are better able to balance conflicting data we obtain through the ear. Data that comes to us only through our eyes tends to evoke a more emotional and less reliable response.

Companies understand this well, and use it to encourage and seduce us into buying their products. If you look at catalogs from an earlier era you will see very few drawings. Instead, you will see detailed written descriptions of the desired product. Today, most catalogs encourage your purchase by means of elaborate and beautiful artwork and, not surprisingly, many of us buy on impulse after seeing something we did not even know we needed. Orthodox Jews do not consider it a coincidence that the image cast on the retina of the eye is upside down. Instead, we recognize this as God's way of hinting to us that what one sees is not necessarily an accurate rendition of what is there, and we are advised to trust information gained through our ears, which includes reading aloud, as being more intellectual and balanced. Information derived via our eyes is more likely to be influenced by our emotions. Other anatomical details reveal insights into the difference between male and female sexuality, the differences between humans and animals, and physical and spiritual roles.

DESCRIPTIVE vs. PROSCRIPTIVE

Once we accustom ourselves to viewing the Bible less as a historic document or a theological textbook and more as an instruction manual for safe operation of the mechanism of human community, many insights into political wisdom are revealed. Biblical laws do not order us what to do in the way that the highway code tells us to adhere to the speed limit. They describe the inevitability of cause and effect in societies of people over time. Once we accustom ourselves to viewing the Bible's laws as *descriptive* instead of *proscriptive,* these rules become more useful to everybody, not just to believers.

For example, Newton's Law of Gravitation is descriptive, not proscriptive. It is mistaken to suppose that until the seventeenth century, Englishmen were free to float above the countryside like untethered helium balloons until Newton ruthlessly suppressed their freedoms with his oppressive new gravity law. Gravity always applied, it just wasn't well understood. One does not have to be a believer in Sir Isaac Newton to be subject to his law. In fact, anybody stepping out of a tall building's window will quickly discover that the law applies to everyone, whether he believes in Newton or not.

Likewise, biblical laws are binding whether we wisely accept them as the rules of the game or whether we attempt to dismiss them with a defiant shake of the fist. The difference is between living what seems to be an absurd and random existence and living in an ordered world of rules that are never easy but always consistent. This is a lot like the difference between a hippie and a physicist: One resents laws while the other is grateful for them. Scripture describes how the world works. It may not strike us as fair or even as desirable, but it is so. The modernist mutinies, confident that he knows a better reality. The traditionalist calmly accepts it and resolves to learn the rules so he can fully enjoy the game.

CHAPTER TWENTY-FOUR

FAITH'S INFLUENCE ON TECHNOLOGY

WHY HAVE THE OVERWHELMING MAJORITY OF SCIENTIFIC ADVANCES TAKEN PLACE IN JUDEO-CHRISTIAN SOCIETIES?

The Bible's underlying political message is not for the establishment of a theocracy. Were that to be the case, the utility value of scriptural politics would be dramatically diminished in today's world.

Rather, the Bible's message is that the key to wise government is accurately understanding the full complexity of human nature. It only makes sense that the Manufacturer's handbook is the best guide to understanding some difficult and often uncomfortable questions, such as: Why have so many of the major natural calamities of the twentieth century taken place in non-Christian countries? Is it because God punishes people who have not embraced Christianity? As a Jew, I certainly don't believe that is the reason. Yet the figures are revealing. I have studied the world's twenty greatest natural disasters (measured by number of fatalities) of the twentieth century. They range from the flooding of China's Yellow River early in the century, a flood which snuffed out the lives of hundreds of thousands of Chinese peasants, to the fifteen thousand people drowned in the more recent monsoon in Bangladesh. Of all twenty, only three have taken place in nations where Christianity has had a profound influence. Two were volcanic eruptions in Sicily and Italy that killed tens of thousands of people; the other was the flooding of Holland during a violent North Sea storm several decades ago.

NON-CHRISTIAN NATIONS AND NATURAL DISASTERS

The question thus stands: Why do so many more people die in natural disasters in non-Christian countries? Phrasing it this way provides the clue. If one measures the prevalence of natural disasters in terms of objective meteorological data, it turns out that Hurricane Hugo, which battered our own east coast a few years ago, was a far more severe storm than the one that ended the lives of fifteen thousand Bangladeshis. Yet Hurricane Hugo killed almost nobody. Perhaps in order to justify some of the Federal Emergency Management Agency's activities, the authorities actually compiled death figures for Hurricane Hugo by counting people who died while in hospitals during the time the storm raged. They also counted people who died from heart attacks during the storm. Even so, it was only possible to indirectly attribute a handful of deaths to Hugo. While certainly sad, this in no way compares to the fifteen thousand Asian peasants who were literally drowned in their homes and fields as the Pacific monsoon submerged their villages.

The dreadful San Francisco earthquake of a few years ago did kill about fifty motorists unfortunate enough to be in their cars beneath the stretch of East Bay highway that collapsed upon them. However, it is important to know that San Francisco's high rise skyscrapers did not fall. In fact, other than the problematic highway, virtually all other buildings and bridges survived the shaker and killed nobody. A few years earlier, a far weaker quake killed thousands in the eastern reaches of the old Soviet Union.

The truth is that God seems to allow nature to expend her fury in an equal-opportunity way. Natural disasters occur randomly around the world regardless of the particular faith of a land's inhabitants. What dramatically changes the *consequences* of natural events such as earthquakes or storms is how a particular society is organized. And this is where the religious culture of the people seems to make a huge difference. Allow me to explain.

DEVELOPING AND USING OUR "FAITH MUSCLE"

When Holland was flooded by the North Sea breaking through its dikes, it was the last time it ever happened. Oh, the North Sea is still as brutal as ever, but it has never again hurt Holland since that original catastrophe. Once the initial crisis was over, the Dutch got together and embarked on the greatest flood control and land reclamation project in history. By the time they were done, the Zuider Zee and the rest of Dutch geography had changed for all time. In a way, one could say that each and every Dutch subject emptied his mattress of saved-up golden guilders and, putting them together with the accumulated savings of his neighbors, built up the necessary war chest to defeat the North Sea. In reality, it was achieved through the magic of the capital market. The Dutch government, acting on behalf of all the people, offered twenty-year bonds. The Dutch eagerly handed in their savings in exchange for a promise by the government to repay the sum with interest after twenty years. Those thrifty and stalwart farmers did not hesitate for a moment.

What made it all possible? What prompted the Dutch to hand over their precious savings in order to build the biggest and strongest dike ever? I think a large component of it was the ability to have faith. Their faith muscle was strong and, like any other muscle, once you have strengthened your faith muscle on one thing, it is strong for any other purpose too. You may have developed your biceps in the gym, but when you also need them to lift the kitchen table, they will not let you down. Similarly, those of us who have developed our faith muscle within the religious observance of Christianity or Judaism find that we can count on that faith muscle being ready and available whenever we require its services in more mundane pursuits too.

What does the word "faith" mean? Surely it implies the ability to function with something invisible as if it were there. Faith with an upper-case "F" means specifically the ability to see an invisible God as clearly as if He stood before us. Faith in general means seeing the future outcome of present events as clearly as if we could contract time at will. Marriage and financial investment are two examples of beneficial human activities that would be terribly difficult for people who lack the capacity to exercise faith.

Nobody actually knows everything there is to know about the person they are about to marry, and they certainly know nothing of the circumstances awaiting them in life. Yet some marry and, looking the future bravely in the eye, march forward in confidence and faith. Others tremble in fearful anticipation; they advance and then retreat, commit and then withdraw, always concerned that the future is not sufficiently visible for determined action.

The field of investments offers similar challenges. If all were clear, there would be no risk, everyone would eagerly offer capital, and there may be no returns. The best investment opportunities always await those with the capacity for faith. Those are the people who can see ahead and spot a trend which, to most others, is still invisible. This is called faith, and it is best developed in the gymnasium of religious experience.

Countries with Judeo-Christian cultures are at an enormous advantage in this area. Unlike so many of the world's religions, both Judaism and Christianity, each with its utterly distinctive theology, do impart a framework of faith to its adherents. Apart from the many other benefits of religious faith, one of the great gifts that religion offers is a spiritual faith muscle. Nowhere is this clearer than in the United States of America. Both marriages and investments have prospered in America largely on account of the advantage that religious faith confers in these areas. It is a gift of Christianity from which all Americans have greatly benefited.

In Bangladesh, as in most other parts of the world, it is a difficult task to get millions of peasants to act in unison and entrust their meager resources to a capital market. This is not because they are peasants, neither is it because they are of Bangladeshi nationality. It is certainly not because of their race or the color of their skin. But it might have much to do with the differences between their religion and America's. Faith may well be a far smaller element of their religion than it is of Judaism and Christianity. In Bangladesh they may not have sufficiently exercised their faith muscles, nor seen their governments act in a manner that fills them with confidence. So when the monsoon strikes, it is each man alone against the forces of nature. Individuals, not surprisingly, emerge as the losers. In America, and other countries with Judeo-Christian roots, it has almost always been different. Individuals are encouraged to entrust their resources to the group in exchange for a solemn promise that those funds will help build preventive and protective measures and, eventually, be repaid with interest.

There is another factor at work here. I understood the favor bestowed upon America by our adoption of Judeo-Christian principles when a friend of one of the members of my synagogue told me the following story. She had taken a long-awaited trip to Indonesia and gone out for a day's boating with a local crew. Unexpectedly, a storm blew up and the motor conked out far away from land. This young American girl and her girl friend were appalled when, with no radio aboard, the crew lay back and did nothing to try and save the boat. The Americans began to plan for survival while their Indonesian guides sat back to await death. No doubt they found the driving life force in the Americans to be unseemly, but that is precisely the point. Culture, that is to say religion, shapes every-thing. That does not mean that the two girls were fervent Jews, they were not. However they had absorbed Judaism's commitment to life in the same way that one can absorb a love for music without ever understanding the complexity of its chords. Marooned at sea, the young American girls were unmistakable products of a Judeo-Christian culture. Over the next few days the American girls attempted to rig sails, capture rain water, and nav-igate; while the boat crew merely watched and told the girls, "If it is meant for us to live we will live, and if it is meant for us to die we will die." Those of us who have been affect-ed by Judeo-Christian culture assume that every human would want to conquer disease and overcome natural calamity. That is not universally true.

Disasters are indeed distributed evenly and randomly around the world. However, human response is so different that we are not surprised to see such different fatality fig-ures. In some cases, the fatality figures are reduced because in the West, under Christendom, it is no longer each human against the fury of nature. Again, both Judaism and Christianity, in spite of vastly different theologies, tend to bring people together. They are both community-building faiths with the result that the cultures they produce are cultures that bind individuals into groups. This is healthier for individuals and it builds better societies. Even insurance companies are directly attributable to religious faith. We can see in the insurance company an attempt to formalize the mutual concern that characterizes groups sharing a common outlook.

JUDEO-CHRISTIAN INFLUENCE ON SCIENTIFIC DISCOVERY

Christianity not only lowers the death toll from natural disasters by contributing to society's ability to resist those challenges, it also contributes to life in the form of technical advance. Well over 90 percent of all the scientific discoveries of the past thousand years have been made in nations where Christianity is the prevailing religion. Virtually every major discovery in physics, medicine, chemistry, mathematics, electricity, nuclear physics, mechanics and just about everything else has taken place in Christian countries. This has been true until recently when almost the entire world has adopted the western approach to scientific research. Now technicians of all races, religions, nationalities, and belief systems regularly push back the boundaries of science by building upon western patents, using western equipment, or studying in western universities. This leaves the question of why western approaches to science have come to dominate the world.

In true rabbinical fashion, I must answer the question of why the overwhelming majority of scientific advances have taken place in Judeo-Christian societies with another question. What is life's greatest, most profound thrill?

We all know that sex is the second-greatest thrill available to human beings. The act of physical intimacy between husband and wife is so profound because it brings us into touch with the infinite soul of another human being, and all humans long for contact with the Infinite. We all hate limits just as we all hate death, the ultimate limitation. Sex as God designed it brings us into contact with the Infinite because getting to know another person in the biblical sense is getting to know a little of the God who created that person. Sex is thrilling because it involves getting to sense just a tiny part of God's infinite quality through one of His creations, one's spouse.

What, then, is life's greatest thrill? It is getting to know God directly. Since this is such a formidable task, sex gives us a tiny taste of that contact. But in the same way sex is an indirect way of experiencing God's infinite qualities by intimately encountering one of God's creations; it is another way of experiencing God's exciting greatness. This is by intimately encountering His creation. The study of the natural world is another way of getting to know God. And for those who study natural science in this way, their exploration becomes a thrilling life purpose. Judeo-Christian culture has been enormously impacted by one monumental sentence, eight simple words making up one great idea. It is a sentence known to almost every religiously raised little Jewish and Christian boy and girl. It goes like this: "In the beginning God created heaven and earth."

That one sentence, totally unknown outside the worlds of Judeo-Christian influence, conveys a powerful truth: that if you study hard enough to understand how the world works, you will better understand the mind of God. Since no other culture links the natural world so closely to God's initial activity, it is no surprise that few other cultures have been similarly incentivized to probe nature. That opening sentence of the

Good Book informed agile and ambitious minds over the centuries that examining the world was a worthy and holy undertaking. It is thus no wonder that the overwhelming majority of scientific discoveries were made, either by people who had absorbed the cultural implications of that sentence, or in many famous cases, by men and women who revered that verse as historical fact: "In the beginning God created heaven and earth."

CHAPTER TWENTY-FIVE

EDUCATION AND THE KNOWLEDGE OF GOD

IS KNOWLEDGE OF GOD A PREREQUISITE FOR EFFECTIVE EDUCATION?

Any student who has been deprived of knowledge of God commences his scientific studies at a disadvantage. One of his handicaps will be the temptation to attribute anything that seems mysterious to coincidence. This trap awaits because a world without God is obviously a world without purpose. It is a world of randomness.

I am not advocating mandatory chapel for all university students, although from time to time I have heard more preposterous suggestions than this from the educational establishment. I am merely observing that many of the discoveries and insights that brought the world from medievalism to modernity took place in universities strongly linked to religion. These were Christian institutions in which God's presence was palpable, and this profoundly affected not only the theology department but also the physics lab and the medical school. One reason is that even just a faint awareness of God prevents the researcher from prematurely leaping to the conclusion of "coincidence." In a world created by God, there can be no coincidence. As I mentioned earlier, the biblical Hebrew language does not have a word for "coincidence." Why have a word for something that does not exist?

ALL CULTURES CREATED EQUAL?

Each one of us who benefits from the giant economic machine that hums away in the soul of America and which brings a measure of affluence to us all owes a debt of gratitude to Christianity. It's not just scientists who are spurred in their discoveries; not just those who can smile at most weather inclemency; but all who benefit from the tranquillity and prosperity of America. As the great historian Paul Johnson has beautifully expressed, "But it was equally the divine plan that God should be worshipped and obeyed and, not least, feared. The fear of the Lord, in short, is the beginning of capitalist wisdom, as of any other kind." Paul Johnson is right.

Only in a tradition that includes a mandate to mankind that we conquer the world and subdue it, have we set out to do so. It is only with global communication and the spreading of that God-based culture, that certain areas of the world have begun to join in the western quest for scientific knowledge and benign stewardship and domination of the world and its bountiful resources.

I recognize that I am violating one of the great taboos of political correctness by suggesting that not all cultures are equal. Note that I am not suggesting anything about race or nationality. I am diffidently but firmly stating that not all religions, or as Elliot said, not all cultures produce the same society. It is true. While we can probably learn something from every culture, and while most cultures have something to offer us, they are not all equally valuable.

There is an attempt to tell school children that the ancient Aztec civilization pioneered open-heart surgery. The teachers omit the fact that the Aztecs cut out people's hearts as a brutal form of torture, not as a life-saving technique. Foolish professors may insist to their gullible students that early Egyptians flew airplanes but saying it doesn't make it true. One of the major foci of modern education is that we must diminish learning of the accomplishments of white, European (or American) males. There certainly have been some major breakthroughs in other cultures (e.g., the Chinese contribution of paper) but there have not been many. The number of scientific discoveries are overwhelmingly a function of Europe, and more recently America.

Modern educators like to focus on cases where the Church repressed knowledge, as in the case of Galileo. What is ignored is that he himself was a "product" of religious universities and a religious society. Furthermore, the suppression of scientific knowledge was in no way confined to the church. Anti-religous Stalinist Russia and the French Revolution, to name just two examples, both executed recognized scientific geniuses.

Today knowledge of God is one of the most conspicuous Berlin Walls dividing our cultural landscape. In religious schools and universities, in traditional synagogues and churches, and in the hearts and minds of the majority of Americans, knowledge of God is considered crucial to proper education. On the other end of the tug-of-war rope is found the educational bureaucracy that expects the state to accommodate every possible bizarre cultural mutation and lifestyle, but finds prayer at graduation an intolerable and fatal compromise of state neutrality toward religion.

A PREREQUISITE FOR EFFECTIVE EDUCATION?

Is knowledge of God a prerequisite for effective education? Again, there are only two sides to this issue. Each side of the national tug-of-war derives a unifying effect from adherence to its own doctrine on this question. Fortunately, we live in one of history's greatest educational laboratories since the Israelites spent forty years in that graduate school wandering the Sinai desert. Nowhere in the world is more variety in education being offered than in the United States. Unfortunately, to taste that variety one must seek out the smaller private schools that, for the most part, receive little or no government funding.

We ought to study whether there are any measurable differences between the quality of education (and its value as preparation for real life) delivered by religious universities and that packaged by their secular competitors. I am confident that the religiously affiliated schools would come out far ahead.

For practical purposes, the problems afflicting elementary, secondary and university education are identical and differ only in degree. But this discussion really has nothing to do with whether prayer is recited in public schools or Bibles are allowed on the playground. These are minor side-skirmishes. Seeing them as the main issue is the same mistake a primitive man might have made had he stumbled across a brand-new automobile mysteriously transported back through time to his century: He would be delighted to discover that he has found a shelter with soft beds. He would be thrilled when the arrows of his enemies bounced harmlessly off the Detroit body work. But he would never know the true miracle of transportation. We miss the point of the real benefits that a religious outlook brings to us in the task of preparing the next generation for its role in the world.

The problems we encounter invariably result from the switch in policy over the past three decades from pro-God to secular. The loudest voices in education today are raised not over falling educational standards and results, but over whether the Bible (even a posting of the Ten Commandments) or teacher or school initiated prayer should be permitted in public schools. Again, we see that Americans are fighting chiefly over God and His role in society. And that is a hopeful sign.

CHAPTER TWENTY-SIX

TRUTH OR CONSEQUENCES

WHEN A FIVE-YEAR-OLD BOY KNOCKS OVER A LITTLE GIRL ON THE PLAYGROUND, THERE ARE TWO APPROACHES YOU CAN TAKE.

We have already discussed the fallacy of equating human beings with animals—a worldview propagated by the radical elements of the animal rights movement and embraced by more and more liberals in society at large. As we continue our examination of the positive role of the Judeo-Christian ethic in American culture, it is vital that we take a deeper look at the practical consequences of the liberal perspective on this issue. The consequences, many of which we are already seeing, are staggering.

If people are nothing but sophisticated animals, then blaming a human for his behavior is inappropriate. Killing and robbing are obviously anti-social and must be discouraged. Since the "criminal" cannot be morally culpable any more than an animal would be, he must have been badly treated by society which caused him to act this way. In the same way as we excuse a caged lion for mauling someone who tormented it, we must excuse the criminal because at some time he, too, was mistreated. Far-fetched? Not really. The "abuse excuse" has become an effective defense weapon in our courts of law, too often drawing a "Not Guilty" verdict in the face of overwhelming contrary evidence.

The secular liberal believes deep down that teaching morality and ethics to young children makes about as much sense as teaching morality to snakes and seals. What is "good" for one person is not necessarily "good" for another. What is "right" is not absolute, but only relative to the situation or to how you feel. Character? Who's to dictate what makes good character?

Is it any surprise that youth crime is soaring?

WHICH APPROACH DO YOU CHOOSE?

When a five-year-old boy knocks over a little girl on the playground, there are two approaches you can take. One assumes that everyone has bad inclinations that need to be restrained; the other is that the child is a "noble savage" and, without external forces influencing him, he would be perfect. One way leads the parent or teacher to condemn that violent behavior and even to punish it, while the second leads to trying to understand the root causes behind the child's aggression. The first approach helps form positive character in the child; the second coddles his aggressiveness and in fact reinforces it. For the last decade the "self-esteem" movement has been fed to teachers and parents. Studies now show that violent young criminals have more highly developed self-esteem than most children their age, which certainly makes sense. After all, their inflated self-esteem justifies their criminal abuse of others. We used to encourage children to have self-respect by demanding that they control themselves, work hard and achieve. Today's adults *give* self-esteem rather than letting children *earn* self-respect. One way they do this is by understanding bad behavior rather than condemning it.

I must emphasize that the second approach does not rule out the first. One can admonish a child while recognizing that he is coming down with a cold, has had a long day, or even has had a dysfunctional home life. But when we opt for understanding only, we do both the child, the little girl, and society as a whole, a grave disservice by averting formation of the child's character.

I have often watched parents respond to such examples of youthful bullying. It is both hilarious and tragic to hear their earnest questions. "Now, why did you do that to Sally?" Or, "Is something bothering you today?" On my end of the tug-of-war rope, the answers to those questions are irrelevant right now. All that matters is that little Johnny must be helped to understand that this sort of conduct is unacceptable. The deep inner causation of Johnny knocking Sally to the ground does not matter as much as teaching him, on the spot, that such behavior is not proper and will not be tolerated. The gift of the Torah on Mount Sinai was predicated on the principle that first the Jews were to accept the rules and the commandments. Later there would be time to understand the philosophies and extenuating circumstances. As a great rabbi once pointed out, Moses did not conduct a symposium on the root causes of Egyptian anti-Semitism.

My mother of blessed memory once had a guest whose four-year-old daughter kept rudely interrupting the adult conversation. The young mother continued to apologize for her daughter's behavior without rebuking the child. Embarrassed, she eventually said to her hostess, "I'm looking foward to her outgrowing this phase." With more forthrightness than diplomacy, my mother immediately told her that while young children naturally outgrow shoes, they need guidance to outgrow bad manners.

My end of the tug-of-war rope believes that people *can* control themselves in a way quite different from animals. The other end of the rope believes that people essentially *are* animals. When animals behave in a way that causes problems, we do try to understand the causes. If the cat scratched you, perhaps you were doing something to annoy the feline. That is just what cats do if you annoy them. If, even subconsciously, Johnny's mother or teacher believes people are just smart animals, then she accepts that Johnny will knock over little girls who do something to annoy him or if he didn't like his breakfast cereal that morning. She must try to understand what *caused* Johnny to push over little Sally. The correct reaction, according to her worldview, is to respond to Johnny's aggression by talking to both Johnny and Sally.

CRIMINALS AS "VICTIMS"

It has been only a short step from there to viewing criminals as victims. Our message to all the little Johnnies in society is that we understand them or we will at least try to understand them. Above all, what they did is not (heaven forbid) evil. It may be antisocial, but the important thing is that there were reasons that made them do it, reasons which explain and perhaps even exonerate their behavior.

The social engineers, the political philosophers and the government bureaucrats who crafted America's crime catastrophe were not evil people. Like misguided people everywhere, they would be horrified to know that their good intentions have produced such atrocities. They were merely rejecting Judeo-Christian-inspired guidelines which formed public policy until approximately thirty-five years ago. They rejected biblical guidelines as primitive and unsuitable for the emerging utopia they were going to create for us. Instead they gave us a hell. They dynamited a house because it contained a leaky faucet. There were certainly problems with the criminal justice system. But in making it conform more closely to the nontraditional and secular picture, they have come close to destroying the whole edifice. Have there been true miscarriages of justices that liberal policies can prevent? Certainly. Nothing is perfect and no idea succeeds unless it also contains at least an element of truth in it. It is important to understand that those same liberal policies have led to other injustices, where victims now feel the system is weighted against them. In a human world there will always be mistakes, intentional and otherwise. That is why it is so important to look at underlying principles rather than base our decisions on individual stories. The underlying principles beckon us to return to the truth or continue suffering the consequences. Individual stories tug at our heartstrings and mislead us into making emotionally based and shortsighted decisions.

A critical technique in the success of liberals has been to redirect people's attention from the spiritual to the material, and from the invisible future (or past) to the visible present. Henry Hazlitt gave us a brilliant example of this technique in his classic tract, *Economics in One Lesson*. In the book's first chapter, a broken pane of glass in a shop

window is misinterpreted by observers as an economic boon. They calculate the stimu-
lating effect on the glass repairman, the increased purchasing power of his wife, the effect
of her purchases on the local economy, and on and on. Their fallacy, of course, lies in forgetting the correspondingly diminished economic circumstances of the shop owner. The
visible and present payment to the glass repairman obscures the invisible future uses to
which the shopkeeper might have put the money.

Similarly, liberals have turned the case of the unjustly punished individual into a
cliché in cinema, theater, and television. Directing our attention to a present and visible
example of injustice, the story line of many a play or film thus conditions us into a dangerous sentimentalism and away from a broader, more mature concern for society as a
whole.

How Liberalism Backfires

As with any breakdown of traditional disciplines, however, the resultant disorder often
turns against the tradition-destroyers themselves. The U.S. in the 1990s has seen crime
gain and hold first place among the issues of public concern. By removing traditional
moral principles from the criminal justice system, liberalism spawned a crime wave that
has affected at least one relative or friend of the vast majority of American voters. By also
inculcating a sentimentalist spirit in those voters, liberals gave every friend or relative of
a crime victim not merely a sense that the system had ill served him, but genuine moral
outrage that society had failed in the most important respect. This indignation is now
turning against the liberals responsible for creating it—much to their surprise. As I write,
news reports proclaim that some cities which have made a conscientious effort to return
to individual accountability and moral values, have seen dramatic reversals in their rates
of crime. Even New York City has witnessed such positive changes. One way works, the
other does not. Why are we so hesitant to go with the one that does?

For their part, the traditionalists in society failed to recognize the underlying unifying principles in the liberal trend. They mistook the new policies as a harmless experiment that stood a reasonable chance of success. Had they understood that the modernists' intention was, in the words of English critic high priest of liberalism Lionel
Trilling, "to subvert the classic Jewish, Christian and natural virtues...to insinuate that
what Jews and Christians have for centuries called sin is actually a high form of liberation," they would surely have rebelled.

Before the Bible gets past its third chapter, it makes clear that God created man in
His image and therefore imbued him with the power of free choice. The Judeo-Christian
perspective claims that man has the ability to choose between good and evil and is therefore accountable for all his actions.

Since secularists maintain that man is the result of millions of random arrangements of amino acid molecules, naturally it would be presumptuous to expect this talking baboon to be able to determine the difference between good and evil. After all, non-talking baboons of the common variety also occasionally rape and kill, and when they do it is invariably an environmental factor such as overcrowding that is to blame. In the October 20, 1998 issue of *USA Today* we are informed of something religious America has known for decades. Guess what? A child's chances of dying from abuse or neglect are eight times higher when a boyfriend of the mother lives in the home. Wow, amazing! Children raised by mothers and fathers who remain married to one another have better lives than children of mothers and fathers who divorce and fornicate. How old-fashioned. But *USA Today* goes much further, it provides an explanation for this discovery. Do you think this statistic endorses traditional morality? You poor misguided simpleton. Of course not. Richard Gelles, a family violence specialist at the University of Pennsylvania notes that in some primate tribes, killing the offspring of the female he is going to mate with is one of the first things a newly dominant male does.

So it isn't nice to do, but is certainly understandable; it is natural; monkeys do it. All the "family violence specialists" in the country will never bring about the domestic tranquillity found in the ordinary Jewish or Christian home. Furthermore, as long as "family violence specialists" derive their wisdom from the basic secular assumption that we are more like apes than angels, they do society more harm than good.

Similarly, when a man or woman or boy or girl misbehaves, he is merely responding to a cultural condition. The felon deserves pity and help, not punishment and correction.

Yes, ideas really do have consequences, and none are more consequential than how we view our relationship with God.

AGAIN, ONLY ONE WAY WORKS

Throughout Scripture, neither God nor His prophets accept excuses; not from Israel and not from her kings. There is atonement and mercy, but there is also accountability and justice. Secular citizens consider the story of Man's fall, the banishment from Eden and Paradise lost, as irrelevant—an almost tribal legend. Traditionalists, on the other hand, understand that God's policy is that man must be held accountable by both family and society for all of his actions. Which side of the tug-of-war one joins makes all the difference to our prisons, our courts, and our streets. Does a criminal act voluntarily, and must he therefore accept responsibility for his actions? Or is he a blameless and amoral creature of instinct who needs to be understood and coddled? Again we can see that how we view our relationship with God has as much to do with penalties and prisons as it does with pews and parsons.

CHAPTER TWENTY-SEVEN

CHAOS IS NATURAL

GOD WANTS US TO OVERCOME NATURE, BOTH
OUR OWN AND THAT OF THE NATURAL WORLD.

Must science and religion always be in conflict?

Many people mistakenly assume so. At the very least they assume that if such conflict is to be diminished, it is religion that will have to adjust.

Look, it is really very simple. Think of science as the maintenance manual that came in the glove box of your new car. It tells you how to change fuses and at what pressure to keep the tires. It is really helpful when you need to know where to find the remote control switch for opening the trunk or how to service the fuel injector. However, you'd be making a serious mistake were you to look to that manual for information on everything you might do with your car. Should you visit your mother? How often? Which route should you take to pick up your date? What should you do or not do in the back seat of the car? How fast should you drive? Is it a good idea to have a drink or two of some alcoholic beverage before driving? What sort of music should you listen to on the car radio? No, these and many other questions are determined by your values and beliefs, not by objective phenomena that the car manufacturer could be expected to know anything about.

Silly and sometimes dangerous consequences ensue when we ask science for answers to the fundamental questions of life that can only be answered in the context of values and beliefs that address the issue of ultimate good. While it is a mistake to view the human being as a material object that is completely understandable and predictable using tools of physics and chemistry, those disciplines do have real value. What is more, their very real value is not confined to just the material aspects of the world. They provide subtle clues to certain spiritual realities, too.

PHYSICS AND HUMAN BEHAVIOR

Let us further examine some basic premises of Judeo-Christian thinking by looking at the physical world. The laws of physics contain many elegant analogies to principles of human behavior. None of this comes as any surprise to this Orthodox rabbi, who believes that one God created both the physical and human worlds and that He set in place laws that apply to each. The monotheistic traditions, beginning with Judaism and strongly reinforced by Christianity, teach that God's act of creation established the laws we recognize as physics, chemistry, astronomy and the other branches of the natural sciences.

Without His intervention, the universe remains captive to the second law of thermodynamics which assures us that chaos is the natural condition. The universe was created by God injecting unlimited energy and intelligence and America was created by devout Christians applying God's principles. In both cases entropy was defeated. Normally, however, entropy is always increasing. Which is to say, without infusion of energy and work according to an intelligent plan, disorder and chaos increase. Think of those booming company towns in jungles around the world that flourished while the oil, gold, or other commodity held out. Once the supply dwindled or political instability made the company abandon its claim, the town was swallowed by the jungle. First the elements worked their destruction on the buildings, then vegetation overran the once bustling community. A few years after being abandoned, the town was almost indistinguishable from the surrounding jungle. Once human beings ceased working and maintaining the little corner of order they had created, chaos took over again.

Even if you have unpleasant memories of suffering through high school physics, bear with me. Entropy, like gravity, is a law that affects all of us regardless of whether we enjoy science or not.

Contemplate the depressing finality of entropy. Imagine me taking a large glass jar and painstakingly filling it with neatly arranged rows of red and green marbles. I cover the jar and shake it. We observe the marbles vibrating and migrating round the jar until, pretty soon, all signs of the original layered pattern have vanished. How long must I shake the jar so as to have the marbles return to their original layers? Consider that each marble can occupy only a finite number of positions in the jar, and all the marbles of the same color are interchangeable. I do not require any marble to return to its original place. In fact, I can drastically reduce my expectations still further and remove the requirement that the original pattern be replicated. I will accept columns, diagonals or any other arrangement of marbles that looks ordered rather than random. How long will it take to shake these miserable marbles into some conformance with my requirements? Longer than most of us are willing to stand there shaking the jar. Order simply refuses to emerge out of chaos by itself.

Consider another example of the same law. Suppose we leave an automobile in a field for a few centuries, then return to inspect the result. What do we find? A heap of iron oxide, some powdered glass, bits of rubber, and so forth. If we attempt to reverse the experiment, leaving the decomposed materials and checking every hundred years or so to see if nature has reconstructed a car, we will remain disappointed forever. We are so accustomed to these processes that we ignore the staggering mystery: Why on earth should a car spontaneously break down into its component parts, but those same parts never recombine into a car?

The entropy principle explains that a kind of natural gravity is at work. It tends to pull things down into their lowest state of order. The marbles will never return to an ordered arrangement, no matter how long or vigorously I shake them. Entropy keeps them in random and chaotic arrangements. An automobile is a most carefully contrived arrangement of glass, metal, plastic, and rubber. Like the marbles, once disarranged, those component parts will never come back together by chance.

The finality of entropy leads us to a consideration of what is "natural." We see that creating order out of chaos always requires energy and intellect. Just maintaining that order requires energy as well. Nature, in this sense, represents the universe without the application of energy or intellect. We all know that the Bible, the founding document of western civilization, opens with God's conversion of primeval natural chaos into an ordered universe. Because the creation occurs at the very beginning, we understand why the Hebrew word for "nature," *teva,* does not appear in the Bible. Random, undirected nature is essentially driven out in the first sentence.

Our two entropy examples reveal that the more natural state is the one with the most chaos and the least intelligible order. Our nonsymmetical scattering of colored marbles is natural, layered patterns of marbles are not. Heaps of iron oxide and broken glass are far more natural than a working automobile. Similarly, a stagnant swamp is more natural than a sparkling marina. God wants us to overcome nature, both our own and that of the natural world. Gobbling one's food is natural; so is relieving oneself wherever one happens to be. Both these behaviors are quite common in nature. Humans are to overcome their natural tendencies and replace them with a higher order of behavior. We are also to try to improve on nature, and the currently popular notion that somehow untouched nature is of a higher value than improved nature is a mistake. A skyscraper is more eloquent testimony to God and the unique creativity He imparted to man than is a mountain. A factory tells us more about God than a forest. A marina reveals more of God's greatness than a mountain and a skyscraper tells us much more than a swamp. Believing the opposite is both a consequence of secularization and a return to primitive pantheism.

THE LAW OF SPIRITUAL ENTROPY

I have observed a corollary to the law of entropy which I think follows from it, and which states that it is easier to destroy things than to build them. For instance, it is quicker and less expensive to demolish a building than to construct one. It is also easier to engage in terrorism than it is to protect against it. This is true no matter what area we examine. Allow four preschoolers, preferably male, into a neat and orderly kitchen and give them free rein. Any experienced mother will tell you that in the time it takes her to answer the doorbell's ring, the kitchen can be converted into a reasonable facsimile of a Bosnian battlefield. Restoring that kitchen to an advertisement for *Good Housekeeping* will take time, perseverance and an intelligent plan.

People spend a lifetime building their reputations; a mere five-minute misstep can ruin what took a lifetime to build. We can shout "This isn't fair!" as long and as loud as we like, but we will do better to accept reality. Reality is simply that each physical law has a spiritual equivalent. Consider a law like inertia, which states that any body in space prefers to keep on doing whatever it is that it is doing currently. Moving bodies tend to keep moving and stationary bodies tend to remain motionless. It is easier to keep a car rolling than to get it rolling in the first place. This is why we need transmissions. All the torque of first gear is needed to get the car rolling; however, once it is moving, we can up-shift to third although it offers far less torque to the wheels. Conversely, it is easier to keep a stationary car still than it is to stop a fast-moving one. That is why the regular brake of the car is a very powerful mechanism for stopping the wheels from turning. However, the parking brake is far weaker—just try and slow down your moving vehicle by using the parking brake.

The spiritual equivalent of this rather inconvenient aspect of how the good Lord saw fit to set up the world is that people with good habits find it far easier to keep those positive traits than do people who are still trying to acquire them. Just think of starting a diet or an exercise regimen. The first few weeks are difficult and painful. But if you keep it up for a while, it becomes far easier. People trying to cease smoking struggle mightily, whereas those who have never started find it difficult to relate to the problem. So it is with most other principles of the natural world such as critical mass, gravity, and particularly, spiri-tual entropy. Being aware of how spiritual laws parallel their physical counterparts helps us understand just how reliable and immutable they really are. America is in the grip of a law's inevitable results as surely as if she were a hot air balloon that has exhausted its supply of fuel for heating the air in the giant colored envelope overhead. Believers and nonbelievers alike are going to descend fairly rapidly.

America, with all its flaws and foibles, has worked well as a nation. How much can we continue to tinker with her foundations before we increase chaos and disorder beyond that which can be corrected? Once before in our history, we ignored a basic foundation of our conviction in this country. Despite proclaiming in the Declaration of Independence that "all men are created equal," we did not act in accordance with our words. Many of the signers of the Declaration of Independence and the Constitution saw the peril in that inconsistency. The Civil War and the turbulent race relations that resulted in our land would have come as no surprise to those men. Read their words and you will know that they understood the dangers of not being true to principle where slavery was concerned.

Over two hundred years later, we are on the verge of abandoning another major principle referred to in the same Declaration. But in this instance I doubt that the founders saw the impending doom. You will recall that they sued for independence from England, "appealing to the Supreme Judge of the World for the Rectitude of our Intentions." Today we are on the verge of turning our back on that "Supreme Judge" and the laws He gave us for running His world.

Once again, I remind you that the laws I describe have little to do with specific theologies. Let's take an imaginary trip to find out the difference between cultures that have adopted Judeo-Christian principles and those that have not done so.

THE TROPICAL ISLAND EXPERIMENT

Decades before our computer-controlled "virtual laboratories," Einstein created his famous "thought experiments." They allowed him to solve problems for which actual laboratory experiments would have proven too expensive, if not impossible, to conduct. Rather than measuring gravity in an elevator dropping down a three-mile elevator shaft, the great physicist showed that we can just as well, and a lot more safely, analyze the problem from the comfort of our desks.

Following his example, then, let us conduct a thought experiment to see if we can understand the origins of our own calendar. The experiment proceeds as follows. We deposit a young boy and girl on an otherwise-deserted tropical island. Taking care that they have enough to eat, and stipulating no health or external dangers, we set up clandestine surveillance equipment and settle back to observe their development over a few millennia.

After a century or two, they will have increased their numbers substantially. By now a full-fledged society, our experiment has them remaining oblivious of any other people or any human history. In what ways will their world resemble ours? Will they be aware of night and day? Assuredly. Will they notice periodicity in the heavens, eventually developing a calendar? Certainly. First they will become aware of the moon yielding a lunar month of about thirty days. Eventually, they will most likely discover that the solar year contains 365 days.

However, it is highly unlikely that they will adopt a seven-day week. Not only is there no visible astronomic seven-day cycle, but seven does not divide evenly into 365, or into thirty, which makes it an illogical choice. They would most likely establish a five-day week, as this would make each year a calendar replica of the preceding one.

Why, then, do we have something as confusing and artificial as a seven-day week when switching it to five would make more sense? Only because we retain a primeval, collective memory that long ago, God initiated a seven-day cycle as a kind of divine circadian rhythm. It is otherwise difficult to account for the wide acceptance of the seven-day week.

In fact, there was an attempt to substitute a five-day week through the old League of Nations, that post World War I precursor to the United Nations. It will come as no surprise that it was atheistic Russia that spearheaded this effort through the League's commission on commerce. They attempted to move the world off a seven-day system and onto a five-day week, understanding full well that a seven-day week spoke of a Creator. The attempt was blocked chiefly by the religious communities of Great Britain and the United States.

MARRIAGE AND FAMILY?

What other conventions, which we take for granted today, will our island community develop? Biology will present us with mothers and children. But will there be marriage? Remember, on this island no deity has proclaimed, "It is not good for man to live alone." There is no collective recollection of Adam, Eve, and their children. Will we find that the conventional family relationships we take for granted in civilization will have emerged from some other source? To put it another way, without a sacred role for marriage, will there be families? Will we find men dedicated to a single woman and the couple then dedicated to its children? Will we find three generations of a family lovingly gathered for a week-long (that is five-day) celebration of their grandparents' wedding anniversary?

I doubt it. There are two reasons for my skepticism. I have no doubt that women would instinctively want one man to love and protect her and her offspring. The alternative would be finding herself at the mercy of a horde. Every bright woman on our island will try to persuade some man to renounce all others in favor of protecting her. Except for the most rabid feminists, women have realized that most of them eventually do want children—often with a fierce desperation. Any woman who has given birth knows that her sisters would want to have the choice not to work at full strength all the way through a pregnancy. Still fewer women choose to handle labor and delivery, the first months of recovery and round-the-clock feedings, then all the other aspects of parenthood all by themselves.

Yes, I believe women might come up with the idea of marriage. However, since marriage is far more in the best interest of women than in men, why should men agree?

Indeed they should not, which is exactly what we find in some of the less wholesome corners of American society where secular liberalism has most left its mark. Why should men agree to the restrictions of marriage? First of all, renouncing the entire field of nubile and available females and remaining exclusively loyal to only one woman is against the sexual instinct. It is also against the genetic interests of men, who best serve the call of their genes by impregnating as many women as possible. That would be the natural way. If we are nothing but material beings similar to animals, marrying and remaining loyal to only one woman makes as little sense for human males as it makes for male dogs.

The second reason I cannot see marriage evolving naturally on the idyllic island of our thought experiment is that even if many men improbably agreed to sacrifice their immediate gratification in favor of their long-term interests, the discipline required for this is more than most of us could summon up. Indeed, we can see in America today that marital fidelity is not easy and it is certainly not all that common. It is no surprise that church-affiliated couples have vastly lower rates of infidelity than those who see no religious component to their vows. It is far easier to stay faithful when you believe that God demands fidelity and is watching. Without marriage, does anyone doubt that society would look very different indeed?

Chaos is natural; it is society without God. It is God who created order in our universe and Christianity that upheld His order as the standard for American society and government. The last thirty-five years have given us a clue as to what our world will look like if we do not reaffirm, and return to, the wisdom and order of His creation.

CHAPTER TWENTY-EIGHT

HEAVEN HELP THE HOME

**PERHAPS THE QUESTION IS NOT
"DID APES BECOME HUMANS?" AS MUCH AS IT
OUGHT TO BE "ARE HUMANS BECOMING APES?"**

Nowhere is the tug-of-war for the soul of America more strikingly visible than in the area of marriage and family.

At one end of the rope are all those who believe that humans and their relationships function best when operated according to the manufacturer's instruction manual, the Bible. Meanwhile, the other end of the rope is being forcefully pulled by all those who, in one way or another, reject all guidance other than their own emotions, experiences, and consciences.

While I love modernity in science and technology, I greatly distrust modernity in nonmaterial matters such as human relationships and human happiness. *Sesame Street* and psychiatric journals tell us that the definition of family has been changed to include almost anything. The traditional view says that God created a world where humans will be happiest and feel most fulfilled when one mother and one father unite in marriage and raise their children together. Our modern culture tells us that the traditional family is at best one option, and at worst an antiquated, repressive phenomenon.

The beginning of the Bible distinguishes between people and animals in a surprising way. God created all living creatures in turn; fish and birds on the fifth day, land animals and then mankind on the sixth. However, mankind is the only one of God's creations that is described as "male" and "female." In other words, according to the Creator, the difference between a lion and a lioness is physical or, at best, instinctive. Mr. Elephant, for all spiritual purposes, is identical to Mrs. Elephant. Man, however, is comprised of two subspecies: man and woman.

Which leads to yet another aspect of the great American tug-of-war of our late twentieth century. Some see the Bible as just one more ancient volume assembled from the ramblings of assorted desert poets. Those holding this view would be little short of insane to regulate their lives according to the primitive views of a bunch of early nomads. Why, the archaic scribes of those scriptural relics probably did not even have indoor plumbing. What could they possibly teach us?

Pulling from the other end of the rope are those of us, both Jewish and Christian, who see the Bible to be nothing less than God speaking to humanity. From our perspective, it would be just as insane to ignore the Bible. One may as well ignore the instruction manual when attempting to operate a complex machine. If there is one complex machine for which the manufacturer's instruction manual is certainly needed, it is the wondrous machine we call marriage.

MARRIAGE: DIVINE HELP NEEDED!

The marriage model designed by the world's greatest matchmaker is based on fundamental differences between animals and humans. At best, a male animal views its female as a commodity. In some species she is nothing more than an asset to help him respond to one of nature's more insistent calls. To the chimpanzee, for instance, females are to be fought over and then impregnated. Frighteningly, the same behavior is already starting to appear among young American males who have been deprived of a religious heritage. But then, why should that surprise us? Without God, we are animals; it follows that we will begin to resemble them. Perhaps the question is not "Did apes become humans?" as much as it ought to be "Are humans becoming apes?" As marriage becomes less relevant to those Americans on the Left end of the rope, our resemblance to the wild kingdom becomes more evident. Without marriage, weaker humans become more dependent on government. In the animal world, weaker animals depend on the zoo keeper to maintain their health and security. Without marriage, men can tend to become predators and rogues. This again is reminiscent of the jungle, barnyard, or zoo. Marriage is almost more important for the preservation of society than it is to the individual male.

Of course a human male can find physical satisfaction without marriage. In all ages this has been possible for a fee or by using force; in our own enlightened times it's willingly offered for free by foolish women to almost any man. For an animal, this is sufficient. It can find physical release and propagate its gene pool. Yet mankind, which can achieve these goals without marrying, still seeks to marry. Men guided by a biblical blueprint are unique in desiring and appreciating women for spiritual reasons. Wives not only provide companionship, love, and sex, but they also help men transcend their lower natures to become true men as God designed them to be.

WHICH PATH SHALL WE FOLLOW?

The lesson of Genesis is that men have only two choices. They can aspire to be real men, or they can emulate animals. Which they choose will be revealed best by how they treat women and their children. If they dedicate their lives to one woman, supporting her, nurturing her and growing into a giver through her, they are men, not animals. If each of their children are regarded as precious jewels to be gradually exposed to a wondrous world, they are men, not animals. Men who use women merely for selfish gratification live by the secular, animalistic worldview. Without the loving, loyal commitment of marriage as God designed it, such men may have spawn but never children.

Which of these two paths any society follows depends on whether the Bible is considered a blueprint or a relic. If you doubt this assertion, just visit locations in America that stand as tribute to each of those incompatible views. Visit communities where people follow God's ways seriously and you will find, for the most part, stable homes, loving parents, and children on their way to becoming model citizens. Compare these beacons of home life with parts of some American cities regarded as crowning achievements of government-sponsored secular fundamentalism—and notice the profound difference. Which path, really, is best for present-and-future America?

It all depends on whether we respect God as relevant to our practical lives. Nothing else is a more reliable predictor of what a home will look like, or what our children will be like. This is what the tug-of-war is about. It impacts every corner of public policy.

Do we see the birth of a baby as a glorious miracle or merely a coincidental and random rearrangement of six dollars' worth of common chemicals? Biblical values tell us a baby is a gift that God bestows upon parents. It is not just the gift of a new life with all its hidden potential to change the world, but it is something far more: It is the gift of being permitted to participate in the acts of creation and nurture themselves. After six days of labor creating the universe, God's last act was the creation of the human being. Through our children, we are permitted to become God's partner in that act, with all the responsibility and excitement that implies. That is what makes the parent-child relationship so wonderfully special. It is also what makes secular liberalism's attempts to interfere in that relationship so sinister.

DAD IS NOT OPTIONAL

For molding, guiding and teaching a child, the wise mother knows how invaluable a father is. The Hebrew language imparts tremendous insight on this subject. Even if you detested foreign languages in school, would never dream of visiting a country where English is not spoken, and cringe at the thought of buying language tapes, I think you will enjoy this—so follow closely.

No scholars of English spend time trying to explain why the word *carpet* is composed of the word *car* and the word *pet*. We would laugh at the suggestion that a woolen floor covering is, in any way, related to an automobile or a domesticated animal. Nobody expects a philosophically coherent explanation for why the "sole" of a shoe is similar to the "sole" one might serve as the fish course and to the word we use to describe the "sole" occupant of a room. Likewise, grammar books may harp on the fact that "sheep" is the word used for both singular and plural while "goose" turns into "geese," but we expect no special hidden wisdom to be shed by this anomaly.

In Hebrew, however, such discussions are enlightening. Any words that have more than one meaning are by definition related, and when a word is built from two other words there is specific meaning in the construction. Words that share a root are always connected. And when certain words appear only in the plural, it is intended to transmit a specific message. For instance, no singular exists in Hebrew for the word "face." It can only be used as a plural: *panim*. This indicates a reality—that no one has only one face. Even if a man is so utterly consistent that his wife sees exactly the same face as do his golf buddies, such a paragon still owns several faces as he matures during his lifetime.

A profound insight to reality is disclosed by there being no singular word in Hebrew for "parent." The word, *horim*, only exists in the plural. An individual is a mother or a father; an individual can valiantly try to fill both roles, but being *parents* is possible only for a couple. We should not really speak of "single parents." You can be a single mom and you can be a single dad, but it is foolish to think you can be a single *parents*. This is a painful reality for the valiant moms and dads who do their best to raise children without a spouse. Feeling and even exhibiting compassion and support for these Americans is highly appropriate. Converting their predicament into normality by using language (single parent) that disguises reality is misplaced compassion. It may help elevate the self-esteem of single moms, but it may also contribute to an increase in their numbers by pretending that dads are superfluous.

While trying to be helpful to those who have either embraced the lie or been victimized by it, we must protect the future by telling the truth. Parenting is an activity similar to the one that conceived the child in the first place; it is incomplete when done without the active, loving, principled participation of a partner of the opposite sex. When a child is bereft of a father, he is, according to the Bible, considered an orphan. All those biblical commands to be kind to the widow and orphan refer not to a child who has neither mother nor father, but rather to the widow and her child.

As the traditional "till death do us part" marriage has been traded for serial marriages or no marriage at all, undesirable patterns have evolved. Statistics about youth and young-adult crime are staggering. An overwhelming proportion of those who have been in trouble with the law did not have loving fathers involved in their upbringing. How much more does one need to know than that? Children who are to become assets to society need to be nurtured and instructed by both a mother and a father. In other words, "father" is not the title one earns for impregnating a woman; any male animal can impregnate. Being a father is far more complex and demanding. Without one, children, particularly boys, stand a pretty good chance of hurting their community more than helping it. Everyone already knows how easy it is for boys raised without a father to become neighborhood predators. What is less known is how frequently girls raised without a father become the prey of those young predators.

The Judeo-Christian view of fatherhood is under attack in our media, in our schools, and on the streets of America's cities. Nowhere is this clearer than in how young men view young women and how they feel about their own seed. Men (and boys) who think women are commodities to be fought over, used, and impregnated have renounced real manhood in favor of animal behavior. Instead of fathers, they are merely sires. Likewise, women who think giving birth to a child is the same as raising one also emulate the animal world where mothers are important only until their young can physically manage on their own. Getting pregnant and giving birth are only the first stages of a lengthy life-affirming process. As adoptive families teach us, pregnancy and birth are the least important aspects of being a mother.

Teenage students who "keep score" and males who do not even regret that they cannot recognize their own children are a terrifying omen of America's plunge into barbarism.

CHAPTER TWENTY-NINE

FATHERS NEEDED

CHILDREN NEED CARING FATHERS. FATHERS NEED TO FEEL NEEDED BY THEIR WIVES AND CHILDREN.

O ne of the hideous consequences of welfare's good intentions is that even good men married to good women can feel a little less needed.

When government taxes its producers in order to provide housing, an income, some security, and almost everything else a woman might have traditionally depended on a man for, there are several consequences—not all of them intended. It is true that some women married to bad men, as well as women abandoned by the men who sired their children, are thus rescued by the largesse of their fellow citizens. It is also true, however, that there are other women who feel little reluctance to become impregnated by men whose role in the lives of their children ends at conception.

Thus one of welfare's unintended effects on our nation has been the encouragement of illegitimacy. From a financial perspective a woman can do better by relying on welfare than on a man with no financial prospects. A vicious cycle is set in motion, where the man has no need to improve himself in order to be attractive to a woman, and women bemoan the lack of good men.

But the damage is not restricted to those at lower socioeconomic levels. Public policies also imperil middle and upper class marriages. There is an awareness hanging in the air that sometimes finds voice when tempers flare. In the man's mind, a woman's voice can be heard saying, "I don't even need you, I'd be better off without you." Even when statistics show that women and children suffer financially after divorce, emotionally, women are encouraged to not believe it will be true in their case. Or they are encouraged to agitate for judicial and legislative reform to change the fact.

For a man, not feeling needed is the first step on the terrifying road to impotence, and there is no worse feeling. It becomes understandable, if not excusable, for a man to abandon the source of the frustration that comes from not feeling needed. So deeply does he resent his unimportance that he feels he must leave his family; they don't really need him, they know it, and they may even have told him so in one way or another.

THE GIFT OF A CARING FATHER

One of the most important gifts a woman can bestow upon her children is that of giving them a caring father. In my own home, my wife affirms to our children the gift of a caring father each Friday night. At the beginning of the Sabbath, Jewish husbands and fathers are supposed to recite the special Sabbath benediction called the *kiddush*. People often ask me why every Friday night it is I who say the kiddush and never my wife Susan, in spite of her excellent Hebrew skills.

There are two answers. The first is that little children develop an instinctive attachment to their mother. We have to work at developing their attachment to their father. Creating opportunities for a child to show respect for his father is one gift a mother gives. Teaching them to interrupt their play to welcome their father home from work is one such opportunity. Reserving certain religious rituals for Dad is another.

DNA VERIFIES GOD'S DESIGN

Feminists may scoff at this and suggest that a "real man" does not need artificial rituals to help his children relate to him. This is their attempt to change reality because they consider it unfair. In fact, many liberal branches of Judaism regard it as unfair that, by Jewish law, the religious privilege of belonging to the priesthood is passed down only through the father's line. How unegalitarian! These liberal rabbis may well regard anyone with a mother or a father from a priestly family as a priest. However, until DNA testing of recent years, they wouldn't have realized that they were attempting to change a reality. Just in the last few years, scientists conducted DNA tests on Jewish men who had a tradition of being priests. Most families with names like Cohen, Katz, Katzenberg, and so on, are all descended from Moses' brother Aaron—in whom the priestly line of Judaism was founded—and are distantly related. Astonishingly, these men shared a common DNA line, thereby supporting the ancient biblical account.

Clearly Jews have for millennia defined priests in accordance with the Bible, restricting it to a male transmission. Otherwise, by this point in time, almost all Jews would share that DNA, for over the centuries many Jewish women whose fathers belonged to the priestly class have married men who did not. I am trying to make the point that there is a reality in the world that cannot be changed, no matter how much we want it to be.

Spiritual laws are as immutable as physical laws. There may be many ways to try to build a heavier-than-air flying machine, but only one way works. You may try installing flapping wings instead of fixed wings and you may try to fuel the machine with coal instead of petroleum. However, such attempts are as doomed as are attempts to discover alternative models for the family.

Children need caring fathers, and fathers need to feel needed by their wives and children; the physical reality that men can neither carry the child during pregnancy nor nurse it afterwards reveals the fact that they do not forge that bond automatically.

HONORING OUR NATION'S FATHERS

But there is also a second reason for why the Sabbath kiddush is said by the Jewish man every Friday night rather than by his wife. Not unexpectedly, the kiddush contains the passage from Genesis that describes how, after six days of effort, God completed His work of creation and rested. However, that is only a small part of the kiddush. The rest is a puzzling reminder of the Israelites' Exodus from Egypt 3,300 years ago. In this section, I announce to my Sabbath table that this weekly anniversary of the creation of the world, the Sabbath, is in memory of the Exodus from Egypt. We recite the kiddush not only to commemorate the creation of the world, but also to commemorate the birth of the Jewish nation. In Jewish life, all acts of commemoration are best performed by a male reflected by the fact that in Hebrew, male and memory share the same word: *zachar*. This may be why so many cultures continue to remember the family name through the male line only. It may also be a reminder that marriages work best when women consider themselves to be joining their husband's family just a bit more than having their husbands join their own. Taking a husband's name is not only the highest compliment a woman can pay a man, it also ensures that each family is remembered into the future through the line of its males. This is yet another way God has created a role for the male to compensate for the indispensable role that nature created for the female. This is a gift of God given uniquely to humans.

Now why would it be necessary each Friday night for every Jewish family to actively recall the ancient event of the Exodus? Because the Exodus marks the birth of the Jewish people as a nation, and a nation that loses sight of its origins is doomed. Once a week is none too often for a people to recall its birth.

Not only is it important for a nation to remain forever cognizant of its origins, but people need to do the same. The all-important bond between father and child is one of the crucial distinctions between man and animal. All creatures maintain some kind of bond with their mothers; only humans recognize their fathers. Which is why the growing number of young Americans who literally do not know their fathers is so troubling. Once again we see the mystical link between male and memory.

Those women who, despite possessing skills, talents, and qualifications desired in the workforce, dedicate themselves to their families and their communities do their husbands an enormous favor. By allowing their men the privilege of supporting them and their family, they confer the feeling of being needed that men yearn for. In addition, those fortunate men enjoy added incentive to succeed financially. To them, work is no longer selfish and intrinsically valueless. Because it is for the benefit of others, it has become noble. No higher motivation to succeed exists.

In exactly the same way, my wife, who is perfectly capable of reciting the Friday night kiddush, helps cement the family structure by allowing me that exclusive role. The delicious and leisured family meal we have awaited all week will not start until Dad says the kiddush. In subtle ways, my children recognize that I am needed. Even more importantly, on some subconscious level, I feel needed. Little wonder that Friday night is a special time for Jewish husbands and wives.

Biologically, women can choose to go at motherhood alone. They need a man for only a very few moments; through scientific advances, they can even avoid contact with a man. Whether a mother decides from the start that her child needs no father or she later ejects the father from the family through divorce, or whether a man walks out, the wisdom and stability of thousands of years is being replaced with the latest trend. Statistics show overwhelmingly that after a divorce, men reduce contact with their families. When men initiate divorce, they not only hurt their wives and children, they also hurt themselves in terms of diminished health and reduced economic prowess. Even more seriously, they impact future American generations in ways impossible to fully appreciate at the moment.

BACK TO THE BLUEPRINT

It is not an accident that while the Bible allows and acknowledges divorce, it does not instruct us to "Be kind to the widow, *divorcee* and orphan." Are we not to act with kindness and compassion to the divorced woman? Of course we are; even heaven is said to weep when a couple divorces. However, the biblical blueprint clearly does not regard divorce as an ordinary and normal part of social life. It is never a good idea to structure legislation on the basis of the exceptions.

Being left fatherless through death is totally different from being fatherless due to a deliberate choice of the father or mother. Interestingly, studies show that when fathers are away for an unavoidable purpose such as war, children do not suffer to the same degree as when the father chooses to leave or is shut out from the family unit. Of course an orphaned child suffers, yet Mom feels comfortable talking about the father. She might say, "Your father would have been proud of you." Although physically dead, these fathers live on in their families. In the case of divorce, however, seldom is the father's name mentioned—and when it is heard it is often in derogatory terms or tones. Furthermore, a community can rally and help those few children who are orphaned. Their numbers are limited. However, when society slides too far down the slippery slope and too many children in a group don't have a father present, the resources of the community are strained beyond endurance. I believe the costs of current secularly based policies will be paid for many years to come. Both ancient Israel and modern America had fathers. To their wise and loyal descendants, they still live.

The American experience of the last few decades has made clear that trying to raise children without fathers does not work. Not surprisingly, male animals form no bond to speak of with their young. Running across their own descendants a few years after birth, animals evoke no recognition at all. For humans, however, God made a delightful provision. Although every lion cub looks pretty much like every other lion in the world, our Creator arranged for every human baby to look more like its mother and father than like any other human on earth. This reflects the reality that real men should bond with their children forever. They recognize that their children impart even more meaning to their lives than their wives were able to do alone. It is the child who whispers to his father, "Fear nothing, try to accomplish everything, for you will live forever."

CHAPTER THIRTY

DIVORCE, AMERICAN STYLE

THE PRETENSE THAT COUPLES WHO DIVORCE IMPACT NONE OTHER THAN THEMSELVES IS SIMPLY UNTRUE.

Are traditional families good only for the individuals involved, or are they necessary and beneficial for society at large?

Of course, individuals are each unique. Statistics and polls reflect group behavior, not individual choices, and it is a mistake to point to individual cases that contradict general patterns and suggest that they prove the patterns wrong. I have yet to hear a serious argument that since cigar-smoking comedian George Burns lived way past the average age, we should encourage Americans to smoke cigars.

But certain trends are discernible as more and more children reach adulthood having never been part of traditional family life. While any one individual always has the freedom of choice to behave in whatever manner he deems suitable for any given circumstance, large numbers of people will respond to that same circumstance more or less predictably. For instance, I may or may not choose to stare at the scene of an accident as I drive past. You have the same choice. However, if we are both part of the same large group, enough people will indulge their human natures making it more likely that you and I will do the same. Even if we don't, we will be impacted. If someone yells "fire" in a crowded theater, each member of the audience has the free will to sit quietly and first evaluate the nature of the peril and the direction from which it threatens. That, however, is not what happens. Enough people will simultaneously rush the exits to cause a panic. The resulting stampede makes it extremely unlikely that you and I will continue to act rationally, and that others won't endanger us.

Insurance companies earn respectable returns by betting on the reliability of their actuarial tables. They cannot predict the behavior, health, or driving habits of any particular person. Once the number of policyholders becomes large enough, however, their predictions become reliable. Given large numbers, young males will drive more recklessly than young females.

If a state, city, or region legalizes gambling, no obligation to gamble is placed upon any citizen. Yet, we can predict with uncanny accuracy just how many families will be impacted by irresponsible adults spending the household money on gaming.

DIVORCE DESERVES ITS STIGMA

Our society incessantly sends a message that being judgmental is wrong. I disagree. There are people I love dearly who are divorced, including close friends and family members. I have, on rare occasion, counseled in favor of divorce in a specific situation. I do not hate divorced people or feel a holier-than-thou attitude when I say that there should be a stigma attached to divorce. No matter how unfair it seems, no matter what the personal circumstances, there must be a stigma attached to divorce so that there will be a recognition that it is a final resort that inevitably hurts both children and society.

Pretending that children from divorced homes are at no disadvantage leads to a society, such as ours, that is increasingly populated by such children. The pretense that couples who divorce impact none other than themselves is simply untrue. Divorce rips families apart, fragments neighborhoods and impairs the whole fabric of human interaction within society. If that sounds like hyperbole, ask yourself when you were last able to remain friendly with both parties after a couple you liked decided to divorce. Why is it no surprise when a neighborhood teenage troublemaker is from a broken family?

IMMUTABLE LAWS OF MARRIAGE

We've all heard claims that it is better for children to live through a divorce than to live in a home full of quarreling adults. That claim, of course, ignores the fact that adults have the option of behaving like adults and recognizing that marriage and having children was a commitment that they *must make* work. But it is time to go back to an earlier claim that divorce does hurt children. Ignoring that fact makes as much sense as questioning someone as to why they assume that someone would suffer if they jump out of a twentieth-floor window. The immutable law of gravity states that one will be hurt if one tumbles out of a high window. Knowing that law allows people to put safety guards on the window or act in other ways to avoid disaster. Could someone's fall be broken by a tree or canopy? Yes. But we wouldn't declare that, because a tree or canopy is present, no window guards are necessary. There is also no use expending energy trying to prove that the law of gravity is an old-fashioned one or wrong. It always was a law and always will be one. The law of gravity describes a phenomenon rather than proscribing a rule.

The Bible is also describing, not proscribing. It states fact: *If, then*. Most children whose parents are divorced *will* suffer. Pretending otherwise only encourages divorce, leaving more children at the disadvantage of a single-mother or single-father situation. While our society is slowly realizing what a calamity divorce is, we are raising more and more children who have no model from which to build a successful marriage partnership of their own. I believe this phenomenon must now be recognized as its own crisis.

While personal experience is persuading more people of the price of divorce, our schools, children's literature, TV shows and movies—all of which shape our next generation—try to make believe that divorce is only a temporary setback. We would do better to recognize the disaster divorce is, and through education and social pressure encourage its use only in the most extreme situations.

It is not unusual, whether in a classroom or in summer camp, for more than half of today's children to be from broken homes. When we look at jail inmates, the percentage who had no fathers to guide them rises astronomically. There is a Talmudic saying that if one is kind when one should be cruel, one will end up being cruel when one should be kind. How much cruelty have we inflicted on innocent children and society at large in an attempt to be kind to husbands and wives who want to divorce? Love and happiness in marriage are the result of a commitment, not of a feeling; we are to run the important aspects of our lives according to our heads, not our hearts. This is one of the crucial messages of the opening passages of the Bible.

By rejecting the message of the first few chapters of Genesis, we have severely undermined God's wonderful institution of marriage. As we have turned away from the blueprint our Creator gave us for successful life, we have bequeathed bitterness upon those who have either bought into the opposing animalistic message or had it shoved at them by the liberal policies of the last thirty-five years. Its legacy consists of the dangerous streets and squalid neighborhoods that altogether appropriately get referred to as the urban jungle. It consists of children whose parents' wealth can buy them anything material in the world but cannot purchase stability, virtue, or respect. The cure is the Judeo-Christian marriage model which can turn animals into men and jungles into shining cities.

CHAPTER THIRTY-ONE

MOTHERS NEEDED

WHENEVER SOCIETIES HAVE DEEMED THEMSELVES WISER THAN GOD BY TAKING THEIR OWN, MORE "ENLIGHTENED" PATH, NATIONS HAVE CRUMBLED AND FALLEN.

I have spoken thus far of the father's noble role as an economic support of his wife and children. Does this strike you as a bigoted notion? What about all the women who go to work each day to supplement their husbands' income so their families will have better economic opportunity? And what of all the heroic single moms who are the sole providers for their children?

It is vital that we be compassionate regarding individual situations. Yet, when we consider society as a whole, we must also recognize that the exceptions must not dictate our overall policy of a nation. A society can uphold only one set of values at a time; we cannot, in an attempt to please everyone, uphold values that contradict themselves.

Thus we must decide whether marriage is necessary for our durability. Choosing to make no statement on the topic is, in itself, making a very eloquent statement. We did not remain silent over the scourge of drunken drivers and the carnage they inflicted on our roads. On the contrary, we made it known in every possible way that we detested drunken driving. We finally felt justified in overriding every individual's freedom to drink whatever and whenever he chose because we realized that such freedom was purchased at enormous cost.

Similarly, with divorce and other areas of sexual morality, society's survival will eventually demand that we override the freedom of individuals to act as destructively as they choose. The cost such freedom imposes on the rest of us is just too high. It may be very nice to say "Let everyone do what they like" but this just doesn't translate into reality.

Short of opting for an entirely libertarian government which would literally do no more than maintain basic law and order and operate the military, our present reality is that every piece of governmental legislation either promotes or discourages certain behavior. We therefore have no choice but to eventually try to determine which behaviors we value and which we want to discourage. Either taxes are reduced for married couples or we are telling people we have no particular interest in them getting and remaining married. Either we cease mandating child care centers in businesses or we are deeming it far wiser for mothers of infants and toddlers to drop them off for the day than to stay at home to nurture these children themselves.

Despite our "enlightened" trend toward government-mandated support of working moms, we are increasingly discovering that children need hands-on parenting. As 1997 cover stories in both *U.S. News and World Report* and *Newsweek* pointed out, day care and baby-sitters may be an improvement over plopping a child in front of the TV while a mother shoots crack in the corner, but they are a poor second to a loving mother reading to and cuddling a child on her lap.

Many parents feel that both mother and father focusing mainly on earning money leaves a huge void in family togetherness and child development. Children need both economic support *and* an attentive parent. Most couples, if they need to designate *one* role for each spouse, will send the father to work and have the mother focus primarily on the children. When the government provides incentives for businesses to hire women, or makes it easier for a woman than for a man to get a loan to start a new business, it takes away the free choice of a married couple to decide for themselves how to run their lives. Government policies such as the "marriage penalty" for taxation work against the couple who would like to have the man be the breadwinner and the wife a homemaker.

GOVERNMENT VS. STAY-HOME MOMS

Let's imagine the following scenario. Mary and Ed Jones marry and start raising a family. They would like to opt for a traditional division of roles. At the same time, our government is not just making possible an opposing outlook, it is actively encouraging it. The government has decided to make it tougher for Mary and Ed to make the choice they really prefer. Will Mary Jones find fulfillment in raising her children, doing volunteer work in the community, and helping her husband in his business? Tough luck. In order to support what it deems to be more important issues, the government has not only raised taxes but forced businesses to provide family leave time and on-site day care. This results in higher prices for goods the Joneses use.

Business is also forced to demonstrate "diversity" in hiring, making it harder for Mr. Jones to get a promotion and raise. Prices are raised even more as women leave positions to stay home with their children and companies must, at great expense, train new employees. But of course, the company is not permitted to ask the aspiring new employee if she intends to get pregnant or leave to raise a family. Mrs. Jones must now go to work to pay for these added expenses. And, after all, magazines and TV shows tell her that she can best actualize her potential outside the home. If you are a traditional family, you are regarded as a relic from the age of dinosaurs.

MEDIA ASSUMPTIONS LEAD TO FAULTY CONCLUSIONS

Our media report that only a minority of families now fit the traditional family mode; but media neglect to publicize that their criteria for a traditional mode rejects anything but a two-child, totally non-working-mother family. The prevailing message is that if you are traditional, you are part of a weird, out-of-touch, tiny minority. In much smaller print the studies say that families with one or three children, or where the mother puts in as little as five hours a week on a job, are not considered traditional. The parameters are drawn so tightly that they exclude almost everyone.

Be aware: When journalists produce reports like these, there is an agenda. They are not merely reporting what they believe to be trends in America. They are actively engaged in an attempt to influence the figures. We are all discouraged when we hear that our values are appreciated by diminishing numbers of our fellow citizens. If everyone in the neighborhood litters, for how long do we expect Mary Jones to persist in teaching her children to pick up their chocolate wrappers? By persuading all the Marys in America that their religious and traditional marital and family dreams are antiquated and rare, we actually help to condemn them to extinction.

Mrs. Jones is made to feel that she must be stupid and repressed to want to be a homemaker. She certainly should not worry about her children if she goes to work. The government will provide longer school days, before- and after-school day care, and legislation to help her get off work when a child is sick. She has to realize that her children will actually be far better off with "professional" care than with the well-intentioned but outmoded attention of a mere mother. Ignored is that Mrs. Jones did not want to go to work in the first place. She felt there was merit in being home when her children came home from school at 3 P.M. and in passing on the family's values about sex, drug use, and manners. Now a teacher will be asked to do it, because working parents have little time for that. But the teacher, instructed by the secular educational bureaucracy, will not teach the parents' values in the areas of sex, drugs and manners; he or she will convey the values of secular fundamentalism—the more "enlightened" way.

Mary, along with her husband Ed, thought it would be better for her to be available to help with homework rather than being assured that her children would be promoted even if they were illiterate. Mr. and Mrs. Jones felt that a mother devoting herself to monitoring a child's development was better than paying taxes for school nurses who would direct a pregnant daughter to the nearest abortion clinic. Of course, the school board will—quite understandably—ask for a raise in local taxes to help relieve the burden on schools which are now expected to address areas of child nurture and instruction previously reserved for parents.

DEVALUING THE AMERICAN MOM

As the vicious cycle continues, mothers feel unappreciated, unneeded, and unsure of just what they have to offer when experts are around to take care of their children. Mrs. Jones may have thought there was value in teaching her children not to litter, to step to the side when waiting to enter an elevator, or to answer the phone politely. If she is exhausted at night after a day's work, it is no surprise that the job of teaching the courtesies that allow us to live together in harmony will cease to be done.

So we have tried for a few decades now to pretend that children can be raised without mothers. We have pretended that one hour of quality time is more valuable than many hours of attention. We've pretended that after working a full day, mothers still have unlimited energy to make a home. In the opinion of an increasing number of people, it has not worked. Just as a child reacts differently if a father dies or a father chooses to leave the family, children know whether a mother is working outside the home so they will have food, or working for her own fulfillment. A surprising number of grown daughters of career women are opting to be stay-at-home moms, not wanting their children to feel second-place in their lives. Individuals can make their own choices. But society must choose *either* to place a higher value on women who work outside the home or on those who work primarily in it. It must choose whether it values licensed business arrangements for baby-sitters and day care or encourages people to make their own arrangements among relatives and friends. Unless the government stays entirely out of business, taxation, and education, it has to make decisions that will encourage one or the other path. It cannot encourage both. Due to the law of spiritual gravity, if it attempts to remain neutral, promoting neither, it invariably ends up promoting those ideas that provide another healthy shove to a society already sliding dangerously down the slippery slope of secularism.

Of course, there are many homes where women courageously strive to raise their children without a man. Circumstances force these valiant women to work in order to support their family while still struggling to give time and energy to their children's other urgent needs. And of course there are wives who absolutely must supplement a husband's income, not in order to afford vacations but in order to afford food. Admiring these women, though, must not obscure the question: Are government policies and social pressure not only encouraging but *causing* more and more moms to *have* to work? And if so, is that detrimental to family and society or not?

Thus we are in a quandary. In many issues we prefer to define whether something is good or bad not on facts, but rather on the perceptions of those involved. What do I mean? Imagine looking into a room where two youngsters are throwing a ball back and forth. Suddenly the ball zooms into a vase that was sitting on a mantle, and the vase falls and smashes into shards. Into the room comes a woman who turns pale as tears fall down her cheeks. The vase had been a wedding present from her best friend, who died a few months earlier.

Now picture the same room, same activity, and the same woman walking in to observe the shattered vase. This time, she smiles because she had always thought the vase was a monstrosity. It had been given to her by an uncle she couldn't stand. In fact, she had often wished for the courage to smash it herself. Same picture, totally different reactions.

In the above case, differing reactions are fine. But there are other times when we expect all decent people to have similar responses. When an airplane crash leaves many dead, or a flood leaves hundreds homeless, or a child is left fatherless when her daddy dies, we, as a society, agree that a tragedy has occurred. We are repulsed if someone explains that the environment will benefit from the decrease in the number of humans who perished in the accident. We do not allow a different perception of the event.

COMPROMISE AND SELF-CONTRADICTION

But we have placed many issues into a limbo area, where in the name of "self-realization," "personal growth" and "individual choice" we are supposed to validate decisions that result in what used to be universally acknowledged as tragedies. For example, when a child is left fatherless because her parents divorced, rather than because of death, all of a sudden we are not supposed to see this as a tragedy—but simply as her parents' personal choice. We have become more like the vase example than like the airplane crash. When a woman opts to be a single mother, we are mocked if we do not approve. Similarly, when a woman suffers a miscarriage and loses a much-wanted child, we encourage her to mourn and we join her in her sadness. But if the pregnancy is ended by choice, we must act as if nothing significant occurred. We continue to compromise and contradict ourselves for the sake of personal convenience, for the sake of personal "freedom," for the sake of not having to be accountable to a higher source or value system. When it comes to moral values, compromise and self-contradiction lead only to weakness, not strength; to bondage, not freedom. Inevitably, compromise crumbles the very foundation on which a society is built.

As a nation, we need to return to our earlier worldview. When a diabetic agrees to have his leg amputated because his life is threatened, it may be a necessary choice. It is not one he makes flippantly or without recognizing the price and pain involved. He certainly does not celebrate. Likewise, even in those rare instances when divorce is the correct choice, it still is a tragedy. We have tried to pretend that divorce is a positive thing, and it is time to face the fact that it is not. Sometimes, necessary; good, never. Does that make the divorced man or woman feel bad? Of course it does, and we can try to ease the pain for our friends when it occurs. But as a society, we must ask them to pay that price rather than forcing children and society to pay the price when divorce becomes routine.

In the same vein, is it a tragedy when parents are forced to relinquish care of their children to others? Of course it is. When a poverty-stricken woman tearfully places her infant in day care so she can go to work in order to be able to feed and clothe that child, we sympathize and even agitate for the government to step in so she need not do so. Why, then, when a different woman drops off her six-week-old baby because she thinks she will be bored taking care of it, are we are expected to withhold judicious reasoning? Once again, we need to decide what values to promote as a society. We have validated and even glorified day care and working mothers. Many city governments will only allow a new corporate building if day care sites are provided. The government has been promoting the concept of earlier and earlier day care, suggesting that even a two-year-old needs professional care to fully develop. If the full misfortune of day care only shows up in ten or fifteen years, the reporter who extolled it will simply sit down to write a different article. The mother who heeded his earlier article will never get a second chance to do something different with her two-year-old.

THE EXCEPTION SHOULD NOT BECOME THE RULE

Clearly one of the results of removing God and His ideas from public policy discussions is that we have lost the capacity for objective reasoning. No longer do we evaluate the action as beneficial or detrimental for families or society; we now subjectivize it, asking only about its effect on individual hearts and emotions.

As for the woman who truly has a calling to be a doctor, scientist or teacher, she may, of course, choose to remain single or childless. She may, as did Golda Meir, former prime minister of Israel, devote herself to a cause while acknowledging that her family will suffer. She may, as is happening more and more, find a husband who appreciates what she has to offer the world and together they may opt for a unique type of partnership. He can be the primary caregiver, while she works outside the home. Or a husband and wife may join the economic and personal aspects of their life together and be partners in all spheres. Perhaps, as is one mother of ten I know, a woman may be one of those amazing people who can exist on four hours' sleep, spend the day at work, and still have sufficient reserves to be a fully-energized mom for the evenings and weekends. But while there is always room for individual creativity and personal solutions, we must not make the mistake of formulating policy on the basis of the exception.

When the government and educational institutions of this country pretend that the majority of women can be relaxed, smiling, and successful wives, mothers, and corporate executives—with each aspect of their life dovetailing into the other—they are lying. They are ignoring the real picture of a harried nurse or marketing executive or secretary who is being asked to be superwoman—and is not. They are ignoring the hordes of children who are growing up without values and direction. I have yet to meet one divorced mother who, no matter how successful her career is, wants the same for her child.

Most of us wish our children to have stable, loving, fulfilling marriages. Most parents want to have time with their children and to convey their values and beliefs to the next generation. Good marriages and strong families don't just happen. They take a great deal of work and guidance. God gave us that guidance in His Word, and history demonstrates that wherever societies have followed the Judeo-Christian family ethic, nations have flourished. But whenever societies have deemed themselves wiser than God by taking their own, more "enlightened" path, nations have crumbled and fallen.

When government interferes in the delicate relationship between husband and wife or parents and children, society suffers. Promoting economic policies that encourage men and women to be rivals rather than partners, pushing programs that glorify the work people do outside of their house more than inside, and training our youth in ways that make successful marriages less likely for them, are recipes for the crumbling of the American family—and of America itself.

CHAPTER THIRTY-TWO

SEX IS EVERYONE'S BUSINESS

SOCIETY FLAUNTS SEX PUBLICLY WHILE CLAIMING IT IS PRIVATE; THE TRUTH IS THAT SEX IS A PRIVATE ACT WITH IMMENSELY POWERFUL PUBLIC IMPACT.

Shakespeare may well have had Hamlet say "to thine own self be true," but Judeo-Christian thought has never had much confidence in the human conscience. The conscience is notoriously elastic, tending seldom to condemn that which we really want to do. This is why Jewish thought much prefers a set of laws to guide us, rather than merely a well-intentioned conscience. Unsurprisingly, the entire body of Jewish law is referred to collectively as the *Halacha,* "the way to go."

The Halacha points out that a durable society and fulfilled human beings are the result of marriage and that marriage is clearly defined as one man and one woman dedicating their lives to one another and to their children. The Halacha specifies that the other person in whom we seek wholeness must be of the opposite gender. Halacha is obviously only mandatory for Jews, but there are other laws that we are told are universal for everyone. Known collectively as the Seven Laws of the Sons of Noah, these laws are indispensable for the survival of any human society. One of the seven establishes courts of law. Another rejects homosexuality as a valid lifestyle. I would not suggest that American law embody all of God's rules to the Jews. For example, although pork is prohibited as food for Jews, I have no desire at all to see hog farmers put out of business. Nonetheless, the Bible does include rules that all human societies need in order to survive. Those details that are more ethical than ritualistic have filtered into the foundations of western civilization and been adopted by Christendom and specifically by the founding fathers of

America. Perhaps that is what lies behind the vitality and family stability of America's people of faith.

Modernity, on the other hand, is often driven by emotion. And when it comes to emotion, that which is before our eyes easily trumps that which we must conjure intellectually. Thus when a man declares his erotic love for another man, Halacha weeps and sighs but stands firm. Although the wayward individual will feel pain, society is entitled to endure and the answer must be a firm negative.

PROUD TRIBUTE TO FREE CHOICE?

In any event, asks the modernist, Who says that one homosexual couple or a thousand homosexual couples will threaten society in any way at all? Just as the voice of Judeo-Christain tradition is about to commence the complex but utterly true explanation of how homosexuality hurts society, modernism catches sight of the two men looking impatiently at their watches and nods approval of their union. Whether of Jewish ancestry or not, that modernist bristles with anger at the suggestion that traditional Jewish values should have any relevance in modern life.

Let me remind you that throughout American history men have roomed together. It was nobody's business whether the students, laborers, or new immigrants were friends, brothers, or lovers. Today's liberal warrior is not asking us to stop discriminating against homosexuals. After all, their income level is often above average. He is not asking us to stop the public stoning of homosexuals, which never has been a feature of American life. He is demanding that we all accept and even endorse their actions as another proud tribute to free choice.

As the rector of one of Judaism's more liberal theological seminaries, the University of Judaism, said regarding the Bible's unequivocal objection to acts of homosexuality: "On the basis of new medical information, we can adjust the law accordingly." In other words, God mistakenly prohibited homosexuality because He was ignorant of forthcoming medical information disclosing how healthy is that particular sexual activity. The only alternative is that the rector of the University of Judaism must consider the Bible to be the mindless ramblings of ignorant desert tribes from long ago. Those who trumpet religious language while rejecting the traditional views that have survived the centuries, provide a patina of respectability to the flouting of centuries of belief. In reality, those who wear the ecclesiastical robes of liberal denominations of both Judaism and Christianity and proclaim that homosexuality is not a sin, must make one of these two choices. Either God and His Word are impotent, ignorant, and irrelevant, or alternatively, the Bible provides the only legitimate insight into the mind of the Creator.

People's pain is always immediate and visible whereas society's durability depends on subtle ideas and complex principles that are always long term and abstract. Without the stability of God's Word, modernism wins every time and every society gradually declines—from affluence to decadence, to depravity and, ultimately, oblivion. Only the Jews have survived for millennia and only on account of Halacha. Religious Jews of all denominations have a unique role to play in this stage of American history by helping to popularize those general aspects of Halacha that could help restore decency and durability to our land. It would be a fitting repayment of the debt incurred by so much goodness bestowed upon Jews by America.

NOBODY ELSE'S BUSINESS?

For centuries America has recognized that sex is truly everyone's business. Drawing from the Hebrew Bible, Roman law, English law, and American law have all prohibited polygamy, incest, and (until recently) adultery. These laws reflected our conviction that we all have a say in what two of our fellow citizens might be doing in the privacy of their bedroom. Yet, during the past three and a half decades or so, too many of us have uncritically embraced the revolutionary idea that sex is nobody else's business.

The ancient Jewish holiday of Passover reminds us that sex is indeed everybody's business. The core observance of Passover, or *Pesach* in Hebrew, is of course the *seder*. As the twelfth chapter of Exodus informs us, the seder was characterized by the slaughter and consumption of the *Paschal,* or Pesach lamb. Although the Paschal lamb is no longer sacrificed, most of the symbolism surrounding the modern seder is intended to capture the centrality of that ancient ritual and its significance to sex.

Three of the basic requirements of the original biblical seder offer clear direction for our own confused times: (1) Each family gathered to slaughter and eat its own lamb; (2) the lamb's blood was painted on the door of the home; and (3) males participating in that original seder had to be circumcised.

One reason why the Passover seder is still the most popular family religious observance among American Jews may well be its biblical roots as a family event. After two hundred years of slavery in Egypt, Jewish family life was all but decimated. On the eve of its birth as a new nation, Israel had to reestablish the family as the fundamental element of society. For their very first ritual as a nation, God gathered them not into political, tribal, or labor groupings but into individual families. This reasserted the bond between husband and wife, the parental home and its children.

Painting the blood onto the front door informed the world that behind that door lived a group of people bonded by blood. That bloody door symbolized a separation between the home of one's blood family and the rest of society. It reminds us today that the bonds uniting those in the family are entirely different from the bonds uniting members of a fraternity, a labor union, or a tennis club. Behind that door a man and woman engage in physical intimacy and behind that door they raise the children who, spiritually through adoption or physically through birth, are the fruit of that special husband-wife union. Behind that door the blood of circumcision is spilt as one generation produces the next. Thus is a great nation forged.

Finally, being an uncircumcised Jew is incompatible with a traditional Passover because circumcision reaffirms Passover's theme—that sex is everybody's business. When an infant Jewish boy is circumcised, there are two main requirements. The procedure must be conducted during daylight and preferably in the presence of many people. Thus every circumcised Jewish male knows that in broad daylight, before other members of his community, a sign was placed upon his penis to remind him that what he does with it is of communal concern.

Since the arrival of the birth control pill about thirty-five years ago, American secularism has been preoccupied with separating sex from life. While obviously not every act of marital intimacy will or should produce life, societies throughout mankind's long history that have strenuously separated the two have not long endured.

Sex education programs for children who cannot even yet read fluently are really indoctrinations into the dogma of recreational sex. Venerable matrons who minimize the emotional torment of abortion and encourage its easy availability as an alternative to birth control, have been unwittingly co-opted into the recreational sex campaign. Colleges that insist on coed dormitories and bathrooms also endanger the future by telling our children that sex is casual and insignificant.

Our society flaunts sex publicly while claiming it is private; the truth is that sex is a private act with immensely powerful public impact. Passover and its message that sex and family tie the present to the future remind us of the peril of pretending that sex is nobody's business.

THE NORMALIZATION OF SIN

In many ways, homosexuality is to us today what abortion was during the 1970s. Back then we were warned of the dangers of back-alley abortionists and self-induced abortions using wire hangers. Our emotions were seduced by tales of girls who were raped or married women who could not handle a tenth child. Nobody ever painted an accurate picture of what America would look like once abortion became common. The most charitable view would be that back in the '70s, abortion rights advocates had no inkling of how far things would go. Nobody suggested that, even as sex education classes proliferated and contraception became easily available, the numbers of abortions would grow astronomically. Nobody thought that twenty-year-old girls would arrive at the clinic for their third and fourth abortions. Nobody whispered that, as a prominent Los Angeles gynecologist told me, wealthy married feminists would abort their future daughters because they wanted only one child and wanted that child to be a boy. Prior to 1970, a young girl finding herself a single mother would sometimes abandon the newborn on the doorstep of a well-off family or perhaps the local church. We even had a sad but accurate name for the little child unfortunate enough to be welcomed into the world in this unloved fashion. Because they were unexpectedly found in the morning, we called them foundlings.

As long as killing unborn children was unthinkable that it could only be done in seedy back-alley "clinics," even abandoning a baby where it would be found and given a home was a momentous decision. Today, however, abortion becomes routine and those who oppose it are made to feel like social pariahs. Not surprisingly, when women have been trained to see abortion as a "minor" procedure, we are finding that even average young women can kill their newborn babies and dispose of the vulnerable little body in a local Dumpster. In one particularly gruesome and well-publicized case, the young woman was assisted in the murder by the child's father. Many of our youth do not even recognize that murdering the infant who only just left their body is wrong. After all, respected elected officials have assured them that, had a doctor ended the baby's life as it was exiting the birth canal, it would all have been fine. Can anyone seriously argue that the lessening of reverence for human life, as exhibited by school yard shootings is unrelated to the nation's change of attitude on abortion? Ignoring the obvious link would be ridiculous.

Today, with the normalization of homosexuality, we are just where we were twenty-five years ago with abortion. Just as nobody foresaw where that campaign would lead, we are now frighteningly ignorant of where today's path will lead. Let me try to peer ahead through the gloom. The propaganda war will continue to win new ground in portraying homosexuals as average, admirable, and persecuted people. Increasing numbers of Americans become indoctrinated into believing that homosexuality is just another lifestyle choice or inborn genetic quality. Pandora's box will open. As our children work their way through a government educational system, they will be trained to believe that homosexuality is entirely legitimate. As politically correct dogma continues to replace reading and math they might even be expected to verbalize this viewpoint in class discussions and to recite it on tests. Their class grades may depend on how vigorously they uphold and defend the pro-homosexuality lifestyle, as is already happening in colleges today.

REAPING THE CONSEQUENCES

Just as in the abortion example, here too we shall reap consequences about which nobody now warns us. Youngsters who are even now prematurely assaulted with sexual references will have this issue thrown in to further damage their psychological health. We should expect a rise in the rate of teenage suicides as youngsters are forced to "decide" early as to their sexual orientation. We should expect a rise in AIDS and other sexually transmitted diseases as well as an increase in sexual abuse by men preying on vulnerable youth. We can anticipate that those who speak out against homosexuality will be increasingly reviled and repressed, while gay and lesbian activists will become increasingly vocal and persuasive in pushing their agendas in the media, in courts, in all branches of government. Already today, when science and homosexuality clash, science has been nudged aside. In the political campaign to normalize homosexuality, psychiatrists who claim to be able to help those who voluntarily wish to leave the homosexual lifestyle are ignored and even spat upon. Any facts that counter the dogma that homosexuality is as much a part of a person as skin color are rejected.

This will also serve as another wedge thrust between the generations. Once children are taught to accept homosexuality, what are they to make of their parents' earlier opposition? In other words, parents of Judeo-Christian morality have only two choices: We must either firmly express our beliefs and oppose the government using tax money to indoctrinate our children against our beliefs, or we must change our beliefs. But retaining our beliefs at home while allowing our children to be taught something else entirely at school is to vigorously drive a titanium wedge into the integrity of the family structure. Parents who believe homosexuality is wrong but who allow their children to be taught otherwise at school will be considered ancient relics and altogether dispensable as mentors and guides to the future.

There is also likely to be an economic impact. Countless decent Americans, reluctant to see themselves as "discriminatory," have been unknowingly conscripted into the radical agenda of homosexuality. Next up is the program to force both the private and public sector to treat "domestic partners" as spouses. Countless Americans who asked themselves what could be so bad about letting each person make his own personal choice are beginning to sense that perhaps there is an impact that may reach into almost everyone's pocket. San Francisco embarked upon the interesting experiment of insisting that any company hoping to do business with or in the city of San Francisco adopt the domestic-partner approach to various employment benefits. United Airlines was invited to shift its operations out of San Francisco unless it modified its policy in this regard. United Airlines has shown that its fiscal stability could not withstand this dramatic expansion of its benefits package. As of the time of writing, United Airlines is taking a "let's wait it out" approach. By implementing one study after another, they are hoping that the crocodile can be kept happy by eating other victims.

The Salvation Army, on the other hand, chose to abandon their San Francisco operation rather than submit to such an abuse of municipal authority. As a religiously inspired organization, it would not allow political correctness to force it to act against its principles. (To the embarrassment of many Catholics, the church did not take an equally firm stand.) So much for the vaunted liberal concern for the poor and homeless. Did the

Salvation Army offer a warm meal and a helping hand to the poorest and weakest members of society? Tough luck. Close them down if they fail to accept and operate by homosexual doctrine.

Interestingly enough, during this homosexual assault on American corporations and their shareholders, few business leaders have dared to voice their concerns for the record. Even if their personal religious beliefs as well as their business experience tell them that the domestic partnership view of benefits is a bad idea, they have been intimidated into silence. This almost takes the form of a religious dogma forced onto the skeptics. In exactly the same way that the church was said to have forced Galileo to renounce his belief in a heliocentric solar system, today's free thinkers are being forced to abandon their belief that homosexuality is not necessarily good for society. Criticizing the strong-arm tactics of the homosexual agenda could be devastating to the well-being of a company's shareholders. Boycotts are just the beginning. From there it rapidly progresses to harrassment, slander, and intimidation of corporate leadership. It is no wonder that with few exceptions, businesses as well as city, state and federal governments have buckled to the unreasonable special-interest demands. Religious fanatics such as today's secularists show little mercy for the free-thinking infidel.

MORAL CLARITY NEEDED

Once again we are faced with the tug-of-war. With no Judeo-Christian basis to our view of right and wrong, with no moral center, it is indeed tough to find grounds to oppose homosexuality. If two men or two women are desperate to publicly affirm their love, it's only right that we allow them to do so, even if it impacts society as a whole. Another expense is just the reasonable cost of doing business in an open, loving, and compassionate environment. Only the telescope of Judeo-Christian values reveals storm clouds on the horizon. Accommodating today's demands of the homosexual political agenda may be no more than an inconvenient expense. Once the storm hits and threatens to sink the ship of state, it is too late to batten down the hatches.

Any attempt to turn back this agenda of citizen-funded homosexual rights will fail without a religiously founded moral argument. If our only argument against a rapidly expanding world of homosexuality is that it will cost money, we will fail. Americans are accustomed to "principle" costing money, and ironically the pro-homosexual crowd has twisted their cause into the "morally right thing to do." After all, the economic argument was used to convince the country that slavery was necessary. Freeing the slaves was the right thing to do no matter what the cost. Discrimination is wrong; those who reject homosexuality are discriminatory; therefore, those who reject homosexuality are wrong. We must repress and correct this wrong, even if it costs money.

The Left will refute all other arguments as well, insisting that prejudice and hatred will cause the problems, rather than homosexuality. We can only challenge homosexuality on the basis of religious faith. Some things are wrong simply because God said so. In this respect it is similar to another boundary which I trust will not be breached anytime soon (although who can tell what delightful treats the modernists have in store for America once the homosexuality battle is as won as the abortion battle?). That boundary is incest. What if society's next step is to scorn those who express revulsion over incest? What will we use then to defend our traditional outlook? Some will cry out that incest is too dangerous on account of genetic problems likely to appear in offspring. Others will denounce incest in terms of potential psychological damage to its practitioners. These and other protests are meaningless unless we are willing to state a simple truth: Incest is prohibited by the God of Abraham, Isaac, and Jacob as recorded in His Bible. While it would not surprise us to hear that a practice forbidden by our God has the capacity to harm His children, we refrain, not because of the potential harm but because of the prohibition. Thus, even if genetic repair becomes available, we still consider incest to be a sin. Even if skilled psychologists develop the ability to immunize people against the psychic damage incest can cause, we still refrain because it is wrong. Period. End of story.

Without this kind of moral clarity, we will be pushed back from each line in the sand that we draw. We will vainly attempt to persuade ourselves that each retreat is really a proud defense as we draw a new line in the sand forty yards back from the old one. In time, the new line comes under attack and since we lack the only ammunition that is still dry, namely a moral center based on God's commands to His children, we finally abandon that line, too. And the game continues, with one side consistently winning all the big battles while the other side reassures itself that the economy is doing just fine.

In this way, even great civilizations perish.

CHAPTER THIRTY-THREE

IS HISTORY
REPEATING ITSELF?

SOMEHOW, LIBERATING OURSELVES FROM THE CONFINES OF RELIGION HAS NOT DELIVERED THE NIRVANA WE WERE PROMISED.

Historian Will Durant, in *A History of Roman Civilization*, points out some fascinating elements of the collapse of the once great, seemingly invincible Roman Empire. Toward the end of its horrifying descent into oblivion, it was briefly propped up by a return to those values that endure. It was too late. Secularism was so entrenched that the effort to instill sanity was soon rejected by the intelligentsia. Still, the experiment shows us that decline can be halted if the will is really there. I believe that America's religious conservatives possess both the vision and the will. Although Rome soon after became a footnote to history, America can step back from the brink and endure.

In the third century, emperor Marcus Aurelius Severus Alexander made the Roman Empire flourish and prosper for the last time. He recommended that the Roman people embrace and live by the morals of the Jews and the Christians. He frequently quoted the Judeo-Christian counsel, "What you do not wish a man to do to you, do not do to him," and had it engraved on the walls of his palace and on many public buildings. He assumed a severe censorship over public morals and ordered the arrest of prostitutes and the deportation of homosexuals. He reduced taxes, forced down interest rates and loaned money to the poor to enable them to purchase and own land.

He didn't last very long. His enemies derisively referred to him as "head of the synagogue," and soon "The majority of the industrial establishments in Italy were brought under the control of the state. Butchers, bakers, masons, builders, glassblowers, iron workers, engravers were all ruled by detailed government regulations."[1]

Derision of morality. Excessive government regulation. Sounds like yesterday's headlines, doesn't it? But it all happened seventeen hundred years ago to the greatest empire in world history—an empire which had just abandoned principles of social organization congruent with Judeo-Christian thought.

SOUND FAMILIAR?

By the beginning of the fourth century, the empire had instituted price and wage controls, effectively eliminating people's ability to trade freely with one another. Says Durant: "This edict was until our own time the most famous example of an attempt to replace economic laws by governmental decrees. Its failure was rapid and complete."[2]

The weakness of this managed economy lay in its administrative cost, Durant observes. He adds that the required bureaucracy was so extensive that some estimates pin its size at half the population.

To support this bureaucracy as well as the "dole," (the traditional name for a system that took money from some citizens to give to others), taxation rose to unprecedented levels. Since most taxpayers sought to evade taxes, the state organized a special force of revenue police to examine every man's property and income and exact severe penalties for evasion. Durant makes the point that this was not because citizens were evil; it was because a government that had lost its moral soul had become the enemy.

In a chapter entitled "Why Rome Fell," Durant writes that a great civilization is not conquered from without until it has destroyed itself within. I am no historian but I am fascinated by the similarities between our own times and those described by Will Durant. Excessive regulation, excessive government size and intrusion, and excessive and abusive taxation policies were only the tip of the iceberg. The essential causes of Rome's decline lay in her people, her morals, her bureaucratic despotism, her stifling taxes, and fall in population. Sexual excesses may have reduced human fertility. Contraception, abortion and infanticide had a dysgenic as well as a numerical effect. The dole weakened the poor and luxury weakened the rich. Immigration brought together a hundred cultures whose differences rubbed themselves out into indifference. Moral and aesthetic standards were lowered by the magnetism of the mass and sexual "freedom" ran riot while political liberty decayed. Government no longer attracted first-rate men.

ONLY ONE WAY WORKS

As we have seen, it is impossible for a culture, or even a family, to equally emphasize two different philosophic approaches. One has to decide which approach is more important; great consequence will attend that decision. For instance, we either believe it more important that children learn to honor, respect, and serve adults, or we believe the reverse. Judeo-Christian thought follows the Ten Commandments, one of which instructs children to behave in very specific ways toward their parents. It is hardly an accident that, as was done during the final years of the old Roman Empire, we today emphasize what adult society must do "for the children." In spite of good intentions, when we inverted God's design of a child's obligation to his parents by emphasizing the child's right to do virtually whatever he pleases, we began an almost irreversible assault on the family's integrity—and on the souls of our children.

How should we require children to behave? Remember our fantasy island a few chapters back? Let us revisit that island, a place where no deity ever proclaimed "Honor your father and mother." Without a Fifth Commandment in their national subconscious, will island children revere their parents? There are no commandments for things we would naturally do such as "Thou shalt eat anything thou wants," or "Thou shalt breathe frequently." Our thought experiment suggests that without the Fifth Commandment it would probably not occur to children to honor their parents. In fact, we all remember how much easier it was to appreciate the parents of a friend more than our own. We can all remember our childhood conviction that other children seemed to be mysteriously blessed by parents ever so much more understanding and reasonable than our own. That is part of the seductive propensity for error built into the human nature; it is probably also the reason God gave us the Fifth Commandment.

Now travel back to real-life America and observe the sad cityscapes peopled by individuals who have utterly severed their links to religion. It is hardly necessary to point out how much better are intergenerational relationships in religious neighborhoods. In areas where the men have abandoned the church while the women have maintained its importance, there remains a strong relationship between grandmothers and their grandchildren. There are those who are so reluctant to concede the tragic failure of secularism that they vainly seek other explanations to account for the correlation between religious affiliation and family structural stability. This exercise is futile because a moment's reflection reveals that the "other factors" so eagerly pounced upon, such as education, income and parental responsibility, are themselves consequences of religiously informed values.

We can examine trends in those parts of our society that jettisoned Judeo-Christian guidance more than a generation ago. For example, atheist regimes, most notably communist tyrannies, almost always oppose any special treatment of the parent-child relationship; Soviet Russia specialized in training children to rat on their parents. The hero of the Young Pioneers (the Russian equivalent to the Boy Scouts), was a youngster called Pavlik Morozov, whose parents were murdered by Stalin after young Pavlik betrayed them for not turning in all the family's food. They were behaving like parents, trying to insure his survival rather than patriotically starving along with the rest of the Russian farmers. Pavlik, however, had not been trained to act like a son, so he betrayed his parents to the state. To the communists, he was a model for other children to emulate.

Likewise, living in Africa at the time, I well recall that African graduates of Moscow's revolutionary Lumumba University were instructed to kill a parent upon their return to Africa. This proved that they were "good communists," and had outgrown family and tribal loyalty. Even during the early days of Israel, as the devoted Zionist, Hollywood playwright Ben Hecht sadly recalled, the Jewish defense force, the *Haganah,* urged youngsters to turn their parents in for associating with the *Palmach,* a rival organization. In our own American society, there have recently been lectures in public schools that encourage children to turn to the government if they have a problem with their parents.

The further to the secular Left the ideologue, the less comfortable he is with the notion that a man loves his own children more than he loves anyone else's, or that children owe their parents more than they owe society at large.

LARGESS DOESN'T NECESSARILY YIELD RESPECT

There is another argument people raise to explain spontaneous arousal of filial devotion. The contention is that since human young are dependent on their parents longer than any other species, they will become more attached. Being cared for will invoke such gratitude in the young recipients of parental benevolence that affection and respect toward parents results automatically. If it were true that largess always generates gratitude and respect in the hearts of the recipients, then those on welfare would constitute the single most grateful and patriotic segment of American society. "Beverly Hills" children, a metaphor for spoiled American children who have only to ask before they are given material things, should be more devoted to their parents and more filled with gratitude than children from more normal homes. As most people with any life experience know, too much giving frequently causes bitterness and resentment, not gratitude. Since it is almost impossible to adequately repay parents for all they have done, the most natural of childhood sentiments is a certain resentment. For this reason, many therapists today earn fine livings listening to patients blame their parents for their own failures. Once again, the Fifth Commandment denies us that indulgence. Instead, it demands from us a life-long loyalty to our parents. Children become truly devoted to their parents only through religious instruction and example.

The two sides of the issue are very clear. The traditionalist believes parents are to children what God is to adults: someone who is both loving and firm. Someone who provides, but also demands. Someone who rewards, but also punishes. Above all, someone who directs you in how to live your life. Thus in the Orthodox Jewish liturgy we have phrases such as "Our Father, our King." Honoring father and mother is placed on a par with honoring God. God declines to place His Presence in any place where parents are not honored, reports the Talmud, the authoritative source for the oral Jewish tradition. The reason is obvious. Anyone incapable of one practice will surely also be incapable of the other.

Sadly, even when parents want to do the right thing, it is difficult. We have created a system that makes it increasingly difficult for parents to raise their children with a traditional view of right and wrong. Parents who, in good faith, assumed it was safe to hand over to government the responsibility of raising their children are discovering that they have lost their children.

THE GENERATIONAL DECLINE OF FAITH

What is the long and winding path that leads from rejection of religion to societal downfall? It is a path that can wind on for as long as four generations, though seldom much longer. Once again, individual families don't necessarily fit the pattern. You need large numbers to see the results. Typically the first generation is raised religiously and traditionally. Its marriages are strong and its home life derives the benefit of the early upbringing of its parents. When they grow and raise their own children it is often with higher emphasis on economic success than on values. Religion becomes more a question of church or synagogue affiliation than daily practice. Without proper grounding in biblical ways, these children are dramatically affected by the university or college they attend. Secularism becomes the religion of the "enlightened." Not surprisingly, periods of intergenerational alienation occur, often caused by the children's choice of mate and lifestyle. Eventually these children have children, and it is this next generation (the "grandchildren") that pays the price for the first steps away from God taken by their "grandparents."

Think of our own times. Great-grandparents or grandparents were usually immigrants from one "old country" or another. Alternatively they might have been farming pioneers or struggled in some way to build their families. However, for them there was always one unwavering constant: their faith. If Jewish, that generation observed the Sabbath and would sooner have died than eaten non-kosher food. For Christians there were different non-negotiable variables. Even on the Oregon Trail, for example, valiant attempts were made not to travel on Sundays. Mistakenly, parents assumed that goodness never had to be learned, that children of good parents would automatically grow up to be good people.

Confident that this was so, they chiefly concerned themselves with getting their children onto the escalator of success. Often that meant sacrifice to gain an education for as many of their children as possible. Those young people achieved success and, because of the homes in which they were raised, grew up to be decent and productive people. However, they saw little connection between godliness and goodness; they certainly did not realize that they were only good and decent because they were raised in the presence of God.

Their children (the "grandchildren") now grew up during the permissive 1960s and 1970s. Not having had the advantage of growing up in a godly environment, they more easily fell victim to the mood of the times. The piety of their grandparents was forgotten as they rebelled against what they felt was the middle-class meaninglessness of their parents' lives. They were alienated from the simple faith and piety of their grandparents, and they rejected the basic but unrooted decency of their parents who had lived through World War II.

Inexplicably, this generation felt as if they lacked certain tools for life. They certainly enjoyed some degree of affluence. They were educated, and they had no shortage of contemporary causes to devote themselves to. But they had no idea of how to commit to or how to maintain a marriage. Furthermore, seeing no link between God and a meaningful life, they considered all lifestyles to be equally valid and functional. Today, *their* children have multiple sexual encounters by their midteens, their children have rising suicide rates, and their children live with the constant threat of callous violence in school or on the street.

Somehow, liberating ourselves from the confines of religion has not delivered the nirvana we were promised.

Family relationships, obligations and responsibilities transcend anything that could possibly be the business of the state. The old adage, "The family that prays together stays together," may well be true. But my chief point here is that successful societies always regard the family as their chief building block. Therefore, the adherence to certain timeless, fundamental principles of strong families—principles which happen to have their philosophical and intellectual origins in God—are necessary for societies to survive and thrive.

CHAPTER THIRTY-FOUR

GOD AND ECONOMICS 101

THE WORLD STILL AWAITS A SOCIETY THAT HAS EMBRACED ATHEISM AND ALSO OPERATES A SUCCESSFUL FREE MARKET.

L et's return to our island community, the land without God or the Bible or a Judeo-Christian heritage, to see whether its citizens enjoy economic prosperity. Doing so may help us see and appreciate the stability and value our Judeo-Christian underpinnings have brought to America's economy and the importance of maintaining those fundamental principles.

What kind of monetary system does our fantasy island have? While our observations will probably reveal the islanders bartering with one another, it is less certain that they will make the leap of assigning value to discs of metal. Since that failed to happen in many parts of the real world that were isolated from Bible-based tradition, we can posit that our island descendants may also not make the leap from barter to coins and capital. Why should they do so? At first blush it is illogical. Why would any man relinquish the products of his time and energy in exchange for metal discs or colored pieces of paper? Just imagine the response of a farmer to the suggestion that he hand over his hard-earned harvest to some stranger who will hand him something he can neither eat nor use to shelter his family. The aspiring capitalist would try to persuade the farmer that everything will work out just fine. He would try to assure him that whenever he, the farmer, requires goods (like shoes for his wife) or services (such as someone to repair his roof), the vendor will gladly accept the same metallic discs and colored scraps of paper in payment. It is no wonder that barter survived for so long. Who would want to be the first farmer foolish enough to make such a transaction?

GOD AND FREE-MARKET ECONOMIES

Can it be that just as the seven-day week is the product of a collective memory of a biblical tradition, so too is money? The oral transmission, handed down from Moses, tells us an amazing thing. Early on in the history of the Jewish people, the patriarch Jacob entered the city of Shechem. The Bible tells us that he was *vayiCHAN* in that city. According to Jewish tradition that means Jacob established a marketplace and currency there. The root, *chn* (in Hebrew, vowels are exterior to the words themselves) is also the root of the Hebrew word for "store" and for a market-based economy. So a *chanut* is a shop, a *chenvani* a storekeeper. This word is not only the etymological origin for the English words "coin" and "gain" but also for the Chinese word for "coin," *ch'ien,* and similar words in many other languages. What strikes us as so unusual about this verb is that the Bible has already introduced us to a noun with the same root. As we said in a previous chapter, all Hebrew words that share a root must be related. We must then take seriously the fact that the earlier word, *CHeN,* means God's favor. In other words, there is a relationship between currency and God's favor. What is it about the free market that would make it find favor in God's eye, as well as be a favor that He bestowed on mankind?

The current popular image suggests that one must choose between being spiritual, like Mother Teresa, or involved in commerce, like Bill Gates. In reality, Mother Teresa was well aware that money is of great help to accomplish her goal of caring for human beings, while Bill Gates's enterprise allows humans to interact more effectively, a very spiritual act.

All human activities can be located somewhere on the spectrum that is anchored at one end by spirituality and at the other by physicality. Praying is near the spiritual end; reading and writing, composing music and making tools might be its neighbors. As the source of great sensual pleasure and of new life, sex might be somewhere near midspectrum, while eating and all other bodily functions belong over toward the physical end. Where do commercial transactions fit on the spectrum? When a man exchanges coins in his pocket for goods he desires, is he performing a physical act or a spiritual one?

One way of identifying a spiritual act is by determining whether a chimpanzee would understand the action. This is because God endowed man with His spirit and so distinguished between man and chimpanzee. When I return home from work and slump into a comfortable armchair, my pet primate undoubtedly sympathizes. As I move to the dinner table and begin eating, he certainly knows what is going on. When I open a newspaper, however, and hold it motionless before my face for twenty minutes, he becomes quite confused. He cannot relate to the pleasure I gain from that piece of paper.

Another criterion for a spiritual act is whether the action can be replicated by a machine. If a human soul is indispensable for a certain process, that process is at least partially spiritual. Music can inspire the soul in man so that he marches off to war or finds a lump in his throat. No machine will choke up upon hearing Mozart's *Eine Kleine Nachtmusik*. No machine exhibits loyalty or can even test whether an individual possesses that quality. Loyalty is a spiritual characteristic.

What of a business transaction? Does it belong on the spiritual or physical side of the spectrum? A chimpanzee would not have the slightest idea of what is transpiring between proprietor and customer at the counter of a store. He can relate very well to grabbing a banana from someone; he can even understand proffering that banana to his offspring. He may imitate someone exchanging metal disks for bananas, but he cannot intellectually initiate and carry through a business deal. Neither do machines exist that can independently effect a transaction. They cannot predict whether a customer will buy something or for how much. Economic exchange takes place only after two thinking human beings will it. The process is spiritual.

Thus, atheism and business are not natural allies. One would have supposed that a philosophy of secular humanism, recognizing no authority, would be naturally drawn to the world of money and power. One would have expected the political Left to excuse what it calls the "greed" of capitalism and to recognize it as nothing other than Darwinian law applied to the life of modern man. Yet, this is not possible; something as spiritual as commerce simply cannot coexist with socialism. The atheist himself recognizes that, to be true to his credo, he must reject the free market because it is appointed by a God in whom he does not believe. The world still awaits a society that has embraced atheism and also operates a successful free market. That this has not happened is no coincidence, but rather a consequence of the spiritual nature of money.

It is therefore not surprising that economics used to be a field of study that belonged with religion and theology. Adam Smith as well as many other eighteenth century economists were religious philosophers before they were economists. Smith wrote *Theory of Moral Sentiments* before he wrote *Wealth of Nations*. When the great universities moved the study of economics from their religion to their science departments, they were actually driving a wedge between capitalism and the moral arguments and spiritual dimensions that underpin its validity. After all, whether a man dissipates his money frivolously or invests it wisely, whether he hoards it or shares it with those less fortunate, and whether he bends rules to earn it depend on his character and on his moral makeup. No wonder that the science that seeks to predict these things, economics, is known as the dismal science. How men and women relate to money depends mostly on the state of their spirit.

OUR DAILY REMINDER

So it is in remarkable harmony with biblical insight that Americans take pride in being the only country in the world to place "In God We Trust" upon our currency. Imagine telling someone who had never visited America that somewhere in our country we engrave the motto "In God We Trust," that we do this in such a way and with such repetition that each American has the opportunity to read those inspiring words several times each day. We then ask our unsuspecting friend to guess where on the American landscape those words are to be found. Wouldn't most intelligent people guess that the phrase is to be found on the walls of churches where it obviously belongs? Yet both the American and Jewish view refutes this common-sense approach. We say that people at worship are already exquisitely attuned to their trust in God. It is precisely during the time we are conducting commercial transactions that we need reminding of this basic fact. Where better to place "In God We Trust" than on the very instruments of our economic creativity, our currency? It additionally reminds us that the only reason for that early farmer to accept these spiritual symbols of faith in return for his entire harvest is because he is part of a community of faith that assures him that those same coins will be accepted by whomever he trades with in the future. That assurance could only have been imparted to people by religious faith.

Wherever the Bible has served as the primary source of wisdom, people have understood the proper role of gold and silver. Both are mentioned extensively in the Bible as having intrinsic value. While shiny beads, salt, or mirrors were at one time or another routinely utilized in trade, they no longer are. Gold and silver have retained their worth. Civilizations based on the Bible learned how to greatly expand trade, and therefore wealth, by employing precious metals as an exchange medium. Naturally, these peoples enjoyed a gigantic head start over those who had to discover this all by trial and error.

By and large, religious people are comfortable with a monetary role for gold. For one thing, it has the capacity to help keep government honest by serving as an inflation alarm bell. Not surprisingly, governments that have deliberately inflated the currency as an underhanded way to impose new taxation generally tried and sometimes succeeded in making gold illegal or at least difficult for citizens to own. Without computers and with a vast geographical area to administer, the British empire kept inflation at bay for over one hundred years. It is said that the Bank of England simply used the price of gold on the merchant streets of London as a barometer to indicate when it was safe for the mint to print currency. People who reject the Judeo-Christian vision of monetary stability do not see why one metal should be granted power over their desire to sometimes ignore fiscal realities. To me it is no mystery. Gold is the very first metal mentioned in the Bible, which tells me (just as it told my earliest ancestors) that gold was imbued by God with a special role in human affairs. It was a special and desirable substance and could serve as a means of exchange. This would assist God's plan for humanity by making us obsessive about discovering and supplying the wants of our neighbors in order to obtain some of that gold. It is no surprise that secularism detests this special role for gold as it detests the freedom from centralized tyranny that gold can offer all people.

CHAPTER THIRTY-FIVE

THE JUDEO-CHRISTIAN ROLE IN AMERICA'S PROSPERITY

THE CHARACTER TRAITS OF BOTH JUDAISM AND CHRISTIANITY ARE THE VERY QUALITIES THAT BEST PREPARE PEOPLE FOR EFFECTIVE ROLES IN COMMERCE.

What other principles of the Judeo-Christian tradition have allowed societies that adopted them to flourish economically? Well, the individual character traits that both Judaism and Christianity promote are the very qualities that best prepare people for effective roles in commerce. Indeed, America's prosperity owes a deep debt of gratitude to those who have lived by biblical, traditional values in the marketplace.

INTEGRITY

I do not think I am going too far to say that all things being equal, any employer will gain from hiring someone strongly influenced by Judeo-Christian tradition. At any rate, whenever I board a jetliner and watch the last-minute engine and airframe checks being done by the maintenance people, I certainly hope that there is a religious ethic guiding those engineers. Am I saying that atheists can never have integrity? Of course not. Atheists can have integrity, but a society needs to rely on a more reliable system than trusting everyone to want to do the right thing. The USSR tried to function as an atheistic economy and failed. In fact, Russian friends have told me that Russia was notorious for the frequency of its airplane accidents. While *Pravda* kept reports of the crashes out of the newspaper, Russians knew that flying was uncomfortable and dangerous. A society can never supervise an airline mechanic or anyone else's work so reliably that they must invariably do an outstanding job. Each supervisor would need a supervisor as well, in a grand hopeless pyramid scheme. Our system works because most Americans, whether church-going or not, still believe that God is watching their every action. At the very least, enough Americans still believe that there is such a thing as right and wrong for the system to work. Fudging airline maintenance records is wrong to most people even if they no longer necessarily agree that Scripture is our source for knowing what is right and wrong in the first place. For how much longer can America and its numerous vital systems survive if fundamentalist secularism continues to indoctrinate America into believing that there is no such thing as absolute right and wrong?

A friend of mine who flew in on a relief mission to the old Soviet Union following an earthquake told me that even new buildings collapsed, killing many. This was not because they did not know how to build to earthquake safe specifications. Officially, the buildings met all sorts of codes. However, each part of the construction team knew that the socialistic policies of the government made it impossible to survive without stealing. It was completely accepted that workers stole cement, paint, nails, and other items they could access. Inspectors accepted bribes to sign forms showing that work had been completed correctly, when in fact it hadn't.

When I speak of integrity I am referring to a person whose actions are consistent with his Judeo-Christian outlook. God's Word expects its recipients to exercise diligence, honesty, decency, fairness, and conscientiousness while forbidding sloth, dishonesty, indecency, unfairness, and sloppiness. Integrity is God's idea. Propagated by obedient Christians and Jews throughout the world, it is arguably the number-one asset in the effort of businesses and governments to make their economies stronger. That is why integrity is one of the most important assets of a system of ethical capitalism. It has certainly helped to build America's economic machine.

FAITH

But integrity is only part of the benefit package that often accompanies biblical faith in America. As mentioned earlier, one of the most important of these benefits is faith itself. Having faith accustoms people to making major commitments without assurance of success. Couples must marry without the help of a crystal ball that would predict all the ups and downs of their future together. Farmers plant and await crops that may or may not ripen. Investing capital, starting a new business, hiring new employees—all involve risk and require faith.

In fact, the very act of accepting metal discs or pieces of paper in exchange for a day of backbreaking labor requires enormous faith. To understand the true dimensions of that faith, observe how things change in its absence. ValuJet, an airline loved by Wall Street, provided economical air travel to select destinations. When one of their planes crashed into the Florida Everglades, the airline collapsed. Why should that have occurred when other airlines have sustained catastrophic accidents and survived? In the case of

ValuJet, the accident was widely perceived as symptomatic of general carelessness. There was a major loss of faith and the market responded. People stopped flying and investors withdrew their capital. When investors lose faith in markets, when depositors lose faith in banks, when citizens lose faith in the currency, economic disaster strikes.

But as long as faith is intact, people will accept intrinsically worthless paper or metal as payment for their goods and services. They do so in the belief that when they require some commodity, a vendor will in turn accept their little metal discs or scraps of paper. As long as the future remains uncertain, people who maintain Bible-inspired faith will always have a great advantage over those who do not—whether as spouses, farmers, or investors.

One of the Hebrew words for a businessman is *Ohmein,* which means "man of faith" and shares the same root with the liturgical "Amen." With no verifiable information that he will be successful selling his wares, the merchant nonetheless purchases inventory. He then delights in selling out his inventory, even vital commodities like food or clothing, in exchange for metal discs. Instead of despairing at how he will now feed and clothe his children, he has complete faith that whenever he wishes, there will be someone who will gladly sell him food or anything else for those very metal discs. This faith would be quite unfounded in many parts of the world in which stores are often without inventory and even food is scarce. Even people with money starve in those circumstances.

Were a businessman to trade on the basis of doubt and suspicion, he would contract little business at all. As we are reduced to a society that contracts deals using more and more legal documentation, our free-market economy is hindered, not helped. The dramatic increase we see in the litigiousness of American society is a consequence of the flight of faith—and a symptom of trouble ahead.

All of commerce and consequently much of human freedom depends on honest transactions conducted in good faith. This is what allows each of us to choose how to spend our energies, time and skills. It allows us to each set our own life priorities independent of any tyrant's control over our lives. But with no presumption of honesty and reliability, free commerce must soon collapse and be replaced by a dictatorial, socialistic economy. With no faith, there is no finance.

SERVICE WITH A SMILE

Judeo-Christian thought also inculcates in people the idea of service. This is a valuable mindset for the ambitious entrepreneur who must focus on filling other people's needs. If he focuses on his wants (accumulating money) rather than on what he can do for others, he will fail. Everybody wants money, but those who pursue it directly become either robbers or bumbling businessmen. The most conspicuous commercial successes are won by those who fill a need in such a way that transcends a customer's level of expectation.

Americans are unaccustomed to the surliness of storekeepers so common in social-ist countries. It is precisely a preoccupation with the needs of others that characterizes the successful entrepreneur. Concern for customers is the hallmark of a business profes-sional; his success is multiplied by the repeat business of customers who find him pleas-ant to deal with.

Not only must the businessman be gracious to his customers, but he also realizes that his employees are his most valuable asset. Recognizing them as spiritual beings, he must not only endeavor to compensate them fairly but also help them find transcendent meaning in their work. Jewish law prohibits an employer from instructing his worker to perform meaningless work. For example, he may not hire the worker to dig a hole one day, fill it the next and thereafter repeatedly dig it and refill it. This prohibition applies no matter how generous the pay may be, because such make-work leaves the worker with no sense of accomplishment and therefore, no sense of the value of his contribu-tion. (It also is extremely poor stewardship of a businessman's assets, a principle taught in both the Old and New Testaments.)

CHARITABLE GIVING

Judeo-Christian teachings that emphasize the virtue of charity would fit well into busi-ness school curricula. Giving charity trains us to loosen the tight grip many of us have on our funds. It encourages us to see the value in sharing our wealth. Indeed, abundant charitable giving makes for a healthy economy.

I once was a guest at a gathering of American evangelical philanthropists and was completely fascinated by how amazing and unique this was. I could think of no other country in the world in which a gathering of godly, wealthy people all shared a preoc-cupation with giving money away. Each year, this remarkable group of Christian mer-chants gave away, in the aggregate, sums larger than the gross domestic product of many of the member nations of the United Nations.

Multitudes of other Christians tithe their incomes to support their churches or para-church charities. Those who do not tithe give what they can. Many give far above a tithe amount. Religious Jews also tithe and give generously to help those in need.

But such generosity is not confined to just the religious. So successfully has this part of Judeo-Christian culture taken hold in America that giving is the done thing among nearly all the conspicuously successful. There are rich folks in almost every industrial-ized country today, but giving away large sums of money is a uniquely American activity. Some may argue that this is only on account of a tax code that allows deductions for charitable contributions. That is putting the cart before the horse. The tax code encour-ages gift giving as a reflection of American values; it does not cause those values, it only reflects them. Not surprisingly, as traditional religious ethics are weakening all sorts of organizations are finding that many of their benefactor's descendants are nowhere as generous as their parents and grandparents once were.

DEFERRED GRATIFICATION

Another Judeo-Christian trait which benefits those who practice capitalism is deferred gratification. The same person who defers sex until marriage and eating until a blessing has been said, finds it easier to practice saving and investing rather than giving in to impulse spending. One of the reasons America has been an economic powerhouse is our tendency to save and invest—both wise principles of biblical instruction—rather than spend and indulge.

However, in the past three and a half decades, our priorities have shifted to elevate the habit of consumer spending. We call it consumer spending because once that money is spent, the asset we receive in exchange does not last very long. Pretty soon we will have consumed it. It might be food, a movie ticket, or a fancy automobile. You might tell me that the fancy automobile is not consumed, it is parked there in the driveway for all to see. Wrong. The car may be parked there in the driveway, but the fancy part of the purchase is quickly dissipating with each passing day. The amount of money you spent for the fancy car over and above what you might have spent on a more basic form of transportation vanishes pretty much as soon as you drive out of the dealer's showroom. A major portion of the purchase price of that car was consumer spending.

Contrast that with saving one's money and starting a business with the accumulated capital. Not only has the money not vanished, it is now going to grow while it provides jobs for one group of people and goods or services for another group. As others outside the company invest their savings in the company, this additional capital provides more jobs and more goods or services, while providing the investor a return on investment that contributes to his own financial self-sufficiency. The more people who retire self-sufficient, the fewer people we will have to support with tax dollars. The fewer tax dollars confiscated from the people, the more dollars there are to go back into the economy. It is easy to see that a society made up mostly of thrifty citizens will rapidly outperform one made up of self-indulgent people.

In America, a family's net worth is very much tied to its cultural vision. A family that is future-oriented scrimps and saves for education and investment, while a family that is present-oriented tends to spend on consumer goods. It is no accident that common features of both traditional Judaism and Christianity include a dislike of debt, a scorning of luxury, and a desire to prepare and provide for the future. This has not only built strong families and eventually large family fortunes, it has also contributed to America's economic strength. It is a model worth emulating, regardless of one's religious persuasion.

INCUBATORS OF CAPITALISM

Returning to our earlier discussion of family, it is worth noting that in addition to being central to the Judeo-Christian tradition, families are also the best incubators of capitalism. Have you ever stopped to think how many poor and/or immigrant families have started with virtually nothing, worked together, and eventually built a fortune? Within such a family the young future business professional learns the value of faith in a dream combined with integrity, diligence, service, and reinvestment of capital. As so many in America's current immigration wave know, it is not wealth that produces family values, it is families that produce wealth.

For these reasons, the world still awaits a society that embraces atheism and also operates a successful free market. It will wait in futility. It is the embrace of Judeo-Christian principles that has allowed peoples to rise from poverty to prosperity.

CHAPTER THIRTY-SIX

THE JUDEO-CHRISTIAN MARKETPLACE

A POPULAR TACTIC USED BY CHAMPIONS OF THE WELFARE STATE IS TO SLANDER THOSE WHO HAVE WORKED DILIGENTLY FOR PERSONAL SUCCESS.

Western civilizations based on the Bible have flourished economically because they understood the role of private property and the role of the law in protecting that property.

Jewish law, extracted from the Bible, imposes 613 rules upon Jews. A disproportionate number of those laws relate to property and money. In fact, no area of law is given as much attention in the Torah as the area dealing with free-market transactions between free and independent citizens. Of the 613 commandments presented in the Torah, only twenty-six apply to that well-known bastion of Jewish observance, kosher food. But for teaching us how to interact with one another during commercial transactions, the Torah offers no fewer than 120 different laws.

The anti-Semite will claim that this is due to the greediness and rapacity of the Jew, but looking at the laws reveals otherwise. Many are instructions for giving charity, others for honest dealing in weights and measures. God recognized the capacity for dishonesty and immorality in the marketplace. He also understood the danger of envy and how it makes socialism look attractive, so many of the laws protect private property and the right of individuals to make contracts between themselves, free of government intrusion such as minimum wage legislation. The Bible is explicit not only about rules governing how an employer may treat an employee, but also on the obligation of an employee to deliver value for his salary. Jewish law frowns on nine-year-olds working in the coal mine and on the government forcing employers to pay a certain minimum salary.

GOD AND PROPERTY OWNERSHIP

Let us be absolutely clear about this. The view as expressed throughout Scripture and all of Jewish theological and moral writing of the past two millennia, unapologetically endorses private property rights. Throughout the eighteenth and nineteenth centuries most churches accepted this principle. As we saw earlier, the Bible records how Abraham purchased a family burial site from Ephron. Its borders were then precisely recorded and it remained in the possession of Abraham's descendants. As the Jews entered the promised land, the land was divided and apportioned to individual families. No part of the holy land was retained by the government. Mount Moriah, the site of the Temple, was reserved as God's dwelling; nobody had the right to keep anyone else away from there. From Mount Moriah came the concept of sanctuary, for it belonged to God, not to the king or to the government.

All the numerous laws of tithing and charity presuppose private property. It is no great moral challenge to give away property that does not belong to you. Every few years a politician who calls for increased taxation to fight the war on poverty is shown to be miserly in his personal charitable giving. Extensive bodies of biblical law also deal with fences between adjoining private properties, damage done by one person's possessions to those of another, and exactly how voluntary trades are to take place. There is no hint of a suggestion anywhere that owning property is inherently questionable. On the contrary, there is the recognition that anything owned by "everybody" is actually owned by nobody. It will be neglected and it will decay.

One of the conspicuous themes around which observance of the Jewish Sabbath is structured is the distinction between property owned by private citizens and public property such as parks and streets. In order to drive home the difference, observant Jews refrain, on Saturdays, from carrying anything at all across a border separating private from public. Scripture records how even kings were severely punished when they seized property that belonged to citizens.

AN EXPERIMENT IN SUBSERVIENCE

We can see the importance of private property ownership in the Judeo-Christian tradition and the early American commitment to the Judeo-Christian ideal. Now think of the philosophy that drives the bureaucrats of the welfare state. Think of the large developments of drab identical blocks of hundreds of apartments that we call public housing but which mostly resemble their cousins in Moscow and other old iron curtain cities.

Were low-income Americans granted ownership of these apartments? Of course not. And not surprisingly, the apartments deteriorated quickly. No distinction was made between those who had a value system but little money, and those who had no money and never would have, because they lacked a value system. By defining people only through a material lens—earning less than a certain amount—those who truly needed a hand up were forced to live with those who only wished to destroy. Too often, public housing, with its physical dangers and associated poor public schools, kept those who wanted to better themselves in a state of perpetual subservience and tenancy. It is little wonder that, twenty or thirty years later, more and more cities have had to level such projects in embarrassed admission that the welfare state is a disastrous answer to the cycle of poverty.

Religiously inspired people try to grant freedom and independence to all, through many church and faith-based projects that provide a means of acquiring food and housing, medical assistance, a job, and ultimately, property of their own. Not surprisingly private programs, like Habitat for Humanity, which screens applicants and demands work from participants, have wonderful results. The state of Michigan likewise found that welfare recipients were more successful at getting off and staying off of welfare when mentored by church members. At the other end of the tug-of-war rope, bureaucrats retain their grip on power by enslaving people to the welfare system. It takes a religious worldview to recognize the wisdom of private ownership of all property. The welfare state of America has bought into this misguided ethic, and we have reaped the consequences. The welfare state of America has bought into this misguided ethic, and we have reaped the consequences. It is a tragic error for those who think of themselves as religious, to condone today's welfare system.

THE VIEW FROM THE ZOO

If there is one political reality to be learned from the past three decades it is that public perception shapes real-life outcomes. One popular tactic used by champions of the welfare state is to slander those who have worked diligently for their success. The slander has worked, leading to a public perception that the rich got that way by stealing from the poor. This perception includes the notion that wealth-producing activities are unseemly and that free-market economic activity causes, rather than cures, poverty. Just as it is wrong for a zookeeper to allow one elephant to eat considerably more than another, so it must be wrong for the government to allow one human or company to acquire or possess significantly more than another.

This view is consistent, of course, with the Leftist view that humans are merely another species of animal. Secularists believe, if they stop to actually think about it, that humans contribute little or nothing to the satisfying of their needs. Like animals, they can only exist on what is already available. In other words, humans consume. Therefore, isn't it only proper of our Beltway zookeepers to equalize distribution and consumption? Unfortunately, our nation's politically correct (but morally incorrect) answer is to take from those who seem to have too much and redistribute the proceeds to those who seem to have too little, just as a responsible zookeeper would do.

In the view of government bureaucrats, entrepreneurs who create and market new technology and products in our country are very smart animals, but animals nonetheless. By some form of skullduggery, under cover of darkness while the zookeepers were not watching, these entrepreneurs somehow seized more than their "fair" share. They are obviously depriving others of that to which they are entitled. After all, there are only so many bones, fish and pieces of meat available in the keepers' bucket.

Thus our government zookeepers attempt to repair their mistakes by the vigilant taxation and prosecution of companies which have been "too" successful. To gain votes, politicians often encourage those who have made self-destructive decisions in their lives to feel scorn for those who deployed self-discipline to become productive. There is no better way than to exhibit a revulsion for what I call ethical capitalism. Today we hear people referring to the 1980s as a period of moral depravity. These individuals consider the miracle of economic enterprise to be the human equivalent of dogs fighting over a bone.

When America followed the biblical blueprint, it was clear that buying, selling, owning property, and being successful in business should evoke no psychological discomfort. Economic activity is another way in which we satisfyingly distance ourselves from the animal kingdom and justify our humanity.

But if we continue to accept the godless alternative, then indeed we do not differ in kind from monkeys or other animals, only in degree. Animals do not create wealth, they merely seize the commodities they need; people obviously do the same. They may employ more sophisticated methods like bonds, debentures, taxation, and penalization of success, but it is seizing nonetheless. Is it merely coincidence that those who most strongly advance evolution as the one and only approach to our origins are also those who most strongly oppose the free market?

Clearly, morally sensitive people must decry this activity. If God created us and touched us with His abilities, then we are qualitatively different from animals. Our ability to speak and to create is unique. Therefore, animals plunder but people profit; the creation of wealth is an expression of our godly origins.

THE HIDDEN MEANING OF THE MARKETPLACE

The marketplace demonstrates how humans relate to each other differently than animals. A dog or a deer sees another dog or deer as something to fight and dominate. The fight will usually be over something quite tangible like territory, females, or prestige. Furthermore, the fight will most likely be a rather lonely ordeal since neither antagonist expects nor receives any assistance from other males in his group. By contrast, a man in the marketplace, living by the Judeo-Christian ethic, views another man in terms of potential mutual benefit. He asks himself the beautiful question that fuels all of commercial enterprise: What can we do for one another? Perhaps he wants to hire me; perhaps he can do something for which I want to hire him. Perhaps he has something I wish to purchase or he might be a customer for my product. This line of inquiry emerges in all its nobility when one recognizes it as the only alternative to fighting.

A store or market is an amazing place. Where else do people voluntarily interact, leaving each happier than he was before? As Ayn Rand observed, one can extract performance from people in one of two ways: with a gun or with money. Most of us prefer the latter. No wonder God smiles upon the free and open marketplace.

CHAPTER THIRTY-SEVEN

A TAX POLICY
THAT MAKES SENSE

THE MODERNIST, EVER CONFIDENT THAT THE
FUTURE WILL EVENTUALLY DISPROVE THE PAST,
KEEPS ON EXPERIMENTING WITH TAX RATES.

What role should government play in collecting money from members of a society and using it for collective services? In other words, what about taxation? What are the specific and timeless principles expressed in the Bible several thousand years ago? What wisdom is contained in ancient texts revered by tens of millions of Jews and Christians? How have we veered from that biblically ordained path?

The first biblical mention of taxation comes in Genesis 41. Bewildered by disturbing dreams of skinny cows eating fat cows and withered stalks of corn, the Egyptian pharaoh unsuccessfully seeks explanations from his courtiers. Finally his butler remembers Joseph, a Hebrew who has been unjustly imprisoned for alleged sexual harassment. Brought before Pharaoh, Joseph interprets the king's dreams as God's forewarning of seven years of plenty followed by seven years of famine.

A PLAN THAT WORKS

Not content simply to interpret the dream, Joseph recommends applying a tax upon the Egyptian economy during its forthcoming seven years of plenty: "Let Pharaoh appoint officers over the land and collect a fifth part during the seven years of plenty." He specifically recommends a figure of 20 percent as the total tax on the country's gross domestic product. Although Joseph was an outsider to Pharaoh's court, an alien ex-convict, his counsel made sense to Pharaoh. Even more surprisingly, "the thing was good in the eyes of all his servants."

It stretches credibility that a Jewish outsider's recommendation to tax an entire country should please the Egyptian monarch. That his subjects also found the recommendation pleasing can mean only one thing: The tax rate they were anticipating, reports Talmudic tradition, was considerably higher than Joseph's 20 percent. Not only were they relieved, but the thought of being able to retain 80 percent of the fruits of their labors threw them into their work with renewed enthusiasm and energy. The Bible reports that Pharaoh was so impressed by Joseph's plan that he empowered the Hebrew to supervise its implementation. The Egyptians were invigorated and, as one would expect, their economy thrived. Their storehouses were full when, as Joseph had predicted, seven years of famine came upon them.

Even though the affluent Egyptians might well have accepted a much higher tax rate because the revenue was to be for their own direct benefit during the later lean years, divine inspiration led Joseph to avoid this trap. In a move that is echoed in American law, Joseph also provided tax exemption for religious institutions. That is to say, land owned by the Egyptian priestly class was not taxed.

One can choose either to view this episode as simply belonging in a college's "Great Works of Literature" course, or to grasp its importance as a divine recommendation for government tax policy. Even when anticipating a long recession, let alone when in the very midst of one, we would be wise to cap tax rates at 20 percent. This is not so much a case of a "moral" tax rate as it is a case of a tax rate that works. Once again, God's rules *describe* reality instead of merely *proscribing* it.

THE BIBLE AND THE *WALL STREET JOURNAL*

This biblical perspective conforms almost precisely to the Crandall Pierce "High Rates, Low Rates—Same Yield" graph which the *Wall Street Journal* has published several times. This graph shows that Americans are willing to yield up to 20 percent of their aggregate labors for the common good. From 1960 to the present, during which time the top tax rate has fluctuated between 28 and 91 percent, figures reveal that revenue has barely shifted away from the 20 percent of Gross Domestic Product that one would expect.

The Crandall Pierce graph confirms what Joseph understood. The human soul, as well as national economies, rebel at taxation that exceeds 20 percent. It is thus not surprising that, in spite of wide variation in tax rates over the past three and a half decades, Americans have willingly paid in tax just as much of their Gross Domestic Product as the Egyptians did 3,500 years ago. When tax rates are too high, our nation's economy suffers and our people find loopholes to avoid paying. We will adjust our work, investment and spending patterns with the unsurprising result that, notwithstanding incessant government tampering, we pay exactly the 20 percent that Genesis 41 recommends.

Recognizing that government does fill certain legitimate public needs, and as such needs revenue, few plead for zero taxation. I constantly poll my lecture and radio audiences and seldom do people tell me that they favor ridiculously low levels of taxation. However, fervent secularists are unwilling to answer one very simple question: What figure do you feel it wrong to ask citizens to exceed as a tax rate? The fervent secularist does not rule out even 90 percent, as Britain's Labor Party has imposed from time to time when they have been in power. In theory, the true secularist actually believes that 100 percent would be appropriate for some citizens who they feel already have too much. Although ordinary, reasonable and religious folks feel that 10 percent is unrealistically low, they do not welcome 30, 40 or 50 percent tax rates. Certain instinctive reactions seem built into us. George Bernard Shaw once observed that even generous men are unwilling to share their wives. That has not changed in the ninety years since Shaw wrote it. Similarly, the fact that even generous men are unwilling to share more than 20 percent of their income is no stain on their characters but in fact underscores their wisdom in economic matters.

IGNORING THE LESSONS OF HISTORY

But the modernist, ever confident that the future will eventually disprove the past, keeps on experimenting with tax rates. And just as he thinks he has succeeded in getting the horse used to living on sawdust instead of oats, the horse disappoints him by dying, thereby ruining the experiment. Undaunted, and with secularism still his credo, the modernist prepares to try yet another theory.

"Whereas my father did burden you with a heavy yoke, I will add to your yoke," recklessly proclaimed King Solomon's son and heir, Rehoboam, as he raised tax rates. The first book of Kings describes how this announcement came after he "forsook the counsel of the older and more experienced men and took counsel with the young men who had grown up with him."

King Rehoboam then sent Adoram, the tax collector, to make good on his threat. "And all Israel stoned him with stones, so that he died.… Thus did Israel rebel against the house of David." It is important to note that this revolt was justified by Jewish law and supported by the prophets. The rebellion was not against the king's right to tax but rather against the excessiveness of the tax. It was originally sparked, explains nineteenth century Rabbi Meir ben Yechiel Michael, by the king's disregard for the taxpayers' sentiments toward the new rates.

In Rehoboam, the Bible previews what would be repeated by liberal politicians throughout history. In chapter 37 of his *Decline and Fall of the Roman Empire*, Edward Gibbon describes the assault on the church during the empire's final years, followed by "…the system of taxation, which fell like a hail-storm upon the land, like a devouring pestilence on its inhabitants."[1] How different American history might be if King George

III had listened to this warning. How different our history might be had our founding fathers not rebelled against Britain's excessive levels of taxation. But what will our future be if we ignore history now? Ours is not the first society to turn its back on the biblical outlook of its founders and suffer the inevitable economic penalty. Ancient Israel, the Roman Empire, and the British Empire are among dozens of examples of great cultures weakened by undisciplined politicians whose governments gorged on ever-increasing taxation of the populace.

The final word on taxation in the Hebrew Scriptures is found in Proverbs 12:24, which declares that "the hands of the diligent shall produce wealth but the lazy will be subject to taxation." According to the eleventh century Rabbi Solomon Yitzchaki, these words warn that excessive taxation hinders productivity and only comes to pass through the laziness and indifference of citizens who decline to resist the oppression. Resisting a government's instinct for excessive taxation requires vigilance and energy. If we fail to exert the necessary vigilance and energy, we shall only have ourselves to blame for the sad consequences.

CHAPTER THIRTY-EIGHT

THE RESENTMENT TAX

NOT ONLY IS THE INHERITANCE TAX IMMORAL,
IT ALSO DISCOURAGES INDIVIDUAL ENTERPRISE
AND THRIFT WHICH, IN TURN,
DAMAGES ECONOMIC PRODUCTIVITY.

Focusing on one specific tax may help shed light on the big picture of the difference between reasonable and economically healthy tax policies and unreasonable, damaging policies. Let's focus for a few moments on the inheritance tax.

The Bible, in the book of Numbers, is the source for the idea that children inherit from their parents. The notion that a king or a government should become the heir to all men is quite at odds with the biblical vision. I am confident that to whatever extent the Bible constitutes an instruction manual to how the world works, it informs us that severing or weakening the economic link between parents and children will wreak social as well as fiscal havoc on our society.

Would our hypothetical "island society" figure this out themselves? Remember, this society acknowledges no God and no Word of God. It is just as likely that the stronger, more powerful men in that society would use the death of an individual as an opportunity to snatch the wealth he had accumulated, leaving his spouse and children weak and dependent. Otherwise his descendants might challenge them for leadership of the island. Only the Bible originates the notion that, unlike lions and ostriches, human parents remain devoted to their children all their lives and can extend that devotion into future generations through a meaningful inheritance.

A well-known insurance company learned this lesson. They ran a commercial showing a happy family, suggesting that men should buy insurance so that their families could do well without them. The commercial was a failure. It was changed to speak directly to the man, with the message, "You can still take care of your family, even after you are gone." No person wants to be told that he is unnecessary. Working to build up a business to provide for your children, or to save money that will help your children get a step up in life, is a tremendous motivational tool. Allowing the government to take everything people have worked for after their death will ensure that people will naturally produce less. Why should they risk working hard for others not of their blood?

THINKING LONG-TERM

Thus, not only is the inheritance tax immoral, it also discourages individual enterprise and thrift which, in turn, damages our economic productivity. It is hard enough to encourage citizens to think long-term rather than short-term, but the fact is that long-term thinkers are good for society. They invest rather than just spend. They commence enterprises that may take a lifetime or longer to reach fruition. They conserve and protect rather than despoil. And one of God's devices to encourage long-term thinking among societies is children.

In his masterpiece *The Unheavenly City,* Harvard professor Edward Banfield wrote:

> The Jewish immigrants were very different from the peasant peoples. Like the native Americans, they were future-oriented. They believed, as had the Puritans, who were in many ways like them, that they were under a special obligation to assist in the realization of God's plan for the future. The idea of making sacrifices in the expectation of future rewards came naturally to them. Even more than the native American, the Jewish immigrant worked to acquire the capital, not only money and other material goods but also knowledge, skill, character, attachment to family and community, that would enable him to rise.[1]

The prophet Isaiah tells that the tendency of people who have no future, of people who think that "tomorrow they die," is to eat, drink, and make merry. This contrasts strongly with what people would do if they knew they would live forever. Without death to condemn everything as pointless, people would commence great undertakings. The gift children bestow is just that: immortality. I can be persuaded to become far more productive than my own immediate needs would demand, but only by the urge to provide for my children. If our government's inheritance tax makes it difficult for my additional work to benefit my children, then I shall just stop being a producer and become a consumer. All of society will eventually suffer from this squandering of human capital.

The concept of family inheritance tells us something of enduring importance about how to link together consecutive generations. Much of what is achieved by our system of ethical capitalism depends on entrepreneurs continuing to build upon the foundations constructed by their parents. It is also true that people will invent, labor and create tire-lessly if they know that in so doing, they are bettering the lives of their children and their grandchildren. How many immigrants to this country scrubbed floors and cleaned toi-lets, content in the knowledge that their children would become doctors? Men and women legitimately seek immortality through their children, which is why the Bible devotes so much space to the complexities of inheritance law. This is to stress that no one other than a man's heirs is entitled to his possessions after his death.

THE RESENTMENT TAX

Considering all of this, it is no surprise that one theory that fills the secularist with glee is the inheritance tax. He believes that marrying and raising children is just one among many alternative forms of human living arrangements. Philosophically speaking, everyone agrees that when a man dies, he no longer legally owns his possessions. Those whose world view is informed by taking Judaism or Christianity seriously, feel that the dead parents' children have a priority claim on the estate. The others argue that this is unfair to everyone else.

Inheritance taxes express an attitude of resentment for every penny a child receives from his parents' estate. Why should only a few prosper by some money suddenly becoming ownerless? It should belong to everybody, because (and here is the crux) there is no significance, other than the merely biological, to the parent-child relationship. Like animals in a zoo, when one animal's food dish is abandoned the others converge to feed themselves.

Invariably, politicians with an anti-God view will happily introduce, and then raise, the inheritance tax. No matter how well-intentioned, no matter how many Sundays they spend in church or Yom Kippurs in synagogue, they are deeply offended that some people should acquire more of a departed citizen's wealth than others merely because an acci-dent of birth made them his children. They feel that when a human dies, his property should belong to all citizens equally. Again, as a result of abandoning biblical principles for more "enlightened" thinking, we get a spiral of ever-increasing, confiscatory taxes that furthermore discourage productive enterprise.

While the inheritance tax interferes with parents providing for the future of their children, there is a flip side as well. The Bible naturally alludes to the need for a social security system. In fact, it mandates one. It is called *family*, and the secret to the economic viability of this social security system is quite simple: There always need to be more people working and producing than there are retired beneficiaries enjoying the yields of the sys-tem. A mother and father can be supported through old age as long as they invest in more than two children during their productive years.

If the secular spokesmen protested that children are unnecessary today because if people invested in mutual funds rather than children to sustain themselves during old age, there could be no complaint. However, they do not. Instead they emphasize the need for a government social security system which confiscates from young workers and gives to older retirees. Social security only works if many more people choose to have children than choose not to. The system requires more producers than takers. If the balance tips, the couple who invested their middle years raising four children, forgoing expensive vacations and restaurant meals, now find themselves subsidizing the retirements of their neighbors who elected to remain childless.

A FAIRER APPROACH

The biblical approach is clearly fairer. The couple who struggled and sacrificed to raise a family should enjoy the largess their children choose to make available to repay the debt to them. The childless-by-choice couple should now live only off their investments and not off the labor of other people's children. Good people will offer them charity if needed—but that is very different from telling them that they are entitled to others' earnings. And, of course, money is only part of the picture. All of us pity the lonely, elderly citizen who has no one to share his last years. A system that discourages cohesive, extended families where children are a blessing, leads to abandonment of the elderly.

For those who cannot, for one reason or other, have children, the Bible provides an alternate path. According to Jewish tradition, a teacher who imparts spiritual value to someone is to be accorded all the respect due a parent, including a financial obligation. This was an ethic with which America was imbued. Certainly we used to hear stories in America, of even crotchety childless aunts being given a home, and students visiting and caring for beloved teachers. Imparting such information has nothing to do with having a teaching credential on the wall. Each of us has the opportunity to impact others whether it is through being a neighbor, mentor, volunteer or through any number of other paths. Time and commitment are the only two requirements. One unintended consequence that results when society encourages people to rely on the government for support at any stage of their life is decreasing ties among people. We may not make friends, stay close to relatives, or join churches and synagogues in order that people will help us when we are in need. But that is a benefit we enjoy. Feeling financially independent of others allows us to leave the forming of lasting interpersonal connections to some vague time in the future.

One of my teachers and rabbinical mentors was the saintly Rabbi Simcha Wasserman. It was always a wondrous mystery to us, his students and disciples, that although the rabbi and his wonderful wife were never blessed with children, one never saw the faintest hint of bitterness at God's decision.

Toward the end of his life, I summoned up enough courage, hesitantly, to ask him about this. He responded with a story. Once he was on a plane and found himself seated next to a professor from the University of Chicago. They exchanged pleasantries and later the professor asked the rabbi where he was headed. Rabbi Wasserman answered that he was on his way to attend the wedding of one of his students in another city. The professor fell silent, so the rabbi asked him how many students he had taught over the years. The professor mentally tallied up more than twenty years at the university and said that he had probably taught several thousand students. In all innocence, the rabbi then said, "Well you must really spend most of your time traveling to your students' weddings." Looking puzzled, the professor said, "What do you mean?" Said Rabbi Wasserman, "Almost every student I ever taught sends me not only an invitation but an air ticket to enable me to be at his wedding. It would be as unthinkable for most of them to marry without my presence as it would be for them to do so without their parents being there."

Rabbi Wasserman looked pensive as he reached this point in the account and he said to me, "Reb Daniel, do you know what the professor told me?" I shook my head. Continuing with wonder on his face, my teacher said, "That professor who had taught many more students than I had taught, had never, ever been invited to even one wedding of a student." Smiling gently at me he said, "So you see, my wife and I were given many dear children after all." He was a godly man.

The secular crowd, however, is determined to erode the relationship between parents and their children. Children must be educated by the state, must eventually work for the state (i.e. pay taxes), and whatever selflessness they engage in must be administered by the state. This highlights another biblical principle. Traditionalists see children as a blessing; modernists see children as a burden. It is no wonder that Planned Parenthood workers routinely get ejected by third world villagers who understand that without the illusion of federal social security, children really do matter. Once again we find that a few minutes of religious and historical research could have avoided years of futile social experimentation.

Yet, when all is said and done, in this age when we reduce political discourse into sixty second commercials, we tend to respond emotionally to a call for saving social security or supporting the poor. Americans, as DeToqueville said over two hundred years ago, are good people. So much of what needs to be done to allow society to continue functioning sounds harsh. But is it?

There is sometimes a disingenuous argument used to discourage religious people from participating in politics. "It's fine to be religious, but keep your religion out of politics," we are told. Disingenuous—because it is only conservatives who must do so. Liberals somehow do get to use religion to buttress their positions. Did you hear liberals saying that even though President Clinton lied to the nation, their faith told them that he was worthy of redemption? I did. More importantly, the argument fails because politics is nothing other than the practical application of our values. For Americans, it is impossible to separate religion from values.

Obviously, in deciding how I am going to vote on issues of welfare reform etc., I consult my religion. While members of society are told that it is their religious duty to support all manner of tax increases in order to care for the underprivileged, the issue is not so simple. Let me share with you my analysis.

There is a saying in the Talmud that if a Jew totally lacks compassion, one should doubt whether he really is Jewish. This is not a legal ruling, but it does make the point that compassion is a deep and intrinsic part of Jewish nature. When Democrats and their media allies talk about Republicans wanting to starve children, or similar nonsense, far too many Jews accept those statements at face value. Leave aside the fact that the people who most often cite Jewish law as support for confiscating income from hard-working, fully functional American families in order to provide a sinecure for needy people—whether or not they are responsible for their state—are the very Jews least likely to regard Jewish tradition as binding. They tend to openly flout Jewish tradition's unambiguous views on kosher food or the Sabbath. Only when they think they can gain a measure of authenticity by appearing to fly in formation with thousands of years of Jewish tradition, do they cloak themselves in scriptural misquotes. If, for a Jew, it is valid to consult the Bible on welfare, it must be valid to do so on rituals as well as euthanasia or abortion. You cannot pick and choose.

Those of us who do consult Jewish tradition on all aspects of our life need to ask ourselves whether an unimpeachable authority on Jewish tradition such as twelfth-century sage Maimonides would approve of welfare. Would he heartily endorse it because it offers a temporary hand-up to those suffering from the vicissitudes of life? Or would he recoil in horror from a system that too frequently strips up to 50 percent of the earnings of the self-disciplined to underwrite the lifestyles of the self-destructive?

THE REAL JEWISH VIEW OF CHARITY

Parts of the Talmud indeed instruct inhabitants of a city to compel one another to provide for the poor. However, the administration of this compulsory charity fund is to be religious, not civil, falling as it does under the local rabbinic court. (Secondly, it is a giving of self as well as a giving of money. There is enormous responsibility upon the givers and the rabbinic authorities to be as vigilant over potential misuse of donors' funds as they are with the needs of the recipients.) This is no endorsement of a government's "war on poverty," for it is not government compulsion but religious and moral obligation. (It is locally administered and care is taken that the recipients are worthy and are moving toward independence. Because this traditional Jewish system is localized, it can in no way be compared to the current vast and wasteful government bureaucracy that demeans those it intends to help.)

Other Jewish sources clearly condemn our current welfare system since they state that there is an obligation upon the rabbinic court administering the charity to make sure that none of the poor are *ramaim*—or "liars"—people who could work but refuse to do so.

Most importantly, Jewish law always speaks in terms of obligations, not entitlements. The recipient is never *entitled* to charity, but everyone is obliged to give some of his earnings to those with less. This may seem like a semantic point, but in fact it underscores a major difference. For example, Jewish sources discuss a community's charitable obligations in terms of food, housing and medical needs. These discussions are sometimes cited as proof that Jewish law demands that society guarantee medical care for the indigent. In fact, instead of placing an obligation to cover medical fees upon the rest of society (as does our current welfare system and proposed socialized health plans), Jewish law places a religious obligation upon individual doctors to care for the poor. However, that obligation is to be weighed by the doctor in light of his other commitments, his income, and according to how worthy he judges the recipient. In addition, there is an obligation upon the receiver of the services: He or she is clearly instructed to work in exchange for his medical care. This allows needy people not only to obtain medical care but also to keep their self-respect. America's welfare system, in contrast, leaves no one feeling happy. A dentist friend of mine takes care of many patients for whom taxpayer money foots the bill. She is incensed when she sees that many of her patients come in with multiple tattoos and body piercing. Rather than feeling charitable when she takes care of them, she feels abused—both as a dentist and as a taxpayer. If these patients can afford "artistic" renderings on their bodies, then we are fools to say that they should not first use their resources for medical and dental care. The patients, for their part, don't even feel grateful to my friend or to all the Americans who pay taxes. They are angry and bitter people, not because they are not getting enough, but because it corrodes the soul constantly to receive without also having the opportunity to give.

When the focus is on every individual's personal obligations, society runs smoothly. Perhaps one of the most damaging and un-Jewish things done in the name of compassion was to turn charity into a legal entitlement. Not only did that make public money easy pickings for the unscrupulous, but it removed human dignity from the equation.

Jewish tradition requires those responsible for distributing funds to the poor to carefully and personally decide how much of the finite funds each recipient will be given and for how long. While every attempt is made to not embarrass the needy individual (an intermediary is often used so that the donor and recipient remain anonymous) there is always a personal touch. No one should be just a number in a bureaucracy.

We are specifically discouraged from creating a class of nonworking people. Welfare does just the opposite, treating the givers (taxpayers) quite cavalierly while treating the recipients in a fashion frowned upon by Jewish tradition.

KINDNESS TEMPERED BY FIRMNESS

Traditionally, each of the biblical patriarchs is especially associated with one character trait. Abraham is epitomized by the quality of *chessed*—doing kind deeds. Talmudic tradition has it that Abraham, through his renowned kindness, attracted thousands of devotees to Judaism. Imagine how many Jews there should have been by the time his grandson Jacob was an old man! Yet, a full three generations later, the Bible indicates a total Jewish population of merely seventy souls. What happened to the thousands of people who by now should have been part of this new monotheistic people?

The Talmud explains these surprising demographics as the inevitable consequence of viewing kindness and compassion as the only governing principles of good. Kindness attracts a following, but justice and structure maintain it. Abraham had focused on the Almighty's capacity for unrestrained love and compassion. His son Isaac introduced an awareness of God's firm hand into Jewish culture; the character trait we associate with Isaac is strength. Many of the disciples drawn by Abraham's gentle nature were later repelled by Isaac's unpopular emphasis on law and structure. It is Isaac's contribution that makes us, his spiritual descendants, capable of denying a child an eleventh piece of candy. Isaac's emphasis on the invisible long-term effects of even a kind-hearted action provided his spiritual descendants with durability. Kindness and compassion provide a soul for society, but it is the structure of law that defines boundaries and allows humans to live among one another. With Abraham's kindness alone there would have been no Jewish people. Isaac added an essential element, one that we need to reexamine today.

I do believe that most Jews and most Americans want to give a hand to those in need. In similar fashion I think that most people are passionately committed to education as a means for providing as many people as possible with a path to success. But I don't think that enough people of faith have reassessed whether the entrenched welfare and educational bureaucracies in this country are harming the poor and illiterate more than they are helping. There is certainly much proof that, in fact, the "help" that has been sincerely given has become a shackle. And of course, when large quantities of money are wasted through carelessness or deceit, there is less available for those who truly deserve and need help. Throwing money at the poor through a malfunctioning welfare bureaucracy may salve our consciences, while at the same time cause lasting damage to those the system claims to help. That is certainly not what my religion requires of me.

CHAPTER THIRTY-NINE

THE POLITICS
OF POVERTY

THE SHORT-TERM PULL IS NEARLY ALWAYS
MORE VISIBLE THAN THE LONG-TERM GOOD.

I occasionally give speeches on college campuses and am often disturbed by a widespread naiveté about money among today's students. Since I am an openly conservative speaker, there are usually a number of students who come not to listen but to protest. Often, their protest is just a variation on the tired old liberal theme that all conservatives are mean-spirited and selfish.

When I attempt to bring the questioner into a discussion of specifics, he will say something along the line that what this country needs is universal health care or increased welfare spending. As I continue to press by asking exactly what he means by universal health coverage, whether it should include liver transplants, inoculations, cosmetic surgery, and body piercing, the student assumes a superior stance and suggests that the concept is important, not the details.

I present my position that the government must deal in details; high-sounding sentiments are worthless for actually accomplishing anything. When I ask what government programs should be cut to pay for the increase in spending, or if taxes should be raised to do so, there is often a blank look on the protester's face. I'm sure this student is aware that if he purchases tickets to a concert, he must pay with money. It is not enough to tell the ticket booth that he just wants to hear his favorite singer and the details of payment are unimportant.

I have reluctantly reached the conclusion that these voting-age students have no idea that the government has no money of its own but must take from somewhere whatever it wants to spend elsewhere. I am not sure if this naiveté is confined to college campuses. For example, while it is reasonable for a person afflicted with a disease, or one who has a stricken loved one, to campaign for increased research in that particular area, that is not a good way for policy to be made.

When Christopher Reeve suffered a spinal cord injury, it pushed that area into prominence. But in all the calls for increased funding, I did not see anyone saying, "Since we need more research on spinal cord injuries, shall we reduce funding for diabetes or for cystic fibrosis? Or perhaps we should spend less on the arts." The assumption seems to be that money is just sitting there and we simply need to withdraw it. Too many citizens fail to understand the simple reality that governments do not produce money, although they may well print it. Only hard-working people, who produce more than they need, actually produce wealth and money. With most taxpayers working the entire months of January through mid-June (as of 1998) to pay for government at all levels, we simply cannot pay any more and remain a free society. But the corollary is that if we want government to spend more on anything, even the most worthy of causes, there are only two choices. Either we must yield more of what we earn by the sweat of our brows, or we must reduce government spending in other areas which, to other citizens, are just as worthy as our pet cause.

This seems so abundantly clear to anyone who lives in the real world that we must ask the obvious question: Why do so many people fail to grasp this basic economic reality? The answer is that the spiritual gravity that brings down individuals, families, as well as great societies is a built-in tendency we all possess. One of its most profound effects is that it causes people to react strongly to the visible while encouraging them to ignore the invisible. The reason this tendency causes damage in our lives is because the short-term pull is nearly always more visible than the long-term good.

CALMING THE SCREAMING CHILD

A good parent balances the child's scream for candy and cookies against the demand of responsible nutrition and the fear of dental cavities. One pull is urgent and all too visible, not to mention audible. The other pull, which happens to be best for the child, is informed by events not yet visible and belonging to the future. Is it any wonder that so many parents yield? It is the easier thing to do! And in any event, who wants to constantly withhold treats from his child?

In exactly the same way, government interacts with a nation's citizens. The treat is always visible and in the here and now. The penalty is usually exacted some time in the future, from some less visible group. When a president or a group of legislators proudly announce plans to right something they perceive as a grave social problem, it usually involves someone else paying the bill. It may well be a monetary cost that will be paid by some large and unidentified group of taxpayers, or it may be a price paid by a future generation of Americans who will have to live in a slightly less benign world. Meanwhile, the benefited parties can be brought to the White House lawn for a public relations photo opportunity. The president tells the world about his compassion and concern for these unfortunate people. He waves the new legislation aloft and proudly declares the end of some injustice. Everyone smiles for the cameras. Everyone, that is, except those invisible people who are left holding the bag.

O YE OF LITTLE FAITH

Why does the future become less important, and immediate gratification more important, as societies slide toward oblivion? As people abandon God-focused faith, they also lose faith in general. Which is to say that as we cease exercising our faith in God, we lose the ability to exercise faith for all the many places in which faith is vital to a successful life. Faith of either variety means the ability to see things not immediately visible.

The Center for the Study of Social Change and Political Change tells us that, after religious professionals (who are, after all, paid to be in church), military professionals and business professionals are the most likely people in America to attend church every week. This is no accident. Both require the ability to see that which is not yet quite visible. The military has to clearly anticipate threats of which nobody else is yet aware, and sometimes it must clearly see victories which to others seem elusive. Business must see the potential for profit in what appear to be hopeless situations. This ability to see the future, as it were, is called faith. General faith springs from the exercise of religious faith.

A family of little faith is doomed. Children will be allowed to spend precious and unrecoverable hours before a television. They will be allowed a virtually unrestricted diet of fats and sweets. They will know little discipline, little postponement of gratification, because the convenience of the present is of far greater priority to their parents than the long-term health and social development of the children. The pleasures and benefits of this indulgent policy are immediately felt; its price will be paid far off into the future. Seeing that ultimate price demands faith the family does not possess.

A society of no faith is equally doomed. They will demand goodies from their leaders who, lacking the faith to say no, gladly indulge the populace in exchange for the votes that keep them in power. They know full well that the price will have to be paid on some future leader's watch. At least it won't be paid on theirs. Whether the issue is Social Security, socialized medicine, rent control making married couples pay more tax than they would pay were they single or any other fiscal policy, too many of us see only the immediate benefits. We have been indoctrinated with the propaganda of compassion. Feeling people's pain sounds noble and good. In reality it serves the need of those who seek to benefit now by making future generations pay the price.

Not surprisingly, only one group of Americans is consistently resisting this massive cultural change in our values: America's religious conservatives. Only they possess the faith to forego short-term snake-oil fixes in order to ensure the long-term fiscal and social health of society. Others may bemoan the economic consequences of practicing the propaganda of compassion, but only America's religious conservatives, both Jewish and Christian, possess the spiritual muscle to attack the malevolence at its root, which is the secular tendency to ignore the invisible. No wonder that Adam Smith and most of the other fathers of modern economics were God-worshiping Christians. No wonder that Keynes and other big-spending fathers of economic modernism were atheists.

Secular liberals today fail to grasp that earlier generations effectively balanced the needs of the present with those of the future; they balanced the visible with the still-invisible. They did so in their families and they did so in matters of public policy. Like wise parents, we Americans tended to make decisions that took the long term into account. We tended to set policies that recognized the impact over the entire complex fabric of society. We never just picked Peter's pocket to pay Paul. Faith allowed us to act wisely and we were rewarded. We could afford a religiously neutral government because everyone knew that the governors were the servants of the governed, rather than the reverse. As long as the governed had faith in God, the governors would obey the imperatives of faith.

SERVANTS WHO WOULD BE MASTERS

But over the past thirty-five years our government has not liked this situation very much. Understanding that the wisdom and power of the governed was derived from Christian faith, they set about diminishing that faith in order to make the governed the slaves of the governors. A government's options are distinctly limited if its citizens are religious, so religion must go. A nation made up of citizens with deep religious faith will never allow its government to plunder tomorrow to pay for today. Citizens with true faith in God will never offer their votes in exchange for assets forcibly seized from other fellow citizens. So those who wish to seek and retain political power over their fellow citizens must first attenuate the religious faith of their populations. In America this means that those in government who view themselves as masters (rather than servants) of the rest of us must do all they can to weaken Christianity.

Those of us who venerate freedom, be we Jewish or Christian, be we religious or secularized, have no option but to pray for the health of Christianity in America. No other group possesses both the faith and the numbers sufficient to hold back the ever-encroaching, sometimes sinister, power of the state.

RICH MAN, POOR MAN

There remains one more vital way in which Christian faith in America serves as a bulwark against growing government size and taxation. You see, the liberal Left likes to use the nation's "poor" to justify its constant cries for higher and higher taxes, demonizing all who resist granting money to the visible at the expense of the invisible. Those who do not want taxes raised still higher to help the poor are not compassionate. Over time, this short-sighted philosophy has robbed the term "poor" of any meaning. Just try asking your friends what it means and you will quickly find out that nobody really knows. Have them tell you a dollar amount, either in assets or in income, below which anybody could legitimately be called poor. Instead of an answer you will usually get a long discussion. This is because the term "poor" would not exist were it not for the Bible. No group of people would, on their own, come up with the concept of charity or the notion of poor. These are both legacies of western civilization's Judeo-Christian origins; unfortunately they have been hijacked by the Left for the purposes of expanding government power.

The main reason it is so difficult to define "poor" is because we are people, not animals. I can already hear you saying "There he goes again," but wait just one moment. You see, it is relatively easy to define poverty in an animal. Say an elephant requires sixty pounds of vegetation each day to remain healthy. Say a lion requires twenty pounds of meat. If either animal receives less than this, it can safely be regarded as poor. They each have less than they need. However, if you speak of what a person needs you start sounding a bit like Karl Marx, who felt that communism would provide all a person really needs. His spiritual heirs discovered that Karl erred. People's ability to produce is finite and limited by their strength, ability, and life span. People's needs, on the other hand, can be infinite. While all individual animals of a species are pretty much alike, no two humans are alike. It is simply not possible to speak of a human's needs. In my case religious education for my children and a boat for me are real needs. I do not need a large car or a fancy house. I do need not to have to work on Saturdays. Other people establish what their own needs are.

RICH IS COMPARATIVE, NOT ABSOLUTE

There is one additional complication in trying to speak of people's needs. We all have limitless desires. This does not mean we are unable to live comfortably within our means, or that we go through life gnawed by discontent. Nonetheless, we would all know what to do with a large inheritance if it were to come our way. In Africa, I have seen lions utterly ignore a herd of impala deer idly strolling by. The deer seemed quite indifferent to the lion and he to them. This was because he had recently eaten dinner and would not have known what to do with the windfall. He rightly reasoned that he could always catch an impala when he was again hungry. Humans are not like that. Our desires are always ahead of our means to fulfill them. To put it directly, wealth and poverty to animals are absolutes; to humans, they are comparatives. An animal either has what it needs or it does not. Since animals are entirely material, establishing their needs is simple. Once you have established the needs of one average-sized family dog, you have established it for most similar dogs. Not so with people whose needs sometimes go way beyond merely staying alive. One person's needs may be quite different from another's.

Try this thought experiment. Arriving home tonight, you find a large duffel bag filled with countless hundred dollar bills. Suspecting that you are becoming unwittingly involved in a drug transaction, you nervously grab the bag and dart into your home, locking the door behind you. To your immense relief, you discover a little card with your name on it which announces that the contents of the bag are a gift to you from the Gore for President campaign. After your trembling fingers have counted out a million dollars, you sit back to contemplate how your life will change. Debts can now be paid off, a few little luxuries of which you have dreamed can be purchased, and your newly enlarged savings account will certainly put a spring in your step. You are feeling pretty good as you go to sleep.

Next morning dawns and your first instinct is to call your best friend to share your good news. Before you can start telling him about the exciting event, your friend bursts into an irrepressible account of how he received a million dollars from the Gore for President campaign. Admit it; aren't you just the tiniest bit disappointed? Getting off the phone, you call your dear Aunt Agatha. Perhaps she will be excited by your wonderful news. It turns out that she too was a beneficiary of the Gore for President campaign. She also is now one million dollars richer than she was yesterday.

The dreadful truth is beginning to dawn on you. Last night, every single American received a duffel bag filled with a million dollars of newly minted one-hundred-dollar bills. Now you are not nearly as excited as you were when you thought yours was the only bank account that had been increased by a million dollars. This is because to humans, wealth is comparative. Wealth means having more than those around you. Knowing that you own far more than a Bangladeshi peasant could even dream of does not make you feel rich; having a million dollars more than your friends and acquaintances makes you feel very rich indeed. Being given a million dollars along with every one of your fellow citizens fails to make you feel rich because, when all is said and done, your buying power will be just what it was before the grand gift. The marketplace will quickly compensate for all those unearned dollars floating around as prices rise to match the extra few trillion dollars of paper promises. Yesterday you could buy a new car for $25,000; today it may cost you $300,000. If everyone's a millionaire, yesterday's $75 grocery basket will simply increase to $800 tomorrow. It's not wealth if everyone else has it too.

POOR IS ALSO COMPARATIVE

Looking over one shoulder and seeing people with a lot less than you makes you feel rich. Similarly, looking over your other shoulder and seeing many people with a lot more than you can make you feel poor. This is one reason most people tend to prefer living among other people with roughly the same quantity of material wealth. None of us enjoys feeling poor and living among people with a great deal more than we have. Similarly, living among friends who own a great deal less than we do makes us feel awkward and guilty. Again, when applied to human beings, rich and poor have no absolute or objective meaning. The word "poor" is comparative and means having a lot less than those around you. You may well have far more money than a Bangladeshi peasant but if you have far less than your friends, neighbors, and relatives, you could feel rather poor.

How then did the word "poor" enter our political vocabulary? Originally, from God's Word, we became aware of an obligation toward those with less than we have. In cultures that have never been touched by the Judeo-Christian tradition, one encounters an almost eerie indifference on the part of those blessed toward those less fortunate. In Deuteronomy 15:4, God assures His people that if they follow His commands as a nation, "there should be no poor among you...." No more than seven verses later, in what appears to be a contradiction to the earlier assurance, we are told, "There will always be poor people in the land." Secular scholarship leaps through the escape hatch of multiple authorship, crying, "Two separate authors wrote those verses!" and assumes that an incompetent editorial board failed to spot the contradiction. Religious tradition, however, far more usefully explains that by following God's guidance, each one of us can train ourselves to look only over the shoulder that makes us feel fortunate, blessed, and wealthy. In this way, there need be "no poor among you."

At the same time, however, nobody need fear that with all these grateful and blessed people around, he will be unable to find anyone on whom to bestow charity. Each of us should view himself as rich and voluntarily help others in genuine need. Those we help may also be wealthy compared to many others in our world, but as far as we are concerned, if they have a genuine need they are worthy recipients of our generosity. Thus society becomes an exquisite tapestry of interlinked human elements, every one of which views himself as rich while simultaneously seeking to help others who have less. This is what America used to look like.

One of the great indictments of the changes that thirty-five years of secularism have inflicted upon us, is that America's so-called poor pay few taxes and give little charity themselves. Secularism has converted an entire class of Americans into people who take but do not give. Secularism promotes the illusion of a static world; it identifies someone as poor and then turns him into a permanent ward of the state. Even well-intentioned secularists fall into this trap because they tend to view reality as a sequence of disconnected snapshots rather than as a continuous video.

THE DISHONESTY OF SNAPSHOTS

The old Greek philosopher Zeno confounded all his contemporaries by presenting this conundrum: The famous runner Achilles is challenged to a race by a tortoise who demands a head start of 100 yards. At the starter's signal, Achilles, who runs ten times faster than the tortoise, sets off and quickly covers 100 yards, reaching the point from which the tortoise began. By that time the tortoise, running at one-tenth the speed, has run ten yards. By the time Achilles reaches the 110-yard point, the tortoise is now one yard ahead of Achilles. By the time the human runner has covered that one yard, the tortoise is now a tenth of a yard ahead of Achilles. No matter how many "snapshots" we examine, Achilles lags behind the tortoise. While it is true that the lead enjoyed by the tortoise is a diminishing one, he does seem to remain the leader and thus, eventually, the winner.

Obviously Zeno and his wily friends knew that Achilles will win a race against a tortoise. What bothered them about this paradox was that they could not find the catch. The catch is that real life is not reflected accurately by a series of snapshots; it is correctly depicted only by a smooth and continuously running video.

In the same way, we could examine a snapshot of ten Americans struggling to get by on minimum wage. It is not a pretty picture. However, were we to revisit them six months later, most would be earning somewhat more for their work. Government statisticians would have to select another ten Americans to produce a snapshot purporting to show that ten Americans are still on minimum wage. While true that there are still ten Americans on minimum wage, it is surely not irrelevant that they are a different set of ten Americans and that the first ten are moving up the economic escalator.

There are only three job skills necessary to find and keep an entry-level job; none of these skills can be taught by government programs. First, show up regularly and on time. Second, obey instruction. Third, keep quiet. These are character attributes and can only be acquired from parents and family who care. Anybody obeying these three rules in America can obtain an entry-level job and keep it. By keeping the position, one quickly becomes trained and worth more to an employer. At that point, the potential inconvenience and expense of finding and training a new employee is countered by the employer raising the wage of his worker. The investment of his time during the first six months at one employer has made him more valuable in this position than a newcomer could be. Thus our fortunate American newcomer to the job market finds himself on the economic escalator. The snapshot we saw of him six months earlier is now meaningless.

Similarly, a snapshot of a successful lawyer photographed a year before she graduates law school may well show someone apparently in need of government assistance. The snapshot will show a young woman working (well, okay, studying) all day without being paid a penny. She may live in just one little room that she shares with another student. She may subsist on macaroni and cheese. The snapshot demands a compassionate response from anyone seeing it, but it fails to show that this woman is only months away from earning an enviable income and in absolutely no need of help from anyone. Least of all should she extract assistance from middle-income families whose total income is considerably less than she will earn in her first year with a prestigious law firm.

Yet government policies use misleading snapshots such as these to convince hard-working and big-hearted Americans that higher taxes are necessary to help the poor. Not surprisingly, as reported in *Forbes* magazine on May 4, 1998, shelters for the poor compete for homeless people in order to justify their budgets. Grand Central Neighborhood Social Services Corp. in New York even ran a marketing special during November 1997 to engage new clients by offering a free breakfast and $5 in cash. What better way to get good people to agree to higher taxes than to play on their natural and biblically inspired compassion for the poor? All that's needed for this to work are lots of warm bodies labeled "the poor" who can be paraded before the well-intentioned and gullible, who then nobly open their wallets.

QUESTION THE SNAPSHOTS

Only our mass abandonment of religious outlook in America makes us vulnerable to the snapshot view of the world and the mass manipulation it allows. Religious people are more intuitively likely to view life through a video rather than through a dishonest sequence of snapshots. We are accustomed to the timeline of history and to the ever-repeating biblical laws of cause and effect. In one way or another we all have been educated to distrust superficial appearances. Show us a snapshot depicting an attractive-looking couple strolling hand in hand and we instinctively ask ourselves questions. We wonder whether this is a devoted married couple anticipating many happy years in one another's loving company, or an extramarital couple caught in a moment of adulterous bliss. We just do not know from the photograph and we are not prepared to join them in their evident joy until we see the video. Secularism takes the snapshot at its face value and dismisses those of us who feel the need to know more as judgmental and filled with hate.

In this way, although genuinely compassionate and charitable, religious Jews and Christians are less vulnerable to the politics of poverty. We recognize that not a single one of us has everything he needs or wants and therefore poverty is more a state of mind than a state of pocket. We also recognize that self discipline and biblical values are the stepping stones to a family's economic growth. From the point of view of a poverty-industry bureaucracy however, religious Americans are an obstacle to the growth of government by the politics of poverty. Thus we see yet another reason why government is no longer neutral to religion but actively hostile. Thus no better metaphor exists for our cultural schism than a tug-of-war between those who see religious faith as part of the solution and those who see religious faith as the problem. The two sides operate within utterly incompatible moral frameworks. One has proven that it works. The other has proven to be a dismal failure.

CHAPTER FORTY

A CALL FOR MORAL SANCTIONS

THE POINT OF SOCIAL SANCTIONS IS NOT TO RUIN
LIVES BUT TO PRESERVE THE COMMON WELFARE.

There is another demand we can make of people only if we recognize the uniqueness of human beings. Judeo-Christian principles insist that people have the ability to control not only their actions but even their thoughts. And that, therefore, people are (and must be) accountable for their actions and thoughts.

This school of thought believes that when the Tenth Commandment prohibits us from desiring (not "taking," an action which is covered in number eight) what belongs to another, God is demanding quite reasonably that we control our thoughts. We are to develop and refine the faculty for dismissing unworthy or potentially damaging thoughts from our minds. While the modernist, particularly in the field of art, may consider unfettered and undisciplined thought to be just one step removed from genius, the Bible directs us to rein in our minds.

The implications of controlling one's thoughts are huge. One arena of life in which much damage is caused by the secular position is that there are no bad thoughts in married life. Mainstream magazines often quote therapists who encourage sexual fantasizing as harmless and at times even beneficial. The truth is that male human nature being what it is, no real live woman, let alone a wife who has borne him a child or two, can possibly match up to the object of her husband's fantasies. Likewise, few middle-aged men would win the Mr. Olympia contest. Why would anyone encourage husbands or wives to engage in behavior that can only make them less content in their marriage?

Children raised with no ability or desire to restrain their fantasies of sensual and material appetites are being condemned to a life of constant dissatisfaction. Dissatisfaction regularly leads to resentment and then envy. It is a short step from envy to a justification for taking what is not rightfully yours, or to exacerbating your problems by blaming them on anyone but yourself.

AWARENESS OF GOD'S PRESENCE

Just as there are thoughts we are supposed to train ourselves not to have, there are other ideas one should keep ever-present. While modern liberalism espouses the liberation of mankind from the baleful and accusing presence of God, the Judeo-Christian position believes that one of the most comforting and helpful sensitivities to develop in oneself and in one's children is an awareness of God's watchful omnipresence.

In a beautiful passage in Genesis (39:7–18), Joseph was in the process of being sexually harassed by the wife of Egyptian nobleman Potiphar. Joseph refused: "My master has withheld nothing from me except you, because you are his wife. How then could I do such a wicked thing and sin against God?" This was Joseph's line in the sand. As the harassment continued, he literally fled the scene to avoid sin. Potiphar's wife, wrathful over being scorned, later falsely accused him of sexual assault but Joseph was indeed sinless in God's sight.

We have raised a generation unaware of God's presence and its potency as an aid to self-monitoring. What might happen, for example, if a gang member were to reject bad influence with a paraphrase of Joseph's words: "God is watching and would not want me to go with you." (Actually, if more of us were to simply *think* this sentiment, what impact might that have on morality in our society?)

Lamentably, we are not likely to witness that heartwarming scene any time soon. In spite of the fact that many studies show considerably less criminal activity among religiously involved families, the anti-God theoreticians feel that the cure is worse than the disease. Under no circumstances can we encourage religion, and we must try to remove it from organizations such as Boy Scouts and Girl Scouts (or at least remove these organizations from our schools). Most ordinary citizens would disagree.

The most serious public policy consequence of this principle is that, in the final analysis, there can never be enough policemen. Once each person's internal monitoring system has been disconnected, everyone needs to be watched all the time. Of course, each policeman needs a policeman, too. Perhaps this is why smaller towns in parts of the country considered to be populated chiefly by Christians have streets and parks that are relatively safe to stroll in at night.

THE PLUMMETING AIRCRAFT

We might ask why we need to always lock the door; why we work for almost half the year to pay our tax bill, and why we hear seven-year-old children using profane language.

The real question we should be asking is, "What did we used to do that kept society so stable, safe, and prosperous?" To use one of our earlier analogies, do not ask what made the airplane tumble out of the sky. The answer is simple: It ran out of fuel. Ask instead where the fuel came from and how it was converted into the thrust that kept the craft in the air.

Similarly, when studying social decay, the question is not what brought foul-mouthed louts to menace shoppers in our malls. Instead, we should ask: Why was a visitor to a theater or department store in the 1950s surrounded by neatly dressed people who exuded politeness and consideration? Why, back then, were our buses, parks, and other public places safe at all hours of the day or night? What made most young people marry and raise children responsibly?

The fuel that used to keep the airplane of society airborne has run out. We are plummeting. Instead of an altimeter in the cockpit, we have statistics on growing rates of illegitimacy. Instead of the queasy feeling in the stomach that comes from dropping too rapidly, we have the discomfort of sharing our streets, stores, schools, parks and roads with ill-mannered, angry, inconsiderate, obscene, sinister thugs. It is the screamed insult and raised finger from another car at a real or imagined driving error. It is loud, rude, public speech peppered with obscenities that would have made a hardened convict blush only a generation ago. Nearly always, it is assault by fear and filth.

POLITICALLY INCORRECT MORAL WEAPONS

How did we once maintain a society that was a model of prosperity, tranquillity, and politeness? Part of the answer is that, as a God-fearing nation, we employed several fundamental moral weapons which we have now become too timid, or too politically correct, to use. These weapons include disapproval, ostracism, and other sanctions.

Let's see how such weapons would relate to the phenomenon of illegitimacy. Thirty-five years ago, the unmarried teenage girl who became pregnant was sent away to have the baby. The shame she brought on herself and her family was deep and lasting. In addition, the bastard child carried the disgrace throughout his life, with diminished career and marriage prospects. As we approach the end of the millennium, our enlightened generation tends to throw up our hands in horror at the thought that ostracism and moral censure should be put to such barbaric use. I would argue to the contrary, on three grounds. First, I suggest that the traditional use of ostracism and censure educated society on the proper ties between people, God, and community, while the abandonment of these tools has led to rampant and dangerous individualism. Second, I maintain that proper and judicious use of social sanctions prevents far more problems and misery than it creates, as do many other forms of punishment. Finally, I argue that no community can succeed without ostracism and censure.

In the "resolution of censure" which society once passed on the unwed mother, everyone objects most vociferously to the clause which ostracizes the bastard. Even if the mother deserves her punishment, goes the line, what possible justification can society have for tainting an innocent child who certainly did nothing to deserve the stigma?

A traditional answer to this takes us back to the story of Noah. Genesis 9:20–27 relates how Noah's son Ham sinned by viewing his father's nakedness and then bragging of it to his brothers. Interestingly, when Noah awakened and determined to mete out punishment, he cursed not Ham (the miscreant) but Ham's son Canaan.

THE COMMUNITY OF GENERATIONS

This Bible passage teaches us two critical facts about the human condition which escape the notice of modern people. First, that civilization depends upon maintaining a "community of the generations." Everything we do honors or dishonors our ancestors and affects the generations to come. Even in our egalitarian society, we know that our positive achievements and monetary success benefit our children. Why should we then expect that our sins will not *harm* them?

Indeed, the biblical account's second—and related—insight is that people care more about their loved ones than about themselves. Men will sacrifice themselves for their wives and brothers will do so for their sisters. But even stronger is the mother's instinct to protect her children. Far from an act of injustice, the ostracism of a bastard is a gesture of profound respect for the mother-child tie, the most critical building block of civilization.

The point of social sanctions, like the point of any other deterrence mechanism, is not to ruin lives but to preserve the common welfare. Anyone urging the return of such sanctions hopes that their very presence will make the need for their use quite rare. Back in the 1950s, the number of pregnant schoolgirls who were stigmatized was tiny, and so was the rate of illegitimacy. The number of vagrants who were harassed out of respectable neighborhoods was minute, and the streets were safe and clean.

The tool of ostracism and social censure was used most effectively to limit both drunken driving and cigarette smoking. In both cases it was not considered sufficient to merely penalize the actions; it was also necessary to brand those who engaged in those behaviors. As a society, we are obviously quite comfortable employing social disapproval as a tool for social improvement. We are just a little queasy about utilizing these undoubtedly effective tools for moral ends.

Recently the citizens of Kennesaw, Georgia, passed an ordinance requiring all households to be armed. They only had to shoot their first robber, a fairly significant gesture of ostracism, to get their point across. This was obviously unfortunate for the robber; it may even have been unfair, since nothing in his hitherto prosperous career had prepared him for the warm Georgia reception he was given. But he could hardly be described as an innocent bystander.

It would, however, be a mistake to conceive of social sanctions as merely the spiritual equivalent of a shotgun. One reason ostracism and moral censure are so powerful is that they may be employed in widely varying degrees of intensity. The patterns of the business world reveal how subtle, carefully nuanced social devices can be just as effective as a scarlet letter. For example, very few companies find the need for written codes of dress, relying on non-verbal communication and even the occasional use of ostracism (e.g., sending an improperly dressed employee home to change clothes), in achieving a high level of conformity to an established norm. Similarly, business can signal full-fledged acceptance, extreme disapproval, or anything in between, through the judicious application of promotions, pay raises, perquisites, and the like. Even such simple indicators as who is and is not consulted about a decision (another minor form of ostracism) can have a powerful impact on a person's self-esteem, status and respect within a company.

A final and most critical point about sanctions: Society requires a religious sense of moral conviction in order to authorize their use. "Noah walked with God" and thus had no qualms about cursing his grandson. Similarly, ostracizing an unwed pregnant teenager and shunning her child requires a Bible-believing, prayerful community, a community based on Judeo-Christian ideals. In that type of community, just as she is publicly disgraced, there will be a warm family who will adopt the child, letting it grow up as their own.

Let's be honest. Thirty years ago, when society looked down on illegitimacy, did anyone think that women someday would have children out of wedlock on purpose and be proud of it? And that they would demand both applause and financial support for their actions? If you are one of the many Americans who worry about all the fatherless children being born, then shaming a few individuals for their irresponsible actions begins to look like the necessary, and ultimately kind, gesture that it is.

MISGUIDED COMPASSION

In my view, and the view of many others, great cruelty has been inflicted by "compassionate policies" of the last few decades on precisely those they promised to help. Many great thinkers in the African-American community such as economists Thomas Sowell and Walter Williams, Supreme Court Justice Clarence Thomas, or leader Ward Connerly feel that a black child born today is, in many areas, worse off than the black child born into the same degree of poverty in 1960. Both are poor; but in the past there was a hope of a future while now there is a promise of hatred and failure. Read the books of courageous black women such as Star Parker or Ezola Foster and you will be embarrassed to realize what harm liberal, socialized "compassion" has caused. If you have not heard of these women, is it possible that your nightly news on TV and newspaper are only presenting one side of the story? Likewise, a "compassionate" education bureaucracy that didn't want a six-year-old immigrant to suffer in an English-speaking classroom too often condemned that child to a life of poverty.

As a Jew, I need to ask myself, "Why is the official secular Jewish leadership so in favor of these failing liberal policies?" Again, religious Jews and Christians have led the way in rightly calling for a return to the moral wisdom that preceded our nation's disastrous social experiment.

PART IV

RECOGNIZING OUR DILEMMA

CHAPTER FORTY-ONE

THE STATE OF AMERICAN JEWRY

THE OFFICIAL VOICE OF THE JEWISH COMMUNITY HAS LONG BEEN IN OPPOSITION TO THE MOOD OF THE MAJORITY OF AMERICANS.

I have attempted to show that, for the past three decades or so, American society has been dominated by the doctrines of the Left. Furthermore, those doctrines have become official policies and have bred tragedy. As the great writer Thomas Sowell puts it, "By and large, the '60s marked the beginning of many social disasters and we are still picking up the pieces." Sowell documents how dependency had been going down for decades before the so-called "war on poverty" began to send it climbing. He shows how the number of murders in America in 1960 was lower than it had been in 1930, 1940, or 1950. Once the Left introduced its theories about "root causes of crime" and the "rights" of criminals, however, the murder rate began to soar, eventually doubling between 1960 and 1970.

The same baleful legacy of liberalism was seen in everything it touched. Thomas Sowell demonstrates how the downward trend in sexual promiscuity among young people began to reverse as soon as the modern "enlightened" and "healthy" view of sex was spread throughout schools under the dishonest title of "sex education." It was not education about biology but propaganda designed to replace the values that children had absorbed from their families. Sowell, a black American himself, bravely reveals the figures that prove that the economic rise of blacks in America was also a victim of the 1960s' brand of secular fundamentalism. That rise was faster in the 1940s and 1950s than in the 1960s or later. How could anything liberalism has achieved compensate for its undermining of such basic institutions as the family, law enforcement, and education, he asks? As Sowell courageously says, "Food stamps are no substitute for a father, busing is no substitute for a decent education, and racial breast-beating is no substitute for being able to walk the streets without fear of hoodlums and murderers."[1]

Some think the pendulum has started its swing back. It is true that vast numbers are repulsed by the violent and decadent behavior promoted by contemporary television, films, and music. There is growing impatience with crime, as evidenced by Washington state's "Three Strikes and You're Out" law being copied around the country. The growing school voucher movement and home school population reflect a major decrease in confidence in our public schools and Left-oriented teaching bureaucracies. Disenchantment with professional politicians has fueled the term-limits movement and reduced respect for public office holders. Unprecedented victories of countless religious conservatives in 1994 and 1996 revealed an embrace of candidates professing a return to religious tradition in Congressional elections. Their liberal opponents have had to pretend to adopt many of their stances in order to hold or regain their own seats in office.

But I do not believe it is the simple swing of a pendulum we are seeing, for the laws of physics cannot be counted on to save a culture. What we are witnessing is the Right side of the cultural tug-of-war beginning to dig in and pull harder. To paraphrase the reluctant architect of the attack on Pearl Harbor, Admiral Yamamoto, religious conservatives in America are like a sleeping giant that has been awakened. America has commenced a major sociological shift. For thirty-five years the Left has pressed its assault on traditional American culture. Never content with its victories, secular fundamentalism has continued its ruthless sneak attack on American society. Traditional America and its many allies are only now starting to fight back.

Paradoxically, in this tug-of-war, the official voice of the Jewish community has long been in opposition to the mood of the majority of Americans. Since the war against Judeo-Christian values began in the early 1960s, official Jewish energy and resources have been disproportionately deployed to the wrong side. And by the wrong side, I mean the side furthest from every single moral principle of authentic Jewish tradition. It is time to expose the dubious scholarship, selective quotations, and spurious interpretations of our holy tradition that some Jewish communal leaders have depended upon to mislead almost an entire generation of American Jews.

One of the most frequent questions I am asked as I speak to audiences around the country is, "Why are Jews so liberal?" The questioners are puzzled even more by the fact that the Jewish families they know socially or through work are often very traditional in their personal behavior. They seem to be living the values that Americans conventionally cherish, yet their political behavior doesn't reflect that. What is going on?

WHO IS A JEW?

In order to understand this, we may first have to realize the following. While it is valid to say that the Pope speaks in the name of Catholicism, no one person or group speaks for all Jews. Statements are constantly being made by organizations that have the word "Jewish" in their name, but one should never assume that they reliably represent Jewish thought or that they even express the views of large numbers of Jews.

Complicating matters is enormous disagreement as to who exactly is a Jew. Someone born into a Latter Day Saint family but who rejects the teachings of the church would not identify themselves as a Latter Day Saint. Being born into a Christian family, but personally rejecting Jesus as Messiah, does not entitle you to call yourself a Christian. Jews from birth, however, never exert any conscious effort to become Jewish—they simply are Jewish. Likewise, it is almost impossible to get "declassified" as a Jew, no matter how many fundamental tenets of Judaism one abandons, violates, or even publicly refutes.

Adding to the general confusion are people like California Senator Diane Feinstein, who was raised a Catholic and never renounced that faith. Feinstein gets a free pass into Judaism by the general population because she married and acquired a "Jewish" last name. To secure political advantage when dealing with the Jewish community, her supporters suggest that she is Jewish.

Something that causes the Jewish community real distress is the vast number of Jews who have intermarried and assimilated during the last fifty years. Many Americans with "Jewish" names, such as Goldwater, Cohen, Weiss, Levine, and Goldberg, are totally non-affiliated Jews or practicing members of other faiths. Since Jewish men more frequently seek a non-Jewish mate than do Jewish women, the Jewish-sounding family name is kept in circulation and thus many of these Cohens, Weisses and Goldbergs are generations removed from their Jewish heritage. A case in point is President Clinton's Secretary of Defense William Cohen, who retains a Jewish name even though Judaism was long since abandoned by his family. One result of the above phenomenon is that many more people are thought of as Jews, than actually are Jewish.

ORTHODOX, CONSERVATIVE, REFORM

Among those actually born to Jewish parents, and among those converting to Judaism and retaining some connection to the Jewish community, there are countless categories. The oldest of the three main denominations is the Orthodox—the most traditional and socially conservative. Not surprisingly, they tend to vote for conservative politicians more than other Jews. The Conservative branch of Judaism (with a capital, not a lower case c) retains some fealty to selected Jewish laws but generally are politically and socially liberal. The Reform movement, founded originally in Germany in the 1800s, rejects Jewish law as authoritative and tends to be very liberal. These are, needless to say, generalizations.

Within these groups are dozens of categories. For instance, there are many Jews I know and admire, who are members of Reform Temples and who object to the extreme liberal politics associated with the Reform movement. I know Reform rabbis who only eat kosher food. I even know some remarkable pro-life Reform rabbis. However, the official policies of the movement are guided more by contemporary liberal doctrine than by ancient Mosaic law.

The official Reform Jewish position is almost always extremely liberal. It is also the movement with the largest following. That is not surprising since it is the least demanding. Affiliating with a Reform Temple can mean anything from being highly involved to showing up once a year or simply paying dues. In contrast, Orthodox Jewish affiliation can entail showing up in synagogue twice daily and usually includes very visible and stringent religious practices. Those secular Americans who want to still identify as Jewish while staying on the periphery of the religion would most probably call themselves Reform or nowadays increasingly, simply unaffiliated. Because of these large numbers, as well as a politically active Rabbinate, Americans can be forgiven for believing that the Reform position is *the* Jewish position. For example, there was a debate covered in newspapers around the country, as to whether the Reform rabbinate would approve of homosexual marriages. While the decision was to table the topic, a large number of the involved rabbis did state that, "We lack any defensible moral or religious grounds to withhold from homosexual couples the opportunity to express the sanctity of those unions in precisely the way heterosexual couples have always expressed it: through marriage."

How can this be? Rabbis lacking religious grounds to oppose homosexual "marriage"? Hello guys: How about God calling the act of male homosexuality an "abomination"? Does that not constitute "defensible religious grounds" for a rabbi? Newspapers' accounts suggested to people that *Judaism* approves of homosexual marriages. Nothing could be further from the truth. Many Americans of Jewish ancestry may well support homosexuality. That is quite different from trying to claim legitimacy from Judaism's unwavering, three-thousand-year-old opposition to sodomy. After all, it is the Bible which proclaims homosexual behavior to be unacceptable. Support of gay marriage may be the view of many Americans, including some of Jewish ancestry, but it is not the view of Judaism nor of large numbers of Jews.

OFFICIAL VOICE OF JUDAISM?

As an Orthodox rabbi, what worries me is that the above statement was issued by rabbis belonging to an organization called the Central Conference of American Rabbis. The subtle nuances of denominational affiliation are lost on many of my Christian friends, just as so few Jews understand the difference between Lutherans and Southern Baptists.

To many Americans, the Central Conference of American Rabbis sounds as if it is the official voice of American Judaism. To many, it probably sounds more authentic than the Sanhedrin. Thus, Jews in America come to be inadvertently perceived as actively supportive of policies that a majority of Americans view as not only anti-biblical, but also destructive to society. It is hard to conceive of a scenario in which this will help Jews or Judaism thrive in America. It is a lot easier to perceive circumstances in which it will hurt.

Reform Judaism, at its inception, not only strayed from Jewish Law but actively rejected it. When the first class of American Reform rabbis was being graduated by Cincinnati's Hebrew Union College in 1883, the menu for the banquet consisted of little neck clams, soft-shell crabs, and shrimp salad—all shellfish dishes. Shellfish so flagrantly violate the Old Testament dietary laws we call *kashruth* (keeping kosher) that they are not eaten even by many Jews who are not fully observant of the Law. To many Jews, eating shellfish is almost akin to eating pork. Thus, without doubt Hebrew Union College deliberately insulted Judaism and designed a way to offend all Jews who cared about tradition. Its inaugural rabbinical graduation was a statement that it found traditional Judaism irrelevant and worthy of mockery. Not surprisingly, an attempt in 1983 to gather the descendants of those original rabbis to celebrate the centennial of the graduation was abandoned. It turned out to be virtually impossible to locate any of that group's descendants who still identified themselves as Jews. Reform Judaism has often been termed the last station on the way out of Judaism and the first on the way in. I think the former is truer than the latter, although there are wonderfully encouraging signs of change among the movement's younger leaders.

In recent years, the Reform movement has moved closer to traditional Jewish customs, encouraging some forms of Sabbath and even kashruth observance. Many reform Jews are learning more about Judaism and drawing closer to their religion, whereas the past generation of reform Jews was predominately moving away from religion. However, as a movement, Reform Judaism still does not believe in one of the basic tenets of Judaism: that the Bible is the absolute and direct Word of God. Since that belief is lacking, Reform Judaism has little or no connection with the Jewish Law to which I and other Orthodox Jews subscribe. So when Reform rabbis speak in favor of homosexual marriage, it comes as no surprise because it follows their long tradition of supporting many things Judaism opposes—and opposing many things Judaism supports.

A friend of mine who is a past president of his Reform temple tells me that since Reform Judaism rejects the principle of religious authority itself, nobody expects temple members to agree with the Rabbinate. Why should they? In the move away from accepting traditional Jewish authority, the Reform rabbis also have no ecclesiastical authority over their congregations. Each member can accept and reject any pronouncement of the rabbis as they choose. So, a statement by the official voice of the Reform movement tells us absolutely nothing about Judaism, and it doesn't reliably tell us much about Reform Jews either.

Similarly, who can blame any American for assuming that an organization called the University of Judaism speaks for Judaism? Can I really expect a resident of South Dakota to know that the above university is run by the Conservative movement of Judaism, and that Conservative Jews are quite different from Jewish conservatives? Seldom making the headlines are smaller Orthodox groups such as Agudath Israel or the Rabbinical Council of America, which on more than one occasion have sided with Christian groups on topics such as the Defense of Marriage Act in 1996. These Jewish groups are often ignored by the *New York Times* category of media.

To Tell the Truth

The whole situation seems a ghoulish imitation of the old television show "To Tell the Truth," in which three people, each claiming to be the same person, challenged the panel to decide which two were lying. That is the sad condition in which the American Jewish community finds itself today. Anyone can claim to speak for the Jewish people, but neither Jewish nor non-Jewish Americans are capable of discerning the validity of the claim. Judaism is often publicly represented by Reform stances. In this way, positions that would make Abraham weep, Moses thunder, and Maimonides despair get portrayed *not* as positions held by Jews who reject large parts of the Jewish tradition, but as *the* Jewish position.

While it has been true for thousands of years that in most generations many Jews reject Jewish teachings, what has changed in the last few centuries is that these Jews insist their views are correct. They claim that *they* are the authentic heirs of Judaism. In fact, Orthodox Jews make them distinctly uncomfortable. Many Reform Jewish friends are being quite candid with me when they confess that they would be more comfortable with their children becoming Buddhists than becoming Orthodox Jews.

Reject the Dogma, Not the Person

It is important here to make a distinction between people and dogma. I grew up in a home that was open to all Jews no matter what their level of observance, and I have emulated my parents in this regard. Pacific Jewish Center, the innovative outreach synagogue in Venice, California, that Michael Medved and I established in 1978 and where I served as rabbi for fifteen years, was known throughout the country as the little *shul* on the beach that welcomed all Jews regardless of their level of observance. All were invited to learn about their faith, but there was never any pressure to adopt religious practice. My wife and I do not grill guests at our house to determine whether they are Sabbath observant, kosher, or heterosexual. We are often aware that they are not one or more of the above. That is a private matter between them and God. In this we follow the example of our founding father, Abraham. We have always seen our role as providing hospitality while making ourselves available as educators and, to the best of our meager abilities, role models.

Yet there is a line that cannot be crossed. When I was growing up, there were members of my father's Orthodox synagogue who violated the Sabbath laws and who ate non-kosher food. But back in those days, they would have loudly objected had someone tried to tell them that what they were doing was perfectly legitimate from a Jewish perspective. Today, the opposite is true. No matter how far from Judaism an action or idea is, there are Jewish groups and rabbis who will attempt to legitimize it. For example, at the time of America's founding, if a Jew traveled by coach on the Sabbath, he knew he was violating Jewish law. Today, there are hundreds of rabbis who will publicly explain that getting on an airplane or in a car on Saturday in no way violates the Jewish Sabbath. While I still welcome that Jew and even that rabbi into my home, I can no longer be silent on the topic. Once someone portrays violations of Jewish Law and tradition as virtuous, it ceases to be a private matter between that individual and his God. In the face of what is now a public distortion of Judaism; it becomes incumbent upon me to clarify the truth, while still distinguishing between that person and his beliefs. One can reject and abhor actions while retaining affection and love for those performing the actions. A Jew who eats pork or supports homosexuality might well find himself welcomed to my *Shabbat* table and we can even avoid those topics during our conversation. When he flagrantly wears a T-shirt proclaiming himself a member of the National Jewish Pork Eaters League or Jews for Homosexual Marriage, I am forced to speak out.

I am perfectly willing to admit that any individual Reform Jew may well be a better person or even a better Jew than I. Only our Creator knows for sure. But that individual cannot rightly claim that his *actions* of eating non-kosher food or endorsing homosexual marriage are aspects of his being a good Jew. A good Jew can only be defined by the extent to which he or she struggles and sacrifices to keep as many as possible of the 613 commandments of the Torah. Only God can decide which laws He considers most important, and that is why I only judge actions and not any individual as a whole. But no Jew can make a valid claim that the sanctity of marriage as a relationship between a man and a woman or keeping the dietary laws are no longer necessary components of Judaism, any more than a Jew can legitimately claim that believing in Jesus is necessary to be a fulfilled Jew. At that point you are speaking about a different religion than the one I practice.

TRADITIONALISM IS NOT HATE

There is an attempt to portray those of us who cleave to the traditions of our fathers as harsh and hate-filled. I must point out that it was Reform Judaism that initially decided to move away from traditional Judaism. It is thus a bit disingenuous for this movement to now cry "unfair" that it is not respected by those who stay committed to the Judaism of two thousand years ago. When one Orthodox rabbinical group issued a statement in 1997 that Reform Judaism was not an authentic portrayal of Judaism, the official spokesmen for Reform Judaism created an uproar. They insisted that Orthodox rabbis had declared that Reform Jews are not Jews. Although this was not what was said, they nonetheless conveyed it this way to their irate membership.

There has also been fallacious reasoning lately that one can mandate respect. Sorry, that isn't true. The law rightly prevents us from physically harming someone with whom we disagree, but the law cannot force us to respect him. I am prohibited from assaulting an adulterer but I cannot be forced to respect him or his stance that adultery is really no big deal. Similarly, some Reform rabbis plaintively call out to their more traditional brethren, "Our Judaism is just as valid as yours, and you are intolerant if you do not believe that," as if that could possibly force anyone to endorse their distortion of Judaism. Having taken a position in opposition to the beliefs and practices of the last 3,000 years of Jewish life, they then profess shock that their beliefs and practices are not accepted by those of us who have retained the tradition. The choice was theirs, and they must live with the choices they made. Though I can (and must) accept and love them as fellow people and fellow Jews, I can no more condone the validity of their positions than I can comfortably wolf down a ham sandwich on the solemn fast day of Yom Kippur.

CHAPTER FORTY-TWO

WHY ARE JEWS SO LIBERAL?

GOD AND HIS WAYS ARE OUT-OF-DATE AND
REPRESSIVE COMPARED TO THE "ENLIGHTENED"
WISDOM OF HUMANKIND.

We are still left with the question, "Why are Jews so visible and prominent in liberal causes?"

Well-intentioned and philo-Semitic Americans, decent folk without an anti-Semitic bone in their bodies, are genuinely puzzled by this question. Why do the descendants of the people who gave the world the Ten Commandments seem more hostile to them than anyone else in America? As I hear from my lecture audiences around the country and from callers to my radio show, this question baffles people. After a great deal of thought and years spent in detailed analyses of countless ancient Jewish texts that predict this trend in my people, the following is my answer.

OUR SEARCH FOR "LIBERATION"

To understand this phenomenon, one has to know that Jewish attraction to liberalism is not new. In one form or another, many Jews have been liberals for more than three thousand years. Talmudic tradition reports that upon receiving the Ten Commandments, the Israelites wept. Their gloom was caused by the realization that the godly revelation they had just experienced now prohibited the lascivious lifestyle to which they had grown accustomed in Egypt. At that moment, liberalism was born: the eternal search for "liberation" from God's seemingly restrictive rules. There are those who will always seek—or if necessary, create—the escape hatch through which those who find God's rules too limiting can flee. Liberalism, under many different names, has always found eager converts.

As Aldous Huxley wrote with candor in *Confessions of a Professional Free Thinker*: "We were opposed to morality because it interfered with our sexual freedom."

Note that I am not claiming that every single Jewish liberal is consciously aware of trying to escape God's rules—of course not. However I shall demonstrate later how this underlying principle fuels all of secular liberalism's adherents. Meanwhile, you should realize that of all religions, few exercise such detailed control over every aspect of daily life as does Judaism. Oscar Wilde defined the cynic as one who knows the price of everything and the value of nothing. Too many Jews see only the price of religious discipline. They correctly note that the Torah instructs how to walk and how to talk, how to rise in the morning and how to retire at night. For those disciples of Moses who wish to know, it speaks of how and when to pray and what and how to eat. It mandates whom to marry and how to make love. It demands that couples try to have children and specifies how to raise them.

Consider how the life of a religious, decent, law-abiding Christian would change were he to become persuaded that God is nothing but an artificial construct of needy people. Should a Christian become liberated from God, he would be horribly impoverished in his spiritual life, to be sure. There may be ethical and moral ramifications down the road. But, in those first few heady days or even years, he might not significantly alter his life-style. At first, he would only see a few extra hours available every Sunday morning since there would now be little reason to go to church. He would still remain a true husband and a devoted father. He would still go to work every Monday morning and deliver an honest day's work for an honest day's pay. He would be just as unlikely to become enmeshed in criminal activity. The tremendous impact of the vanishing of God might even be concealed in his generation.

THE LURE OF LIBERALISM

Now imagine how I would be affected by the disappearance of God. Do you have any idea how curious I am about the taste of a McDonald's cheeseburger? There is only one reason I have not yet tried it—God said no. Were I persuaded that there is no God, it would take only a millisecond for me to head for my local McDonald's. So many people seem to love oysters and lobster. They cannot surely all be wrong. With no God around to spoil things for me, I would finally find out for myself just how satisfying these culinary favorites can be. Many other sensual adventures would beckon tantalizingly and I happily, with no God, could think of no reason to refrain. I would no longer have to explain to my boss or clients why I couldn't work on Saturdays or for a third of the month of September during Jewish religious holidays, and yes, wow—I could even attend baseball games on Friday nights. Everything down to my physical relationship with my wife would be impacted within the first days of my decision to throw off Torah observance.

Even non-observant Jews would benefit. You need only think of entertainers like Woody Allen to know how obsessed with God are even those Jews who have long since shrugged off any intimate relationship with Him. Most vacationing Jews who order bacon and eggs for breakfast invariably glance around guiltily as if expecting Moses, or at least their rabbi to suddenly walk into the hotel dining room.

Like keen athletes, some descendants of Abraham see lifestyle-enhancing benefits in a religious regimen. However, many non-observant Jews desperately pursue liberalism, *often unconsciously*, as a way out of their Covenant. This is the true purpose of liberalism, and Jews are its disproportionate champions because, more than anyone else, they desperately yearn for an escape from having to accept the seeming rigors of Jewish law. Those Jews who observe kosher food laws, the Sabbath, and marital laws know that it isn't easy. Many of those who don't observe these laws still feel lingering guilt and resent any suggestion that they are still as binding as they were on the day they were given on Mount Sinai.

Adhering to some of God's rules suggests that the Jewish soul owes allegiance to them all. Is God your boss or isn't He? Better to reject them all than feel obligated to abide by any. Once eating lobster is normalized, eventually homosexuality and abortion are also permitted, even if it takes a few generations to get there. The more you need to rationalize that eating lobster is actually all right the more your need to insist that everything else is all right too. How intoxicating and liberating the rejection of God's Law can seem for Jews! How appealing is liberalism.

This explains why non-observant Jews often lead the fight for the acceptance of homosexuality as a normative lifestyle. The only timeless stand against sodomy is the Bible's. With regard to abortion, any suggestion that anyone other than the woman concerned should enjoy veto power over the next generation concedes the existence of an external authority on values. Modern liberalism simply means becoming "liberated" from the external authority of God. God either does not exist or He is irrelevant, so He and His ways are out-of-date, out-of-touch, and unnecessarily repressive compared to the enlightened wisdom of humankind.

Many Jews and non-Jews who reject God's authority on how we live and on how we organize our families and our society still purport to believe in God. For the most part they embrace a uniquely American forms of atheism which applauds a lying, philandering, scandal-ridden president who leaves church with a Bible clutched under his arm only to rush across town and address a defiant, fund-raising gathering of ultra-Left Hollywood abortion activists. America's unique form of atheism enables people to arrive at their houses of worship in order to participate in a gay pride service. This form of atheism declares, of course, that religion and God are important, but that their importance is either confined to the ethereal or that God and religion should be formed in our own image. Sure we believe in God, says the liberal. In whatever form He, She, or It may take for each individual.

WHERE DO YOU STAND?

We cannot ignore the fact that for every church and synagogue opposing liberal doctrine there is another church or synagogue ardently backing it. For this reason, each and every American citizen must accept the responsibility of examining carefully where he or she stands rather than rely on a person's religious title to choose that spokesman as their representative. In Civil War days, when the church was one of the main inspirations for emancipation activity, other religious leaders regularly quoted the Bible to represent pro-slavery views. Similarly today, religious leaders with titles such as bishop, minister, pastor, and rabbi can be found on both ends of the tug-of-war. While those few who openly and honestly declare themselves atheists are clearly on the opposite side from religious traditionalists, the New Age spirituality found among liberation theologians in both Judaism and Christianity muddy the waters. For the most part, these are well-intentioned folk who want to "fix the world" but have no intention of making themselves subservient to God's revealed wisdom. Instead, most of the programs on their agenda happen to conflict with traditional understanding. They have been devastatingly effective in their anti-traditional activism because they have usurped the nomenclature of the church. Aware of how responsive Americans are to God's Word, they turned that admirable trait to sad ends.

Liberalism often employs enough religious language to express concern and compassion, suggesting a moral basis for its ideals. For instance, Left-leaning clergy of both the Jewish and Christian traditions frequently quote the Bible to support high taxes. However, all the Bible yields for these purposes are vague references to "justice" and "charity," requiring monumental interpretive efforts in order to produce the desired conclusions. As we have seen, however, specific and authoritative Jewish texts address the issue of taxation quite unequivocally and leave no doubt as to the disastrous impact of Left-wing economic policies.

In his Farewell Address, George Washington referred to religion and morality as the "firmest props of the duties of men and citizens." It was Thomas Jefferson who grounded the Declaration of Independence with four references to the Creator. But when First Lady Hillary Clinton, prodded by her fraudulent spiritual gurus, issues a call for "a new politics of meaning" to cure the "spiritual vacuum" afflicting America, nobody really believes that she means a return to Judeo-Christian values. Secular humanists in and out of the White House, in ecclesiastical costume and out, have learned to use phrases such as "We need to make room in the culture for a public discussion of our common spiritual life.... We need to rediscover together what is truly sacred." The best response to this nonsense was that of Jewish conservative columnist Charles Krauthammer: "Rediscover? For most Americans there is no need to rediscover the transcendent. They live with it. It is called religion."

On the Left flank of today's political landscape are leaders posturing as Old Testament prophets. Only a few short years ago they might have been protesting everything American, promoting free love, free speech, and free drugs as they occupied university buildings from Berkeley to Harvard. Today's political opportunism requires a more acceptable image, and few images are more convenient than that of an Old Testament prophet. Denouncing the establishment from the pulpit feels more important and, yes, more legitimate than doing so from the colleges and cafes. This is especially true nowadays when the "establishment" has so little self-confidence that it not only tolerates Old Testament denouncers, it positively lionizes them. It took considerably more courage to play Elijah to Ahab and Jezebel than it does today to play the role of angry clergyman.

Posing as an Old Testament prophet is rather convenient because it grants one the right to tell other people what to do while leaving the prophet himself immune to moral scrutiny. So-called "Prophetic Judaism" has always served as a cloak to conceal the hypocrisy of Jewish liberation theology. Liberation theologians of all stripes have always understood America's love for the Word of God and its affinity for the language of transcendence. Understanding that we are moved more by calls of conscience than by expediency, they have simply usurped the nomenclature of the church for their own agenda.

Well, my God and the God of my fellow religious conservatives has a great deal to say about the real world. I do not only listen to God in order to find out which psalms to recite when the celebration of the New Moon coincides with Sabbath. When God's view and my personal yearnings clash, I know that I should be the one to submit. I try to listen to God on absolutely every detail of life. I am not strong enough to always obey, but I always later regret my weakness. In common with all other truly religious Jews and Christians, I am not a free spirit. I am a servant—a servant of the Creator. Jews have always been seduced by liberalism in such numbers because we have so much more law to become liberated from than other faiths. Liberalism—rejecting God—is simply more emancipating for Jews than for anyone else.

JEWISH GUILT

Why can't Jews simply cease being Jewish when they abandon the tenets of the religion? Why do they insist that they are still good Jews even though they are writing their own definitions as to what that means? Why do so many of them insist that their liberalism is an expression *of* their Judaism? Why do some of the Jews whose grandparents long ago rejected the authority of the Torah's rules on Sabbath observance or kosher food insist on having animal rights or homosexual Passover seders (that conform to none of the rules for the seder) rather than just ignore Passover altogether? Well, many of them do. Vast numbers of Jews whose grandparents abandoned traditional observance have become totally assimilated, have intermarried, or converted to other religions. They have nothing to do with any form of Judaism. Other Jews have retained a cultural connection, or are comfortable with their level of observance whatever it may be.

But there are many Jews, no matter how removed from Jewish tradition, who still feel Moses peering over their shoulders. Jewish guilt is a wondrous reality. It is tremendously difficult for the Jewish soul to throw off the dozens of generations that preceded it. Many of the Jews who regularly eat pork do so either defiantly or self-consciously. They would love nothing better than to be liberated from their guilt feelings. That can only happen if they convince themselves that they are, in fact, doing the right thing. "Old-fashioned," "stubborn" Jews like me really bother them. I have witnessed this on many occasions when I find myself at a lunch meeting with a non-observant Jew. For me, it is never a big deal to sit and drink coffee while my secular Jewish associate tucks into his non-kosher meal. For him it is invariably a big deal. More than once I have had a business meeting interrupted when my companion erupts into a lengthy denunciation of Jewish tradition. I respond by assuring him that the law of Moses is still alive and strong in his heart because, were that not the case, he would respond far less defensively to my luncheon choice. He could, as non-Jewish businessmen do, ignore my actions, or simply say, "Oh, I don't keep kosher." Yet, he finds my keeping kosher disturbing. To him it is a condemnation of the fact that he doesn't. Hundreds of Jews who have become Orthodox as adults have told me that their non-Jewish friends and business associates evince interest or at least respect towards the changes in their lives. Jewish contacts, on the other hand, display hostility and ridicule towards them for adopting a new (very old) lifestyle. I have proven this further by experimentation: I have informed secular Jewish lunch companions that I have recently adopted a vegetarian, macro-biotic diet so I shall not have more than a glass of water. This announcement is invariably greeted by congratulations on my wisdom and self-restraint. My companions often tell me that they know that they too ought to switch to a strict diet. When I then blow my cover and laughingly confess that my diet is actually inspired by the Torah's kosher laws, I discover that my joke has backfired. Secular Jews just have no sense of humor. They simply fail to see how hilarious it is when every ridiculous rule or foolish fad earns their respect unless it happens to come from God, in which case they condemn it as outmoded, regressive, judgmental, primitive, and dangerous.

The fact that so many secularized Jews feel a need to justify their abandonment of tradition is, for me, one of the surest signs that something momentous happened to the Jewish people 3,300 years ago at the foot of Mount Sinai.

THE JEWISH NEED FOR PURPOSE

But Jewish guilt isn't the whole answer. There is, I believe, a yearning for God found at the core of every Jew. Those who do not find the correct path do not ignore that yearning. Instead, in the search for truth, they wander along false avenues. In the past this has led to disproportionate Jewish support for socialism and communism. In our times, as both of those doctrines have proven compassionate in theory but cruel in reality, liberalism and secular humanism have taken their place. Liberalism flourishes in the secular Jewish community for two reasons. First, as I just stated, the liberal attempt to perfect the world obscures the conviction, deep in every Jewish soul, that God expects Jews to abide by all His rules and that through Him alone will the world attain completion. Second, also deep in the Jewish soul, is a need to do more than exist. Just as some souls have a need for music while others yearn for artistic expression, the Jewish people, as a collective group, strive to improve the world. This has led to the introduction of monotheism and much of the moral system by which the world survives. It has led to the disproportionate number of scientists, business leaders, and thought generators of Jewish heritage who have immeasurably benefited mankind. It has even led to an amazing number of Jewish converts to Christianity, who not only convert but move into the leadership of many Christian activist movements. I do not think it is coincidental that the highly effective leader of the American Center for Law and Justice (ACLJ), Pat Robertson's legal answer to the ACLU, is Jay Sekulow—a devout Christian who was raised as a Reform Jew. Likewise, religious Christian Lou Sheldon, the tireless and beloved head of the Traditional Values Coalition, was born to a Jewish mother. A Jew, even when, and possibly especially when, he abandons traditional Judaism still yearns to impact the world. Some Jews accomplish this through medicine, business, or other means. That yearning has also led to a disproportionate number of Jewish activists in secular and decadent movements. The majority of Jews are decent, moral people. But those who aren't are not going to merely think incorrectly; they are going to agitate for their destructive views to be accepted in the name of *tikkun olam,* improving the world.

SELECTIVE SYMPATHY OR THE OFFICIAL VOICE

Having explained why individuals of Jewish ancestry may be radically liberal, we still have another question. Why do so many official voices of the Jewish community line up at the liberal end of the tug-of-war?

The standard answer that Jewish leadership prefers to give to this question, is that because Jews have been a persecuted minority for so long, we empathize with other downtrodden people. We assume liberalism to be a kinder, gentler philosophy than conservatism. Liberalism seems to be morally superior, and in fact, many warm hearted, well meaning Jews have been told so by their rabbis and the leadership of Jewish organizations.

Each year, Jews read the words in the Passover seder: "Remember that you were once slaves in the land of Egypt." The Egyptian experience was the first in a long sequence of oppressions. Jews have retained that feeling in our national consciousness, leading to an ability to identify with the underdog. For individual Jews this is definitely an appeal of the politics of compassion.

But, while this may be true on an individual level, it is unconvincing when applied to the community at large. Indeed, the Jewish organizational establishment does not support all underdogs. It sympathizes very selectively, too often identifying with whichever side comes closest to opposing traditional Judeo-Christian values. Thus, prominent Jewish organizations were far more vocal in their sympathy for the Los Angeles rioters in April 1992 than for the hard-working, family-minded Korean shopkeepers, many of whom were active Christians. No major Jewish organization raised funds to assist the Koreans who were surely the victims of what could only be described as a pogrom.

This was selective sympathy at its worst. Having often been victims of rampaging mobs throughout our history, surely Jews should have stood in solidarity with and raised money for these innocent Korean victims. But they did not.

Likewise, Jews constantly position themselves as standing against censorship. Yet, how many Jewish organizations protested the decision by the University of California at Monterey student book store not to stock any books by "dead white males"?

When the local Jewish old age home informs Jewish communal leadership that a raise in the minimum wage will impair their ability to take care of their residents, the leadership supports the increase anyway. Why does compassion not insist that being able to house and care for our own elderly be the Jewish priority?

Jewish groups pick and choose their issues very carefully. Invariably, the majority of so-called Jewish organizations, and certainly the large nationally known ones, will line up not with the underdog but with secular liberal dogma. And they tell themselves that they are doing the morally correct thing.

SECULAR HUMANISM IS A FAITH

But wait a minute—isn't morality a characteristic of a religious faith? We all consider our faith to be morally superior; that is one of the reasons we remain totally committed to our faith. Well, liberalism is a religious faith. Or to be more accurate, it is an anti-religious faith. Just as you cannot be a Jewish Christian because they are two separate faiths, you cannot belong to both the faiths of secular humanism (modern liberalism) and Judaism. You do have to choose. In the same way I tell my children that I can only ally myself with the conservative political movement or the Republican Party to the extent that they coincide with Judaism. At any point, now or in the future, that Judaism and the Republican Party part ways, my allegiance is clear. Judaism triumphs. For me, conservatism in America in the 1990s is an outgrowth of my Judaism. In another time or place in history I might well be on the side of those advocating other policies if those policies are closer to authentic Jewish tradition. Today in America however, there is no doubt at all that vast numbers of Jews are being misled into believing that modern liberalism is identical to Judaism.

CHAPTER FORTY-THREE

REPLACING RELIGION WITH POLITICS

JEWISH ORGANIZATIONAL HOSTILITY TO CHRISTIAN
CONSERVATIVES HAS LESS TO DO WITH RELIGION
AND MUCH TO DO WITH POLITICS.

I constantly explain to audiences that for too many Jews, liberalism has become their de facto religion. Judaism comes in second at best. What makes me say this?

Jews voted for both Dukakis and Clinton twice as enthusiastically as did the rest of America. The spokesmen for groups like the Gay, Lesbian and Bisexual Veterans of America or National Gay and Lesbian Task Force are all too often Jewish. Many of the member organizations of the Religious Coalition for Reproductive Choice are Jewish. The membership of the American Civil Liberties Union (ACLU), a champion of ultra-liberal causes, is disproportionately high in Jews. The ACLU's leadership is almost reminiscent of a temple board meeting.

LEFT-EYE MYOPIA

When the media want a comment from a women's organization, they routinely seek a spokeswoman from the National Organization for Women. Most Americans would be forgiven for believing NOW's membership is so large that the organization can speak fairly for the nation's female population. Unfortunately for this theory, there happens to be another women's group with a far larger membership. But you will seldom hear of Concerned Women for America being approached for a comment because the media are not really looking for a representative female comment, but rather for a liberal female comment. Similarly, female Republican elected officials and other conservative female activists didn't seem to matter when "The Year of the Woman" was pronounced. Despite their significant numbers and contributions to society they were inconvenient to the liberal world view and thus ignored.

In her book *What's Right For All Americans: A Fearless Los Angeles Schoolteacher Challenges the Black Political Establishment,* black schoolteacher and activist Ezola Foster speaks of the discrepancy between most American blacks, who supported and were proud of Clarence Thomas's nomination to the Supreme Court, and the hostile liberal stance of the NAACP (the National Association for the Advancement of Colored People). Likewise, most retired Americans join AARP (the American Association for Retired Persons) for discounts on prescription medicine and other perks, not as an endorsement of the organization's far-Left politics. These groups, as well as many other American organizations, were long ago hijacked by liberal activists who earned their academic degrees from the radicalized universities of the 1960s and 1970s. As these organizations veered to the Left, their constituents were either unaware or absorbed their Left-wing world view as the only acceptable viewpoint for their particular interest group.

Unfortunately, many Jewish organizations have suffered from the same dynamic. Often staffed by radicals of similar ilk, these groups have misguidedly allied themselves with the far left reaches of the Democratic Party. Great effort is expended to maintain that connection.

An effective tactic used extensively by secular fundamentalists is to present only one side of the story. Before the 1996 elections, a Florida rabbi from the Conservative branch of Judaism (religiously between Orthodox and Reform though politically to the Left) scheduled a debate between a Jewish conservative and a Jewish liberal. The board of directors canceled the debate for fear that the Jewish conservative might make the stronger argument, thus encouraging attendees to vote Republican. In other words, they preferred keeping their members ignorant rather than run the risk that being fully informed might lead them to vote differently from how the Jewish organizational structure thought best.

The policy of "left-eye myopia" is transparent. Much of the media, along with Jewish organizations, scrutinize unevenly and see only what they want to see.

Geoffrey Fieger, a hopeless Democratic candidate for governor in the 1998 elections, compared Orthodox rabbis to Nazis. I am sure he is an embarrassment to his party, and I personally don't hold the Democratic Party responsible for his statements. Why do I, like so many other conservatives in this country, suspect that were he a Republican, Jewish groups nationwide would be pointing to him as proof that every Republican was tainted?

Did you hear about the time Hillary Clinton looked out on a group of youngsters and said that this country would not be on the right track until Americans looked on all children and saw the face of Jesus? Hillary really did say that; most Americans never heard about it. How might the *New York Times* have responded had that statement been made by Newt Gingrich? After all, such a statement coming from a Republican would have demonstrated a blatant lack of respect for Jews and other non-Christians, would it not? Coming from a Republican leader, it would have made headlines and been repeated for years. Why, then, did not only the media, but Jewish organizations, only report Hillary's statement as a minor footnote? Why did Jewish Federations around the country not agonize over the inevitable repression of minorities should Hillary's husband be elected? Instead, the media, other liberal groups, and the usually vocal Jewish groups constantly on the lookout for bigotry, made light of her statement.

Amazingly, Jewish groups have even continued to honor Mrs. Clinton even after her open support for Palestinian statehood. The fact that she was warmly received at a United Jewish Appeal event after such political comments tends to support a contention of mine. If America's liberal Jews had to choose between a conservative America that genuinely guaranteed safety and security for Israel and a secular liberal America that threw Israel to the wolves, Israel would lose. If the deal offered to American Jews was become pro-life in exchange for Israel's survival, the answer would be a resounding "no way."

"IF YOU'RE CONSERVATIVE, IT NEVER HAPPENED"

My experience reveals the same bias. I was privileged to speak at the Republican National Convention in August 1996. After I returned home to Seattle, my speech in San Diego was covered by the local Seattle TV stations, the *Seattle Times,* the *Eastside Week,* and other Washington State papers. Seattle's *Jewish Transcript,* always on the watch for Jewish Seattle-ites who make the news, had not one word to say regarding my appearance. You must understand that I was not at all peeved; only amused. With the national exposure I did receive, there was nothing I needed from the *Jewish Transcript.* But the incident certainly helps to highlight the syndrome—the Jewish community ignores conservatives. When a local doctor wrote a letter to the editor asking why my speech was ignored, his letter was likewise disregarded, although the tiny local paper's editor did courteously call me to inquire whether it was true that I felt neglected. I like her and indicated that I felt no animus at all. Neglected? Sure, but no animus. In the same year, another Orthodox rabbi addressed the Democratic National Convention. Not surprisingly, Jewish papers throughout America stated that it was the first time an Orthodox rabbi had ever spoken at one of the major conventions. My appearance had been eradicated without a trace— political revisionism in action and the farthest thing from objective journalism. If it were not so childishly funny, I'd say I had been purged in the finest Stalinist tradition.

This tendency of the sixty or so Jewish weeklies to print only news which supports their views is quite common throughout America's Jewish communities. They are often published by local Jewish Federations which, rather than representing the entire Jewish community, sometimes represent only the liberal Jewish community. For instance, a study in Indianapolis showed the Indianapolis Jewish community to be especially conservative. Yet the local Federation issued a statement opposing home schooling, an issue of total irrelevance to the local Jewish community (except for the local Jewish home schoolers themselves) but of relevance to the teacher unions who are key to the liberal coalition. A survey by the Jewish Council for Public Affairs (an arm of the Jewish Federation) showed many such discrepancies. For example, 68 percent of community relations council leaders felt that racial, gender and ethnic quotas should be a factor in university admissions and hiring, while only 47 percent of donors to the federations thought that way. Twenty percent more leaders than donors objected to religious displays on public grounds. For decades the Jewish Federations of every major city have been sources of almost legendary generosity to all citizens. They have made many of us proud to be Jewish. It would be tragic if their legacy should now be squandered by them switching their mission from helping people to indoctrinating them with anti-religious propaganda.

WHAT IS YOUR RELIGION?

When a representative of the American Jewish Committee, Hyman Bookbinder, told the press that House Speaker Newt Gingrich was a "disaster for what we Jews believe in," it is interesting to ask what he actually meant by that phrase. In fact, one can make sense of his reply only by recalling that liberals have tried to equate Judaism with liberalism. His answer included affirmative action, welfare, prohibition of prayer in schools, no private school vouchers, abortion rights and rights of homosexuals. I think it would have been more accurate had he claimed to speak for circumcised liberals rather than for Jews. Bookbinder's list has far more in common with the concerns of the Democratic Party platform than it does with those of Judaism.

Likewise, The Jewish Telegraphic Agency ran a story entitled "Christian Right: a Threat in Local Elections," by Debra Nussbaum Cohen. She warned that candidates endorsed by the Christian religious Right "who have been winning local political races around the country, pose a serious threat to Jewish interests." By way of explanation, she added, "Once on school boards, for example, they advocate school prayer, teaching creationism in science classes, removal of books with content they consider profane, and eradicating AIDS education in favor of teaching abstinence."

The items on both those agendas are either in direct opposition to Jewish law, or items of interest and debate but certainly not belief. Yet these Left-wing dogmas have been elevated in parts of the Jewish community to a sacred status so that it is now virtually heretical to oppose them. Knowing how heretics are treated will give you a clue as to how the Jewish establishment reacts to Jewish conservatives.

School vouchers is a particularly illustrative case of Jewish commitment to liberalism. Studies repeatedly commissioned by communities concerned at diminished Jewish commitment, consistently show that one of the strongest barriers to assimilation is a Jewish education. However, most Jewish day schools are foundering in a sea of red ink. Faced with costs of upward of $5,000 in tuition bills, many parents with large families who want such a religious foundation for their children simply cannot afford it. School vouchers could well be the most important development in strengthening the Jewish community. It is quite difficult for anyone professing concern for Judaism and Jewish survival not to become a vigorous advocate of no strings attached school vouchers.

What would you expect Jewish communal leadership to do? Would they embrace an obvious solution to the growing educational problems in spite of its being a conservative solution? No, of course not; Jewish leadership considers loyalty to the Democratic Party and its allies in the National Education Association to be more important than their own children's educational opportunities. Now that is real commitment—a religious commitment—a unwavering commitment to the fundamentalist faith of secular liberalism.

"NOT REALLY JEWISH"

The following occurrence amused me. An acquaintance recounted a conversation she had with a secretary at the Los Angeles Jewish Federation when she called to find out if the Federation could give her information on the pending local school voucher initiative. She was emphatically told that school vouchers were bad for the Jewish community and all Jews should oppose them. When my friend replied that well-known Jewish spokesmen Dennis Prager, Michael Medved and I were in favor of the vouchers, she was told, "Well, they're not really Jewish." So, to an employee of the Los Angeles Jewish Federation, a body charged with representing about half a million Jews, voting with the liberal establishment was more significant than keeping kosher, observing the Sabbath, praying in *teffilin* (phylacteries), and teaching Torah.

This woman's statement not only disenfranchised me, it ignored the traditional and religious Jewish community which supported the voucher initiative. In spite of broad-based support that included religious Jews, evangelical Christians, and many members of "minority" groups, Initiative 174 failed that year in California. Friends of mine in Orange County told me it was defeated largely by the activism, resources, and media connections of the Los Angeles Jewish community.

Once we see that much of the Jewish establishment has linked itself, as a religious conviction, with the Democratic Party, we can begin to understand why the Christian Right is treated with such hostility. As religious conservatism reinvigorated the Republican Party, secular Jews went on the assault. The truth is that Jewish organizational hostility to Christian conservatives had less to do with religion and much to do with politics. The Jewish Left's strategy was first to note the increasing presence of Christian conservatives energizing the Republican Party. The next step was to demonize these religious conservatives, thus suggesting that the Republican Party was steeped in anti-Semitism. The final stage of their nefarious campaign is to suggest that only liberalism stands between America's Jews and frightening images of Christian-inspired terror.

CHAPTER FORTY-FOUR

THE REDEFINING OF JUDAISM

CALLING LIBERALISM JUDAISM DOES NOT MAKE IT SO.

By now, the game should be apparent. Jewish groups have redefined Judaism to mean liberalism. They have then proceeded to define anti-liberalism as anti-Semitism. This is not only intellectually dishonest, it is utterly reprehensible. Anti-Semitism is often an unfair charge because it is undefined—which leaves the accused with no way to clear himself. If he did not do something to hurt Jews, then he must have said something to offend Jews. If he cannot be proven to have said anything nasty about Jews, then maybe he thought something we Jews might find offensive and naturally we claim to know what was in his heart. If he ever makes a foolish or boorish remark, anything else he may do or say is irrelevant. The unfounded charge of "anti-Semite" brands the victim and leaves the accuser absolved. It is time for us to recognize the charge of anti-Semitism for what it often is: a political weapon intended to bludgeon critics of liberalism into silence.

THE RELIGION OF LIBERALISM

You may think I am exaggerating. I find it hard to arrive at any different conclusion. When *Jewish Heritage* published an article in May 1997 titled "Christian Right Takes a Wrong Turn," its writer, Judith Peiss, was infuriated by the views of Tim LaHaye, a Christian author, on the unabashedly liberal American Civil Liberties Union (ACLU). LaHaye said that the ACLU was "the most effective humanistic organization for destroying the laws, morals, and traditional rights of Americans." Ms. Peiss argued that since the leadership of the ACLU is Jewish, LaHaye's characterization of the group is anti-Semitic.[1]

When Jews sided with Christians, they also had to be demeaned. Even the American Jewish Committee publication, *Natural Adversaries or Possible Allies? American Jews and the New Christian Right,* which, while aggressively liberal, at least attempts to be fair, revealed its own bias toward "adversaries" rather than "allies" by boasting how Jewish groups seldom let an opportunity slip by to sue religious Christians. For instance, the report claims, "When Arkansas passed the Balanced Treatment for Creation-Science and Evolution-Science Act [1981], Jewish agencies quickly joined the fight for judicial relief." It continued, "Only the Rabbinical Alliance, an organization of the ultra-Orthodox, joined in a convoluted philosophical brief on behalf of the creationists."[2]

What puzzled many sincere Christians was that Arkansas is not known for its large and conspicuous Jewish community. Why did a bill for which Arkansas had voted make New York Jews so angry? Furthermore, why was their side waging a noble war for "judicial relief" while the *ultra-Orthodox* (my emphasis) rabbis were only capable of advancing "convoluted" philosophical arguments?

As my political involvement increased and I spoke more frequently to large audiences around the country, I was to hear this complaint again and again: Any policy despised by the liberal establishment, even if good for Jews and in sync with traditional Judaism, is immediately condemned by secular Jewish leadership as violating Jewish principles. Those supporting the proposed policy become vilified as anti-Semites.

Look at it this way. If the voters in small Illinois and Texas towns vote out of office the only school board candidates with Jewish names, are they practicing anti-Semitism or prudence? Like so many Americans, these voters live rather conservative lives. They attend church regularly, they work hard at their jobs and, above all, they are trying to raise G-rated kids in an X-rated culture. It turns out that in the two cases I am familiar with, the Jewish school board officials were not only the most ardent advocates for condom training, they also regularly led the assault against graduation-day prayers. What do you expect a town of religious conservatives to do when they perceive their traditional cultural standards to be under liberal attack? They naturally voted according to how they perceived their interests. When we Jews practice it, we call it democracy; when Christians do it, we call it anti-Semitism.

It is crucial for Jews to understand that *those Texas and Illinois voters do not dislike Jews or Judaism—they very much dislike liberalism.* They are protecting their children from a liberal assault, not waging an anti-Semitic battle. Not entirely without justification, they attribute much of the decline in the quality of their daily lives to liberalism's four-decade domination of America's public policy.

Similarly, when women's groups proclaim that they need a liberal female to represent them as president, or black organizations claim that only a black person can represent them, such beliefs are regarded as reasonable. I certainly know that many Jews will vote for someone simply because he has a Jewish name. But let a Christian say that he wants to vote for a Christian and accusations of bigotry fill the air. This is quite astonishing, especially since being born black, female, or Jewish tells us nothing of a person's views. Yet when someone speaks of Christian values, he describes a world view. If women, blacks, Jews, and Christians want to "vote for their own," it seems to me that the Christian is the only one honestly acting on a philosophical rather than on a gender or racial level.

It cannot be stressed enough that Judaism is defined by what God instructed—not by what some, or even many, Jews might do. The majority of Jews may desecrate the Sabbath. That is irrelevant as to whether Sabbath observance is an inherent part of Judaism. Christmas trees do not become a Jewish observance just because many Jews set one up in their living rooms each December. Secularism and liberalism do not become Jewish values just because late twentieth-century Jewish organizations adopt them. If Judaism were dependent on the majority of Jews, it never would have made it as far as Mount Sinai. Jewish wisdom, handed down since the time of Moses, tells us that only 20 percent of Jews chose to leave Egypt. Given the choice of staying with the dominant culture of the day or going into the desert in order to worship God, 80 percent of Jews chose to stay behind. This scenario has been repeated often throughout Jewish history. A small group of Jews stay faithful to Judaism, while a majority of Jews fall away from observance. Within two or three generations the connection of this majority to Jewish roots is usually totally broken. We are possibly watching the dramatic shrinkage of America's Jewish community in our time.

Secular humanists may call their religion Judaism, but as Abraham Lincoln once stated, if you call a dog's tail a leg, the dog still has only four legs. Calling liberalism Judaism does not make it so. If calling homosexuality a sin makes one an anti-Semite, then I place myself with Moses and Aaron in that category. If opposing a woman's right to do what she wishes with her (pregnant or not) body makes one an anti-Semite, then I will classify myself as one along with Sarah, Rebecca, Rachel and Leah. If denouncing the act of a male lying with a male as a sin is termed hate filled bigotry, so be it. If liberalism equals Judaism, then almost all Orthodox Jews and Jewish texts, including the Old Testament, are inherently anti-Semitic. And Christian conservatives are deemed anti-Semitic for cherishing concepts that they share with Orthodox Jews all over the world. This dishonesty cannot continue much longer without eventually costing the Jewish community some of the very best friends it has ever had.

MAKING ENEMIES OF OUR FRIENDS

Imagine the confusion of a God-fearing Christian conservative who honors those who disobeyed German law during the Holocaust in order to save Jewish lives. His religious beliefs inform him that an unborn baby is a human life, despite the law of the land claiming otherwise. In this belief, he is emulating his heroes of fifty years ago who insisted that a Jewish person was a human being despite laws proclaiming otherwise. With no referendum in which he could participate, the American Supreme Court, by judicial fiat, imposed a ruling that is as morally repugnant to him as were the Nazi's laws to decent Germans. Consequently, this Christian supports candidates who believe as he does. His actions in trying to uphold his beliefs are greatly inspired by his contempt for those who looked the other way during the Holocaust.

To his utter astonishment, as he stands by the courage of his convictions, Jewish leadership brands him an anti-Semite because of those beliefs. Imagine how utterly bewildered a Christian Nebraskan might have been when Congressman John Christensen, in the 1994 Nebraska congressional race, was viciously attacked in a sermon given by Reform Rabbi Aryeh Azriel of Temple Israel. The *Omaha World Herald* carried the following report:

> The rabbi's sermon included the statement that some Jews worship on sacred days "to spite Hitler, to spite David Duke and Louis Farrakhan and Pat Buchanan and Lyndon H. LaRouche and the skinheads and the tombstone vandals and their ilk." Departing from a prepared text, the rabbi added the name of Christensen, the GOP nominee for the U.S. House of Representatives from Nebraska's second district.
>
> Rabbi Azriel, explaining why he mentioned Christensen, said, "I think with some of his views, including his view about the right of women to choose what they do with their bodies, he can be a threat."[3]

How can the Jewish community credibly condemn Holocaust revisionism when a statement like this is not repudiated from the rooftops of every synagogue in the country? Was Hitler's crime the opposition of abortions for Jewish women? One might think so from Rabbi Azriel's words, which imply Hitler must not have been such a bad guy after all. And no mainstream Jewish organization other than my own Toward Tradition, protested or condemned Rabbi Azriel's perfidy. This type of venomous assault and despicable insult of decent people's religious beliefs, bodes no good for Jews in this country. It is nothing less than an attempt to intimidate religious Christians, silence them, and politically disempower them. It is certainly radically inconsistent with the traditional Jewish defense of political and religious tolerance.

Surely one of the most bizarre and incomprehensible phenomena in contemporary political life is this assault that secular Jewish representatives are carrying out against religious Christian conservatives. Influential Jews, well-known Jewish groups, and powerful

Jewish publications seem to be single-minded in their attack. They are targeting Christian political candidates and the Christians who back them on both the local and the national level. This would be just another angle on "politics-as-usual" were it not for the fact that Jews are waging war against these people entirely on the basis of their religious beliefs. Let's not pretend that this is merely politics; it is bigotry—precisely the kind of bigotry that many of these Jewish organizations were formed to fight in the first place.

To attempt to intimidate people of other faiths into being afraid to speak openly of their beliefs is, in my mind, one of the most foolhardy things the Jewish community has ever done. It is wrong. It is immoral. It is hypocritical. And it is dreadfully unwise politics. Let us pray that it doesn't come back to haunt us.

Many years ago, gentiles sought reasons and excuses to hate Jews. Today many Christian Americans search for excuses not to hate Jews. Liberal Jewish leadership provides them with precious few. On a whole range of issues, the current Jewish establishment has played into some of the worst and most persistent anti-Semitic stereotypes, conducting itself in a manner that is arrogant, defensive, hypocritical, shortsighted, selfish, and contemptuous of other Americans and their rights.

The Bible lauds the ability to turn enemies into friends, admonishing us, "Do not rejoice at the fall of your enemy." One important reason for this warning is that rejoicing makes it harder later to win his friendship. It is one thing to object and oppose political positions in a responsible and respectful manner. However, even those Jews who absolutely believe in liberal positions are playing a very dangerous game in order to secure their goals. By over-using the anti-Semite charge, we could succeed in accomplishing exactly the opposite of turning enemies into friends. We could instead convert temporary and well meaning critics into silently resentful and permanent enemies.

Throughout Jewish history, responsible rabbinical leadership has always questioned the wisdom of a minority Jewish population conspicuously opposing a majority. Sometimes it is necessary but more often it is not, even when our position is the moral one. The point is that sometimes an unpopular moral stand can invite violence and destruction. Sometimes this is a sad necessity, though more often discretion is the better part of valor. However, in America's cultural tug-of-war, the vocal position taken by the official Jewish voice is anti-biblical, which makes it nothing but the gravest folly. There is no Jewish moral imperative for advocating liberalism and there is certainly no political wisdom in doing so. So why are Jewish organizations doing so? Because it is their faith.

PARANOID PROGAGANDA

The arguments that Jews use among themselves on some of these issues go something like this: If you remain silent when they discriminate against homosexuals, do not be surprised if they come after you next. This whopper depends, of course, on the monumental mythology that the Nazis disliked homosexuals as intensely as they hated Jews.

But the question is not about discrimination or about the private practices of adult American citizens; it is about forced public endorsement and acceptance of homosexuality as a valid lifestyle. And on the issue, the real question we Jews should ask ourselves is why we should antagonize a minimum of the 60 percent of Americans who consider homosexuality wrong, in order to ingratiate ourselves with a mere 1 or, at most, 2 percent of the population who are actively homosexual? If one answers that it is the principle that is important, not the politics, then I must point out that the Constitution of the Jewish people, the *Torah*, is fairly unambiguous in its opposition to homosexuality.

Similarly, it is claimed that if we do not side with women who wish freedom over *their* bodies, how can we Jews ask for help in defying tyrants wishing to torture and mutilate *our* bodies? The contorted logic of confusing violence and torture with refusal to allow a controversial and life-destroying medical procedure is apparent. And as we have seen, Jewish law hardly endorses abortion. The secular Jewish voice is almost guaranteeing that as our land continues its swing back to conservatism, Jews will be seen as more part of the problem than as part of the solution.

I once enjoyed lunch with a Jewish communal leader, influential in a Jewish Federation which claimed to represent the forty thousand or so Jews who lived in his particular metropolitan area. Our discussion revolved around the question of whether it was good or bad that the official posture of the Jewish Federation was indistinguishable from that of the Democratic Party. He was utterly convinced that Jewish values were defined by whatever was the current liberal mantra.

Like far too many Federation leaders in cities across the country, my friend was a Jewish cultural orphan—utterly disconnected from his spiritual origins and all but illiterate in Jewish learning. He was as familiar with the great works of Maimonides, Rashi or the Vilna Gaon as he was with the writings of Saint Thomas Aquinas. Which is to say, not at all. I carefully painted a scenario for him in which his organization's love affair with liberalism could pose real danger to real, live Jews. History has shown that during the last two thousand years, we Jews have demonstrated a tendency to get ourselves thrown out of our host countries. Without excusing our persecuters, I observed, it is surely imprudent to act in ways that deliberately antagonize a major part of the population. This is particularly true when these ways are explicitly at odds with thousands of years of Jewish scholarship and tradition.

I could support Jews standing up for a Jewish value regardless of whom it offends. Were any Jewish Federation to issue a proclamation that the Jewish community affirms that the Bible is the Word of God, I would passionately support them in this proclamation regardless of whom it offended. But people who claim to represent all the Jews of a city by vigorously espousing causes opposed by both Jewish tradition as well as by most of our Christian neighbors, only serves to refute the myth of Jewish intelligence. I concluded my argument to my liberal friend by explaining that it made no sense whatever to support liberalism if there was even the slightest possibility of it endangering Jews.

My friend's response chilled me. I literally felt a tremor go through my body as he calmly explained that even if it actually hurt individual Jews, it was important that the Federation stand up for its values. This response echoed within me like a haunting tune all day until I finally realized why. Eighty years earlier, a Russian rabbi had pleaded with one of his congregants, Leon Bronstein, to avoid involving so many Jews in the Russian Revolution. The congregant, known to his comrades as Leon Trotsky, defiantly informed the rabbi that it was his "Jewish values" that guided him toward socialistic revolution. The rabbi famously murmured, "Yes, it is the Trotskys who make the revolutions, but it is the Bronsteins who pay the price."

In other words, those Jews who abandon Jewish tradition usually embrace socialism (of which liberalism is a variant) as their new religion. When they succeed in their goals, it is often the other Jews—those who remained faithful to their faith—who are left to bear the brunt of the unhappiness caused by socialism. No, today's expanded influence of secular liberalism, along with Jewish prominence in America's social revolution of the late 1900s, is not good news for the Bronsteins or for any other Jew.

WHO ARE THE REAL ANTI-SEMITES?

Many of our worst enemies are of Jewish ancestry themselves. Being Jewish by birth does not automatically make you a lover of Judaism or Jewish values. Instead of saying that we must protect our own, we should be the first to denounce anti-Jewish behavior on the part of some Jews. We have to do it because everyone else has been intimidated into silence for fear of being labeled anti-Semitic.

Why are so many of those who have done the most to introduce filth into the popular culture Jewish? Or is it anti-Semitic to ask this question? Judaism opposes not only obscene but even unrefined language. The Talmud provides examples of how the Torah avoids anything remotely resembling vulgarity. But think of the celebrated Jewish names that this genre brings to mind. In radio, TV and comedy we have Howard Stern and Roseanne Barr. In printed pornography we have Al Goldstein, founder of *Screw* and *Eros* magazines. One of the pioneers of live, comic vulgarity was Lenny Bruce. What supreme Jewish value is served by the dearth of Jewish voices protesting this cultural pollution? Why have so few rabbis or communal leaders protested additional offerings of the Weinstein brothers like the despicable movies *Kids, The Crying Game* and *Pulp Fiction?* If nothing else, such protest would indicate that at least some Jews share the concern for decency shared by most Americans.

Who has done the most to inject anti-Semitic images into the popular culture? Just think of mean stereotypes such as the notorious JAP, or Jewish American Princess. Is it the work of Jesse Helms, Pat Buchanan or Newt Gingrich? No, it is the work of Jewish artists like Woody Allen, Roseanne Barr, Philip Roth and Howard Stern that portrays Jewish women as unresponsive, selfish, and materialistic. This unflattering picture has little basis in Jewish tradition and even less in reality. The heroic film critic, Michael Medved, attributes the Jewish male's cultural assault on Jewish women to the masculine insecurity of Jewish men who generally do not excel in those defining masculine activities in American life such as football, hunting and repairing cars. Such demeaning of women comes from the liberal Left, not from the conservative Right.

NBC's top-rated sitcom *Seinfeld* was another example of how Jewish entertainers routinely demean Judaism in ways that few gentiles in America have ever done. Two episodes will suffice to illustrate not only the trend but also the Jewish community's curious response. One, which has become known as the *Brit* episode (a *brit* is a ritual circumcision traditionally performed by a highly trained and qualified *mohel*) featured a rude and unsavory *mohel* who dangerously botched the job.

Another episode's storyline involved the despondent female lead seeking the counsel of her nerdy-looking rabbi, who listens to her problems only later to betray her confidence with her neighbors and on his radio show.

Saturday Night Live, produced by another Jew, Lorne Michaels, featured a skit about a Passover seder. A sacred and popular part of any seder is when the revered prophet Elijah makes his invisible appearance. In *Saturday Night Live*'s version, however, Elijah appears as an aging hippie who immediately begins making vulgar and suggestive advances to the family's teenage daughter. It would be unimaginable for any gentile American to have produced entertainment this hateful toward Judaism; if they had, the loud protests of Jewish organizations would have led the news for weeks afterward.

Not only were these undeniably anti-Semitic portrayals foisted on America by Jews who are often fawned upon for their "contribution" to Jewish life, but they are also defended by the very Jewish agency whose entire reason for being is to protest anti-Semitism. As reported by the *Jewish Telegraphic Agency,* the Anti Defamation League of Bnai Brith's spokesperson, Myrna Shinbaum, said, "Taking into account that [these shows are] comedy, we don't believe any offense was intended." But we are awfully quick to take offense when conservatives say anything about Judaism.

IT IS ENOUGH FOR US...

To paraphrase the popular refrain from the Passover seder, *dayenu*—it is enough for us— it is enough for us that the Jewish establishment is seen to oppose attempts to reign in pornography and blasphemy in art and entertainment. It is enough for us that some of the most notoriously foul-mouthed and obscene-minded entertainers are Jewish and earn no reproof for their public aggrandizement of filth. It is enough for us that those who speak for the Jews are seen to be advocates for criminals through the efforts of the largely Jewish American Civil Liberties Union. It is enough for us that Jewish groups are seen to be outspoken opponents of educational choice. It is enough for us that so many of the enthusiasts for the radical homosexual agenda, increased immorality, and expanded abortion rights are Jewish. It is enough for us that we boasted to the world on the morning after the 1992 presidential elections that we voted for President-elect Clinton at twice the rate of the American population at large. After all, what was there to boast about the fact that more than 80 percent of Jews voted for the man whom nearly 60 percent of American voters rejected? And they say we have high IQs.

Promoting a destructive liberal agenda in the name of Judaism is heinous. The Left is in the process of hijacking the good name that Judaism has enjoyed in America for two hundred years and is about to despoil the good name in pursuit of its political agenda. Those so frantically opposing America's religious conservatives should not mislead the public into believing that they are acting in the name of Judaism. They are not. They are acting in the name of liberalism and in its interests alone.

CHAPTER FORTY-FIVE

THREE SPECTERS

MOST JEWS ARE CLEARLY NOT NEUTRAL ON THE SUBJECT OF THE CHRISTIAN RIGHT.

Am I trying to say that there is no such thing as anti-Semitism? No. I am saying that we abuse the charge. How serious, actually, is the problem of anti-Semitism in America? After all, one of the most ubiquitous allegations made against Christian conservatives is that they are anti-Semitic. I know Jews who absolutely line up with the Republican Party on the majority of economic and moral issues, yet will not vote Republican because of its association with the Christian Right. In 1997, the American Jewish Congress's Annual Survey of American Jewish Opinion found that 95 percent of American Jews believe anti-Semitism in the United States is a "very serious problem" or "somewhat of a problem." The polling data showed that Jews saw the main sources of anti-Semitism as the "religious Right" and Muslims.

As for portions of the Muslim community, particularly the "Black Muslim" group in America, I would probably poll in exactly the same way. I put "Black Muslim" in quotations so as not to confuse Muslims who happen to be black with the openly anti-white, anti-Jewish, militant "Black Muslims." Newspapers of that group run articles suggesting that Jewish doctors infect black babies with AIDS, an allegation reminiscent of the blood libels of Europe—and potentially very dangerous. At the same time we have to recognize that this element is a fringe of both the Black and the Muslim community, not its core.

As for fear of the Christian Right, I think that fear of that community has been orchestrated as I said above, for political reasons. Let's examine it more closely.

Most Jews are clearly not neutral on the subject of the Christian Right. There are

It is as unfair to condemn as anti-Semitic a Catholic priest who mentions this fact as it would be ridiculously unfair to condemn Don Feder himself. It is also unfair to expect ordinary Americans somehow to know that all these Jewish organizations listed have rejected the Torah as the defining document of Jewish values and morality. To me it is tragic that no similar list exists of traditional Jewish organizations that condemn the one-and-a-half million abortions that take place each year in this country. Those organizations do exist—they just have not felt the urgency to join in and help one end of the tug-of-war. I hope they will soon do so, since the disproportionate number of Jewish organizations pulling hard on the other end of the rope is quite noticeable.

Is it anti-Semitic to attack ideas that the Jewish community holds sacred? It obviously was anti-Semitic when ancient Romans conquered Israel and outlawed circumcision, Jewish study, and the observance of Jewish holidays. Those three observances are classic fundamentals of Judaism. But when Christian conservatives lambaste liberalism in America today, this bears no resemblance to the Roman edicts of old. Today, when liberalism and its sad effect on America is discussed, there is always some misguided Jewish leader who pops up like a Jack-in-the-box to protest the attack on "Jewish ideas." Just because many Jews consider the doctrines of secular liberalism sacred does not mean that attacking those ideas is anti-Semitic. As I said before, one must distinguish between Jewish ideas and ideas adopted by some, or even many Jews.

The Jewish community tends to regard the term "anti-Semitism" as both a pea shooter and a nuclear missile. It is the very first weapon for which to reach as well as a weapon with tremendous fire power. We have become trigger happy, which not only uses up ammunition but makes it hard to attract attention when you really need help. Every school child knows the story of the boy who cried wolf. So many times had he warned the community of a non-existent peril that when the threat was eventually authentic, nobody believed him. It is true that during certain historical periods, some factions of the Christian church hurt and killed Jews, but it is also true that in America, Christianity has not been a threat to Jews. Furthermore, America's Christians have worked meticulously to distance themselves from negative portrayals of Judaism in the past. While acknowledging the past, let us concede that obsession with a problem can indeed lead to paranoia. Overly vigilant caution can lead to cries of "wolf." I think American Jewry has reached that point. The danger, of course, is that the townspeople got rather sick of that boy who cried wolf, and when he truly needed their assistance, they had learned to ignore him.

I am not saying that there is no such thing as anti-Semitism. I am only urging my fellow Jews to determine in a fair-minded manner exactly what we mean when we hurl that slur—to be intellectually honest and carefully selective when we feel we must do so.

CHAPTER FORTY-SIX

JEWISH DOUBLE STANDARD

WE HAVE A SAD AND POTENTIALLY FATAL TENDENCY TO PUNISH FRIENDS AND REWARD ENEMIES.

Not only is anti-Semitism an overused and inaccurately made charge, it highlights another point. The American Jewish Committee mentioned in one of its publications that Rabbi Alexander Schindler, then president of the Union of American Hebrew Congregations (of the Reform denomination of Judaism), blamed the Christian Right for an "outbreak of anti-Semitic acts." The report goes on to say, "Privately Tanenbaum (of the American Jewish Committee) told Reverend Jerry Falwell that he regretted Schindler's words...."[1] Had any Christian leader accused a Jewish organization of causing hostile actions against Christians, I don't think that a private apology by another Christian leader would have sufficed. And it shouldn't. In that case, as in others, the Jewish community has been guilty of establishing a double standard on bigotry. An editorial in a 1996 edition of the *Forward* (a prominent and somewhat fair-minded New York Jewish weekly) mentioned a voter guide book that gave religious leaders sample sermons. The *Forward* was not referring to the Christian Coalition's voter guidebook, which Jewish groups regularly denounce as trampling on the separation of church and state. Rather, the much-admired booklet was put out by the National Jewish Community Relations Advisory Board and was endorsed by many Jewish organizations. In other words, a voter guidebook whose results may have encouraged conservative and Republican voters was blasted as immoral and as crossing the church-state boundary, but one meant for rabbis to promote Democratic turnout was fine.

Most human beings succumb to a double standard. We allow for weaknesses in ourselves yet expect others to be perfect. My room may be a mess, but I get annoyed when my child's room looks the same. I sometimes make a foolish remark in public, but when my business associate makes an equally foolish remark, I mention it time and again. Too many Jews demand that America exhibit sensitivity to everyone except, of course, Christians. They are fair game.

POLITICALLY CORRECT BIGOTRY

Yet, any time the Jewish communal leadership feels that a possibly anti-Semitic comment was made (assuming, as we saw before that it is a Republican, a Christian or a conservative making it), it is quick to demand a public apology. Not only that, but they call on Christians to join them in the call against anti-Semitism. Yet, when some celebrity makes an anti-Christian comment, as Jane Fonda recently did, no Jewish organization protests the bigotry. In a widely reported speech in June 1998 Fonda told the National Press Club in Washington, D.C., "Christian conservatives don't care about children that don't look like them. They don't care about children that are not white, middle-class Christians. As far as they are concerned, others can be eliminated." Imagine the hue and cry had Jane Fonda said, "Jews don't really care about blacks, as far as Jews are concerned, blacks can be eliminated." Does anybody doubt that Jewish organizations would have extracted a tearful apology worthy of the great actress herself? Does anybody doubt that Jews would have enlisted the help of Christian groups to condemn those comments? Does anybody doubt that Christian groups would have gladly joined the condemnation?

As a matter of fact, Jewish organizations, joined by honchos of the entertainment industry, urged unabashed censorship against journalist William Cash who wrote a mildly unflattering article about Jews in Hollywood in the *London Spectator*. His point was merely that Jews were highly over represented in the entertainment community and that to Americans, this seemed irrelevant whereas in England it would be news. The fury that these Jews unleashed against the *Spectator* very nearly ended Cash's career. There were cascades of letters to the editor of the *Spectator* from countless Jewish entertainment luminaries like Barbra Streisand followed by advertising boycotts organized by American Jewish organizations.

Yet, since Jane Fonda just engaged in anti-Christianism rather than anti-Semitism, not one major Jewish organization found reason to protest. The deafening silence of Jews when Christianity is insulted raises very real questions about the moral seriousness of Jewish protest. How can our leaders be so hypersensitive to the most microscopic of perceived anti-Jewish slurs, yet so entirely indifferent to flagrant and vicious anti-Christian insults? What message are we trying to send? What message are we sending without trying?

Jews often denounce Christian leaders who encourage their flock to vote for representatives who will reflect their moral values. Their shrill outbursts include routine and unflattering comparisons to Adolph Hitler. When a network of Baptist ministers in Texas complained to the rabbis of several Reform temples about their routine bashing of evangelical Christianity and its spokesmen, they were ignored. In an effort to bring greater understanding and end the public denunciations of Christianity emanating from the Reform rabbis, one minister acquaintance of mine sent a letter to the rabbis explaining the situation and requesting a meeting. At the time he called me, he had written four letters and left four phone messages over two months and was still awaiting a response or even an acknowledgment of his concern. Is it anti-Semitic of him to describe the frustration he feels at how he and his religion are being treated? Even after ADL national director Abraham Foxman conceded that the publication, *The Religious Right: The Assault on Tolerance and Pluralism in America,* had overstepped the bounds of truth and decency and issued an unprecedented apology to Pat Robertson, Ralph Reed and others, there was not much of a change in the tone found in the ADL statements that issued forth in the following months and years. (I should mention that I was referred to in the book as a "strident west coast rabbi." One of my speeches to the Christian Coalition was misquoted in a pathetic attempt to discredit me for hobnobbing with Christian conservatives.) I believe this tiny sampling of Jewish communal conduct that I have presented constitutes a double standard. The only question to be asked is whether this kind of behavior is likely to improve or damage the way many people feel about Jews.

JEWS AND RELIGIOUS HATRED

I see no sense in the argument I have often heard that a black person by definition cannot be a racist. When Colin Ferguson sprayed a Long Island railroad car with gunfire, killing and wounding at random because he hated white people, he was being no less a racist than the Ku Klux Klan member who at the turn of the century lynched a black man only because of the color of his skin. Similarly, Jews sometimes act as if they cannot be guilty of religious hatred because they have so often been the victims of it. I beg to differ. Imagine how Christians felt when they saw Reform Rabbi Balfour Brickner's comment in an article about the "religious Right" in the *National Jewish Post and Opinion:*

> The minions of this all too earthly choir are everywhere, active and a threat. If they succeed in their goals, our freedoms will be seriously curtailed, if not eliminated, and our physical lives could be at risk. After all, it was a demented "Christo-fascist" who shot to death Dr. David Gunn and it is religiously driven Christians who blow up family planning clinics.[2]

Does this not remind you of the incendiary libel perpetrated by the Nazi Party against the Jews as the Nazis solidified their power base in the late 1930s and early

1940s? How can a rabbi, of all people, generalize like this? "Christo-fascist"? "Religiously driven Christians who blow up clinics?" Indeed? There have been a few instances of unstable people who have shot abortion doctors or damaged clinics. In each case, the action has been immediately condemned by churches all over the country. Rabbis and Jews would be outraged if Americans would point to traitors Julius and Ethel Rosenberg, and the overrepresentation of Jews in the Communist party at that time, as proof that Jews are unpatriotic. When a skinhead newspaper views Leona Helmsley's conviction for tax evasion as a lesson that Jews are dishonest, it is expressing bigotry and hatred. Rabbi Brickner and the *National Jewish Post and Jewish Opinion,* which published his words, were guilty of no less. Yet the double standard that the liberal Jewish community reserves for itself places restrictions only on others.

In 1997, *Reform Judaism* magazine featured a cover story on Pat Robertson, the head of the Christian Coalition. The unsubstantiated character assassination in the article matched the deliberately unflattering photograph selected to go with the piece. Any reasonable reader would concede that had a Christian magazine run this type of story about a rabbi, it would rightly have been condemned in the strongest terms as blatant anti-Semitism. Apologies would have been demanded, although in the case of *Reform Judaism* and Pat Robertson, none were offered.

OUR STRANGE SILENCE

The 1995 movie *Priest* was a heaven-sent opportunity for Jewish organizations to protest anti-Christianism as vehemently as we expect Christians to protest anti-Semitism. Because it was both well made and well acted, *Priest* presented a disturbingly persuasive picture of Catholic religious leaders who are either hypocrites, drunkards, or both.

During the 1980s, only Michael Medved and Dennis Prager protested *The Last Temptation of Christ,* a major motion picture that twisted history in order to present a distorted, historically dishonest story of Jesus. Not one Jewish organization offered support to the Christian groups who were horrified by this assault on their Christian faith. This is particularly sad given the distinctly Jewish names and Jewish communal prominence of those who produced this horrible movie. Imagine the Jewish community's response if a Christian-owned company had made a film like this about some well-known Jewish leader or about a black leader like Martin Luther King Jr. It is surely appropriate for us to express equal outrage when the target of bigotry is another faith.

When it came to *Priest,* there were a few courageous Jewish leaders out there who stepped to the defense of Catholics. Movie critic and syndicated talk show host Michael Medved, then president of the prominent Los Angeles synagogue that we founded, frequently called for an apology by Disney for *Priest's* insult to Catholics. Rabbi Abraham B. Hecht, president of one of the country's leading Orthodox Jewish organizations, the

Rabbinical Alliance of America, also vigorously condemned the film.

It was appropriate for Jews to join the denunciation of *Priest*. After all, the head of Disney as well as the heads of its distribution subsidiary, Miramax, are Jewish. We may feel that making such an observation is in bad taste. If non-Jews make the same observation we no doubt will immediately recognize them as anti-Semites. However, this kind of intimidation will not stop many Americans from making that observation. Neither will it stop them from seeing as insulting that the companies just happened to choose Good Friday as the date for the film's national release. (This date was later changed to April 19 after complaints by the Catholic League.)

Anti-Christian bigotry, whether in politics, movies, TV shows, or elsewhere, really does provide us with both an opportunity and an obligation. It is the opportunity to finally lay to rest the three specters that stop Jews from fairly evaluating the issues that the Christian Right brings to America's attention. It is the opportunity to show that while there are undeniably Jews who view Christianity (indeed all religion) as a menace, there are also Jews comfortable with allying themselves politically with other religious conservatives. It is the obligation to show that we Jews, along with other citizens, recognize the stake we have in preserving the moral health, the tranquillity, and prosperity of the United States.

SUSPICIOUS BENEVOLENCE?

Some Jewish leaders try to rationalize the contempt they display toward religious Christians. They acknowledge the consistent friendship that Israel and Jews have enjoyed from Christian conservatives but claim that the motivation is flawed. They argue that since Christians support Israel for theological reasons, their support deserves no recognition and even less gratitude. They dismiss the financial, political, and moral support given in the fight to free Soviet Jewry, or to combat true anti-Semitism, by claiming that since American Christians are benevolent toward Jews for biblical reasons, that benevolence is suspect.

Not only would Jewish tradition regard this ingratitude as sinfully immoral, but it also highlights a major flaw in the secular liberal's understanding of his own religion. Ever since the Torah was given on Mount Sinai some 3,300 years ago, Jewish emphasis has been on deed, not thought. We believe that only God knows what is in man's mind. Indeed, all too often we barely understand what is in our own mind let alone someone else's. For this reason, we leave it to God to judge motivation; we are instructed to judge one another purely on the basis of actions. Given a choice, would you rather have as a neighbor someone who does not love you in his heart but whose neighborly behavior is nonetheless scrupulously correct? Or the scoundrel who really loves you in his heart, but kicks your cat, swears at your children, and scratches your car? This is why we owe gratitude to Christianity in

America for the hospitality Jews have found on these shores, regardless of the reason for that hospitality.

There is another reason I denounce Jewish liberals who find something lacking in a friendship based chiefly on a sense of religious obligation. A friendship based on firm and unshakable foundations of religious conviction is much more reliable than a friendship based on the emotions of the moment. For instance, marriages in which the spouses share a sense of religious obligation endure far more reliably than those based on a romantic fling. After I had officiated at my 100th wedding, I pointed out that marriages that start off with a sense of law and obligation nearly always proceed safely to a lifetime of romance. However, all too often, those that start only with romance end with law and obligations at the hands of divorce courts.

Jews need more friends whose devotion rests on deep religious conviction and fewer whose friendship depends on transient political alliances. I think it is time for the Jewish community to take a deep, hard look at the situation in which we find ourselves. Do we want to discourage the one type of friend whose friendship is basically guaranteed by unchangeable conviction? The majority of Christians in this country are philo-Semitic because they have memorized and believe the words from Genesis, "And I will bless those who bless you (the Jewish people), and those who curse you I will curse."

REWARDING OUR ENEMIES

The Jewish community has been very remiss in acknowledging its friends. Politically, Republicans have been better and more consistent friends of Jews and even of Israel than Democrats. One of the best, although perhaps one of the most controversial, examples of this tendency, was the Jewish community's enthusiastic participation in bringing down President Richard M. Nixon. Regardless of whether one liked him personally, and regardless of whether he privately disliked a number of Jews, there is no question whatsoever that Israel survived its Yom Kippur war of 1973 entirely because of Nixon's (not universally popular) decision to resupply the Israeli military machine. In contrast, the Jewish community adored George McGovern. At the time, he was not only Nixon's opponent, he was also chairman of the Subcommittee on the Middle East of the Senate Foreign Relations Committee. In that capacity, George McGovern stridently complained that the administration might be over-hasty in resupplying Israel.

To most historians it is quite clear what likely would have happened to the desperate State of Israel if two-thirds of American Jews had gotten their way and George McGovern had been president at the time. In spite of this, there was no change in political posture on the part of most Jewish organizations. At the same time, we Jews stayed in line with the liberal Left and punished politicians who favored a strong and prepared American military—even as we called for military assistance to the beleaguered Jewish state.

The result of this policy of punishing our friends and rewarding our enemies is that it allows us to be taken for granted. It assures the Republicans that there is nothing they can do to win the Jewish vote while simultaneously assuring the Democrats that there is nothing they could do that would jeopardize our loyalty to them. We have a sad and potentially fatal tendency to punish friends and reward enemies.

In each of his four campaigns, Franklin Delano Roosevelt won about 90 percent of the Jewish vote. He was a revered and loved icon in the Jewish community. Yet it was almost as clear then as it is now that FDR had little interest in attempting to stop or at least slow the carnage of the Holocaust. He routinely ignored the evidence and the pleas of Jewish leaders as well as the requests of Jews in his administration to bomb the death camp railway systems. In spite of this, FDR remains almost beyond criticism in the Jewish community.

Perhaps one of the most important examples of how we reward our enemies and punish our friends is the saga of the two Jesses—Jesse Jackson and Jesse Helms. One represents, at an absolute maximum, 12 percent of the American population. It is the only part of the population that harbors significant anti-Semitic attitudes and it is the only part of the population in which those attitudes are on the increase. He has also established bonds of friendship with some of the least-savory Arab leaders in the Middle East. The other Jesse represents at least the 32 percent of the population, perhaps considerably more, identified by Gallup as born-again Christians. He is a consistent friend of Israel in the Senate and his constituency have proven themselves to be consistently philo-Semitic. Inexplicably, Jesse Jackson is fawned upon by the entire Jewish community. Most recently he was honored by one of the national rabbinical associations, in spite of his notorious reference to New York as Hymietown. Meanwhile, also inexplicably, Jesse Helms is depicted in the Jewish community as one of the dark forces threatening Jewish interests.

BITING THE SYSTEM THAT FEEDS US

Finally, we must note the hostility displayed by Jewish intellectuals, academics and politicians to the American free market—the very system of private enterprise that lifted generations of Jews from tenement slums to lavish mansions. One of the most pervasive and enduring myths is that Jews owe their economic success to the labor unions. Even the most cursory examination of the historic facts will reveal that Jews did not acquire their enormous affluence and influence in America because of union-instigated raises in the minimum wage. Jews prospered as business owners and employers. They succeeded as unfettered entrepreneurs, not as downtrodden piece workers. It was our free market system, above all, that unleashed the energies of a people and facilitated, far more than did the unions, the progress from pushcarts to board rooms.

Yet, in spite of overwhelming evidence that Jewish material success, as well as the

Jewish community's unmatched institutions such as hospitals and schools, owe a debt of gratitude to the institution of American business—Jewish leadership is disproportionately, illogically, anti-business. Jewish organizations unthinkingly ally themselves with anti-business policies, institutions and politicians. Again, a classic case of rewarding our enemies and punishing our friends.

TIME TO UNITE WITH CHRISTIANS

In that large country located between downtown Los Angeles and the Hudson River, there is growing impatience with die-hard, anti-religious liberalism. America's religious conservatives, growing both in number and in significance, are wondering why they abandoned the fields of politics, economics, education, and culture to the Left. This is why I believe a responsibility exists for American Jewish conservatives, be they Orthodox, Reform, Conservative or unaffiliated, to identify themselves proudly. We should publicly distance ourselves from the Judaism-equals-liberalism equation. We should recognize that much of what the Jewish community decries as anti-Semitism is really anti-liberalism, and we should proclaim it as such. We should unite with Christians against anti-Christian bigotry just as firmly as we stand against anti-Semitism.

Even if you absolutely disagree with me on the role of religion in America, it cannot be stressed enough that the behavior of some in the Jewish community has crossed the line of decency. Whether one's politics tend more to the liberal than to the conservative, or vice versa, integrity and honesty demand cogent arguments rather than scare tactics, and reasoned discourse rather than character assassination. This has always been the Jewish way. Now is not the time to abandon that tradition.

CHAPTER FORTY-SEVEN

THE DELUSION OF ANTI-SEMITISM

THE AVERAGE AMERICAN JEW IS TRULY UNAWARE OF HOW UNUSUAL AMERICA IS.

The poll on Jewish opinions revealed another interesting fact about Jews and their views of anti-Semitism. Forty-seven percent of those polled disagreed with the statement that "Virtually all positions of influence in the United States are open to Jews." This poll displays a startling discrepancy between reality and the Jewish perception of reality. It also reveals a huge gap between how other people picture Jews and how we view ourselves. Nowhere is this more striking than in questions that explore whether we are a privileged or a discriminated-against group in America. Other people correctly see us as part of the influential and elite power structure of the country while we consider ourselves victims of insidious, continued discrimination. At dinner parties wealthy Jewish executives will talk of how they had to combat anti-Semitism every step of the way. "Jews still can't make it to the top of Fortune 500 companies," we assure one another. "This sure is a tough country in which to be a minority."

DISPROPORTIONATE REPRESENTATION

These feelings and conversations exist despite our disproportionate representation on the Forbes 400 list and despite the fact that our average income is considerably higher than that of any other identifiable ethnic group in the country. In education we do remarkably well. At the time I'm writing this the presidents of six Ivy League schools are Jewish. Not bad for an oppressed minority. On what basis do we claim to be denied admittance to the establishment? If anything, we are conspicuously over-represented in the mainstream of American society—not only in entertainment, media and business but also in the political power structure. As I write, there are at least twenty-five Jewish members of the U.S. House of Representatives, which means we are over-represented by a factor of more than two. There are ten Jews in the U.S. Senate—over-representation by a factor of four. Two Jewish justices sit on the United States Supreme Court—over-representation by a factor of ten. If the Jews polled are right that anti-Semitism threatens American Jewry with serious discrimination—manifested by positions of power being closed to those of the Jewish faith—then how many Jews in Congress and on the Supreme Court would be needed to allay their fears? How many Jews would need to reach positions of power and prominence in business and in the professions to prove that anti-Semitism is no longer a major threat to American Jews? In fact, after promising us an administration that would look like America, President Clinton delivered one that looked more like Tel Aviv.

COMPARED TO WHOM?

It is an absolute given that in any society, people who stand out as different in any way will experience friction. The only question is whether it will be friction like that experienced by the Tutsis in Rwanda or the Ibos in Nigeria or, for that matter, the Jews of Germany, or something quite different and basically manageable. We talk so casually about the dreadful scourges of racism and anti-Semitism in America today. But I must ask: compared to whom? Who gets along better with one another, American blacks and whites or French-and-English-speaking Canadians? Who gets on better, Jews and Christians in America or Flemings and Walloons in Belgium? There is simply no question that outside the political theology of victimization, created and rewarded by thirty-five years of liberal government policy, ordinary Americans of all races and religions get along better than people in every other non-homogenous country in the world. Certainly, no group is less entitled to self-pity than American Jews. Yet, in spite of obvious grounds for gratitude, we carry around a grudge and seem intent on convincing ourselves that virulent anti-Semitism keeps us down.

By any measure of prominence, influence, and achievement, American Jews are off the scale. Why do we continue promoting the delusion of anti-Semitism, particularly since all that this silly activity can accomplish is increase precisely what it is meant to discourage? People do recognize an elitism in America. People may have certain resentments toward the so-called WASP phenomenon, but it is tolerated if not exactly relished. At least WASPs have the graciousness not to claim to be a persecuted minority. But we Jews—absolutely comparable to Episcopalians or anyone else in terms of prestige and potency—claim to live in a country that hates us. We demand privilege yet we respond with petulance.

COMPARED TO WHERE?

To those who contend that America is overrun by anti-Semitism, as many Jewish agencies do, I must ask another question: Compared to where? England? France? Germany? Canada? Argentina? Where, exactly, would we American Jews rather live?

As long as Jews are identifiable as a separate group, there will be some people who dislike us. There are some people who dislike Asians; there are people who dislike those who wear glasses; there are people who dislike anyone taller, thinner or richer than they are. It is childish to think you can mandate a world filled only with love. Indeed, for American Jews, love is presently more of a problem than hate. As Irving Kristol puts it, the main worry of the American Jewish community today is not that non-Jews want to persecute us—it is that they want to marry us.

How then do we explain the poll results? I would like to offer a few suggestions. At the risk of sounding like an amateur psychologist, I do think it is worth pointing out that a huge percentage of the Jews surveyed were intermarried and most were irreligious. It is fair to suppose that a fair number of those polled had converted to Judaism upon marrying a Jew. It is very plausible that these people are more sensitive to being different and are finding anti-Semitism because they are looking for it.

WE FIND WHAT WE LOOK FOR

Two stories brought this idea to light for me. My close associate, Yarden Weidenfeld, was walking down the road in his neighborhood accompanied by a newly religious friend. It was the Sabbath and both men were wearing *yarmulkes* (head coverings), so were recognizable as Jews. Living in a rural community without sidewalks, they were strolling on the side of the road. As a car rounded the curve and overtook them, the driver tooted his horn. Yarden simply regarded the horn as a warning blast to let him know there was a car coming, or perhaps as the equivalent of a wave from a neighbor. His friend, however, immediately tensed up and said, "They saw our yarmulkes and were trying to scare us." One incident, two perspectives.

In 1996, a small explosive device detonated outside the Jewish Community Center in my home town of Mercer Island, Washington. To the credit of the Jewish community, the local newspapers, and the police department, the incident was not blown out of proportion. There was a concerted effort to acknowledge that, while it might have been an anti-Semitic statement, the blast also might have been the work of teenage hooligans from on or off the island. At this point there has been no repetition of the event and no further clarification. Yet, minus conclusive evidence, human nature urges each of us to decide for ourselves what really took place. For many Jews the automatic assumption was anti-Semitism, when an equally plausible guess might suggest that the blast was no more than foolish, illegal mischief with the location chosen solely for its proximity to the freeway. One incident, two perspectives.

Like all people interacting in the world, Jews are going to have unpleasant encounters. Being passed over for promotion or being snarled at by a customer or store clerk, can lead to personal introspection or be accepted as a natural part of life. If one is looking for it, such normal events can also be interpreted as anti-Semitism. Polls such as the one the American Jewish Congress conducted only highlight how prickly and out of touch the Jewish community in America can be.

ASSUMING THE WORST

Jewish organizations, by continuously basing their fund-raising efforts on the threat of anti-Semitism, in fact train Jews to expect anti-Semitism. In their book *Jews and the New American Scene,* Earl Raab and Seymour Martin Lipset rightly contend, "Despite scary direct mailings from the Simon Wiesenthal Center, anti-Semitism will recede ever further." I have the greatest personal respect for Rabbi Marvin Hier, head of the Wiesenthal Center. But he, along with the rest of the human race, is subject to the phenomenon of seeing something more when you are looking for it. Have you ever learned a new vocabulary word, then suddenly you notice that word everywhere? Or purchased a new car and realized that you now notice the same-model car wherever you go? If your job is to see anti-Semitism, you will find it. Such mass mailings from Jewish organizations not only encourage insecurity and paranoia in the Jewish community, but they also may even *cause* an increase in anti-Semitism. These childishly fearsome direct mail pieces promising to defend the recipient from scary anti-Semites in exchange for a contribution, may be mailed to Jews but they are seen and detested by many non-Jews.

Let's look at a parallel case in the African-American community. In 1996 Americans were told of an epidemic of church burnings. Many organizations announced a resurgence in racism and the National Council of Churches and the Jewish Anti-Defamation League ran ads decrying "the fires of hate." A conspiracy of white supremacists was suggested.

In June 1997, the National Church Arson Task Force finally confirmed what some had suspected all along. There was no epidemic, no conspiracy. A number of churches burn down every year, and the number in 1996 was no greater than normal. Many of the burned buildings were abandoned buildings that had formerly housed churches. Often, when the arsonists were found, they turned out to be mentally disturbed individuals who didn't have a clue what the edifices had been or what a white supremacist was. Blacks themselves were implicated for these arsons in disproportionate numbers. In all, two of the churches in the data examined seemed to have been burned from racial motivation. Of course, two is too many. But there was no resurgence of racism. As fearless journalist and best selling author, Michael Fumento, pointed out the good will of the American populace was manipulated in order to increase fund raising for, and the prominence of, the Center for Democratic Renewal.

Interestingly, after the issue was brought to prominence, a rash of arsons did break out, of both black and non-black churches. These were copycat arsons, attributable to the earlier media attention. Rather than diminishing the burning of churches, the media play increased it.

Jewish newspapers frequently splash news of a bomb threat or defacement of a synagogue on their front pages. When the bomb threat turns out to be from a disturbed Jew rather than from a neo-Nazi, that fact is left for the back of the paper. If you read the literature from some Jewish groups you could believe that skinheads are around every corner. Could this attention in fact be increasing the viability of anti-Semitic groups? When the phrase "anti-Semitism" is encountered at every turn in the Jewish community, Jews come to believe it. Whether right or wrong, if you repeat information often enough people will accept it. That in no way makes it true, though it does risk becoming self-fulfilling prophecy.

Imagine the young Jew raised on the conventional liberal diet of competitive victimization. Much of what he hears during his early years at temple and Hebrew school revolves around how everyone hates us. Thus, his own religion seems to have nothing to offer but the opportunity to be persecuted. Hardly a very good reason to stay involved. Furthermore, every gentile is a potential Cossack or Nazi. He mustn't tolerate any expression of Christianity without registering offense.

Then our young friend reaches college, and what does he discover? Jews in Ivy League schools are approximately ten times over-represented, with 25 percent to 35 percent of the student body. In some schools like the University of Pennsylvania, Jews make up the majority of the student population. Not much evidence there of the anti-Semitic discrimination he was warned about. Not only that, but all the prettiest girls are willing to go out with him. He now resolves the cognitive dissonance in one of two ways: (1) He concludes that his rabbi and Hebrew school teachers were lying about rampant anti-Semitism (and if so, they probably lied about most everything else they told him too); or (2) He persists in his warped image of reality, viewing all non-Jews with suspicion. Either way he is alienated; in one case from his own people, in the other from everyone else.

I don't want to minimize the difficulties faced by religious Jews in the early twentieth century. Many who started a job on Monday morning lost it the following Saturday because they observed their Sabbath. Blue laws, which prohibited stores from opening on Sundays, proved an additional hardship for the Jew who, according to his religion, could not work on Saturdays and, by the law of the land, could not work on Sundays. There were quotas that limited the number of Jews accepted into medical schools. Many clubs, hotels, and employment opportunities were closed to Jews. Particularly in the Bible belt, the Jewish child sat uncomfortably in a classroom where a teacher invoked Jesus' name in the opening prayer session and sometimes even told that child that he was condemned to hell. Instances like this still happen occasionally today.

AN UNUSUAL PEACE

But (and this is a very big but) while it is true that American Jews have experienced real difficulties, it is crucial to note that the American Jewish community has lived for an historically unparalleled length of time with no pogroms or massacres, with no official government sanctions, without even a special Jewish tax levied against them. A cursory overview of Jewish history will reveal this peaceful state to be highly unusual. Has there been religious discrimination in America's past? Of course. But the cry of religious discrimination, like its counterpart of racial discrimination, has turned into a convenient bludgeon with which to destroy rather than improve. We need to remind people that this is the country not only of slavery and hotels closed to Jews, but also the land where an Orthodox Jew served for sixty years as legal counsel for Father Flanagan's Boys' Town, and where a white, Christian manager relentlessly encouraged Jackie Robinson to excel in baseball.

I am convinced that Jewish safety and prosperity in our nation is due to the uniquely American combination of firm Christian belief without a specific church's reigning hand. For each story of discrimination, there is a matching story of respect for a Jew who respected his own religion. The average American Jew is truly unaware of how unusual America is. By going to the extreme of seeing anything and everything as discriminatory, we run the risk of damaging the very safety and prosperity we now enjoy.

Do we really want to promote a secular, liberal vision for America, making "separation of church and state" into dogma and thereby lessening the positive influence Christianity has in America? Do we really want to destroy the foundations of a system that has worked so well for us? My answer is clearly no. I greatly fear the prospect of a "post-Christian" America. This is not despite anti-Semitism, but because of it.

CHAPTER FORTY-EIGHT

NO OFFENSE

JEWS HAVE ABSOLUTELY NO BASIS ON WHICH
TO DEMAND THAT A CHRISTIAN GROUP
BETRAY ITS OWN BELIEFS.

---

ot only do Jewish groups and individuals brand religious Christians indiscriminately as anti-Semites, they go further than that. I occasionally hear Jewish groups demanding that statements of Christian faith be rescinded because they hurt Jewish feelings. Such demands cause me to cringe.

Some statements in Jewish prayers and books make our claim to being a people with a special connection to God. There are certainly phrases which would be uncomfortable to explain to non-Jews, particularly if the non-Jews were seeking to be offended. Many times through our history, these sentences have been quoted out of context in a deliberate attempt to provoke hatred of the Jewish community. Likewise, Christians may hold to certain beliefs which are difficult for Jews to comprehend, and these beliefs are often quoted out of context to vilify the Christian community. How would we Jews react if official church groups *demanded* that Jews rescind tenets of our faith? Yet more and more I hear Jewish groups loudly proclaiming offense over certain expressions of Christian belief.

Here is the bottom line: the American Constitution does not grant anyone the right to tell me that I may not say my prayers according to my conscience. Just as important, neither does it allow me to stop anyone else from saying their prayers or stating their beliefs, according to their conscience.

AGREEING TO DISAGREE

Several years ago a firestorm erupted when a Baptist minister told his followers that God doesn't hear the prayers of Jews. Does a Baptist minister believe God doesn't hear my prayers? So what? He is entitled to his belief, as long as that belief does not lead to action against me. And American law prohibits him or anyone else from acting against me for holding any of my beliefs or for having no beliefs at all. His view on whether God hears me is irrelevant to me because I don't believe this man has a better understanding of God than I do. Does he find the preceding sentence offensive? Will he demand a retraction? I doubt it. Perhaps we can agree to rely on the words attributed to Voltaire: "I disapprove of what you say but I will defend to the death your right to say it."

Just as we Jews have our rights to freedom of expression, so do Christians. As long as these expressions of belief do not lead to illegal action against the other, there is no cause for complaint. Certainly, Jews have absolutely no basis on which to demand that a Christian group, some of whose predecessors founded this country with its tradition of free religious expression for Jews, betray its own beliefs. It really should not threaten any Jew when a Christian expresses doubt about whether God listens to Jewish prayers—the Jews most threatened by this theological idiosyncrasy are typically those who are least likely to personally test whether God hears their own prayers. For all they actually know from personal experience, the Christian may be right. Again we see that Jewish hostility toward Christianity comes mostly from those Jews least involved in their own faith although they will frequently remind anyone listening that they are both "proud and good Jews."

One of the convictions of evangelical Christians is that they must "spread the gospel." In other words, proselytizing is not a hobby for evangelical Christians; it is a tenet of faith. As I stated before, my view is that we Jews should do everything we can to equip our own people with conviction in and knowledge of Judaism rather than trying to silence other faiths. I for one, have no doubts as to whether my religion can hold its own in the marketplace of ideas.

ABSURD DEMANDS

A gracious leader of the Southern Baptists, James Sibley, once told me that he was instructed by a prominent national Jewish group that Baptists must stop proselytizing and must proclaim that messianic Jews who believe in Jesus are not Jewish. What an absurd demand! It is a terribly dangerous precedent for us to seize the prerogative to instruct an established church in America to revoke its theology. And how in the world can a Baptist decide who is Jewish and who is not? Jews themselves can't agree on that issue. In similar fashion, the Jewish community registered offense when the Catholic church declared the Jewish born but raised as an atheist, Edith Stein, a saint. What a blatant interference with Catholic internal religious doctrine. It makes as much sense as it would for the Vatican to inform Jerusalem who it may elect as the next Chief Rabbi of Israel.

Rabbi Leon Klenicki, interfaith affairs director for the Anti-Defamation League of B'nai Brith, provides another example of a misguided attempt to muzzle Christians. Speaking of the Southern Baptist resolution calling for a mission to the Jews, he said, "Especially after the Holocaust, Christians have no right to talk about a mission to the Jew." B'nai Brith orchestrated a mass mailing of postcards demanding a retraction of the resolution. As a Jew in America I believe I have no right to tell any Christian what parts of his theology he may or may not follow. Evangelical activity is as much a part of Christianity as circumcision is of Judaism. We really must stop dictating to other religious groups on the basis of what we find offensive. What is certainly offensive is even to suggest that as a result of a murderous madman called Hitler, American Christians must renounce their religious practice.

It is amazing to me how the Catholic church and many Protestant denominations have conducted honest internal examinations of their own churches. In the backwash of the Holocaust, there has been growing Christian concern over anti-Semitic church teaching. The Lutheran church recently recanted large portions of Luther's teachings and the Catholic church has made a huge reversal in its positions regarding the Jews and significantly changed its liturgy. The Jewish response to these sensitive self-examinations and changes on the part of our Christian neighbors has been to churlishly press for more. Are we never satisfied? Is there never a point at which we should say "Thank you, we appreciate all you have done to make us feel comfortable?"

There has never been a reason in America to suspect the benign attitude of the majority of Christians. Yet Jewish leadership continues to display anger toward our Christian fellow citizens—at least to those who are politically conservative.

Another example of attempted Jewish interference in the tenets of another faith is a preoccupation with the assertion that only those who believe in Jesus can go to heaven. What difference in the world can it make to Jews whether Christians believe Jews will or will not make it to heaven? As long as Christians take no violent steps to hasten Jews' arrival there or to make life in this world uncomfortable, why should Jews protest Christianity's internal doctrine? Yet each time some unfortunate Christian clergyman makes this innocuous statement, the entire machinery of the organized Jewish community grinds into action to ruin the poor man's career. What makes this entire charade so distasteful is the irony that those Jews most incensed by this Christian claim are the very Jews who do not believe in heaven in the first place.

Orthodox Jews, on the other hand, who do believe in an afterlife, are seldom bothered by this Christian view. On occasion one of my children calls a sibling an uncomplimentary name. My response to the insulted child is, "If she told you you're an elephant, would you believe you were?" Religious Jews are confident in their faith. They are sure that their arrival in heaven has more to do with God's will than with man's pronouncements. It is not a positive sign for the Jewish community that we have degenerated to the point where we now scream "I'm offended" more frequently than Chicken Little cried that the sky was falling.

A KEY DIFFERENCE

Many Jews will disagree with my remarks. They will say that I am naïve, that there is a sinister component to Christianity. After all, look at our history. A psychologist member of my congregation once told me of a woman who came to her because she constantly felt as if she was in danger. She could not sleep at night or venture from her apartment, which was equipped with multiple locks. My friend learned that before the woman had placed new locks on her apartment, it had been broken into twice, her car had been stolen, and the woman herself had been mugged. My friend replied that she was having a reasonable reaction considering the neighborhood she lived in and reassured her that she was not paranoid.

Similarly, when a Jew fears anti-Semitism, it is presumptuous to claim that he is being entirely paranoid. Too many times in Jewish history, the Jew has found himself persecuted, forcibly expelled from his home, even imprisoned or killed. But the very emotionality of the Holocaust allows it to be turned into a potent political weapon.

CHAPTER FORTY-NINE

CHRISTIANS AND THE HOLOCAUST

HISTORY SHOWS THAT NO SOCIETY THAT HAS PERSECUTED OR EXPELLED ITS JEWS REMAINED POWERFUL.

S ince Christianity is playing the key role in opposing the spread of liberalism in America, anything that comes between the Jewish and Christian communities serves the purposes of liberalism. One way dysfunctional Jewish leadership has threatened one of history's most blessed Jewish communities has been to denigrate Christians in the context of the emotionally laden subject of the Holocaust. It is interesting to note that those very same liberal Jews who claim that they cannot trust Christians because of the Holocaust are exactly the same Jews who are remarkably indifferent when shown proof that liberal Senator Dodd consulted Nazi gun control laws when he wrote America's very first such laws. That certainly raises suspicions that the Holocaust may be being used to manipulate emotions, rather than confronting honest concerns.

Now the Holocaust is a terribly difficult as well as a painful topic to discuss. The Talmud says that one should not try to comfort a mourner while his dead lies before him. In other words, when a highly emotional state exists, attempting to talk logically is futile. This is the state that exists regarding the Holocaust. There are Holocaust survivors still alive. Almost every Jew today remembers or knows of a relative or family friend who died in the Holocaust. Not only is the tragedy very recent, but we need to realize the long collective historical memory we Jews have of affliction.

A story is told of Napoleon's visit to Russia before France and Russia went to war. While touring, he came across a darkened synagogue filled with Jews, who were sitting in utter desolation on the floor and weeping. Turning to his guides, Napoleon demanded to know what horror the Czar had perpetrated against his Jewish subjects. The guides insisted that no anti-Semitic decrees had been passed recently. Disbelieving, Napoleon entered the synagogue and asked what tragedy had occurred. The Jews responded that their Temple had been destroyed. When Napoleon angrily asked who was responsible, he was told that the Temple being mourned was built by King Solomon and had been demolished well over 2,500 years earlier by the Babylonians. Napoleon is said to have turned to his Russian guides and warned them that any people with the capacity to mourn tragedy for millennia is a people who will outlast both Russia and France.

To this day, Orthodox Jews still mourn the loss of our Holy Temple and the closeness to God that it made possible. Jews continued to incur tragedies, including the destruction of the second Temple by the Romans in the year A.D. 70, the expulsion of the Jews from Spain in 1492 and from England in 1290, and the numerous occasions when Jews were given the choice of converting to other religions or dying. All these national disasters are traditionally remembered in a three-week commemorative mourning period that falls during the summer. The culmination of this mourning, the most tragic day of the Jewish calendar, is the ninth of the Jewish month of Av, the anniversary of the destruction of both the first and second Temples. It was on this day that Napoleon happened to stumble into the Russian synagogue.

There has been no shortage of tragedies to commemorate in Jewish history. If a Jew can still bring tears to his eyes when he thinks of an ancestor killed in medieval times, it is no surprise that he still has an instinctive reaction toward the medieval church, which was often the instigator of, or at least an accomplice to, the violence. But although the Holocaust is difficult to discuss dispassionately, I still think it is time for a reassessment.

I do, however, want to make three points clear. First, although most parts of medieval Europe were certainly governed by religiously empowered authorities, the populations, particularly those elements that regularly delighted in pogroms, were mostly wild mobs. Let us remember a key difference between modern America and medieval Europe. In Europe, a politically and economically powerful clergy ruled largely illiterate mobs. In America, a powerless clergy presides over deeply religious, sophisticated, and educated Christians. In Europe there were centuries of pogroms; such has never been the case in America.

Let's face up to another fact. Life in America has accustomed us to peace among various religious groups. In contrast, European religious life has been unpleasant for many people over the centuries. While, as a Jew, I mourn for my own people, historically Christian denominations in Europe tended to also persecute each other. If we are relying on European memories as our guide, not only Jews, but Catholics, Baptists, Lutherans, and other groups have reason to distrust one another. For example, the life story of the famed scientist Johannes Keppler, who was a Lutheran, contains more than its fair share of entire communities of Lutherans being exiled and persecuted by the Catholic church. Life was pretty unpleasant for everyone back then. Jews may have been more consistently and cruelly victimized, but if every group that has faced religious persecution through the ages brought that suspicion and hostility to America with them, this country would be far less pleasant to live in today.

It in no way diminishes the horrors of the Holocaust to acknowledge other examples of man's inhumanity to man. Let's not forget the massacre of the Armenians by the Turks, which Hitler was quoted as saying proved to him that genocide was possible. Stalin's war against his own population, Pol Pot's massacres in Cambodia, and the killing fields of Africa (for which the final total of deaths may never be known) are among pogroms that the world has known.

As to the Holocaust itself, we need to concede a third point. Although Jews and Christians correctly see in the rise of Nazism a failure on the part of the church, Hitler was made possible by the triumph of scientific naturalism in Europe, not by organized religion. Nazism was, after all, "National Socialism," and any form of socialism has intellectual roots in the secular Left, not the religious Right. While centuries of anti-Semitism by the church certainly made Hitler's task a little easier, we also must recognize that in Lutheran countries such as Denmark, Finland, Norway, and Sweden, devout Christians, and often the church leadership itself, turned the rescuing of Jews into a religious mission. That fact cannot just be dismissed as irrelevant. Many Catholic and Protestant church leaders in Europe realized that Hitler hated God and the church. Many lost their lives. Only a society in which the church had already been weakened could breed Nazism. This is one of the reasons that I insist Jews should do everything in their power to support and encourage American Christians in their task of taking back the culture.

TIME FOR HONEST REASSESSMENT

We must recognize that we often do not know the whole story. The January 1997 issue of *Crisis Magazine,* a journal for which I am an occasional contributor, discusses Pope Pius XII's actions during the Holocaust. The magazine makes the point that the Pope was personally responsible for saving thousands of Jewish lives, providing shelter for many of them in his personal residence. In fact, the chief rabbi of Rome and Dr. Nahum Goldmann, president of the World Jewish Congress, both praised the Pope for his actions at the time. What happened between the end of World War II when the Pope's pro-Jewish actions were still well known among Jewish leaders and now?

Today most Jews base their understanding of what happened not on fact, but on a fictional play by Catholic hater Roff Hochhuth. His *The Deputy* heaps blame on the Catholic church. Hochhuth's revisionist version of history has become widely accepted. No one argues that Catholics in Europe might not have been able to do more. That is always true for all of us. But the intense criticism aimed at Pope Pius XII starts to sound hypocritical when the Jewish community venerates President Franklin D. Roosevelt and American Reform Rabbi Stephen S. Wise, both of whom, it can be argued, did far less than the Pope to save Jews.

Sadly, secular Jewish leadership has started judging American Christians exclusively in terms of what European Christianity did or did not do to save Jews from the Nazis. This is both wrong and simplistic. It is wrong because retroactively applying current thinking to past conditions seldom yields useful results. Condemning those founding fathers who owned slaves in the eighteenth century is neither informative nor constructive. In no way does this data serve to invalidate the Constitution written by those men. In spite of Vatican II, nobody can honestly dispute that Jews were at least heavily involved in the death of Jesus. That is just a historical fact. But in no way does this legitimize killing Jews today. In the same way, it is equally wrong to attack American Christians today because their church and its members did not do as much as we would have liked in war-torn Europe half a century ago.

In the first half of the eighteenth century, vicious pogroms were carried out against the Church of the Latter Day Saints in Illinois and Missouri. Large numbers of Mormons were brutally murdered by hordes of rampaging mobs. The Mormon prophet Joseph Smith was himself massacred during these pogroms. Many of these bloody and horrifying massacres took place in towns with Jewish communities and synagogues. I have been unable to find a single record of any Jews inviting terrified Mormon victims to take refuge in their homes. I have not been able to locate a single record of Jewish communal protest against these pogroms.

I am not blaming Jewish Midwesterners of the 1830s for their silence. It is entirely conceivable to me that any Jew resisting that murderous mob might have been putting his own family at terrible risk. I *am* saying that it is wrong of misguided Jewish leadership to attack Christian leaders for not risking their own members' lives to save Jews during the Nazi era. It is especially foolish (at best) and evil (at worst), to do so without at least gratefully acknowledging the many Christians who in fact did risk, and in many cases sacrificed, their own lives to hide and save many Jews during this horrifying period. Furthermore, we can learn something from a category of Holocaust literature that tends to circulate only among Orthodox Jews. Published by religious Jewish publishing companies, this literature is made up of first-person Holocaust accounts written by deeply religious Jewish survivors. Unlike the well-known works of fiction written mostly by irreligious Jews, these books, despite the atrocities which fill them, are uplifting testaments to faith in God and the levels people can reach when they retain their vision of Him. Despite every effort to treat Jews as animals, the Nazis were not capable of eradicating the Divine spark from those Jews who clung to their God. I have been surprised, in reading some of these accounts, to find that some Jews looked for devout Christians when they needed to find someone they could trust. While there was no guarantee that they would not be betrayed, many European Jews knew that the superstitious and irreligious peasantry was more of a threat than the religious—particularly Protestant—person of faith. In America, we forget how different Europe was from this country. If we must relive the Holocaust, instead of just dwelling on the savagery, let us at least spend time reliving the religious heroism of many Jewish victims and the selfless heroism of many Christian rescuers.

UNHERALDED HEROES

Today's Jewish schoolchildren should be inculcated with gratitude toward those Christians who suffered during the Holocaust in order to save Jewish lives. Yet the self-less role of these Christians are largely ignored. Those who did save Jews are honored as "Righteous Gentiles." I believe that it is time to change that phrase for two reasons. One is that it implies an oxymoron, suggesting that we would not normally expect the two words to be found together. "Look here, I've found one—a real live righteous gentile!" (I wonder how we Jews might react to an annual award bestowed each year by a Christian organization on an "Honest Jewish Businessman.") Secondly, speaking of "Righteous Gentiles" does a disservice to those many Christians who saved Jews specifically *because* of their Christian faith. They were "Righteous Christians," not "Righteous Gentiles." Far too few Jews understand that Christian values were often the very reason these unher-alded heroes were willing to risk their lives.

There is one famous case in which the Jewish community enthusiastically jumped on the bandwagon to acknowledge a debt. That is the case of Oskar Schindler of *Schindler's List* fame. Gratitude is absolutely due him. But the energy expended to recog-nize his actions only reveals the lack of thanks to many others. Although I have declined to see the film, my understanding is that Mr. Schindler was not a particularly religious or, for that matter, a particularly moral man. Is the movie meant to suggest that religious morality is irrelevant as long as one is saving Jews? In any event, what about those who saved Jews and did so because they were driven by Christian values and morality?

CORRIE TEN BOOM

It is in no way denigrating to Mr. Schindler, or to anyone else who risked his life to save Jews, to ask why a certain book has been ignored by the Jewish community. Like many Jews of my generation, I grew up avidly reading libraries of books about the Holocaust. Imagine my surprise when, as an adult, I found a riveting, true story that I had not only never read but had never even heard of. As I began asking around, I learned that none of my Jewish friends or the thousands of Jews in my audiences had heard of this excellent book either.

Furthermore, a call to the Holocaust Museum in Washington, D.C. revealed that the book was not carried in their gift shop nor in any other Holocaust museum in America.

Was this an obscure and hidden volume? Not at all. The book is widely known and read in Christian homes and schools around the country. It has been made into a movie—*The Hiding Place,* by Corrie ten Boom, which tells the true story of how she and her family hid Jews during the Holocaust. It is well written and unbelievably heart-rending.

Why then has it been ignored in the Jewish community? Why has it been in effect censored from Jewish reading lists on the Holocaust? Why was the movie version actually picketed by Jewish groups? I can only surmise that this reaction results from *The Hiding Place* not conforming to the stereotype of religious Christians to which the Jewish community has succumbed. Unlike Herr Schindler, who saved Jews for whatever reasons he personally felt, the ten Boom family's activities were directly motivated by their belief in Jesus. In her words: "Lord Jesus, I offer myself for Your people. In any way. Any place. Any time."

It is clear that Corrie ten Boom and her family desired to show all people, including Jews, what they fervently believed to be the truth of Christianity. Yet their saving of Jewish lives was not predicated on the Jews' accepting Christianity. In fact, the ten Boom family accorded great respect and effort to accommodate those Jews who wanted to keep kosher and observe the Sabbath while in hiding. Sadly, this Christian family's kindness was discovered; the Nazis hauled them away to their infamous prison camps where all but Corrie died. Fortunately, the Jews they had hidden escaped capture. Corrie's father, Mr. Caspar ten Boom, a revered Dutch citizen well into his eighties during the Holocaust, was told by the Nazis that they would release him if he would promise to stop his activities in sheltering Jews. His daughter recalls the scene:

> The Gestapo chief leaned forward. "I'd like to send you home, old fellow," he said. "I'll take your word that you won't cause any more trouble."
>
> I could not see Father's face, only the erect carriage of his shoulders and the halo of white hair above them. But I heard his answer.
>
> "If I go home today," he said evenly and clearly, "tomorrow I will open my door again to any man in need who knocks."[1]

Shortly thereafter Caspar ten Boom died, isolated from his family in the Gestapo prison. This great man's philosophy is made clear earlier in the book. When he first tried to shelter a Jewish baby, a pastor tried to warn him of the danger. Mr. ten Boom replied, "You say we could lose our lives for this child. I would consider that the greatest honor that could come to my family." Corrie herself spent years in concentration camps and lost her sister and nephew to the Nazis for their crimes of saving Jewish lives. Corrie ended her days recently in Southern California, unrecognized and unthanked by a Jewish community obsessed with *Schindler's List.* We owe her an apology.

Like all true stories about the Holocaust, *The Hiding Place* has some chilling scenes. It is difficult to fathom how inhumane people can be. But the Jewish community has not rejected books on the Holocaust because of gruesome German behavior. They have, to my dismay, rejected this particular book and the movie derived from it. Is it because this true story forces an admission that devout Christians can be true friends of the Jewish community? How much truer friend can we have than the ten Boom family?

"In this household," said Caspar ten Boom, "God's people are always welcome."

The Jewish world must recognize that there are Christians who sincerely want Jews to convert but will use no force other than the force of argument to gain it. In my mind, any Jew who talks of the "threat of the religious Right" but has not read *The Hiding Place* has no credibility whatsoever. The Jewish community constantly insinuates that those of us who believe in a political alliance with the Christian community are naïve. They imply that no matter how friendly devout Christians are to us, it is only because they want our conversion; once this is not forthcoming their friendliness will end. *The Hiding Place* will force them to reexamine their views.

I strongly encourage these Jews to also read Corrie ten Boom's other book, *In My Father's House,* in which she details what gave members of her family the strength to risk and eventually lose their lives in order to save Jews. The book opens with an amazing account of her grandfather being told by his pastor that he should have a regular prayer group to pray for the Jewish people and the land of Israel. I personally see it as a mark of shame for the Jewish community that these books are not mandatory reading in every Jewish high school.

HAKARAT HATOV

Hakarat Hatov, gratitude, demands that even Jews who have never set foot in the United States be profoundly grateful to America. This country's participation in World War II prevented more Jews from being obliterated in Hitler's gas chambers, and it helped bring about the State of Israel in 1948. The vast majority of America's soldiers, of course, were Christians. The twentieth century shows me that the United States may well be the instrument by which God kept His promise to the Jewish people of never allowing them to vanish. It is hard to see how Judaism would have survived World War II without the United States of America entering the fight and then providing fertile soil for Judaism to replant itself. When Churchill spoke of "the new world coming to the rescue of the old," he was referring to America's aid to Europe. But one old world that was rescued was considerably older than Great Britain. We Jews do owe an eternal debt of gratitude to

America and her religious Christians which at the time of World War II made up a comfortable majority of America's population.

With all this in mind, it is at best unfair, and at worst malicious, to condemn Christians of today's America for pogroms of yesterday's Europe. All Jews should thank God every morning—not just for creating the world but also for creating the United States of America. This is all demanded by Jewish history and, I would argue, by Jewish law's emphasis on the obligation to express gratitude—Hakarat Hatov.

HOLOCAUST MUSEUMS

I find myself in the uncomfortable position of knowing that I must question some Holocaust museums and programs around the country. The obvious and only question to ask is whether they help or harm the Jewish people. This is a legitimate question and the answer is far from obvious. Their purpose, particularly since most are partially funded by American taxpayer money rather than solely by contributions, has to be the discouraging of hatred between people. Certainly, they should encourage concern for Jews. Yet, some Christians, who initially supported them with good hearted generosity, now see them as promoting a hatred of Christians.

I hope I am not the only American Jew to question aspects of the Holocaust Museum in Washington, D.C. I personally do not feel completely comfortable visiting one of the world's most eloquent cries against prejudice which simultaneously promotes anti-Christian propaganda. Although the museum was constructed with private funds, it does stand on land donated by the American people, the most Christian nation on earth. Therefore it is hard for me to understand why the producers of the film shown to Holocaust Museum visitors, a copy of which I have seen, seem so determined to devote much of the short documentary to the denigration of Christianity.

While the historical role of the church in anti-Semitism is undeniable, is it wise to focus only upon that—and utterly exclude discussion of Stalin's atheistic virulent anti-Semitism or Hitler's own rejection of the church? For example, the video shown repeatedly to the crowds who throng to the museum leads the viewer to believe that Hitler considered himself to be acting as an agent of the Catholic church. Consider this line at the climax of the film: "Enter Adolf Hitler, Austrian born and baptized a Catholic." Imagine how we Jews would react to a Christian presented film on Stalin's murder of twenty million Russians in which the narrator solemnly intoned: *"Enter Karl Marx, Stalin's ideological father, born a Jew."* Surely Jews would be right to claim that this information, though undeniably true, was not crucial to the story and was thus intended to be hurtful. Not mentioned in the Holocaust museum's video is Hitler's all consuming hatred of the Pope and Catholicism. Are we unintentionally causing resentment among Christians? Surely, that can be no help to Jews.

Consider these words which the above film attributes to Hitler himself: "In defending myself against the Jews, I am acting for the Lord. The difference between the church and me is that I am finishing the job." Although I am a student of World War II and am very familiar with many little known details of Hitler's life including his spiritual odyssey, and although I searched diligently, I was unable to locate this phrase among the records of Hitler's writings and speeches. At the time of writing these words, I have no reason to believe that Hitler actually spoke the words that the Holocaust museum puts in his mouth. Selecting this as *the* only clip of Hitler's rantings to be shown in the fifteen minute film could justifiably be seen by Christians as an attack on them. How, exactly, is this slap at Christianity supposed to help Jews? Hitler was a great manipulator. In speaking of *Mein Kampf,* Konrad Heiden, the famed biographer of Hitler stated, "The book may well be called a kind of satanic Bible. To the author—although he was shrewd enough not to state it explicitly himself...the belief in human equality is a kind of hypnotic spell exercised by world-conquering Judaism with the help of the Christian Churches."[2]

In other words, Hitler saw Judaism and the Christian church on the same side of the battle—opposite him. He manipulated the deep well springs of anti-Semitism that existed in Europe, for which the church shares the blame, but he was not an agent of Christianity.

I am additionally disturbed by the fact that Jewish leadership has allowed the Holocaust to be co-opted by the political aspirations of the homosexual movement. The well researched book, *The Pink Swastika—Homosexuality in the Nazi Party* shows that while some homosexuals did die, they were never targeted by the Nazis in the same way that Jews were. In fact, when a militant homosexual group made a well publicized trip to Jerusalem's Yad Vashem Holocaust Museum, they were met by Jewish Holocaust survivors, one of whom shouted, "My grandfather was killed for refusing to have sexual relations with the camp commandant. You are desecrating this place..."[3]

The book painstakingly details the extent to which homosexuality was rife among the *perpetrators,* not the victims, of the Holocaust.

Not only do many Holocaust museums promote the Judaism-equals-homosexuality equation as far as persecution goes, (sometimes that is a condition of funding) it further misleads visitors into believing that Jews and homosexuals go together like peanut butter and jelly. Leonard Peikoff, Ayn Rand's protégé, wrote a scary but important book called *The Ominous Parallels: America Today and Pre-Hitler Germany.* He illustrates how the traditionally minded Germans hated the Jewish-dominated Expressionist theater and its blatantly flaunted homosexuality. The political Left, shaped in part by Jewish intellectuals, artists and entertainers, demanded the new. The Germans reacted by revering tradition and began to flock to the artistic heroes of an earlier era such as Richard Wagner. In other words, secularized German Jews were perceived, not entirely without reason, as fueling a modernist assault on German traditionalism. They were seen to have radicalized most of the culture including the universities. Finally, other Germans reacted in what they saw as a move of self-defense. This in no way explains or excuses the vicious fury of events such as Kristalnacht. What is clear however, is that Nazis were assisted in the early stages of their assault by the high visibility of Jews in the war on conventional decency.

For several years now Orthodox Jews, along with most traditional Americans, have been dismayed and mortified by one Broadway play after another linking the themes of Judaism and homosexuality. Not only does this kind of entertainment, often produced by secularized Americans of Jewish ancestry, camouflage true Judaism's uncompromising opposition to homosexual practice, but I believe it also does much worse. In America's cultural tug-of-war, several indicators exist that reveal which end of the rope different people are pulling. It is not only inaccurate but potentially dangerous to tell all America that Jews pull the end of the rope in company with those who promote forcing Americans to deny their religious beliefs about homosexuality. Increasing numbers of tolerant and decent Americans are beginning to see the growing alliance of the Left. It is made up of teachers unions (in contrast to teachers), homosexual activists, big government advocates, rabid secularists, radical feminists, and abortion enthusiasts, among others. How can it possibly help Jews to convey the impression that this alliance also includes American Judaism? It does not. Significant numbers of American Jews are Orthodox and do not subscribe to any of these socially destructive policies. Many other American Jews are not particularly religious but are traditionalists nevertheless. The problem is that the loudest Jewish voices, those heard overwhelmingly by most Americans, are stout allies of the Left's agenda.

Would anybody be reckless enough to issue a guarantee that Americans will never tire of the assault they are enduring on conventional decency? Will Jewish prominence at the Left end of the cultural spectrum serve the Jewish community well, or will it come around to haunt us? It is hard to see how it could help and easy to see how it could hurt.

History shows that no society that has persecuted or expelled its Jews remained powerful. God does avenge His people. But no society that allows anyone, including Jews, to rebel against God, has lasted either.

JUDAISM IS TO BE LIVED

As I mentioned earlier, religious Jews have kept alive the memory of tragedies and persecutions for thousands of years. In daily, weekly, and holiday prayers, and especially in the three weeks of mourning that usually fall in July or August, the pain is intensely felt. Weddings, live music, and other joyous occurrences are avoided during this time. In contrast, the "liberated" branches of Judaism have minimized those prayers and ignore that special time of commemoration. They have forgotten their past.

I know that religious Jews have been advocates for and participants in establishing Holocaust museums and programs. Since the topic is still so emotionally tinged that is understandable. But I think it is worth questioning if it is wise. Museums of brick and stone will never keep alive the memory of the Jews who lost their lives. Like the remembrance of Jews who lost their lives thousands of years ago, the memory of Holocaust martyrs will only be kept alive by those who retain a connection to Judaism. Neither will a Holocaust museum on every block end anti-Semitism. That is a quixotic hope. Yes, the museums and movies move many to tears. But I have heard, as I am sure you have too, of teenagers departing a Holocaust museum or a screening of *Schindler's List* laughing.

As a community, we should be alert to the Holocaust becoming an icon of communal atheism. For many, remembering the Holocaust has become a secular Jewish observance. This is not only a disservice to those millions who died with prayers on their lips, it is also a disservice to those members of America's Jewish community still eagerly seeking an answer to the question, "Why be Jewish?" Constantly emphasizing the Holocaust sends a message to our youth that being Jewish equates with suffering and dying. It doesn't. Being Jewish means having access to a life enhancing way of living. It means having a relationship with the Creator. Judaism is for the living; it is joyous, powerful, and vibrant. It is possible that our still-fresh pain is leading us to emphasize the wrong things. It is certainly time for American Jews to seriously reevaluate our communal, social, political, and religious priorities. Focusing on the depth of Jewish living can only honor all Jews who died for their religion.

ASK: "WHO AM I?"

Without intending to ape socially popular existential anxieties, every Jew should occasionally ask himself, "Who am I?" Do I view myself chiefly as an American or as a Jew? The same type of question was posed to John F. Kennedy and other Catholics in this country. Was their allegiance primarily to the Pope or to America? A similar question, answered hysterically rather than rationally, was the cause of Japanese citizens being sent to internment camps during World War II. I think the answer is hinted at by how differently Jews refer to themselves from the way other Americans do. There are African-Americans, Polish-Americans, Chinese-Americans, but there are American-Jews. Nobody ever speaks of Jewish Americans, least of all American Jews themselves. I think it important for us Jews to recognize that in this specific, we truly are different from most other Americans.

In other countries where we Jews have lived, the government answered clearly, "You are tolerated, but you are not full citizens." It was Napoleon who introduced a novel concept. He offered the Jewish community full rights as citizens dependent on their being full Frenchmen. "As a Jew—nothing; as a Frenchman—everything." In Germany, the

Reform Jewish movement dealt with this same dilemma. Their solution was to be a Jew in the house and a German in the street. German Jews went so far as to remove two-thousand-year-old references to rebuilding the Holy Temple in Jerusalem from their prayers, replacing them by citing Berlin as the New Jerusalem. Reform Judaism still calls its houses of worship temples instead of synagogues, as they consider defunct the eternal Jewish yearning for a rebuilt Temple in Jerusalem.

What does this have to do with Jews in America? As an American citizen, I am accorded equal rights before the law. I certainly appreciate and support the constitutional system that ensures this equality. However, that existential question needs to be asked by every Jew. Am I first a Jew or am I first an American? Although as an Orthodox Jew, there are lots of ways I don't easily fit into the culture, I am perfectly comfortable recognizing that America is primarily a Christian nation, and I am grateful for my good fortune in being here.

You may point an accusing finger at me and say, "Well and good, but as a Jew you fit into the Judeo-Christian tradition. Were you, for example, a Sikh, you wouldn't be so quick to defend a Christian America." Let me respond with a story.

When my father, a native South African, was studying in one of Europe's pre-World War II *yeshivas* (a school of higher Jewish learning), he went on a winter break to see Finland. In these pre-MTV days, the guests at the inn where he was lodging looked to themselves for entertainment during the long evening hours. One guest said that, despite the freezing temperatures, he could hypnotize one of the group into opening the thick windows. Incredulous, one man volunteered to be hypnotized into opening the windows on the stroke of midnight. As the evening progressed, this man began backing away from the fireplace, where everyone else was huddled. Sweat ran down his face, and he loosened and then removed his jacket. As the clock reached 11:45 he undid his sweater and began asking if everyone else was as warm as he was. Finally, at midnight he raced to the windows and flung them open.

Now, this man did not open the windows because he was hot. He was hot because he needed to open the windows. In other words, I am making the case for gratitude to the Christian foundation of America, not because I can be tolerably comfortable living in a country that follows a Judeo-Christian path. I am making that case because I believe Jews have had unprecedented comfort living in America only because of that Christian heritage. The same is true for that Sikh, my Muslim friend, as well as my atheist acquaintance. They are all better off in a Christian America as far as the important things are concerned. They and their families will be physically safer. Their ability to prosper and support their families, and their ability to worship according to their faith, are all advantages that flow to American citizens on account of America's Christian heritage.

Indeed even the safety and security enjoyed by American Jews for over two hundred years is because of America's religious nature. During its day in the sun, the Jewish Defense League had a slogan: "Never again!" referring to the Holocaust. While some of its members, including its founder, the late Rabbi Meir Kahane, were religious, that particular slogan revealed a very un-Jewish arrogance. The fate of our people is not and has never been in the hands of man, but always in the hands of God. For us to yell "Never again!" while waving a defiant fist in the air is a frightening act of Jewish hubris. What makes us so certain that we possess the power to ensure that it will never happen again? In reality we do not. What assures us that God would never allow it to happen again?

THE HOLOCAUST IN PERSPECTIVE

It is unreasonable to ask anyone who endured the Nazi death camps to suffer through an intellectual and dispassionate analysis of the horror. Surviving victims themselves will learn nothing from me in this discussion and are respectfully requested to skip ahead. But the rest of us desperately need finally to come to terms with some uncomfortable realities.

We should look at the theological implications of our ideas. For anyone who believes in God, we have only three choices as we contemplate the Holocaust: (1) God was powerless to stop evil men from perpetrating the Holocaust; (2) He decided to stand by and allow evil men to commit this unspeakable calamity; or (3) He made it happen. Are there any other alternatives?

No religious Jew can adopt the first explanation, which violates every principle of an all-powerful God. The second explanation is merely a more gentle version of the third and leaves us with the same fundamental question of how so many innocent people could be made to endure such hideous and tragic suffering. We are all naturally too diffident to insist that God made it happen, but as religious Jews we should be equally diffident about insisting that He did not.

How could the innocent be made to suffer tortures most of us cannot comprehend? One answer is that this is precisely why we are encouraged to concern ourselves with society's deteriorating moral conditions. We may be living moral lives as individuals, but when a storm finally breaks, it washes away the innocent with the guilty. Think of all the noble Americans who actively opposed slavery, yet had their lives and families destroyed by the Civil War. Think of those who have lived moral and even chaste lives, who nonetheless innocently contracted AIDS through blood transfusions and died. Think of all the law-abiding and gentle citizens who have lost their lives at the hands of the crime epidemic, although they had nothing to do with the evil policies that helped bring about the epidemic.

There is a legitimate view in traditional Judaism that the answer to anti-Semitism is not less Semitism, but more.

In his monumental and authoritative work on classical Jewish thought, the *Meshech Chochma,* Rabbi Meyer Simcha Cohen of Dvinsk made the following frightening and prophetic declaration:

> It is the nature of Providence that the Jews will live peacefully for periods of about two hundred years. After that, a tempestuous wind will arise and spread its shock waves. It will eradicate, wither, destroy and mercilessly inundate, until they will run and flee, scattered and alone, to a distant place. There they will again unite as a nation. They will become great and their wisdom outstanding. Then the time will come again that they forget that they are strangers in an alien land. They will think it is their original place and cease yearning for God's spiritual salvation, in its appointed time. In that place an even stronger tempestuous wind will arise and remind them in a thunderous voice, "You are Jews! Who has made you into important people? Go now to a land that you do not know." This will be the cycle of the predicament of the Jewish people and their survival among the nations.

In 1985, Rabbi Abraham Joseph Englander commented on these words. This is what he said: "These words were written in the early part of this century [long before Nazism] and in retrospect they seem to be prophetic. Recent history has made this perfectly clear. The greatest push for acceptance triggered the greatest rejection. Germany was the hotbed of the Reform movement which was bent on rejection of the Torah and the complete assimilation of the Jewish people into German society. And it was from Germany that the greatest rejection came."

In other words, assimilation produces unhappy consequences for Jewish communities no matter how many faithful Jews are part of the group. Anti-Semitism is an indication that a community's loyalty to Judaism is slipping. Anti-Semitism points up weakness in our community rather than just flaws in our tormentors. When, God forbid, things go awry for a Jewish community, they go awry for everyone, not just for those who renounced their religious commitment. Certainly, no one is forced into the position of persecuting Jews. That is why Pharaoh and the Egyptians, Haman and his followers, and Hitler and the Nazis deserved punishment. They did not need to volunteer for the job of punishing the Jewish people. But God has the final word as to whether those who do wish harm to the Jews, succeed or not.

All my experience with American Christians reinforces for me the words of both Rabbi Englander and those of Rabbi Cohen of Dvinsk. Christians here in America are really very comfortable with religious Jews. They are considerably less so with those of our people who have rejected the faith of our fathers and replaced it with the faith of secular humanism. If you think you have experienced anti-Semitism from some American Christian, my advice to you is embrace Judaism with serious religious commitment and revisit your Christian acquaintance. I think you will find things much improved. The correct and traditional answer to anti-Semitism is not less but rather more Semitism.

To me, faith in God is strengthened, not weakened, by the events of the Holocaust. The very fact that it occurred in Germany rather than, say Poland, is astounding. German Jews had served in the Kaiser's army with distinction during World War I. German Jews had risen to cultural and economic prominence in Weimar, Germany; even the country's most influential daily newspaper was Jewish-owned. It almost makes me think of the *New York Times*. Germany was the land of culture, art, and music; Jews had participated wholeheartedly in developing these national treasures. And Germany was the country in which Jews were nearly fully assimilated—it was almost impossible to identify Jews in the street.

Instead of Germany, Poland was a more likely nation to spawn the Holocaust. It was there that millions of Jews stood out with their distinctive costume and adherence to the faith of their fathers. It was in Poland that generations of anti-Semitism had bred a fanatical distrust and hatred for Jews. Culture was at a premium in Poland and Jews had acquired very little prominence and power. Had the Holocaust been launched by Poland, I would have considered it an almost natural event—something to have expected from the historic and social condition of Polish Jews. The sheer incomprehensibility of Germany unleashing its fury on Jews makes it a shocking testament to God's involvement in all of history and particularly in World War II. In spite of its truth, this is a very unpopular perspective on the Holocaust for the American Jewish community. I say "in spite of its truth" because there are records of holy rabbis, who themselves lost their lives sanctifying God's name in the Nazi inferno, explaining how their unendurable suffering was a tragic fulfillment of divine promises found in Deuteronomy, chapter 31, verse 17. Do we think God was just kidding when He said, *"This people will rise up and stray after the gods of the people among whom they live, they will forsake me and break my covenant which I have made with them. Then my anger shall be kindled against them in that day, and I will forsake them, and I will hide my face from them, and they shall be consumed, and many evils and troubles shall befall them; so that they will say in that time, 'Are not these evils come upon us because there is no God?'"* Why is it so unacceptable among parts of today's Jewish community to view the Holocaust through the same eyes as many of the holy sages who perished fifty years ago in that very conflagration?

CHAPTER FIFTY

DISAGREEMENT OR DEMONIZATION?

ELEVATING THE SEPARATION OF CHURCH AND STATE INTO IMMUTABLE DOGMA IS THE MEANS BY WHICH AMERICA IS ABANDONING ITS FOUNDATIONS.

Are there areas where Orthodox Jews and religious Christians do not agree? Of course. Neither group is monolithic, so members of each group disagree among themselves. Particularly since politics is a very concrete application of beliefs, two people whose starting point is identical may end up in different places. As humans, we do the best we can, but we are fallible. An Orthodox rabbinical colleague of mine may very well oppose a specific piece of legislation I support, or vice versa. As long as we agree on the fundamentals, we can respectfully debate the issue. I certainly have areas where I disagree with groups speaking for the Christian Right. There is a difference, however, between polite disagreement and assault. There is a difference between liberals who use their Jewish origins as a club to bash Christian conservatives and those of us who sincerely come out on different sides of an issue.

Opposition to prayer in public school unites Jews who are normally on opposite sides of issues in many other arenas. It is the one subject on which the majority of Orthodox, Conservative and Reform rabbis agree. But the agreement is hardly unanimous, especially among the Orthodox. For instance, the Lubavitcher Rebbe, the great Rabbi Menachem Schneerson, with whom I discussed these matters during early 1974 and who was the sole and undisputed leader of a definable and activist group of Orthodox Jews, was unequivocal in his support for prayer in school. The rabbi whose guidance I follow, Rabbi Avigdor Miller, is likewise a supporter. So this is an issue that divides the Orthodox world itself. While various Orthodox leaders come out on different sides, there is respect for the opposing opinion.

While no Orthodox rabbi could support homosexuality any more than he could support serving pork at Bar Mitzvahs, prayer in school is not an issue of Jewish law but a matter of judgment. Reform rabbis take the dogmatic liberal line that schools should have no religious component, and they may utilize the cry of anti-Semitism and cruelty to minorities to support their claim. Orthodox Jews who oppose prayer in school are more likely to feel sympathetic towards the pro-school-prayer side but feel that their first concern must be the Jewish child in the classroom and not America as a whole. There is a world of difference between these two approaches. One treats religious Christians who want prayer returned to the schools with esteem; the other attempts to depict them as evil monsters.

I personally would argue that the Orthodox community should seriously rethink the issue. I am of the opinion that the first concern of all Jews, including Orthodox Jews, should be to recognize the peril for all of us, Jew and non-Jew, of living in a society with no religious values. All religious people perceive the impossibility of education without recognition of a Supreme Being. King Solomon got it right when he wrote in Proverbs 1:7, "The fear of the Lord is the beginning of knowledge...." American educational policy used to take that into account.

As recently as the 1950s the Supreme Court declared, "We are a religious people whose institutions presuppose a Supreme Being."[1] Only ten years later we abandoned that road, when the same court declared it illegal for the following prayer to be said in public schools: "Almighty God, we acknowledge our dependence upon Thee, and we beg Thy blessings upon us, our parents, our teachers and our Country."[2]

We Americans no longer have the luxury of pretending that we can affirm the first statement while forbidding the second. In prohibiting the above-mentioned prayer, Justice Hugo Black stated:

> It has been argued that to apply the Constitution in such a way as to prohibit
> state laws respecting an establishment of religious services in public schools is
> to indicate a hostility toward religion or toward prayer. Nothing of course,
> could be more wrong.[3]

Justice Black, and those on the Court who agreed with him, were the ones who were wrong. There was a fallacy in thinking that religion could be removed from our schools. The Left claimed that the result would be a benign neutrality. They have been proven mistaken. Since nature abhors a vacuum, the religions of moral relativism and secular humanism have simply replaced the religions that were expelled.

While this Supreme Court decision banning the recitation of the New York State "Regents Prayer" at public schools was greeted with an outburst of enthusiastic applause from national Jewish organizations and leaders, a few Jewish voices were raised in dissent. Among the first of these was the following letter, published in the *New York Times* on July 4, 1962.

Lest it be thought that all rabbis concur with the recent statement by the New York Board of Rabbis praising the Supreme Court Decision on prayer at public schools, I wish to express my dissent from, and utter dismay at, this strange alliance between teachers of Judaism and the spokesmen of atheism or secularism who secured and applauded the verdict.

As spiritual leaders of the people that gave birth to the immortal vision of the days when "the earth shall be full of the knowledge of the Lord as the waters cover the sea," we can scarcely, I submit, be jubilant about outlawing the acknowledgment and worship of God from any area of life, least of all from schools, which pre-eminently fashion the outlook of our future citizens, without making a travesty of Jewish thought and history.

For many centuries devout Jewish parents have taught their children, long before they could read or even speak properly, to include in their simple morning prayers the verse from the Hebrew Bible: "The beginning of wisdom is the fear of the Lord," so as to instill in them the conviction that knowledge or education without a religious foundation is worthless.

The United States is now probably the only country in the world outside the Iron Curtain to brand as an offense the public acknowledgment of God in schools. How can rabbis, heirs to the Prophets of Israel, rejoice over this?

Freedom cannot be maintained without religion, just as the brotherhood of man requires the Fatherhood of God. A generation of heathen hedonists, worshiping the idols of happiness and material success, will be unable to evoke the Herculean strength necessary to contain the mighty tide of godlessness in the defense of liberty. Furthermore, even statistics show that only children reared in a wholesome religious atmosphere are likely to develop the maximum immunity to the scourges of juvenile delinquency corroding our society and undermining its security.

"The wall of separation" between state and church must be constructed with ample gateways to prevent the divorce of education from religion if that wall is not to lay siege to our civilization and starve it to death.

These are purely my personal views, but I have no doubt that they are shared by many of my colleagues, whether they are members of the Board of Rabbis or not.

New York, July 1, 1962
Rabbi Immanuel Jakobovits
Fifth Avenue Synagogue
New York City

Shortly after the publication of this letter, Rabbi Jakobovits was appointed Chief Rabbi of Great Britain. His move to London deprived America of his heroic stands and he quickly became a favorite moral mentor to Prime Minister Margaret Thatcher under whose administration Rabbi Jakobovits was honored with a knighting and became Lord Immanuel Jakobovits.

Most secularized Jewish leaders are opposed not only to Christian prayer in school but also toward any recognition of a Divine Presence. They oppose just as violently any suggestion of a school prayer to the God of Abraham, Isaac, and Jacob. Violent, versus respectful, Jewish opposition to school prayer, comes from those Jews least likely to be regular worshipers themselves. It is based on the fallacy that Jews must be allowed to blend into the environment. To my mind, being forced to stand apart may even have benefits. One of the members of my congregation, who along with her husband became an observant Jew well past middle age, credited Christian prayers in school with her insistence on identifying as, and marrying, a Jew. Her parents gave her little knowledge of her religion, but their insistence that the prayers the teacher said were not hers, made enough of an impression to let her know that Judaism counted, both to them and to her. Today we are so busy making sure that our Jewish children don't feel "different" throughout their schooling, that it is truly illogical to tell them that the difference matters when it comes to choosing a spouse. The meaning of the word *Ivri* or "Hebrew" implies a willingness to stand separate and, if necessary, alone. Suffering through a two-minute school prayer hardly resembles the kind of sacrifices loyal Jews have made over the centuries in order to live up to their mission.

CHECK THE CONSTITUTION

Most Jews, even those who abhor the liberal agenda for America, often share the belief that the separation of church and state is of paramount importance. This has been elevated to such a doctrine that I constantly come across people, including reporters and community leaders, who speak of the constitutional right to a "separation of church and state." As an immigrant, I have read the Constitution and must report that no such right exists. If you are shaking your head and disagreeing with me, put down this book and go read a copy of the Constitution. Only one of us can be correct in this matter. The phrase, which you must now agree is absent from the document that guides our country, is quoted constantly as if it is the sole and overriding concept upon which America was founded.

Elevating the separation of church and state to a creed suggests that the reason Jews are secure in America is government secularism. Nightmare scenarios are presented as the inevitable consequence of relaxing vigilance regarding separation of church and state. The church, Jews persuasively argue, has been the source of much anti-Semitism over the millennia. Hence it now becomes the sacred duty for every caring Jew to oppose vigorously any attempt to lower the wall of separation between church and state in America, lest the same fate befall us. Elliott Abrams, in his book *Faith or Fear,* traces the history of the Jewish community concerning this issue. Originally, Jews quite reasonably feared that they would be discriminated against because of their religion. There has been a shift, however, towards rejecting the need for any religious base at all. What started as a positive, understandable concern can, if taken too far, become a dangerous obsession or paranoia. If an overweight person chooses to diet, the decision would be applauded. But if the diet continues to the point of anorexia, it becomes harmful. Likewise, an America starved of biblical faith could become harmful.

There is a constant struggle in any society to balance ideas. In America, freedom of speech has to be weighed against inciting violence or purveying pornography. Allowing business owners to operate with no regulation at all is weighed against the possibilities that they will abuse that freedom. I believe that the Jewish community's championship of "separation of church and state," while initiated with good intentions, has now become sinister and has crossed the line to becoming a debilitating problem.

The problem is that this phrase is used to prevent almost any religious expression in the public square. As we have seen, almost all of the anti-Christian attacks mounted by secular Jews relate to homosexuality, abortion, prayer in school, and the teaching of purely materialistic evolution. Jewish liberals say that Christian conservative beliefs on these issues, when acted upon in the public square, violate the First Amendment, interpreted to mean "separation of church and state." That is no more true than it would have been when the Reverend Martin Luther King Jr. used his religious beliefs at the ballot box in order to improve America. Had today's climate of intolerance for ideas derived from religious sources been prevalent in the 1960s, Martin Luther King Jr.'s movement would never have descended the steps of the church and made it into the streets of America.

Personally, I think that elevating the separation of church and state into immutable dogma is the means by which America is abandoning its foundations. As such, many Jews are unwittingly pursuing the path that is by far the more dangerous. We are still fighting the last generation's wars; meanwhile, times are changing. It could be crucial for American Jews to be part of those changes.

THE ROAD BACK

THE ROAD BACK

RESTORING THE BIBLICAL BLUEPRINT

SOME OPTIONS ARE
SIMPLY NOT REAL OPTIONS.

e who do see America sinking into the morass of cultural depravity and, ultimately, economic and political decline have, at the end of the day, only one concern. We who worry about America's continued viability ask only one important question: Is it too late?

If America is just another piece of real estate, larger but otherwise no different from any other country, then history suggests that it is indeed too late; much too late. If, on the other hand, America is indeed similar to ancient Israel, then the answer is assuredly no. It is late, but not too late; there is a road back.

If Israel's durability as a cultural entity is due to her devotion to God's biblical blueprint, then America can borrow some of that durability by returning to her own biblical blueprint. If those comfortable with a biblical blueprint win the tug-of-war, America will survive. If those who reject the biblical blueprint win, America will surely follow Britain, Spain, Rome and Greece off the center stage of world history.

A LINE IN THE SAND

Regardless of the color of our skin, our economic condition, our gender, or even how we worship God, we should all determine, deep down within ourselves, whether we believe that there exist any absolutes in life. We need to decide whether there are any lines in the sand that society dare not cross. Since the 1960s we have told ourselves that Judeo-Christian principles were walls that imprisoned us, and that they could be safely jettisoned.

Only with the passage of time have we now come to see that they were walls all right, but they were not prison walls. They were fortress walls. Once we decided that the Judeo-Christian walls that constituted fortress America's outer defenses could be breached, we guaranteed that each successive inner wall would eventually be besieged and ultimately toppled.

Almost forty years have gone by in a blur of shattered standards. One societal norm after another has been first ridiculed and then laughingly discarded without even a eulogy. No sooner has one been consigned to the dustbin of our culture than the assault on the next is mounted. Some call it the freeing up of national repressions and others refer to it as the overdue liberalization of a puritanical nation. Actually it is a fierce secularism relentlessly penetrating our defenses. In reality it is not at all liberating, it is the frightening spectacle of a mighty nation committing slow suicide.

What might the American serviceman of World War II have said had we informed him that fifty years after his adventure, large numbers of U.S. soldiers would be undeployable due to pregnancy? What do you say about one of our great educational institutions, Princeton University, granting tenure to bioethicist Peter Singer who believes and teaches that it is ethical to kill infants who are born with major birth defects? How are we to decide which changes are innocuous even if startling, and which are so dangerous that they condemn us to impending extinction?

My answer is that one can choose to sheathe a skyscraper with glass, stone, or aluminum. One can install opening windows or air conditioning. The many choices are liberating. However, no responsible engineer would rejoice in his liberation by designing a skyscraper in the shape of an inverted pyramid. Defending his reluctance to make a bold new statement in architecture, he would patiently explain that he is not at liberty to ignore the law of gravity. Some options are simply not real options. Certain innovations are not audacious expressions of artistic freedom, they are dangerous violations of reality that imperil the entire enterprise. It would be reckless to construct bridges, buildings, and boats while utterly disregarding laws of physics, such as gravity and friction. It would be equally reckless to form families or societies while utterly ignoring the laws that describe how human cooperation works, as presented by the Creator.

DATA STAYS, MATTER DECAYS

What is the difference between those areas in which innovation is refreshing as well as safe and those in which innovation and change threaten long term survival? While it is nearly always safe to experimentally modify matter, tampering with the pure data is inevitably perilous. What do I mean by the terms *data* and *matter*?

It may be easier to make this distinction if we understand the difference between the two. Allow me to provide some examples. Software programs, for instance, are data; keyboards and monitors are matter. Musical tunes and compositions are data; the orchestras that play these tunes and the compact discs upon which they are recorded, are matter. Blueprints for buildings and bridges are data; the buildings and bridges themselves are matter.

Three crucial rules tell us all we need to know about data and matter:

1. Data is indestructible and lasts forever; matter decays, deteriorates, or dies.
2. Data demands total accuracy; matter can tolerate imperfection.
3. Data always precedes matter.

Let me demonstrate the truth of these three observations. If I destroy the plastic disks upon which my software was delivered, I have really destroyed nothing. Microsoft will happily supply another set of disks at almost no cost. Were I to destroy my computer, however, Toshiba will sell me another one but for full price. Matter is destructible but data is indestructible. Burning blueprints does not rip visions out of the minds of architects. Burning books does not destroy ideas. Data is indestructible, even if you destroy the matter on which it is carried. For generations tyrants have discovered that you cannot wipe out an idea by killing those who believe in that idea.

Now let's see how data demands complete perfection while matter tolerates error. A broken key on my computer keyboard only slightly hinders me from creating spreadsheets and essays. However, just one faulty line of code in an operating system would render my entire computer system useless. A few hundred pounds of concrete accidentally omitted from the construction of a bridge or skyscraper is unlikely to cause any serious problems. However, a design calculation in error by only one decimal place could spell disaster. Our ideas must be accurate and true even if our implementation of them is far from perfect.

Lastly we should see how data must precede matter. A business plan is the data; a factory, a warehouse, a store, inventory and trucks are the matter of the business. Nobody would invest in a new business that had a manufacturing facility, delivery truck, and cash registers but no idea of what it would make and to whom it would sell its product. However, we often invest in an idea. Entrepreneurs with good plans but no material assets such as machines or buildings, find it far easier to raise capital than those with matter but no data. Data must always precede matter.

Let's now apply all three data/matter principles to one example. Consider the creation of a baby. There are two separate events to examine. One is its conception and the other is its birth. If you are not certain which of these two events is the matter event and which is the data event, you need only contemplate the question asked by most women upon hearing of a birth. After discovering that mother and baby are both well and inquiring as to the gender of the newborn, most women ask, "How much did the baby weigh?" I suspect this expresses their wonder at the sudden arrival of seven or eight pounds of screaming protoplasm that simply was not here yesterday. In other words, they are moved by the sudden appearance of matter, which is certainly what a birth is. A conception, on the other hand, is the creation of almost pure data. No computer disk stores as much data in as little space as is found in a fertilized human ovum. All the information about the new person as well as information about that new person's future descendants is packed into something quite tiny. All that data is so densely packed into so little space that a fertilized egg could rightly be seen as almost pure data.

This example follows the three rules of data and matter. First, the genetic information created at conception is found in the cells of mother and father and would be hard to destroy, while the resulting human will not live forever. Second, the slightest genetic error at conception can have dreadful consequences, which is why wise pregnant women refrain from ingesting anything even remotely harmful. After birth, however, even a scratch or a cut involving the loss of millions of cells will be repaired and will not imperil the child. And third, obviously, conception must precede birth.

RESTORING OUR CULTURAL DATA

The data that produced the United States of America is eternal, just as is the data that produced ancient Israel. But eternal data does not produce matter that is eternal—all matter comes to an end. Even the data that produced the old Soviet Union was eternal; eternally wrong, but eternal just the same. The ideas that fueled the Bolshevik revolution were the same eternal ideas that built the Tower of Babel. Those bad ideas are always guaranteed to produce short-lived societies. The data depended upon by America's founders seems to produce very long-lived societies. The resulting societies, as judged by history's story of Israel, come to grief only when the data is abandoned, weakened or modified.

The question is this: Have all the wrenching changes that have been inflicted upon American society these past thirty-five years been merely innocuous meddling with matter, or have they been potentially fatal tampering with the data? Have we merely repainted the ship of state or have we tampered with its engines and flotation systems because we considered the previous systems too slow and confining?

As America has cast doubt upon the value of child-rearing by indoctrinating millions of young women that life is most fulfilling for them in the workplace, we just may be modifying our society's cultural code into a bizarre and doomed mutation. By building educational institutions founded on the lie that no absolute, objective truth exists, we may have modified the blueprint from which safe bridges and stable structures have been constructed. When ugliness and animalism replaced beauty and noble aspiration in our art and entertainment, we may have scrambled our cultural software beyond recovery.

The great technological achievements that made America the greatest power on earth were only possible because we relentlessly modified matter as we determinedly preserved the data. The integrity of the data made material growth possible just as a healthy child keeps growing from a genetically reliable conception. Were we to brutally employ some horrific genetic engineering to modify a five-year-old child's genetic and data makeup, we would not be surprised to see him languish and perhaps die. In the same way, these past three-plus decades have seen us reach into America's spiritual nucleus and twist our essential data into unrecognizable nightmares of its original perfection. The resulting mutation seems horrible and doomed. The Left seeks to extricate us from the predicament by distorting our national genetic structure into ever more bizarre mutations in the hope of finding one that works. I believe we should first restore it to its original working state and then discuss changes that may be necessary.

Abolishing the religiously inspired vision of man's uniqueness has cost America dearly. As an experiment, it must surely be judged a disaster. It has ruined our streets, impacted our national productivity, imperiled our capacity for self-defense, and damaged our schools and children. Only by recognizing the link between the deterioration of society during the past thirty-five years and the demotion and extirpation of religion will we find a way to rebuild.

CHAPTER FIFTY-TWO

FOLLOWING OUR FOUNDERS

WE MAY DIFFER ON THEOLOGY,
BUT WE DO NOT DIFFER ON THE BASIC DECENCIES
THAT FLOW FROM JUDEO-CHRISTIAN THOUGHT.

Along with growing numbers of ordinary Americans, I have come to realize that if I want my children to benefit from the same blessings I have been fortunate enough to enjoy, I have no alternative but to become involved with turning back the tide. I am firmly convinced that we all have been swept into the war. Like the family living at Manassas when the Civil War broke out in its fields, we are involved whether we like it or not. In this case, because of spiritual gravity, not choosing a side is effectively joining the liberal side. Two hundred fifty years ago a great member of the British Parliament, Edmund Burke, said, "All that is necessary for evil to prevail is for good men to do nothing." Burke understood the power of spiritual gravity. The other side has the natural advantage, we have the biblical blueprint.

Turning the tide will take resolve, courage, and faith. It will take cooperation among those of us who, despite theological differences, recognize that America exists only by Providence. We must follow the example of our founders who forged a union by focusing on areas of common concern, rather than on areas of major dissent. If we allow religious differences to stop us from working together politically, we will not be able to resist the advance of secular humanism. As long as people share the same moral vision for America's public square, it is less important whether that vision is fueled by Catholic, Protestant, Jewish, Mormon, Buddhist or Moslem faith. We must not allow secularism's high priests to separate us from one another on the basis of material distinctions such as skin color, gender, or bank account. We should acknowledge only differences based on spiritual or data differences. One set of data is a three-thousand-year-old system that produced ancient Israel and modern America. The other leads to secular humanism, atheism, socialism and communism. And therein lies our tug-of-war.

ONLY TWO CHOICES?

But wait, are there really only two choices? What happened to all the famous shades of gray? Must all Americans choose from only these two alternatives? Is there nothing between embracing Judeo-Christian political principles and rejecting them in favor of atheistic liberalism? Of course there are a million variations and countless shades of gray, but only in the areas of human implementation. You and I can choose to live our lives in a myriad of different and fascinating ways. Practical living offers limitless choices. Philosophies however are different. In choosing doctrines, life offers a strangely limiting duality. God's phrase in Deuteronomy 30:19 "Therefore I set before you this day life or death, blessing or curse, so choose life" starkly invites us to select from a menu of only two items. It reflects the duality that we find in light and darkness, good and evil, up and down, and indeed in the wave and particle theories of light itself. We can light a room so dimly as to find ourselves somewhere between light and darkness. However we still recognize "dim" to be somewhere between light and dark rather than as a value in itself. The trajectory of a projectile might be any angle somewhere between straight up and along the horizontal. Yet in calculating its path, we still resolve its motion into only two component parts. I might well judge my behavior at that party last night, as being somewhere between good and evil. I might even determine that it was an improvement over my behavior at last week's party. Nonetheless I recognize that I am judging my behavior by a framework of only two absolute doctrines.

Yes, as individuals we may each choose our path from a bewildering array of choices and we each must live with the consequences of that choice. As a nation however, we must choose a national doctrine from the only two available. In other words, as a nation we either subscribe to Judeo-Christian principles in public policy or we must subscribe to the public policies of secular atheism. Thirty-plus years of experience tells us that our choice may be between a society filled with wasted human potential, crack babies and criminal predators, while elevating the separation of church and state to the status of Holy Writ, or a society in which that separation is understood as our founding fathers understood it, acknowledging a Creator and the primacy of religion without establishing a national church.

Perhaps you are worried by the old canard that religion has been responsible for more taking of life than anything else in history? Well, it simply is not true. In only the twentieth-century, atheism in both its forms of fascism and communism, has been responsible for killing far more humans than all the religious wars of the first nineteen centuries.

Living in the real world, as we do, does not allow us the luxury of making perfect choices. Sometimes we must pick the least-bad alternative. Christians, Jews, and all others need to recognize the peril America faces and work together, despite the differences that separate us. We may differ on theology but we do not differ on the basic decencies that flow from Judeo-Christian thought—and which make it possible for different people to live together.

IT'S A LONG ROAD

Stopping America's ship from sinking and making her ship-shape again will take a very long time. Much damage has been done these past three or four decades; even if we began earnest repairs tomorrow, it would still take ten to twenty years to achieve our goal. It is vital that we recognize that the repairs will be painful and protracted. Do not try to rush the job. Impatience will alienate future allies and jeopardize success.

Shortly after commencing a daunting task is the moment when discouragement is most likely. Have you ever summoned a handyman to repair a small but annoying crack in your kitchen wall? Peering in a little later you are shocked to find the entire wall ripped open, dripping water pipes jutting out of what looks like a canyon and broken plaster the dominant decorative theme of the kitchen. You desperately wish you had just learned to live with the little crack rather than having precipitated this major renovation. By the end of the day the handyman departs and you gingerly tiptoe into your kitchen not knowing what to expect. Surprise! A flawless wall highlights a gleaming kitchen and you are delighted with your cleverness at having hired such a competent handyman. Here is an important rule of reality: Commencing any task of repair inevitably causes an initial impact far worse than the original problem. The trick is to persevere along the lines of the original plan. Just think of a visit to the dentist after enduring a minor but persistent pain. After only a few minutes in the dentist's chair you wish you had left well enough alone. The minor pain was insignificant when compared to what is now being inflicted upon you. Only once the treatment is complete do you feel gratitude to the dentist for having banished the original pain. If discipline in your home has faded and the children are running wild while you and your spouse are in retreat, you might decide to take matters in hand. For the first few days, while you tackle the problem, you will wish you had learned to live with the kids' rambunctiousness. Finally, if you persist, normality returns.

Commencing the daunting task of restoring America means that there will inevitably be times when we will wish we had left well enough alone. It may appear to be getting worse before it gets better. That is fine. We know the biblical blueprint and persistence will pay off. Little by little we will once again see America adopt that ancient and effective blueprint as our society's road map.

THE EFFICACY OF PRAYER

During the difficult times ahead, let us remember how prayer can help.

We live in times that are proving the efficacy of prayer. Rigorously controlled experiments have shown that patients whose recovery is being prayed for heal more rapidly than others. Not only are these studies carried out in statistically significant numbers but they also demonstrate that even if the patient is unaware of the praying being done on his behalf, his recovery is nonetheless accelerated. These studies rule out any possibility of psychosomatic effect. Which is to say that we have always known that a God-fearing patient enjoys an advantage in recovery if he knows that others are praying for him. Today we now know that there is objective improvement in his condition regardless of whether he himself is God-fearing or whether he even knows that others pray. Thus anyone interested in the subject today can access research that links prayer to the medical welfare of an ill patient.

America is an ill patient today. How could prayer not help? Above the fireplace in my front parlor hangs a print of the wonderful painting by the famous Arnold Friberg, *Prayer at Valley Forge*. In almost photographic detail, it depicts George Washington on his knee beside his horse during that fateful winter. It never fails to bring a lump to my throat when I stare at the founder of our country praying to the God of Abraham, Isaac, and Jacob. Prayer helped to bring America into being. It later sustained us during dark days. For instance, President Lincoln and Secretary of State William Seward proclaimed a national fast day on August 12, 1861. Here is part of what they said:

And whereas, when our own beloved Country, once, by the blessing of God, united, prosperous and happy, is now afflicted with faction and civil war, it is peculiarly fit for us to recognize the hand of God in this terrible visitation, and in sorrowful remembrance of our own faults and crimes as a nation and as individuals, to humble ourselves before Him and to pray for His mercy.

Therefore, I, Abraham Lincoln, President of the United States do appoint the last Thursday in September next, as a day of humiliation, prayer, and fasting for all the people of the nation. And I do earnestly recommend to all the people, and especially to all ministers and teachers of religion of all denominations, and to all heads of families, to observe and keep that day according to their several creeds and modes of worship, in all humility and with all religious solemnity, to the end that the united prayer of the nation may ascend to the Throne of Grace, and bring down plentiful blessings upon our Country.

It would be hard to imagine a contemporary prayer that sounded more like the prayers of the Old Testament prophets.

We really have no choice but to pray and encourage a return to an America steeped in Judeo-Christian values. It is either that or taking our chances in a society with no values at all. For all Americans the former carries certain risks, but the latter spells certain doom. For now, we should not be deflected by theological debate from the life-saving tasks awaiting us. There is work to be done. We must ensure that America will continue to be part of God's plan for the world.

NOTES

CHAPTER FIVE

1. William J. Murray, *My Life Without God* (Nashville, Tenn.: Thomas Nelson, 1982), 49.

CHAPTER NINE

1. John Maddox, *The Economist Yearbook* (1998).

CHAPTER THIRTEEN

1. American Jewish Committee, Board of Governors and National Council (9 September 1996), remarks of Martin S. Kaplan, "Survey of the Religious Right."

CHAPTER FOURTEEN

1. Benjamin Franklin as quoted in *The Making of America*, W. Cleon Skousen, The National Center for Constitutional Studies, Washington D.C. (1986).

CHAPTER FIFTEEN

1. Catherine Millard, *The Rewriting of America's History* (Camp Hill, Penn.: Christian Publications, Inc., 1991), 439–446. Reprinted from the Congressional Record of the 83rd Congress, Second Session (8 March 1954).

CHAPTER TWENTY-THREE

1. P. J. Hill, *Cultural Dynamics,* vol. vii, no. 3 (November 1995).

CHAPTER THIRTY-THREE

1. Will Durant, *The Story of Civilization,* volume 3 (New York: Fine Communications, 1972).

2. Ibid.

CHAPTER THIRTY-SEVEN

1. Edward Gibbon, *The Rise and Fall of the Roman Empire* (London: Methuen & Co. LTD., 1911).

CHAPTER THIRTY-EIGHT

1. Edward Banfield, *The Unheavenly City* (Boston, Mass.: Waveland Press, Inc., 1970), 57.

CHAPTER FORTY-ONE

1. The Forward of March 20, 1998, as quoted in *The Coalition* (May 1998).

CHAPTER FORTY-FOUR

1. *Jewish Heritage* (May 1997).

2. Naomi Cohen, *Natural Adversaries or Possible Allies? American Jews and the New Christian Right* (New York: 1993), 38–39.

3. "John Christensen's Restraint," *Omaha World Herald* (23 September 1994).

CHAPTER FORTY-FIVE

1. National Jewish Coalition Bulletin, "What is a Nice Jewish Boy Like You Doing in a Place Like This?" (October–November 1995).

2. Don Feder, "Making Sense of Jewish Liberalism," speech delivered to the Heritage Foundation (19 February 1993).

CHAPTER FORTY-SIX

1. Naomi Cohen, *Natural Adversaries or Possible Allies? American Jews and the New Christian Right* (New York: 1993), 10.

2. *National Jewish Post and Opinion*, "What's Right, What's Left?" (3 May 1995).

CHAPTER FORTY-NINE

1. Corrie ten Boom, *The Hiding Place* (Uhrichville: 1971), 128.

2. Konrad Heiden, introduction to *Mein Kampf*, by Adolph Hitler (Boston: Houghton, Mifflin Co., 1971).

3. *The Jerusalem Post* (30 May 1994), as quoted in *The Pink Swastika*, 462.

CHAPTER FIFTY

1. *Landmark Decisions of the United States Supreme Court*, Harrison and Gilbert, ed. (San Diego, Calif.: Excellent Books, 1991), 48.

2. Ibid., 37.

3. Ibid., 44.